Palgrave Studies in Minority Languages and Communities

Series Editor: **Gabrielle Hogan-Brun**, University of Bristol, UK

Worldwide migration and unprecedented economic, political and social integration in Europe present serious challenges to the nature and position of language minorities. Some communities receive protective legislation and active support from states through policies that promote and sustain cultural and linguistic diversity; others succumb to global homogenisation and assimilation. At the same time, discourses on diversity and emancipation have produced greater demands for the management of difference.

This series publishes new research based on single or comparative case studies on minority languages worldwide. We focus on their use, status and prospects, and on linguistic pluralism in areas with immigrant or traditional minority communities or with shifting borders. Each volume is written in an accessible style for researchers and students in linguistics, education, anthropology, politics and other disciplines, and for practitioners interested in language minorities and diversity.

Titles include:

Jean-Bernard Adrey
DISCOURSE AND STRUGGLE IN MINORITY LANGUAGE POLICY FORMATION
Corsican Language Policy in the EU Context of Governance

Durk Gorter, Heiko F.Marten and Luk Van Mensel (*editors*)
MINORITY LANGUAGES IN THE LINGUISTIC LANDSCAPE

Nancy H. Hornberger (*editor*)
CAN SCHOOLS SAVE INDIGENOUS LANGUAGES?
Policy and Practice on Four Continents

Anne Judge
LINGUISTIC POLICIES AND THE SURVIVAL OF REGIONAL LANGUAGES IN FRANCE AND BRITAIN

Yasuko Kanno
LANGUAGE AND EDUCATION IN JAPAN
Unequal Access to Bilingualism

Janet Muller
LANGUAGE AND CONFLICT IN NORTHERN IRELAND AND CANADA
A Silent War

Máiréad Nic Craith
EUROPE AND THE POLITICS OF LANGUAGE
Citizens, Migrants and Outsiders

Máiréad Nic Craith (*editor*)
LANGUAGE, POWER AND IDENTITY POLITICS

Bernadette O'Rourke
ATTITUDES TOWARDS WEAK AND STRONG MINORITY LANGUAGES
Galician and Irish in the European Context

Anne Pauwels, Joanne Winter and Joseph Lo Bianco (*editors*)
MAINTAINING MINORITY LANGUAGES IN TRANSNATIONAL CONTEXTS
Australian and European Perspectives

Susanna Pertot, Tom M. S. Priestly and Colin H. Williams (*editors*)
RIGHTS, PROMOTION AND INTEGRATION ISSUES FOR MINORITY LANGUAGES IN EUROPE

Vanessa Pupavac
LANGUAGE RIGHTS
From Free Speech to Linguistic Governance

Miquel Strubell and Emili Boix-Fuster (*editors*)
DEMOCRATIC POLICIES FOR LANGUAGE REVIVAL: THE CASE OF CATALAN

Linda Tsung
MINORITY LANGUAGES, EDUCATION AND COMMUNITIES IN CHINA

Glyn Williams
SUSTAINING LANGUAGE DIVERSITY IN EUROPE
Evidence from the Euromosaic project

Forthcoming titles:

Nkonko M Kamwangamalu
LANGUAGE POLICY AND ECONOMICS IN AFRICA

Dovid Katz
YIDDISH AND POWER
Ten Overhauls of a Stateless Language

Peter Sercombe (*editor*)
LANGUAGE, IDENTITIES AND EDUCATION IN ASIA

Graham Hodson Turner
A SOCIOLINGUISTIC HISTORY OF BRITISH SIGN LANGUAGE

Palgrave Studies in Minority Languages and Communities
Series Standing Order ISBN 978-1-4039-3732-2
(*outside North America only*)

You can receive future titles in this series as they are published by placing a standing order. Please contact your bookseller or, in case of difficulty, write to us at the address below with your name and address, the title of the series and the ISBN quoted above.

Customer Services Department, Macmillan Distribution Ltd, Houndmills, Basingstoke, Hampshire RG21 6XS, England

Language Rights

From Free Speech to Linguistic Governance

Vanessa Pupavac
University of Nottingham, UK

palgrave
macmillan

First published 2012 by
PALGRAVE MACMILLAN

Palgrave Macmillan in the UK is an imprint of Macmillan Publishers Limited, registered in England, company number 785998, of Houndmills, Basingstoke, Hampshire RG21 6XS.

Palgrave Macmillan in the US is a division of St Martin's Press LLC, 175 Fifth Avenue, New York, NY 10010.

Palgrave Macmillan is the global academic imprint of the above companies and has companies and representatives throughout the world.

Palgrave® and Macmillan® are registered trademarks in the United States, the United Kingdom, Europe and other countries

ISBN: 978–1–4039–4086–5

This book is printed on paper suitable for recycling and made from fully managed and sustained forest sources. Logging, pulping and manufacturing processes are expected to conform to the environmental regulations of the country of origin.

A catalogue record for this book is available from the British Library.

A catalog record for this book is available from the Library of Congress.

10 9 8 7 6 5 4 3 2 1
21 20 19 18 17 16 15 14 13 12

Printed and bound in Great Britain by
CPI Antony Rowe, Chippenham and Eastbourne

To Mladen, Jelena and Carl

Contents

Acknowledgements

I am indebted to Gabrielle Hogan-Brun, who invited my original project, and to Margaret Appleton, who inspired my interest in language and culture. I thank Louise Askew, Tarak Barkawi, Andreas Bieler, Bill Bowring, Tony Burns, Jane-Marie Collins, Alex Danchev, Mark Duffield, John Fitzpatrick, Hillary Footitt, Devon Curtis, Catherine Gegout, Catherine Goetze, Rania Hafez, Richard Harris, Dennis Hayes, James Heartfield, Ben Holland, Gulshan Khan, Kenan Malik, Adam Morton, Sara Motto, David Norris, Chris Pierson, Vladislava Ribnikar, Verity Robins, Rizwaan Sabir, Lucy Sargisson, Raymond Tallis, Rod Thornton, Stefano Saccomani, Mark Wenman, Stefan Wolff, Hicham Yezza and Kevin Yuill for their encouragement, ideas or comments on earlier drafts. It is fantastic to see Priya Narayanan and others taking up free speech matters. I am grateful for the feedback I received on papers presented at seminars at the Universities of Bristol, Edinburgh and Leeds, the London School of Economics and the School of Slavonic and East European Studies early on in the project, as well as the Centre for the Study of Social and Global Justice at the University of Nottingham. I thank, too, the anonymous reviewers for their valuable suggestions on my manuscript. Tony Simmonds and his fellow university librarians were very helpful in dealing with my numerous inter-library loan requests so quickly.

Chapters 2 and 8 includes excerpts from the following publications:

Vanessa Pupavac (2006) 'Language Rights in Conflict and the Denial of Language as Communication' *International Journal of Human Rights,* Vol. 10, No. 1, March, pp. 61–78.

Vanessa Pupavac (2006) 'Reconstructing Post-Conflict Cultures: A Case Study of Bosnia', in Colin Wright and Christina Demaria (eds) *Post Conflict Cultures*. London: Zoilus Press, pp. 133–50.

Vanessa Pupavac (2005) 'Multiculturalism and Its Discontents in SFR Yugoslavia and Bosnia: A Critique of the Multiculturalist Rights Model' in Nigel White and Dirk Klassen (eds) *The UN, Human Rights and Post-Conflict Situation*. Manchester: Manchester University Press, pp. 213–37.

Vanessa Pupavac (2003) 'Politics and Language Rights: A Case Study of Language Politics in Croatia', in Gabrielle Hogan-Brun and Stefan Wolff (eds) *Minority Languages in Europe: Status, Frameworks, Prospects*. Basingstoke: Palgrave Macmillan, pp. 138–54.

Vanessa Pupavac (2000) 'Socialist Federal Republic of Yugoslavia's Multiethnic Rights Approach and the Politicisation of Ethnicity' *Human Rights Law Review*, Vol. 5, No.2, pp. 3–8. (Permission is given by Oxford University Press).

In my thanks, I am conscious that not everyone will agree with what I have argued here. Responsibility for the content and for any errors is mine. This book would have been impossible to write without two periods of study leave from the School of Politics and International Relations at the University of Nottingham. Finally, I thank Mladen, Jelena and Carl for their patience and impatience, their 'wine-handed' jokes and speech demands.

Abbreviations

AAA	American Anthropological Association
ACALAN	African Academy of Languages
ACTA	Anti-Counterfeiting Trade Agreement
ADL	Anti-Defamation League
AVNOJ	Anti-Fascist Council for the People's Liberation of Yugoslavia
BBC	British Broadcasting Company
BiH	Bosnia and Hercegovina
BNP	British National Party
CELP	Committee on Endangered Languages and their Preservation
CERD	Convention on the Elimination of All Forms of Racial Discrimination
CPS	Crown Prosecution Service
C-SAP	Higher Education Academy Subject Network for Sociology, Anthropology, Politics
Dayton Agreement	General Framework Agreement for Peace in Bosnia and Herzegovina
DBIS	Department of Business, Innovation and Skills
DIUS	Department of Innovation, Universities and Skills
EC	European Community
ECHR	European Court of Human Rights
ECPHR	European Convention for the Protection of Human Rights and Fundamental Freedoms
EDL	English Defence League
ELF	Endangered Language Fund
EU	European Union
FAIFE	Information and Freedom of Expression Committee
FEL	Foundation for Endangered Languages
FRA	European Union Agency for Fundamental Rights
GBS	Society for Endangered Languages
HRW	Human Rights Watch
ICCPR	International Covenant on Civil and Political Rights
ICG	International Crisis Group
ICISS	International Commission on Intervention and State Sovereignty
IFLA	International Federation of Library Associations and Institutions
ILI	Indigenous Language Institute

ILO	International Labour Organization
IMF	International Monetary Fund
LHR	Linguistic Human Rights
MDG	Millennium Development Goal
MLE	mother language education
NATO	North Atlantic Treaty Organization
NGO	non-governmental organisation
OAU	Organisation of African Unity
ODIHR	Office for Democratic Institutions and Human Rights
OHR	Office of the High Representative
OSCE	Organization for Security and Cooperation in Europe
PRSP	Poverty Reduction Strategy Paper
RP	received pronouncement
SCAF	Supreme Council of the Armed Forces (Egypt)
SFOR	NATO Stabilization Force
SFR Yugoslavia	Socialist Federal Republic of Yugoslavia
SSEES	School of Slavonic and East European Studies
TINA	there is no alternative to the market
TUC	Trade Union Congress
UN	United Nations
UN CRC	UN Convention on the Rights of the Child
UNDP	United Nations Development Programme
UNESCO	United Nations Educational, Scientific and Cultural Organization
UNGA	United Nations General Assembly
UNHCHR	United Nations High Commissioner for Human Rights
UNHCR	United Nations High Commissioner for Refugees
UNHRC	United Nations Human Rights Council
UNICEF	United Nations Children's Fund
WWF	World Wildlife Fund

1
Contesting Human Rights, Language and Politics

Introduction

Speech is core to our humanity. In a key sense, we 'talked ourselves' free from biological determinism (Steiner, 1998, [1975], pp. 245–6; Tallis, 1999, pp. 272–3; Vygotsky, 1986, [1934], pp. 68–95, p. 256). Speech is obviously fundamental to our capacity to assert political rights, and determine, 'what is just and unjust' (Aristotle, *Politics*, 1992, p. 60; [350bc, 1253a16]). Rights therefore mean little if they do not relate to speech.

But what are language rights? What language or speech is defended? How do language rights relate to each other? Arguments that languages share core foundations support beliefs in our common humanity against racial thinking. Conversely, arguments that languages may differ in fundamental ways support beliefs in human diversity and plurality. Such concerns inform contemporary language advocacy:

> The world's languages are dying. Ninety percent of them are expected to disappear in the next hundred years. (Nettle and Romaine, 2000)
>
> Linguistic rights are the quintessence of minority rights... language is one of the most important vehicles through which most cultures are expressed.... The prevention of inter-ethnic conflicts goes hand in hand with the establishment of an adequate system of protection for linguistic rights. (Vollebaek, 2008)
>
> People who lose their linguistic and cultural identity may lose an essential element in a social process that commonly teaches respect for nature and understanding of the natural environment and its processes. (Terralingua, in Skutnabb-Kangas, 2009, p. 39)
>
> any reduction of language diversity diminishes the adaptational strength of our species because it lowers the pool of knowledge from which we can draw. (Bernard, 1992, p. 82)

> Linguistic neoimperialism entails the maintenance of inequalities between speakers of English and other languages, within a framework of exploitative dominance. (Phillipson, 2009a, p. 137)
>
> state failure to provide mother tongue education may 'constitute international crimes, including both genocide and crimes against humanity'. (Skutnabb-Kangas and Dunbar, 2010, p. 12)
>
> we cannot stop short by assuming that once someone has access to a language, they have access to doing what they need or want to do through language. (Pennycook, 1998b, p. 86)
>
> Hate speech is a direct attack on the right to be and to think differently. It might not stop at rhetoric, as it has the potential to shape the minds and attitudes of individuals who will believe they have the right to undermine other people's rights. A democratic society cannot afford the freedom to oppress. Instead, we have to identify how to strike the adequate balance between rights and freedoms. (Boe-Buquicchio, 2010)

These quotations illustrate how international language rights advocacy has expanded beyond civil freedoms to encompass protections for specific languages, linguistic identities and discourse. Safeguards are sought to stop cultures becoming homogeneous. Advocates fear 'the degradation of mankind into a single huge speech community speaking a uniform language' (Janhunen, 2006, p. 27). Even liberal theorists, suspicious of cultural claims undermining human rights, concede the specific challenge of language in human rights thinking (Vincent, 2010, p. 228). The 1990s established new human rights frameworks to protect historically marginal groups. Language rights literature follows these human rights developments. Most literature is written from advocacy perspectives, seeking to expand global language rights and enforcement mechanisms on states. Criticisms usually concern the need for more robust provisions and enforcement mechanisms, and defence of human rights gains against any retreats in the war on terror. But there are implications for political and civil freedoms in the expanding global human rights governance.

This study explores international language politics in an age of limits, where advocacy characteristically takes the form of demands for more governance, not more freedom. Evolving global human rights frameworks draw on the moral and political legitimacy of earlier struggles. Human rights during the Cold War were associated with the political prisoner of conscience, suffering state persecution for championing civil and political freedoms. Prominent figures included Soviet dissidents against totalitarianism, and opponents of the Apartheid regime or military dictatorships. Their courageous struggles resonated with earlier historical struggles, from the Haitian rebellion against slavery to struggles for national independence, universal suffrage and equality (Fanon, 1967; Grovogui, 1996; James, 2001, [1938]; L'Ouverture, 2008, [1793–1802]; Paine, 1996, [1791]).

The profile of human rights was boosted in the 1990s, as they became the site of political hopes against declining alternative political projects, and the dominant market relations. Human rights were championed as part of cosmopolitan ideals, seeking to develop global civil society and transcend the world of state power politics. Yet human rights changed their character as advocacy moved from oppositional politics to codifying law over the *demos*. Human rights became part of expanding official governance, revising relations between states, state and citizen, and the public and private spheres. Western governments incorporated human rights into their foreign policies, and challenged the post-war international order based on national sovereignty and non-interference in the internal affairs of states. Liberal theories of justice and international policy-making developed the concept of Responsibility to Protect, legitimising rights of humanitarian military intervention against states, violating human security and human rights of their populations (ICISS, 2001; Rawls, 1999). Meanwhile, human rights were professionalised as a career, distinct from oppositional political activism. Human rights postgraduate qualifications sprang up, alongside short courses training civil servants or non-governmental staff. These developments have fostered fears that human rights are losing their 'revolutionary and dissident purposes' and becoming 'obscured in ever more declarations, treaties and diplomatic lunches' (Douzinas, 2000, p. 380).

My core argument is that international language rights are shifting from freedoms of speech to linguistic governance. Influential advocacy is ambivalent about human subjectivity, linguistic creativity and freedoms, and is legitimising developments antithetical to humanist emancipatory politics. The language rights literature has criticised the rise of global English as part of globalisation, but has not applied the same critical eye to global governance. Indeed, language rights advocacy has been attracted to political solutions expanding global governance, antithetical to rights of self-determination and humanist emancipatory politics. International language rights advocates invoke international law to counter globalisation and linguistic imperialism, but their strategies legitimise a form of legal imperialism, analogous to the linguistic imperialism they attack. Expanding human rights regimes, making particular models of justice universal laws, marginalise individuals as political subjects, and delegitimise political contestation over different visions of the good life. The institutionalising language rights against the demos inverts the meaning of human rights, and effectively assumes, 'the manuscript-assumed authority of the dead... .over the rights and freedom of the living', that the radical Paine's *Rights of Man* rage against (Paine, 1996, [1791], p.10).

My study brings interdisciplinary critical studies to global language rights debates. International studies have critically analysed the rise of expert-led global governance, eroding the principles of legal equality between states, national self-determination and citizens' rights under global human rights regimes (Chandler, 2002; Chomsky, 2000; Duffield, 2007; Grovogui, 1996; Lewis, 1998; Mieville, 2005). Global human rights governance increasingly follows security imperatives against emancipatory political ideals. Strikingly, common human rights arguments today exude pessimism, not only over the fate of many individuals in political danger, but over humanity as a species. Even those arguing for fundamental human rights often hold a rather degraded view of human nature as predatory (Ignatieff, 1998, p. 18). Earlier radical proclamations of the rights of man believed in our humanity, but today's language rights advocacy appears mistrustful towards the mass of humanity and democratic politics. Expanding human rights regimes effectively doubt individuals' moral capacity as citizens to engage in unregulated political speech or even personal discourse and relations. Conversely, I identify myself with a libertarian political and civil rights tradition, which supports language rights as freedoms of speech and expression. These freedoms are being degraded under contemporary global human rights governance and national legal developments.

Contesting language

Language theories have commonly been characterised as those tending towards essentialism (language reflects reality) nominalism (language makes reality) or conceptualism or personalism (the individual speaker making language). There is a strong nominalism in contemporary language approaches, giving centrality to language making the human world. Linguistic nominalism parallels strong legal nominalism in contemporary human rights, and constructivist international relations theories (Donnelly, 2003; Reus-Smith, 2001).

Another core feature of today's language rights advocacy is its wariness towards Chomskian linguistic theories of an underlying core universal grammar, shared by all humanity at the deep structure of languages (Chomsky, 1988; McGilvray, 2002, pp. 27–32). Chomskian theories focused on identifying common sub-cultural features that suggest limits to how languages may differ, notwithstanding their diverse creative development (Chomsky, 2002). Universal grammar theories complement critiques of biological racism, emphasising our common humanity and the innate human capacity for language (Chomsky, 1959; Vygotsky, 1986, [1934]). Symbolically, the civil rights campaigner Martin Luther King invoked the idea of creating 'one language' in his struggle against racism (Sunnemark, 2003, p. 53). Common myths – including myths of a lost universal language – have been identified across continents, but whether or not a common language existed prehistorically cannot be established. Nevertheless, plausible theories have developed for the hand as the common origin of human consciousness and symbolic communication (Tallis, 2003). Thinkers from Aristotle to Vico to Marx have long linked the origins of human language to tool use and the language of gestures (Berlin, 2000; Holborow, 1999, pp. 13–51; Tallis, 2003; Vico, 2002 [1725]; Vygotsky, 1986, [1934]). In any case, appeals to our common humanity should not stand or fall on elusive historical facts, but on its validity as an ideal *per se*. As the philologist Cyrus Gordon argues, 'These are big ideas that mankind must absorb (as attitudes, not as historical or anthropological facts) and apply if our planet is to be worth living in' (Gordon, 1971, pp. 85–6).

The scope of a significant core universal grammar has been debated and challenged in linguistics (Steiner, 1998, [1975], pp. 99–114). Empirical challenges have been joined by ethical objections in a context where language advocacy associates a focus on Saussurean *langue* (language structure) with a denial of *parole* (language use) (Saussure, 1974, [1916]). Language advocates have accused universal grammar theories of legitimising cultural homogenisation and language death (Janhunen, 2006, p. 27). Such accusations overlook how their approaches concern different levels of analysis and suggest '[d]iversification from an underlying unity' (Chomsky, 2006). Today's antipathy towards universalism contrasts with the earlier idealised association made by political radicals and progressives.

Overall, language rights advocacy today identifies with Whorfian cultural relativism, rather than Chomskian universalism. The Sapir-Whorf hypothesis from anthropology suggests that different languages embody and shape different world views (Sapir, 1949; Whorf, 1956). Whorfian ideas especially influence ecolinguistic advocacy over threatened languages, which combines ecological and linguistic concerns. Human diversity is equated with diverse language forms, each language expressing a world view (Skutnabb-Kangas, 2009, p. 39). Simultaneously, human subjectivity and linguistic creativity are implicitly circumscribed by language structures – language shaping people, as opposed to people shaping language.

Influential post-structuralist approaches have criticised structuralist approaches for essentialising language, but develop their own linguistic determinism. '[T]here is nothing outside the text', Jacques Derrida famously declared (Derrida, 1976, p. 158; in Tallis, 1988, p. 17). Or, 'It is the world of words that creates the world of things', Jacques Lacan argues (1977, p. 65; discussed in Tallis, 1988, p. 15). The idea of language creating the world might suggest confidence in human subjectivity. Instead, post-structuralist approaches exude pessimism over our self-expression. Linguistic creativity is questioned, whether of the romantic genius or the ordinary speaker, judged against ideals of perfect selfhood, authorship or conscious speech (Barthes, 1967, 1977; Derrida, 1973, pp. 77–82, pp. 94–5, pp. 145–6; Derrida, 1976, pp. 7–8, 166; discussed in Tallis, 1988, pp. 179–89 and Tallis, 1999, pp. 276–89, pp. 461–6). Contestation of speakers' agency as fictions, and emphasis on speech as habitual and socially conditioned, end up coinciding with Whorfian and behaviouralist theories, notwithstanding their distinct philosophical starting points.

Behaviouralist theories of sociolinguistic conditioning were fundamentally challenged by Chomsky, drawing on earlier ideas of linguistic creativity (Chomsky, 2002; Humboldt, 1999, [1841]). Language is the expression of conscious speakers involving intentionality (Chomsky, 1959). We initiate speech, and do not simply speak following habitual patterns (Humboldt, 1999, [1841], pp. 26–9, 62–3; Tallis, 1999, pp. 320–2, p. 341). Words relate not only to other words, but to extra-linguistic realities, although post-structuralist or nominalist approaches may minimalise these ties (Tallis, 1988, pp. 49–65). As speakers we make and remake language. Speakers, audiences and the linguistic and extra-linguistic context orientate meaning (Tallis, 1999, pp. 287–9). It is not merely linguistic convention that makes stone not food, even if the old lady in the stone soup folk tale is temporarily fooled by the tramp into believing so (Hunia, 1979). The term 'poison' relates to an extra-linguistic world based on specific observable, physical properties, which cannot simply be linguistically removed (Tallis, 1988, pp. 80–1). Nuanced triadic or dialectic approaches to language usefully seek to understand language as constituted through mediations between conscious subjects in social relations, a language (*langue* and *parole*) and objects/world (Tallis, 1988, pp. 114–16). They seek to avoid the one-sided accounts of essentialism (language reflecting reality), nominalism (language making reality), and personalism (the individual speaker making language) (Tallis, 1988, pp. 103–6; Vygotsky, 1986, [1934]). Here I am inspired by dialectic philosophies of language, human subjectivity and linguistic creativity (Humboldt, 1999, [1841]; Tallis, 1988; 1999; Vygotsky, 1986, [1934]).

In different ways, the linguistic theories influencing language advocacy question human subjectivity and linguistic creativity, and see language as circumscribing thinking. These theories are troubled over language's arbitrary and rule-bound character. Yet these same features are crucial to the possibility of human language and creative social meaning-making. The arbitrary relation between signifier (sound value) and signified (concept value) does not mean that reference or meaning is impossible (Tallis, 1988, pp. 66–8; 1999, p. 289). Language's arbitrary sound relation to the world allows infinite creative linguistic expression and representation (Tallis, 1999, p. 289). Simultaneously, a language's rules allow socially meaningful linguistic exchanges. Together they underpin linguistic originality: Humboldt's 'regulated freedom', or Chomsky's 'rule-governed creativity' (Chomsky, 2002, p. 68; Humboldt, 1999, p. 144). We continue communicating and interacting with each other and the world, notwithstanding philosophical despair over obtaining perfect relations and correspondences. Suggestions that the signifier cannot even reach the signified (Derrida, 1973, pp. 77–82, p. 140, pp. 145–6; Derrida, 1976, p. 50) hint at the theorist's feelings of social isolation and difficulty reaching a public (discussed in Tallis, 1988, pp. 87–96, 181–9; Tallis, 1999, pp. 462–3).

Other aspects of contemporary linguistic theories suggest despair over the possibilities of human solidarity and overcoming discrimination and violence. For example, linguistic relational sound contrasts are sometimes interpreted as encasing linguistic meaning in relational oppositions. Effectively, linguistic means are conflated with meanings. But the relational contrasts of linguistic forms do not determine that linguistic content is inherently negative and oppositional (Tallis, 1988, pp. 79–82). Not least, meanings are not merely linguistically determined, or bound to a language system of negative oppositions. 'Language is not ideological in itself through its system or its structure, but in its context of use,' the Marxist linguist Marnie Holborow argues (Holborow, 1999, p. 192). If earlier Marxist linguist theories see language as an 'effect and not a cause' (Gramsci, 1985, p. 210), post-Saussurean linguistic theories give language a causal role.

The linguistic system's contrastive character is taken in influential post-Saussurean theories to suggest that human thinking is binary and founded on difference (Barthes, 1967; 1977; Derrida, 1976; Spivak, 1976). Meaning is ascribed negatively, and not positively present, but endlessly elusive in an endless chain of meaning, fixed only through force (Derrida, 1982; Tallis, 1988, pp. 87–95). One dimension of human thinking as oppositional is thereby made paramount, while other dimensions are marginalised. These ideas are extended to suggest that human meaning-making is inherently discriminatory and violent. Major twentieth century political philosophers Simone de Beauvoir, and Jean Paul Sartre, drawing on Alexandre Kojève, propose identity as constructed against an other (de Beauvoir, 1972, [1949]; Sartre, 1995, [1946]). Such identity theories have influenced post-colonial theories, most famously Edward Said's *Orientalism* (Heartfield, 2002, pp. 57–67; Malik, 1996, pp. 227–236; Said, 1991, [1978]). Binary models pervade contemporary advocacy and policy interventions, organised around models of victims and perpetrators.

Linguistic theories questioning human linguistic agency have implications for democratic politics, founded on ideas of individuals as moral subjects, able to think, speak, and decide consciously for themselves. Post-structuralist approaches, grounding language in discriminatory difference and seeing meanings as exclusionary, suggest the impossibility of overcoming exclusionary social ideologies and practices. Some approaches despairingly conclude that language has alienated humanity from nature, and contaminates human experience of the world. Scepticism is epitomised in explorations of language's violence, or the inexpressibility of horror (Derrida, 1976, p, 37, p. 112; Derrida, 1973; Derrida, 1990; Foucault, 1972, p. 216, p. 229). Language's sickness has been a familiar European cultural theme since the late nineteenth century (Murdoch, 1989, pp. 64–80; Steiner, 1998, [1975], pp. 185–96). The perception of linguistic failure became a significant western philosophical response in the wake of the Holocaust, articulated in Theodore Adorno and Max Horkheimer's *Dialectics of Enlightenment* (1997)

[1944], and George Steiner's *Language and Silence* (1969). Linguistic despair over humanity's imprisonment in language, and language's association with discrimination and violence, are evident in strands of language rights thinking, notably in post-humanist ecolinguistic advocacy. Disillusion with language is paralleled by scepticism towards the free exercise of political speech, and informs the turn to law and the language of rights.

Contesting law, human rights and liberty

The language of rights is the quintessential form in which political demands have been formulated and legitimised in modern society, so it is unsurprising that language advocates make claims as rights. Modern law's specific character has been analysed from diverse perspectives: from mainstream legal theorists like A.V. Dicey (1959) [1889] or H.L.A. Hart (1961) to critical theorists like Franz Neumann (1986) or the Marxist Evegeny Pashukanis (1978) [1924]. Its legitimacy is founded on the people as authors of the law through a social contract, bringing together individual rights, agreement and law. Ideally, the close connection between the law and the people is reinforced by each law passed. For each law, embodying the will of people as contracting subjects affirms their moral, political and legal agency, and individual rights. In turn, enforcement of the law does not rely on coercion – coercion becomes the exception or last resort – but citizens' internalisation of legal norms (Hart, 1961). Citizens are taken to have internalised the law, because the law embodies their will and agreement. This is an ideal representation of law, but the degree to which laws do, or do not, conform to this ideal of citizens as legislators, and engage citizens as active moral subjects, has important political ramifications. Even Thomas Hobbes's *Leviathan*, which prioritises security, conceptualises the sovereign legislator as having to engage with the people's interests, rather than merely ruling them (Fitzpatrick, 2001, pp. 96–8; Robin, 2004, pp. 31–50). The social contract models of law nicely parallel the idea of language as an implied social contract (Douzinas, 2000, pp. 308–9). As such, they are particularly appropriate to language rights thinking, for bringing together speech, law and rights.

However, today's human rights models are distinctive, and depart fundamentally from classic social contract understandings of rights (Locke, Hume and Rousseau, 1947). Human rights theories criticise the rational, autonomous individual of natural rights and social contract theories as a fiction (Mackinnon, 1987; 1993; Milanović, 1992; Pateman, 1988; Santos, 1987; 1995, pp. 60–71). Human rights models are envisaged as a progressive innovation from classic models of rights-holders having the capacity to guarantee their own rights. Making rights contingent on capacity casts doubt on weak marginal groups having their interests recognised as rights. Effectively, the very groups who most need rights protection lack capacity, and are thereby excluded from rights. Yet even radicals previously related rights to the capacity of groups to establish their claims through political struggle (Fanon, 1967, [1961], pp. 160–2).

Contemporary human rights advocacy seeks to empower marginalised groups, both overcoming the flaws of the classical model and going beyond a protectionist model. Its alternative inclusive model of rights is consciously addressed to the moral claims of those who lack capacity. Rights are seen as empowering, by signalling the moral worth of the rights-holders to themselves and the rest of society. Positive affirmation of the rights of particular marginal groups (women, children, minority ethnic groups or others) is seen as enhancing their self-esteem and social status. Advocates seek to entrench their interests as fundamental rights, by whatever theoretical or policy means are necessary, so that states cannot ignore their claims or treat them as discretionary.

It is worth revisiting Isaiah Berlin's classic essay 'Two Concepts of Liberty' on negative and positive liberty, to understand the character of rights and freedoms, which are at stake in language rights debates (Berlin, 1969, pp. 118–72). Berlin's concepts on negative and positive liberty, drawing on J.S. Mill's *On Liberty* (Mill, 1985, [1859]), distinguish 'freedom from' and 'freedom to' (Berlin, 1969, p. 121). The negative sense relates to the question 'What is the area within which the subject – a person or group of persons – is or should be left to do or be what he is able to do or be, without interference by other persons?' (Berlin, 1969, pp. 121–2). Negative liberty is commonly associated with the first generation of human rights and civil liberties against state interference or persecution. In language rights terms, freedoms of speech and expression, recognised in article 19 of the Universal Declaration of Human Rights 1948, are linked to negative liberty.

Positive liberty relates to the questions: 'Who governs me?' 'By whom am I ruled?' 'Who is to say what I am, and what I am not to be or do?' (Berlin, 1969, p. 130). Berlin derives the positive sense from individuals' aspiration to be their own masters:

> I wish to be a subject, not an object...deciding, not being decided for, self-directed and not acted upon by external nature or by other men as if I were a thing, or an animal, or a slave incapable of playing a human role, that is, of conceiving goals and policies of my own and realizing them. (Berlin, 1969, p. 131)

In essence, 'freedom is self-mastery' (Berlin, 1969, p. 146). But our self-mastery and sense of ourselves are bound up with our relations with others, and the group's autonomy and freedom from external governance (Berlin, 1969, pp. 154–62):

> the group...must itself have a sufficient measure of 'negative' freedom – from control by any outside authority – otherwise recognition by it will not give the claimant the status he seeks. (Berlin, 1969, p. 158)

Berlin outlines how aspirations for self-realisation may be inverted into external governance over the individual by guardians, claiming to act in the true self's interests (Berlin, 1969, pp. 133–4). Coercive interventions may become justified against individuals, or populations, towards ideals of rational civilisation or nature. Express wishes may even be contravened in the name of enabling people to realise their true selves, as defined by the expert, advocate, community elder, enlightened despot or guardian (Berlin, 1969, pp. 132–3, p. 142). A dualism is thereby set up between the empirical self and the model self, whether that is an ideal rational self or an ideal authentic member of the nation, ethnicity or indigenous culture. In Berlin's words, a 'monstrous impersonation' of the subject of rights takes place (Berlin, 1969, p. 133). Such abuses are evident in European colonialism's denial of self-government in the name of civilising populations or preserving their traditions, as under British colonial native administration.

Even the benign paternalism of a third-party advocate, acting for the frail empirical self in the name of true self, degrades people's subjectivity. Such therapeutic governance denies people as self-realising individuals with the capacity to choose their own ends:

> to manipulate men, to propel them towards goals which you – the social reformer – see, but they may not, is to deny their human essence, to treat them as objects without wills of their own, and therefore to degrade them. (Berlin, 1969, p. 137)

Berlin was an influential critic of totalitarian socialist and fascist regimes, but he notes how liberal philosophies are not immune from liberal despotism (Berlin, 1969, p. 137, pp. 153–4). Notoriously, Mill contended, 'despotism is a legitimate mode of government in dealing with barbarians providing the end be their improvement' (Mill, 1985, [1859], p. 69). The calls of romantic nationalism, or indigenous rights, for authentic being also have their despotic potential over individuals (Berlin, 1969, p. 159). Berlin is sympathetic to the claims of cultural particularity against universalist models of perfection. But his pluralism does not assume like Burkean conservatism, that individuals must embody their tradition and culture, or that the desire to escape from one's tradition and culture is irrational (Berlin, 1969, p. 161). For Berlin, political freedom is meaningless, if it is deemed inherently irrational to speak or act against one's own station or culture (Berlin, 1969, p. 161). Berlin's pluralism believes our capacity to choose our ends is necessary for our sense of our own subjectivity (Berlin, 1969, pp. 171–2).

Berlin proposes a pluralism of ends, which affirms both Mill's 'experiments in living' and Humboldt's diversity, grounded in individuality, originality and freedom (Berlin, 1969, p. 170; Humboldt, 1999, [1841]; Mill, 1985, [1959], pp. 120–1). Berlin's pluralism recognises political contention and contingency over rival moral and social ends, and opposes bureaucratic goal-making:

> human goals are many, not all of them commensurable, and in perpetual rivalry with one another. To assume that all values can be graded on one scale, so that it is a mere matter of inspection to determine the highest, seems to me to falsify our knowledge that men are free agents, to represent moral decision as an operation which a slide-rule could, in principle, perform. (Berlin, 1969, p. 171)

Berlin believes humans have conflicting ends, and therefore the possibilities of conflict and tragedy haunt the human condition (Berlin, 1969, p. 169).

Contemporary language rights advocacy shares Berlin's concerns that democracy does not guarantee individual or minority positions against the majority. However, its advocacy appears closer to Burkean conservatism than Berlin's liberalism in its treatment of cultural or linguistic identity as universal ends. Multicultural rights governance follows expert-led policy approaches, which assume the universal validity of rights, harmony of values and interests, along with their material realisability (Berlin, 1969, p. 167). They do not uphold the scope of self-government, moral autonomy and personal freedom envisaged by Berlin (Berlin, 1969, p. 165).

Key critical legal studies are sceptical towards legal multiculturalism, which they distinguish from a multiculturalism of undetermined social relations and lived experiences. First, they note the paradox of cultural relativism, whose 'very assertion of incommensurability of particular cultures, relies inherently on overarching determination, on a quasi-totality', namely culture (Fitzpatrick, 2001, p. 49). Second, they note the tensions between cultural relativism and a system of cultural legal pluralism under the state (Fitzpatrick, 2001, pp. 49–50). Critical legal approaches have been wary of the juridification of multiculturalism and human rights, associating it with disciplinary governance (Douzinas, 2000; Fitzpatrick, 2001; Žižek, 1999a; Žižek, 1999b, pp. 215–21; Žižek, 2005). Such critiques share with political philosophies, from Mill and Berlin's liberalism to Sartre's ethics of responsibility, an underlying apprehension towards state-orientated, or rule-based, theories of justice, and their implications for moral subjectivity (Berlin, 1969; Mill, 1985; Sartre, 1948). Official recognition of multicultural difference is compatible with denial of human rights, as Soviet and colonial history testify (Douzinas, 2000, p. 380; Heartfield, 2011). Critics seek to distinguish between human rights limiting 'institutional practice' and 'institutional human rights', sanctifying or policing social identities and values against 'social indeterminacy and existential self-creation' (Douzinas, 2000, pp. 368–75). Bureaucratic human rights governance represents a hollowed-out pluralism of multicultural identity forms, by an essentially western international community of responsible states and non-governmental organisations, 'making a determinative pronouncement about all other cultures – something which, of course, contravenes the principle of incommensurability itself' (Fitzpatrick, 2001, p. 49). Critiques of multicultural governance are relevant to strategies of global linguistic human rights governance.

Marxist critiques of human rights

Critical legal theories are influenced by Marxist critiques of law. Famously, Marx condemned human rights as individualistic, egoistic, bourgeois rights (Marx, 1972, [1891], pp. 16–17). Marx's *On the Jewish Question* located human rights in the alienating property relations of the market:

> Liberty of man as an isolated monad, withdrawn into himself ... the rights of man to liberty is based not on the association of man with man, but on the separation of man with man. It is the right of this separation, the right of the restricted individual, withdrawn into himself ... The practical application of man's right to liberty is man's right to private property. (Marx, 1844, discussed in Bowring, 2008, p. 117).

Marx's *Capital* further analyses how capitalism undermines traditional hierarchies, ties and privileges, and frees individuals to enter fluid market relations of exchange of equivalents (Marx, 1976, [1867], pp. 280–6; Meszaros, 1970; Mieville, 2005; Pashukanis, 1978, [1924]). We are not formally bonded as under feudalism. Instead we enter the market as formally free individual subjects, who contract out our labour power. Capitalism's market relations thereby advance principles of freedom and equality. But capitalism's production relations depend on unequal relations of exploitation. Individuals sell their labour power and become subject to production relations, which work employees to create surplus value above their labour's costs (ibid.). Surplus value is alienated from individual workers and accumulates as capital. Simultaneously, individuals are alienated from their own lives as their life activities become subjected to the demands of capital accumulation. 'Right can never be higher than the economic structure of society and its cultural development conditioned thereby', Marx argues in his *Critique of the Gotha Programme* (Marx, 1972, [1891], p. 17). An equal right represents 'a right of inequality' in unequal social conditions (Marx, 1972, [1891], p. 16). As such, Marx suggests the limits of law's socially transformative role.

Marx, nevertheless, observes the progressive dimension of modern law in its development of democratic rights, whereby individuals are authors of the law to which they are subject (Bowring, 2008; Heartfield, 2002; Pashukanis, 1978, [1924]). Marx argues:

> Democracy is the solved riddle of all constitutions. Here not merely implicitly and in essence but existing in reality, the constitution is

> constantly brought back to its actual basis, the actual human being, the actual people, and established as the people's own work (Marx, [1843–1844] in Marx and Engels, 1975, p. 29, discussed in Bowring, 2008, pp. 102–3).

For Marx, modern law's more democratic character under capitalism is not accidental, but is linked to the development of the market, where the contract becomes the core economic social, political and legal form (Heartfield, 2002; Heartfield, undated; Marx, 1976, [1867], pp. 280–6; Mieville, 2005; Pashukanis, 1978). Marx recognises the historical significance of political emancipation, notwithstanding capitalism's alienating relations of production and private property (Marx, 1844). Political emancipation realises a public space for political social struggles, seeking to overcome these alienating relations and restricting conditions. Human rights are therefore not necessarily only individualistic, but are potentially sociable in carving out a space for political and civil freedoms and social experimentation, as the Birkbeck Law School have explored (Bowring, 2008; Douzinas, 2000, pp. 169–74). However, Marxist theories see political emancipation under the state and law as inherently limited, because the state and law remain intermediaries between individuals and themselves (Marx, 1844). Marx envisaged proletarian dictatorship as temporary on the way to the ultimate withering away of state and the law, for the full un-alienated flourishing of relations between individuals. Here Marx echoes the long philosophical yearning for freedom from the state and the polity (Arendt, 1998, [1958], p. 60). It is in this respect that the Marxist legal theorist Pashukanis characterised bourgeois law as the highest form of law, and contested the idea of developing Marxist law (Mieville, 2005; Pashukanis, 1978, [1924]), a position abused under Stalinist rule (Bowring, 2008, pp. 20–30).

Demands for recognition of a shared public sphere under the secular state are different from human rights advocacy seeking official recognition of difference, which would have been an anathema to Marx. Marx's *On the Jewish Question* suggests that identity recognition represents a retreat from political emancipation towards a quasi-theological, albeit ecumenical, state, which would inhibit the struggle for broader human social emancipation (Marx, 1844). Earlier civil and political rights thinkers, like Thomas Paine, commonly associate official recognition of difference with privilege, and its removal with advancing political emancipation and equality (Paine, 1996, [1791]). Today's identity advocacy reverses earlier progressive democratic political concerns to defend the common people against the privileged minority.

Legal critiques have drawn on Marx's critique to suggest that contemporary human rights approaches embody the interests of liberal capitalism (Bowring, 2008, pp. 20–4; Douzinas, 2000; Fitzpatrick, 2001, pp. 183–218; MacIntyre, 2006, pp. 145–58; Marx, 1844; Mieville, 2005, pp. 302–14; Yuill,

2006, pp. 187–208; Žižek, 1997; 1999a; 2005). Critics distinguish substantial freedoms from the formal freedom of choices within existing capitalist relations. Liberal international law models legitimise the inequalities of the international political economy, and ignore how international human rights regimes advantage core states against periphery states. Human rights' correctives to capitalist production and market relations do not transcend their inequalities. Instead, they expand external governance of populations, rather than increasing their substantial freedom or equality. Consequently, human rights expansion has been described as neoliberalism or a form of post-liberal politics.

Political content of law

Influential critical legal studies are concerned over the marginalising of politics in human rights approaches. They want to reassert substantial historical political understandings of human rights as against procedural accounts of human rights (Bowring, 2008; Douzinas, 2000; Žižek, 2005). Within the Birkbeck School, Douzinas is concerned that human rights have become reduced to individual legal, bureaucratic solutions (Douzinas, 2000, p. 380), while Bowring is concerned that human rights philosophy has become separated from the world and political action, elevating the role of the critic over political struggle (Bowring, 2008, p. 144). Bowring wants to reassert the practical use of human rights in present political struggles, against post-modern impasses, or human rights as a quasi-religious kingdom to come (Bowring, 2008, p. 147). Political engagement and membership of a political community give content to human rights, and meaning to speech rights (Arendt, 1968, pp. 290–302; Bowring, 2008, pp. 142–3; Burke, 1986; Douzinas, 2000, pp. 147–81; Marx, 1844). Importantly, human rights subjects are active agents of their rights when they are grounded in political struggle. However, the procedural groundings of international human rights regimes involve distinctions between expert third-party advocates and human rights victim subjects. In this division of the human rights subject, human rights become a form of 'politics without politics', reduced to expert administration (Bowring, 2008, p. 126). Simultaneously, legal presumptions shift from liberal ideals of citizens as autonomous rational subjects to individuals unable to act without professional mediation, and in turn increasingly circumscribe their personal relations (Reece, 2003; 2009; Yuill, 2006, pp. 199–201). The prevailing human rights approaches cast doubt on people's moral agency and have been tempted to foreclose the diversity of outcomes that democratic politics allows. International human rights regimes elevate the role of global expert elites, and exclude mass participation – indicative that contemporary human rights advocacy shows mistrust of majorities. Such fears of the majority contain unsettling echoes of the older crowd theories against the masses, notwithstanding their evident political differences (Le Bon, 1995, [1895]; Ortega y Gasset, 1961, [1930]).

If key critical legal approaches affirm the potential of conscious collective politics, and seek more democratic politics (Bowring, 2008; Žižek, 1999a), other critical strands end up marginalising political legal subjectivity and reasserting a transcendental ahistorical view of law. Post-structuralist theories, like other critical legal theories, question standard accounts of law, assuming law's legality and non-violence (Fitzpatrick, 2001, p. 77). They draw on Friedrich Nietzsche's *On the Genealogy of Morals*, which argues that the social contract, deriving from creditor–debtor relations, established the sanctity of promises through violence (Nietzsche, 1996, [1887]). Derrida, following Nietzsche, sees violence as inherent to legal order, with its origins in the primal horde against the father, or revolutionary overthrow of the preceding order (Derrida, 1992, pp. 33–5; Fitzpatrick, 2001, p. 78). Derrida's account of law as violence emphasises its originality and creativity against a natural law tradition. Declarations of rights represent originating actions, which assume their existence as an accomplished state (Derrida, 1992; Žižek, 1991, discussed in Fitzpatrick, 2001, pp. 79–81). Here we may compare the political philosopher Hannah Arendt's assertion of human subjectivity, individuality, and the originality of political action against its degradation under modern behaviouralist accounts (Arendt, 1998, [1958]).

Post-structuralist accounts pick up on Rousseau's doubts over the foundations of law. Rousseau's social contract argues: 'a people, since it is subject to laws, ought to be the author of them' (Rousseau, 1968, [1762], p. 83). But, Rousseau observes, the people's identity and authorship are in doubt. Rousseau raises the paradox that 'men would have to have already become before the advent of law that which they become as a result of law' (Rousseau, 1968, [1762], p. 87; Fitzpatrick, 2001, p. 79). Rousseau concludes that a lawgiver, some higher external authority, is required to confer law on the people, analogous to God creating human subjects (Rousseau, 1968, [1762], pp. 80–8; Fitzpatrick, 2001, p. 83).

Rousseau's account suggests law as the agent, rather than law being the outcome of competing political forces. Democratising pressures fostered ideals of people as authors of law, against counter-pressures circumscribing those democratic forces. Political struggles witnessed people as authors of law in unprecedented ways, even if their role reflected brief revolutionary moments, as witnessed at points in the English Civil War, the American, French, Haitian and Russian Revolutions, anti-colonial and anti-Apartheid struggles or the recent Middle Eastern uprisings (Grovogui, 1996; Hill, 1975; James, 2001, [1938]; L'Ouverture, 2008, [1793–1802]; Reed, 2007, [1919]). Against post-structuralist despair over law's foundations, Arendt suggests that democratic principles of 'mutual promise and common deliberation', as simultaneously a beginning act and an organising norm, could save founding acts from arbitrariness and become the organising law of future action (Arendt, 1973, pp. 213–14).

Post-structuralist accounts follow Rousseau's concerns that modern law developed in the name of the people, but under restricted electoral laws that denied the majorities' participation in the authorship of law (Fitzpatrick, 2001, pp. 82–3). Post-structuralist critiques capture the contemporary experience of law as external to the self. But their critical readings of law tend to marginalise any Tom Paines who struggled for political and civil freedoms. Law becomes tainted by primordial, original, undemocratic sin, whereby law's undemocratic past necessitates its future undemocratic character (Derrida, 1992). Rekindled hopes in human rights therefore become appeals to transcendent authorities, instead of appeals grounded in emancipatory democratic politics.

Post-liberal discourse approaches to law

Important ideological differences exist between different strands of contemporary human rights advocacy. Nevertheless, they commonly show a preference for law over politics, and a tendency to reduce politics to policy endorsement. Bowring's *Degradation of the International Legal Order?* (Bowring, 2008) explores how political understandings of human rights have shifted towards discourse approaches, ambivalent towards political speech. On the one hand, significant discourse approaches ground human rights in human communication. On the other hand, significant discourse approaches ground human rights in the limits of human communication. These approaches, though distinct, both complement expanding human rights governance.

Communication approaches come under diverse models and designations, including deliberative democracy, democratisation, democratic governance or social constructivist approaches. They share underlying influences from social psychology, which developed as a discipline to address the challenges of mass society through studies, such as John Dewey's *Democracy and Education* (1916) and *Freedom and Culture* (1940). Social psychology explored the capacity of the masses for democracy and advocated policies to educate the masses into democratic norms. Communicative approaches emphasise the reformist, educative function of law, and value the role of human rights in communicating new social norms. Most loosely, expanding human rights norms represent soft law, 'sending a message' to the public to change their behaviour (a favourite phrase of British government advisers of the last decade). At their strongest, human rights represent hard law, mandating policies as enforceable non-negotiable requirements or prohibitions, domestically encompassing criminal and civil law enforcement, and internationally encompassing a range of sanctions and military action.

Human rights governance, involving the promotion of expert-led policymaking, follows developments in other fields (Bowring, 2008, pp. 104–8; Cowan *et al.*, 2001, p. 13; Habermas, 1971, pp. 112–13; Habermas, 1995; Yuill, 2006, pp. 196–208). Expert governance tends to circumscribe ordinary people's public exercise of reason, as the social theorist Jürgen Habermas has analysed (Habermas, 1995; Rawls, 1973, pp. 95–8, 136–42; Yuill, 2006, pp. 196–208). Simultaneously, human rights promotions support the juridification of informal relations in the private sphere, as Habermas has further explored (Habermas, 1987, pp. 357–68). Habermas' own theories on communication and deliberative democracy involve similar tendencies to circumscribe politics, as Bowring has in turn explored (Bowring, 2008, pp. 104–8; Habermas, 1997; 2001). These approaches give us procedural descriptions, assuming harmonious democracies, susceptible to external evaluations, conditionality and targets (Bowring, 2008, pp. 119–30). However, they overlook questions of conflicting interests, or the political struggle for rights, or why individuals should participate in politics if expert reason determines policy (Bowring, 2008, pp. 119–30). Human rights advocacy, consistent with an elite model of politics, has retreated from political activism, and increasingly embraced professional lobbying or litigation for minority groups (Martel, 1999). Advocates' relation to ordinary people is increasingly didactic, as human rights educators in the classroom. Symptomatically, the human rights sector has become professionalised and characterised by human rights professionals, with a postgraduate qualification in human rights rather than a background in political activism. Linked to the wariness towards majorities and national political processes, there has also been a tendency among advocates to look to international and regional organisations, such as the European Union or Organisation of Security and Cooperation in Europe (OSCE) (Grin, 2003a; Packer, 2003; Holt and Packer, 2007).

I now want to consider human rights approaches based on incommunicability, which are linked to post-structuralist theories, discussed above. They recognise problems of power and powerlessness, yet their underlying pessimism over language is accompanied by pessimism over democratic politics and political speech.

Grounding human rights in pain and the impossibility of language

Key strands of contemporary advocacy ground human rights in an ethics of care and the commonality of pain against the failure of language. Approaches based on radical sympathy are advocated as ethically superior, and more inclusive for encompassing the most vulnerable, as opposed to approaches based in *logos*, the capacity for political speech and its antagonisms (Douzinas, 2000, pp. 354–5; Turner, 1993). Yet this appeal is ambivalent for humanist politics. In denying speech in favour of the cry of pain, we are, in Aristotle's understanding, questioning ourselves as political, speaking beings, and reducing human rights subjects to speechless animals.

Consider human rights appeals through 'the pain, suffering and death of others' (Perrin, 2004, p. 138; discussed in Bowring, 2008, pp. 145–6).

'[T]hought, experience, language: all are inadequate to the disaster'; language 'always falls short of making one suffer what the other has suffered', a sympathetic critic observes (Perrin, 2004, p. 139, p. 141). Yet speechless appeals effectively invite responses, not from fellow political subjects sharing a common political struggle, but from degraded 'bare forked' creatures. Indictments against language may legitimise fatalism or political quietism, or undemocratic solutions, as the philosopher Jean Paul Sartre warns (Sartre, 1967, p. 210, discussed in Murdoch, 1989, pp. 64–80). 'Something must be done' imperatives become individual petitions to authority, rather than collective political self-determination. Indeed, Sartre's warning, 'to distrust the incommunicable; it is the source of all violence' (Sartre, 1967, p. 211), is prophetic of the advocacy images which compelled demands for humanitarian war in the 1990s.

Failures of language and political imagination were not the inevitable response to human rights violations after the Holocaust. Against language's indictment, writers such as Primo Levi found imaginative language to write about the Holocaust experience, which gave victims dignity and individuality, and reaffirmed humanity and the possibilities of speech (Levi, 1986; 1988). Nor was it the prevailing response during the Cold War, with its elevation of the political dissident or dissident poet, championing freedom of speech and conscience. Thus writers saw themselves as preserving the truth in the face of totalitarian persecution (Akhmatova, 1989, [1935–1943], pp. 98–117). Equally, opposition to the Apartheid state demanded political speech, not silence, in the face of what Non-Aligned Movement countries regarded as the worst post-war racist crimes against humanity. Anti-Apartheid political writings emphasised people's collective political resistance, rather than the individual torture victim, and literary works focused on ordinary individuals' integrity and humanity against systematic racial degradation (Coetzee 1983; Paton 1958). Thus, campaign literature might symbolically relegate documentation of torture to an appendix (Brooks and Brickhill, 1980). Conversely, the 1990s' post-Apartheid responses and accounts of ethnic conflict made descriptions of physical humiliation, torture and killings more pivotal.

Earlier Cold War human rights appeals ennobled humanity, in their representations of prisoners of conscience as Christ-like martyrs, sacrificing their lives for political truth. Changing representations from the political human rights dissident to the depoliticised traumatised human rights victim arose against declining collective political engagement and declining social progress (Pupavac, 2008). The US national demoralisation over defeat in the Vietnam War, the end of the post-war economic boom and the stalled civil rights movement are the context for representations shifting to victim identities in the 1970s. In Europe, representations changed later, but sharply, from the mid-1980s, following the demise of collective working-class politics. Similar shifts occurred from political solidarity to victim advocacy in Latin

America (Ronsbo, 2004), South Africa (Jensen, 2008), the Middle East, the Balkans and other conflicts (Hughes and Pupavac, 2005; Pupavac, 2002).

Humanitarian and human rights advocacy in the 1990s became characterised by empathetic solidarity for traumatised victims, assuming governance of their interests over rights of self-determination (Pupavac, 2001; 2004). Trauma frameworks have assumed individual and collective therapeutic mediations to address perceived psychosocial cycles of trauma, violence and dysfunction among populations. Therapeutic governance of identity and communication has included sponsorship of official truth and reconciliation commissions and collective narratives of pain. The linguistic human rights turn therefore involves doubts over the psychosocial capacity of populations and unregulated informal relations. At heart, discourse approaches to human rights are ambivalent about speech and other civil liberties. 1990s appeals tend to degrade humanity into brutalised abusers and abused, even as they seek to engage the feelings of the targeted public. Appeals become a form of disaster pornography, with western human rights voyeurs vicariously stimulated by images dwelling on rape and torture (Burman, 1994). And cries of language's failure overlap with frustrated consumer desires to experience authentically.

Traumatic appeals to power legitimise paternalistic therapeutic governance, but it is questionable whether they advance political freedoms and rights (Pupavac, 2008). Here human rights advocacy converges with humanitarian action, but their convergence in the 1990s arguably undermined both human rights and humanitarianism, and furthered the rise of global governance, legitimising western military humanitarian interventions, or wars conducted in the name of human rights victims, whether in Kosovo or Afghanistan (Chandler, 2002; Chomsky, 1999; 2000; Laïdi, 1998, pp. 109–10, 119–21; Pupavac, 2006; Vaux, 2001). Even those attracted to radical human rights and humanitarian politics criticise unequal relations in international human rights advocacy, and the problem of who claims to speak on behalf of human rights victims (Douzinas, 2000, p. 131).

Enforcing global human rights regimes

Legal transports are not inherently problematic. Societies exchange much with each other: culture, religion, politics, science, mathematics, materials, goods and inventions (Bowring, 2008, pp. 183–205; Donnelly, 2003, p. 71). Against cultural relativist positions, eighteenth-century Haitian slaves did not reject human rights as French, but appropriated them against their French slave-owners (Grovogui, 1996, James, 2001; L'Ouverture, 2008, [1793–1802]). Equally, twentieth-century anti-colonial struggles appropriated ideals of political rights, developed in European political struggles, against the European colonial powers. Furthermore, human rights have established roots in various national legal traditions (Bowring, 2008).

But assertions of global law in a world of international inequalities are problematic for emancipatory politics. For who is empowered to determine human rights on behalf of human rights victims (Douzinas, 2000, p. 131)? An earlier political era was wary about expanding positive international law because of its potential for abuse by power. Instead, modern international law was underpinned by the principle of non-interference in the internal affairs of states to restrain the Great Powers (Berlin, 1969, p. 170; Lansing, 1921). A proactive system of international law licenses powerful states, with the greatest military and economic capacity, to intervene against weaker states. Critical studies suggest international law has been degraded and abused by the strongest states over the last decade (Bowring, 2008; Chandler, 2002; Chomsky, 1999; Douzinas, 2000; Fitzpatrick, 2001; Žižek, 2005). As such, human rights governance represents a form of legal imperialism asserting a new standard of civilisation against weaker countries (Fitzpatrick, 2001, pp. 200–1; Grovogui, 1996; Lewis, 1998). Cultural rights, rather than checking global governance, are accused of legitimising its regulation of local diversity (Chandler, 1999; Fitzpatrick, 2001, pp. 196–8, p. 217). Yet critiques of law as violence are peculiarly absent from the linguistic imperialism literature, whose strategies support expanding global legal governance. This neglect is surprising, considering how their critiques parallel each other. Linguistic imperialism critiques charge linguistics with neglecting the violent history accompanying the rise of global English and how power and violence adhere to global English (Phillipson, 1992), but they may be accused of overlooking the violent history accompanying the rise of international law and human rights (Grovogui, 1996; Heartfield, 2011; Mieville, 2005; Sellars, 2002).

International human rights proponents have promoted rights of intervention, which are problematic in an unequal world, where those with greater material capacity may assume the power to determine how human rights regimes are interpreted and enforced. Western states have given themselves the right to go to war in the name of humanitarianism and human rights from Kosovo to Libya against existing international prohibitions, making human rights into 'rights of death' (Douzinas, 2000, p. 374). The expanding human rights frameworks thus empower, rather than restrain, powerful states and their non-state actors to determine the interests of weaker subjects. Yet human rights subjects under global governance are not in a position to hold their erstwhile advocates accountable when the advocates' decisions are detrimental to the subjects' interests.

Nevertheless, some critics see the potential to use international legal remedies and reclaim international human rights from their appropriation by Great Powers. Bowring suggests that international law could be used to indict western politicians for their decisions to go to war in contravention of the UN Charter. Bowring has acted in human rights cases before the

European Court of Human Rights (ECHR), and has had some legal successes on behalf of victims in the Chechnya conflict against the Russian state (Bowring, 2008, pp. 79–88). However, his study also testifies to how unequal state power relations influence international law enforcement. Others remain sceptical about expanding global human rights governance and the potential of its remedies (Chandler, 2002; Chomsky, 2000; Duffield, 2007; Mieville, 2005; Žižek, 2005).

Outline of themes

This study explores historical, political and theoretical aspects of language rights. Chapter 2 discusses the different generations of human rights. Earlier language rights related to freedom of speech, non-discrimination or rights of communication. Later language rights have related to social and economic claims for support and cultural linguistic identity protections. Human rights advocates state the indivisibility of the three generations of rights, but tensions exist between them. Underlying mistrust of democratic politics drove human rights advocacy to seek minority rights protections beyond the reach of politics. Contemporary language rights involve readiness to circumscribe politics through law.

Chapter 3 traces back language rights politics to Enlightenment and Romantic debates. Enlightenment thinking emphasised speech rights, while Romantic thinking emphasised national language rights. Language rights advocacy broadly follows the counter-enlightenment and conservative Romantic tradition. However, today's language rights advocacy, as Chapter 4 discusses, differs from earlier Romantic ideals embodied in Humboldt's theories of human subjectivity and linguistic creativity. Later Boasian linguistic anthropology and the Sapir-Whorf hypothesis suggest linguistic determinism rather than linguistic creativity. Language rights advocacy, influenced by the Boasian anthropological tradition, retreats from earlier Romantic beliefs to more fatalistic models of cultural linguistic conditioning and adaptation.

Chapter 5 considers the problem of Babel. Rights to translation have been linked to language communication rights, but have increasingly been advocated as language identity rights. Translation theories have shifted from belief in linguistic creativity towards more pessimistic ideas, suggesting the limits and violence of translation. The post-modern philosopher Jacques Derrida's essay on Babel's linguistic imperialism attacks the Babel builders as colonial oppressors (Derrida, 2007, [1985]). But, rather than siding with the oppressed subjects, his deconstructivist approach sides with a jealous God against humanity. Ultimately, anti-translation theories, despite their identification with political radicalism, end up echoing nationalist thinking on language purity and, endorsing linguistic governance against linguistic freedom.

Chapter 6 discusses linguistic imperialism. Linguistic imperialism theories represent Romantic critiques of modernity. Their opposition to assimilation differs from earlier Marxist critiques of capitalism and anti-colonial nationalist approaches. Linguistic imperialism critiques, focused on global English, miss the anti-modernising strands of British colonial rule. Colonial language policies did not necessarily seek to impose the imperial language on subject populations (Pennycook, 1998). British colonial authorities were nervous about the disturbing influences of modernity, and feared the creation of 'deracinated' natives. Instead, colonial language policies sought to maintain native cultures and languages, as part of colonial native administration against anti-colonial nationalist politics.

Chapter 7 considers language politics, from the aspirations of anti-colonial opposition to the problems of post-independence nation-building and language planning. It discusses the anti-colonial and negritude writings, focusing on the ideas of Cesaire, Fanon and Senghor, and how their attitudes towards language are distinct from later post-colonial thinking. Nationalist ideals went further than earlier historical ideals of nation-building in seeking to realise national justice. However, national development aspirations and progressive language planning were frustrated, and former colonial languages continue to dominate.

International language rights advocacy and linguistic imperialism critiques reject modernisation, and follow sustainable development approaches seeking to promote indigenous languages. However, tensions exist between advocates' sustainable development models and their global human rights governance strategies, which require comprehensive state provision to protect minority languages. While their critiques often invoke counter-culture philosophies, their rights strategies are essentially institutionalising solutions, opposed to counter-culture ideals. Linguistic imperialist approaches fail to offer a progressive critique of contemporary global power relations. Instead, their strategies may be analysed as a form of legal multicultural imperialism, legitimising expanding global governance over weaker societies.

International linguistic human rights advocacy seeks official recognition of difference. Chapter 8 considers how international conflict management strategies promote recognition of difference, through exploration of language politics in Social Federal Republic (SFR) Yugoslavia, and the successor state of Bosnia. The case illustrates problems with the institutionalisation of difference, whether under socialism or global (therapeutic) governance. Language rights advocacy has not given sufficient consideration to the problems raised by linguistic identity rights. Ratification of a maximalist position for ethnic groups endorses difference over commonality, and non-communication over communication. Ironically, external state-building in Bosnia, with its public regulation of cultural linguistic identities, embodies a bureaucratic model of politics and human subjectivity, restricting freedom of speech and cultural expression, and undermining the potential to transcend differences and envisage new social and political visions.

Chapter 9 discusses ecolinguistics and post-humanist rights advocacy. Ecolinguistics is distinct from earlier Romanticism in its fundamental questioning of human moral subjectivity and linguistic creativity. Ecolinguistic advocacy seeks global maintenance of linguistic diversity, making analogies between biological diversity and linguistic diversity. Advocates express passionate concern over language death, and seek to protect indigenous language communities from assimilation. Yet ecolinguistic governance strategies also express doubts over the capacity of indigenous peoples, for self-government and imperatives to manage indigenous relations. Ecolinguistic governance would change the character of indigenous communities and indigenous languages in ways which contradict advocates' counter-culture ideals of authenticity and de-institutionalisation.

Chapter 10 discusses the limits of free speech under expanding speech governance. The last two decades have seen the development of global technologies which offer expanded opportunities for global communication and expression challenging national restrictions. But fears over the new media's capacity to disseminate hate speech are fostering speech prohibitions in the name of cultural and victim protection. The UN Human Rights Commission (UNHRC), the Council of Europe and OSCE, as a security organisation with a key international role in minority rights governance in Eastern Europe, are leading initiatives to harmonise national hate speech legislation. Hate speech legislation and codes are creating rights not to be offended, which empower conservative cultural elements against freedom of expression. The chapter highlights how responses in the wake of the Salman Rushdie affair support more formal and informal regulation, rather than freedom. Furthermore, the very minorities whom advocates of hate speech legislation have sought to protect have found their freedom of speech threatened by the blurring of speech and action under hate speech and counterterrorism legislation.

Finally, the book evaluates recent attempts to reclaim political speech and action against both repressive regimes and expanding technocratic expert governance marginalising citizens as political subjects. The afterword highlights how the 2011 Arab Awakening became caught up in tensions between demands for international human rights intervention and self-determination. While the 2011 Occupy movement struggled to escape from a culture of linguistic governance. The book concludes with the call for freedom of speech and expression against expanding linguistic governance.

2
The Rise of International Linguistic Human Rights and the Legal Governance of Politics

Linguistic human rights advocacy

The language of rights is central to how language problems are approached today. Policy documents and academic literature put language rights at the heart of their analysis. Language rights-based policies are displacing traditional language planning, while sociolinguistic studies have become studies of language rights. Language rights are also increasingly discussed as *human rights*, inspired by the remarkable expansion of international human rights advocacy over the last couple of decades. Human rights have been looked to as values for a 'godless' or post-political age (Klug, 2000; Laïdi, 1998). In recent decades radicals and reformers have turned to law to address the spectrum of social concerns, disappointed with the inability of politics and economics to change societies globally (Bowring, 2008; Brown and Halley, 2002; Grigg-Spall and Ireland, 1992; King, 1997; Klug, 2000; Shute and Hurley, 1993). This turn to law contrasts with earlier left-wing scepticism towards law, which highlighted undemocratic legal power, legal abuses and miscarriages of justice (Griffith, 1977). International law is particularly associated by human rights advocates, with non-violence, and international politics with war and state violence (Robertson, 1999). This pattern was observed over seventy years ago by the international relations historian E.H. Carr (Carr, 1939, p. 219). Significantly, anthropology, influential in language advocacy, reversed its historical opposition to international human rights, and now commonly promotes indigenous human rights, including language rights (American Anthropological Association, 1999; Dembour, 2001; Engle, 2001; Messer, 1993; Scheper-Hughes, 1995; Turner, 1997; Wilson, 1997).

A broad shift to approaching language rights as international human rights is clear from 1990. Existing documents such as the International

Convention on Civil and Political Rights (ICCPR) 1966 were given wider scope. New documents were codified, such as the UN Declaration on the Rights of Persons Belonging to National or Ethnic, Religious and Linguistic Minorities 1992 and the European Charter for Regional or Minority Languages 1992. Commentaries on international linguistic human rights and comparative studies of national language rights have mushroomed over the last two decades (for example, Hogan-Brun and Wolff, 2004; *International Journal on Minority and Group Rights*, 1996/1997; Kontra *et al.*, 1999; Shuibhne, 2002; Skutnabb-Kangas and Phillipson, 1994; Skutnabb-Kangas *et al.*, 2009b; Varennes, 1996; 2001a). Initiatives seek to expand existing linguistic human rights, whether through drafting new documents such as the Universal Declaration of Linguistic Rights presented to UNESCO in 1996 or through expanding interpretation and enforcement of existing provisions (Skutnabb-Kangas, 1999, pp. 206–13; Skutnabb-Kangas and Dunbar, 2010).

My discussion critically examines core assumptions in international linguistic human rights advocacy, which are arguably not taken seriously enough and remain largely unchallenged (de Swaan, 2004, p. 575). Adoption of an international human rights approach to language problems is seen as more radical than the traditional language planning approaches, because it recognises problems of power and powerlessness, and seeks to empower minority language communities, not just treat them as service recipients (De Varennes, 2001b; Grin, 2005; Hamel, 1997a; Kontra *et al.*, 1999; Shuibhne, 2002; Phillipson, 1998; Skutnabb-Kangas, 1998; Skutnabb-Kangas and Phillipson, 1994). Concerns are repeatedly expressed that existing international human rights instruments are inadequate, or treated as soft law, and not (yet) enforceable (Grin, 2005; May, 2003; Rannut, 1999, p. 112; Réaume, 2003; Skutnabb-Kangas, 1998; 1999, pp. 204–12; Skutnabb-Kangas and Dunbar, 2010). Yet efforts to address language wrongs through the language of rights do not necessarily make linguistic human rights governance emancipatory. Linguistic human rights advocacy is commonly sceptical towards prescriptive grammar (Skutnabb-Kangas, 1998, p. 20), but its proposed rights governance is highly prescriptive.

Earlier rights movements focused on defending civil and political rights, freedoms of speech and association. However, contemporary human rights approaches, codifying more and more concerns as fundamental universal rights beyond politics, have anti-democratic implications. Politics is ideally the sphere where one comes together to speak reason with fellow citizens as peers (Arendt, 1998, [1958], pp. 26–7). Expanding human rights governance, codifying particular social justice models as formal mandatory norms, circumscribes politics (Laitin and Reich, 2003). Simultaneously, the public exercise of speech and association is undermined (Arendt, 1998, [1958], pp. 3–4). To put speech 'at stake', and marginalize the *polis*, is further to jeopardise individuals' subjectivity as *zoon politikon* and *zoon logon ekhon* ('a living being capable of speech') (Arendt, 1998, [1958], pp. 3–4, 26–7; Berlin, 1969, pp. 131–7). Equally, expanding human rights governance delegitimises alternative political visions and societies failing to follow the globally codified norms. Thus, linguistic human rights advocacy strategies, expanding 'law's empire', have implications for civil and political freedoms (Morgan, 2002), notwithstanding the attractive language of rights, empowerment and identity recognition.

International linguistic human rights framework

Language rights or linguistic human rights follow the dominant currents in the human rights sector. The term 'language rights' has been associated with state legislation and state language planning, while the growing reference to 'linguistic human rights' is associated with international law (see, for example, Kontra *et al.*, 1999). The terms language rights and linguistic human rights may therefore denote different sources of law, although strict demarcation of terms is not maintained in the literature, and will not be here. The distinction between national and international rights is significant, but is often blurred, especially in the writing on EU language rights policies. Increasingly, language policy literature shares the perspectives of linguistic human rights literature, conceptualises national language rights as deriving from international human rights obligations, and formulates language rights as supranational rights.

Importantly, the term 'linguistic human rights' signals a view of international law as supranational law, transcending nation states (Phillipson, 1998, pp. 109–10), against the classic understanding as the law of states (Brierly, 1928; Brownlee, 1971). Traditionally, international human rights documents were not treated as part of international law. Instead, human rights declarations were viewed as merely aspirational and not enforceable. International human rights advocacy in the 1990s challenged traditional law models, arguing that the state was too often a site of oppression, and national sovereignty a cloak for human rights abuses (Cassese, 1994; Rawls, 1999; Robertson, 1999). Human rights advocacy has sought recognition of international human rights as supranational rights, overriding the principles of national sovereignty and non- interference in the internal affairs of states. As language rights commentator Niamh Shuibhne outlines:

> Contemporary human rights law envisages that participating states surrender a considerable degree of sovereignty and thus stands in marked contrast to the original inter-state system. (Shuibhne, 2002, p. 190)

In this vein, the draft Universal Declaration of Linguistic Rights 1996 seeks modification of the international system as a state-based order:

> this Declaration takes language communities and not states as its point of departure and is to be viewed in the context of the reinforcement of international institutions capable of guaranteeing sustainable and equitable development for the whole of humanity. (Universal Declaration of Linguistic Rights, 1996, Preamble 2)

There is readiness to treat existing human rights as supranational law – the UN Special Rapporteur on Article 27 ICCPR has sought for minority rights protections to be enforceable irrespective of domestic recognition (Shuibhne, 2002, p. 232). There is also a push to categorise human rights violations as crimes against humanity, a trend evident in linguistic rights advocacy (Skutnabb-Kangas, 1998; Skutnabb-Kangas and Dunbar, 2010).

Thickening human rights regimes have moved from a focus on protecting civil and political rights against political persecution to encompass the spectrum of global concerns, manifested in rights-based approaches to development, child welfare, the environment and so on. Comprehensive visions of the good life are being elaborated, as advocates categorise their global concerns as fundamental rights, correspondingly expanding the positive duties on states, communities and individuals. International human rights are further becoming incorporated into the global governance of countries through internationally negotiated post-conflict settlements, or Poverty Reduction Strategy Papers, which have replaced the former structural adjustment programmes (Chandler, 1999; 2002; 2010; Duffield, 2007; Harrison, 2004; Pender, 2002).

Language rights advocacy has followed the three generations of rights, namely civil and political rights, economic and social rights, and cultural or identity rights. When earlier human rights thinking focused on civil and political rights, language rights were primarily conceived in these terms. As human rights advocacy has taken up third-generation cultural rights, language rights have shifted to identity protection against assimilation. Thus, the OSCE envisages the objective of rights protection to be:

> one of 'integrating diversity', that is the simultaneous maintenance of different identities and the promotion of social integration. This implies a pluralist, multicultural model of societal organisation based on the principle of non-discrimination (as opposed to an assimilationist or exclusivist approach). (Holt and Packer, 2001, p. 102)

Meanwhile, language rights provisions in existing international documents are being re-interpreted to support identity maintenance.

Table 2.1 Key relevant international documents

UN (1948) Universal Declaration of Human Rights
UN (1965) International Convention on the Elimination of All Forms of Racial Discrimination (CERD)
UN (1966) International Covenant on Civil and Political Rights
UN (1989) UN Convention on the Rights of the Child
UN (1992) Declaration on the Rights of Persons Belonging to National or Ethnic, Religious and Linguistic Minorities
UNESCO(2002) UNESCO Universal Declaration on Cultural Diversity
UN (2007) United Nations Declaration on the Rights of Indigenous Peoples
Universal Declaration of Linguistic Rights (1996)
International Labour Organization (ILO) (1957) Indigenous and Tribal Populations Convention
International Labour Organization (ILO) (1989) Indigenous and Tribal Peoples Convention

Individual language rights are seen as inadequate and requiring recognition of collective language rights for their realisation (Hamel, 1997b, p. 127). The draft Universal Declaration of Linguistic Rights follows, 'the principle that linguistic rights are individual and collective at one and the same time' (Universal Declaration of Linguistic Rights, 1996, Preamble 2). After all, language is not something enjoyed alone, but in community with others. Even if thinking is 'a silent dialogue of myself with myself', and requires solitude, communication is required for developing the faculty of thought and a community of people (Arendt, 1992, pp. 40–1). However, contemporary linguistic human rights advocacy has not focused on collective rights to freedom of speech, expression and association. Rather, advocates seek to secure minority language communities, and facilitate their right to use a specific language (Del Valle, 2003, p. 2; Hamel, 1997a, pp. 7–8; May, 2001; 2003; Phillipson, 1998; Skutnabb-Kangas, 1998; Réaume, 2003; Varennes, 1999, p. 127). Their expanded model of fundamental rights codifies identity recognition. The argument runs briefly as follows. Identity is fundamental to the human personality and dignity; therefore identity should be recognised as a fundamental right, and states required to support people's identities. Language is one of the core constitutive elements of our humanity and identity, so language rights should be treated as fundamental, constitutive rights (Skutnabb-Kangas, 1998, p. 5). Language rights are not, therefore, derivative of civil and political rights or discretionary privileges, but constitute fundamental rights in themselves (Réaume, 2003; 2003, p. 283; Shuibhne, 2002, p. 201).

Advocates also support non-state definitions of linguistic identity, whether defined internationally or by groups themselves (Pennycook, 1998b, p. 86). They actively seek to foster minority identities and prevent language loss. Securing the conditions for the use and maintenance of a specific language is regarded as part of fundamental rights, not merely enrichment claims (del Valle, 2003, p. 344; Réaume, 2003; Phillipson, 1998; Shuibhne, 2002, p. 191; Skutnabb-Kangas, 1998; Skutnabb-Kangas and Phillipson, 1994). Furthermore, linguistic diversity is theorised in terms of biodiversity (Fill and Mühlhäusler, 2001; Maffi, 2001; Skutnabb-Kangas *et al.*, 2003; WWF and Terralingua, 2000), as I discuss in Chapter 9. Just as biodiversity is regarded as crucial for the planet's survival, so too is linguistic diversity. As such everybody has a stake in preventing language shift and loss. The European Bureau for Lesser Used Languages has therefore argued that cultural and linguistic diversity should be treated as fundamental rights (Shuibhne, 2002, p. 245). Some advocacy further believes a firm duty to learn and maintain one's mother tongue should be recognised as part of preventing language shift (Skutnabb-Kangas, 1998, p. 21).

International human rights documents reflect shifting thinking. The UN Charter 1945, the Universal Declaration of Human Rights 1948 and the ICCPR 1966 refer to non-discrimination and freedom of expression. The ICCPR 1966 provides that persons belonging to ethnic, religious or linguistic minorities 'shall not be denied the right, in community with other members of their group...to use their own language' (UN ICCPR, 1966, article 27). Positive actions are only expected of states insofar as they are necessary to access civil and political rights, for example, employment of a court interpreter to ensure a defendant understands the proceedings. In contrast, later international human rights provisions require states actively to maintain linguistic identities, not simply to refrain from discrimination. The UN Declaration on the Rights of Persons Belonging to National or Ethnic, Religious and Linguistic Minorities 1992, for example, requires states to '*protect the existence* and the national or ethnic, cultural, religious and *linguistic identity* of minorities within their respective territories, and shall *encourage conditions for the promotion of that identity*' (UN, 1992, article 1, emphasis added). Towards this end, the 1992 Declaration requires states to '*take measures to create favourable conditions* to enable persons belonging to minorities *to express their characteristics and to develop their culture, language,* religion, traditions and customs' (article 4, emphasis added). Likewise, the Council of Europe's European Charter for Regional or Minority Languages 1992 expects positive affirmation of linguistic identity in both public and private usage. Again, the Council of Europe's Framework Convention for the Protection of National Minorities 1995 considers states should not only:

> respect the ethnic, cultural, linguistic and religious identity of each person belonging to a national minority, but also create appropriate conditions enabling them to express, preserve and develop this identity. (Council of Europe, 1995, Preamble)

The OSCE also refers states to documents such as the Oslo Recommendations Regarding the Linguistic Rights of National Minorities (1998) or The Hague Recommendations Regarding the Education Rights of National Minorities (1996), which they treat as 'expert interpretation of binding, legal obligations and political commitments' (Holt and Packer, 2001, pp. 105–6). Again, the UN Declaration on the Rights of Indigenous Peoples 2007 seeks to secure communities against assimilation and wants states to provide indigenous peoples with access to education in their own culture and language (article 14). Earlier international provisions were less concerned with linguistic security than with integration. Thus, an earlier 1957 ILO convention on indigenous populations states that 'Appropriate measures shall, as far as possible, be taken to preserve the mother tongue or the vernacular language' (article 23(3)). Nevertheless, the 1957 ILO convention envisages 'a progressive transition from the mother tongue or vernacular language to the national language or one of the official languages of the country' (ILO, 1957, article 23 (2)).

Linguistic human rights advocates seek to expand global linguistic identity rights through drafting a Universal Declaration of Linguistic Rights. The draft contains clauses on maintaining and developing one's culture, and expanded rights of language use (Skutnabb-Kangas, 1998, pp. 10–11; 1999, pp. 206–12; Universal Declaration of Linguistic Rights, 1996). The draft proposal refers to linguistic rights supporting 'a satisfactory sociolinguistic balance' (Universal Declaration, 1996, article 2 (2)). The drafters believe that:

> All languages are the expression of a collective identity and of a distinct way of perceiving and describing reality and must therefore be able to enjoy the conditions required for their development in all functions. (Universal Declaration of Linguistic Rights, 1996, article 1)

Accordingly, the drafters want recognition that: 'All language communities are entitled to have at their disposal *whatever means are necessary* to ensure the transmission and continuity of their language' (Universal Declaration

Table 2.2 Key relevant European documents

Council of Europe (1950) Convention for the Protection of Human Rights and Fundamental Freedoms (ECHR)
Council of Europe (1992) European Charter for Regional or Minority Languages
Council of Europe (1995) Framework Convention for the Protection of National Minorities
Council of Europe (2003) Additional Protocol To The Convention On Cybercrime, Concerning The Criminalisation Of Acts Of A Racist And Xenophobic Nature Committed Through Computer Systems

of Linguistic Rights, 1996; article 8.2 in Skutnabb-Kangas, 1999, p. 207, emphasis added). Individuals are considered under the Declaration to have the right to use their language, both in 'private and in public', as 'inalienable personal rights which may be exercised in any situation' (ibid.). Legal commentary within the field supports expanding rights, although broader human rights literature has more mixed views. Influential legal commentator Fernand de Varennes has argued:

> There is a growing legal acceptance in treaties that states have a positive obligation to provide public services, benefits and privileges in the language of a specific minority in appropriate circumstances. (De Varennes, 1999, p. 127)

In this vein, the UN Human Rights Committee's 1994 General Comment on article 27 of the 1966 Covenant interprets the right as encompassing positive state duties, not just non-discrimination (Skutnabb-Kangas, 1998, p. 10). Consider, for example, how the 1966 Covenant refers to 'free assistance of an interpreter *if* he cannot understand or speak the language used in court' (International Covenant, 1966, article 14, emphasis added). Under this provision, a member of a minority is entitled to interpretation assistance in court to facilitate understanding and participation in legal proceedings, not as recognition of his or her distinct linguistic identity. Legal commentary notes how:

> these provisions are grounded firmly in the principles of natural justice, relating only to instances where an individual cannot *understand* the language used by the relevant official authorities; they do not introduce any right of *choice* of language. (Shuibhne, 2002, p. 224, emphasis in original)

Legal commentators are disappointed where the European Court of Justice or national courts recognise only rights of comprehension, not linguistic identity choices (Shuibhne, 2002, p. 224; De Varennes, 1996, pp. 38–40; 70–4). Nevertheless, there is more readiness to recognise linguistic identities, even if a fundamental right has not been established. The Committee of Experts on the 1992 European Charter expects courts to recognise linguistic identity, as it states in its report to Croatia:

> It should be underlined that this provision [article 9], whereby the Parties undertake to guarantee the accused the right to use his/her regional or minority language, goes beyond the right of the accused, as laid down in article 6 paragraph 3.e of the European Convention on Human Rights, to have the free assistance of an interpreter if he cannot understand or speak the language used in court. This measure goes further in the sense

> that speakers of a regional or minority language may use that language before a court of law, *even if they are capable of communicating in the official language*, thereby creating or enlarging the space for the use of these languages in the public sphere. (Council of Europe, 2001, paragraph 62, emphasis added)

The 1990s witnessed international and regional human rights frameworks evolving into regulatory regimes, globalising models of justice to which national law and policy were expected to conform. Maintaining linguistic diversity, rather than defending freedoms, drives today's language advocacy (Ives, 2004a; 2004b; 2004c; 2004d; May, 2001; 2003; Phillipson, 1992; 2009a; Skutnabb-Kangas, 1998; 2001). Human rights frameworks are prominent in qualification for EU accession and governance of post-conflict societies such as Bosnia (Chandler, 1999). Yet multiculturalist policies codifying identity rights entrench social differences, and exacerbate social tensions, as shown by former Yugoslavia and Bosnia (discussed in Chapter 8).

Grounding linguistic human rights?

Language rights literature has predominantly been written from an advocacy perspective, and consequently assumes that recognising rights must advance political and social justice. However, if we understand that law historically shows both progressive and repressive strands, we cannot assume that expanding human rights is necessarily emancipatory. Unfortunately, the sincerity of endeavours elaborating detailed regulatory mechanisms does not guarantee the progressive character of human rights; or, indeed, the compatibility between the different generations of rights, including efforts to establish a fourth generation of ecological rights.

The linguistic human rights literature rarely raises the problem of how language rights are grounded, and shares the impatience of much human rights literature with such questions. A characteristic contribution speaks of how 'We should begin, not with a theoretical anxiety about the nature and origin of rights, but rather with a political question about what protection rights can afford us' (Mendus, 1995, p. 17). Classically, human rights were derived from natural rights, but natural rights theories may be criticised as giving ahistorical accounts of law. Belief in individuals' natural rights historically developed in the political and social transformations of the seventeenth and eighteenth centuries and the individualism arising from the breakdown of feudal order and privileges. But the accompanying secularism ironically undermined the origins of natural rights in a religious providential order, even as sovereignty and the authority of law was passing from the monarch to citizens (Dicey, 1959, [1889], p. 183 and p. 203). So human rights have a specific historical, political cultural foundation, as opposed to a universal grounding.

The few language rights studies raising theoretical concerns note the neglect of the subject. In the late 1980s, the lawyer Denise Réaume observed: 'a singular inattention to the development of a principled theoretical grounding as an important aspect of human rights' (Réaume, 1991, p. 57; discussed in Shuibhne, 2002, p. 188). Surveying the field a decade later, the language rights specialist Shuibhne similarly observed how 'theoretical frameworks are rarely constructed in the language rights context specifically', in one of the rare contributions to the subject (Shuibhne, 2002, p. 189). An excellent collection of essays on *Language Rights and Political Theory* by Will Kymlicka and Alan Patten came out a year later (Kymlicka and Patten, 2003). The editors suggest that existing linguistic human rights claims have not been substantiated and seem 'more like the conclusion of an argument than the argument itself' (Patten and Kymlicka, 2003, p. 36). This perception is evident in advocacy declaring: 'there should be no need to debate the right... It is a self-evident fundamental *collective* human right' (Skutnabb-Kangas, 1998, p. 22). Within the collection, Réaume seeks to piggy-back linguistic group rights onto human rights as reciprocal moral claims and human interests (Réaume, 2003, pp. 284–5). However, overall the collection suggests that international human rights could or should offer only minimal standards.

Insofar as advocates have raised the theoretical grounding of language rights, discussion has been preoccupied with formalising language rights as fundamental rights, that is, entrenching claims, as opposed to actually theoretically grounding them. Writing twenty-five years ago, Leslie Green dismissed the problem, arguing: 'we need not seek timeless, transcendental proofs of the existence of fundamental rights, and it is just as well as we will not find them' (Green, 1987, p. 647; discussed in Shuibhne, 2002, p. 197). Indicatively, Shuibhne refers to establishing language rights as fundamental rights, 'by whatever theoretical means' (Shuibhne, 2002, p. 194). The subordination of discussion to this objective leads to the subject being set aside, or fudged through official recognition, when theoretical efforts flounder. Shuibhne, having raised the problem of grounding fundamental rights, then brackets the matter, referring to, 'language rights – as fundamental rights, *however so derived...*' (Shuibhne, 2002, p. 223, emphasis added). Instead, she places hope in their official recognition as fundamental rights, declaring that, 'EC language policy could clearly be reconstituted more coherently to express the value of language rights as fundamental rights' (Shuibhne, 2002, p. 261). She describes, 'the recognition and protection of language rights as fundamental rights' as, 'an underdeveloped facet of EC language policy, causing a deficit that should be remedied' (Shuibhne, 2002, p. 263). Official legal recognition may seem a neat solution, and identifying theoretical problems may be seen as semantic nit-picking. Yet formal declaratory resolution evades problems with the form of law being promoted by contemporary human rights advocacy, and is symptomatic of a broader technocratic approach to law, politics and social justice apparent in the European Union (Menendez, 2004).

Anthropology and human rights

Legal anthropology notes that human rights' lack of consistent theoretical grounding has not prevented their practical use, but has given more attention to the problem of grounding human rights (Wilson, 1997). This attention is linked to overcoming anthropology's historical scepticism towards human rights (Handwerker, 1997; Messer, 1993; Scheper-Hughes, 1995; Turner, 1997). Famously, the American Anthropological Association in 1947 made a statement declaring itself against international human rights, invoking cultural relativist critiques of human rights as embodying western economic individualism (AAA, 1947; Barnett, 1948; Dembour, 2001; Engle, 2001; Steward, 1948; Washburn, 1987; Wilson, 1997, pp. 2–5). Anthropology has stressed how culture shapes personality, and has contested the classical grounding of human rights in a universal human nature (Wilson, 1997, pp. 4–5). Traditionally, anthropology sees a community's (legal) norms as grounded in its culture. Relativist understandings of the incommensurability of cultures, languages and world views challenge ideals of universal human rights. Indeed, authoritarian governments have invoked cultural relativism and cultural imperialism to reject international human rights as a western imposition (Wilson, 1997, pp. 8–9).

Anthropological studies note the ironies of groups demanding recognition for cultural difference in the universal discourse of human rights (Wilson, 1997, pp. 9–10). Strategies appealing to a universal discourse of human rights, and asserting universal needs for linguistic identity recognition, are at variance with the anti-universalist aspects of linguistic human rights advocacy. To counter cultural relativist opposition, anthropological advocacy has been interested in finding human rights norms in traditional cultures. A situated ethics has attracted language advocates like Alastair Pennycook, who are ambivalent about imposing western rights frameworks onto non-western societies (Pennycook, 1998b). Nevertheless, critics have argued that the deduced norms are not strictly human rights, but forms of human dignity, or constraints on arbitrary exercise of power, normally related to obligations to deities, as opposed to individuals (Wilson, 1997, p. 6; pp. 13–14).

Anthropology has also been attracted towards efforts to ground human rights in human frailty (Rawls, 1973; Turner, 1993; Wilson, 1997, p. 5). Ideas of humans as incomplete without social empowerment to support their self-realisation fit with advocacy concerns to establish special protections for vulnerable linguistic identities (Pennycook, 1998b; Skutnabb-Kangas, 1999). Yet anthropological unease exists over approaches echoing paternalistic models of saving natives, or treating individuals as blank sheets until written on by external authorities (Kuper, 2003). There is some dissent towards approaches treating people as frail, and fixing people into victimhood statuses (Gledhill, 1997; Holborow, 1999, pp. 84–6). Different societies might not identify themselves in terms of ontological frailty (Wilson, 1997, p. 15). Such advocacy globalises contemporary western risk consciousness as a fundamental human characteristic. But the idea of universal human vulnerability has arisen in a particular historical, cultural context (Bracken, 2002; Furedi, 2003; Hacking, 1995; Holborow, 1999, pp. 80–6; Lasch, 1984; Summerfield, 2001). Grounding human rights or language advocacy in ontological frailty embodies contemporary western post-liberal cultural assumptions against its past assumptions of independent character. Prominent language advocates are inclined to see individuals and groups as vulnerable, whereas sceptics are more likely to follow earlier ideals of 'people as independent beings, capable of acting in their own best interests' (Davies, 1997, p. 248).

Linguistic imperialism and ecolinguistics studies condemn Anglo-American hegemony and assumptions of the superiority of global English and modern industrial societies (Maffi, 2001; Phillipson, 1992; Skutnabb-Kangas and Phillipson, 1994; Skutnabb-Kangas *et al.*, 2003; WWF and Terralingua, 2000). Yet language advocacy treating people as powerless victims denies people's historical political agency, and elevates the (western) advocate saviour, as Holborow observes (Holborow, 1999, p. 86). For its advocacy uncritically looks to international law-making and global governance, whether through the United Nations, the European Union, or bodies like the OSCE. Strikingly, linguistic imperialism critics and linguistic human rights advocates rarely cite their fellow linguist Chomsky's critiques of western foreign policy (Chomsky, 1999; 2000). Reluctance may exist because Chomsky's theories of universal grammar clash with advocates' emphasis on linguistic difference, while his critique of human rights imperialism clashes with their global governance strategies. Nevertheless, Chomsky believes in linguistic diversification from an underlying unity, and is interested in advocacy over endangered languages, although wary of human rights power politics (Chomsky, 2006).

Law and culture

Even if claims to cultural difference have been accommodated in international human rights regimes, questions remain over the extent to which social progress may be advanced through human rights. Legal advocacy needs to take into account the contingent character and capacity of law in different social conditions, as Montesquieu's pioneering eighteenth-century comparative legal study *The Spirit of Laws* suggests (Montesquieu, 1949, [1748]). The language theorist Peter Ives does not pursue critical analysis of linguistic human rights advocacy, but his Gramscian theories of organic political movements and translatability of ideas also suggest problems with the translatability of law across different societies with different prevailing conditions (Ives, 2004a, pp. 107–9). Studies have observed a relationship between a country's legal norms and its social, economic and cultural conditions and means of production (Arendt, 1972, pp. 63–76; Dicey, 1959, [1889]; Geertz, 1983, p. 215; Heartfield, 2002; Mieville, 2005; Neumann, 1996; Pashukanis, 1978; Weber, 1954). The relationship between modern human rights and developed capitalist relations suggests that rights enforcement will be strained under the traditional agricultural and patrimonial relations prevailing in many developing countries. So, while linguistic human rights advocacy is strongly influenced by anthropological ideas of language as culture, its normative model departs from previous anthropological understanding of the limits of law, where social and cultural ways of life are at variance (Malinowski, 1945, p. 45).

Put bluntly: 'law is culture and culture is law' (Grossfeld, 1990, p. 41). If older constructivist approaches emphasise how law reflects social relations, later constructivist approaches emphasise law as shaping social relations (Geertz, 1983; Milanović, 1992; Santos, 1987). Idealist interpretations of legal social constructivism have informed expanding universal human rights since the 1990s. Cultures are not islands, and the western origins of human rights concepts do not preclude their incorporation into other cultures, or their use by oppressed groups (Donnelly, 2003, p. 71; Wilson, 1997, p. 10). The Haitian Revolution, of slaves against French rule asserting the rights of man, testifies to emancipatory political appropriation (Grovogui, 1996; James, 2001, [1938]; L'Ouverture, 2008, [1793–1802]). Nevertheless, there are problems with globalising legal norms where the historical conditions underpinning those norms have not been globalised. Namely, predominantly agricultural societies and post-industrial societies have very different capabilities for realising legal entitlements (Pupavac, 2009). Importantly, rights change their character where they have to be enforced against the prevailing social conditions. Problems complying with international human rights regimes in poorer, weaker countries legitimise more external governance and its related unequal power relations (Lewis, 1998).

Ironically, expanding human rights governance accelerates the spread of global English, which linguistic human rights advocacy seeks to combat. Consider how Bosnia's constitution, with its human rights annexes, was drawn up by US negotiators under the Dayton Agreement in 1995, and then translated into Bosnian/Croatian/Serbian (Chandler, 1999). Under international supervision, English now pervades Bosnian society, from public institutions to the non-governmental (NGO) sector to higher education and the media. Meanwhile, ecolinguistic proposals to support vulnerable language communities, arising from collaboration between the language advocacy organisation Terralingua and the World Wildlife Fund

(WWF), imply even more intense governance of communities (WWF and Terralingua, 2000). But treating indigenous people as endangered exotic wildlife species to be preserved is deeply problematic for anti-racist emancipatory politics (Butcher, 2003; 2007; Kuper, 2003; Wilder, 1997).

The human rights literature pointedly highlights abuses of power, but has generally been reluctant to interrogate the power relations within human rights advocacy (Wilson, 1997, pp. 16–17). Similarly, while the linguistic imperialism and language advocacy literature has explored the power relations of global English (Ives, 2004a), it has neglected those implied by international linguistic human rights governance. Their advocacy for human rights conventions converges with legal positivism, against earlier critiques of law as forms of power and violence (Wilson, 1997, p. 8). While their human rights accounts sometimes slip into simplistic dichotomies between the tainted world of politics and the disinterested world of human rights, where power relations are seemingly absent. They may acknowledge that western states dominated the drafting of the Universal Declaration of Human Rights 1948. However, they treat the post-Cold War human rights system as having been developed by a global civil society of westerners and non-westerners, including indigenous peoples (Merry, 2001, pp. 35–8). Concerns over the violence of law, or human rights embodying western perspectives and interests, are put aside or relegated to footnotes (Merry, 1992; Pennycook, 1998b, pp. 73–4, p. 79; Skutnabb-Kangas, 1999, p. 217), in the imperative to codify more social, cultural and linguistic rights. Today's human rights system is considered to be 'a product of negotiation and discussion rather than imposition', making it a more egalitarian 'pluralized, flexible, and responsive system' (Merry, 2001, pp. 40–1). Nevertheless, questions of power remain in human rights governance. Moreover, cultural rights legitimise more intrusive external governance of communities. The language of empowerment is no guarantee of progressive, egalitarian politics.

Law over politics

Shuibhne speaks of the importance of establishing language rights as fundamental rights because, 'it aids the entrenchment of protection for related claims, taking them outside the discretionary arena of administrative policy' (Shuibhne, 2002, p. 194). Yet the thrust of human rights arguments in recent decades has not ultimately been against administrative power. Indeed, language rights advocacy presupposes an enhanced role for the state in regulating individual subjectivity and communal relations, although anti-state sentiments are common, especially in international linguistic rights literature. Rather, imperatives to ground language rights as fundamental rights appear underpinned by distrust of the indeterminate nature of democratic politics and informal social relations. International language rights codes represent expert-made law over the *demos*. People's ability to live with diversity is doubted and is assumed to create conflict:

> Owing to its conflictual and threatened character, ethnic, linguistic, and cultural diversity cannot simply be left to itself, and emerges as a necessary area of policy intervention in modern societies. (Grin, 2003b, p. 180)

Leaving policy contingent upon political contestation is seen as too risky, not just in undemocratic states, but in democratic states too. Advocates fear that democratic politics works against minorities. Linguistic rights advocates struggle to imagine political subjectivity outside ethnicised terms. People's ability to transcend their own position and empathise with others is mistrusted. Demands to entrench language rights as fundamental rights effectively seek to put them beyond both democratic contention and administrative discretion. Again and again, fears of democratic majorities are expressed in the human rights literature. Key language rights academic François Grin believes that 'a classical limitation of democracy is that in its elementary form of majority rule, it is insufficient to safeguard the rights of minorities' (Grin, 2003a, p. 157). Another language rights advocate, Angeline Martel, speaks of democracy as 'a fiction, an ideal unrealized where, traditionally, activism and lobbying have been the almost exclusive domain of the major interests in society' (Martel, 1999, p. 50). Mainstream interests are presented as antithetical to those of minorities: 'The democratic processes that guide policy are essentially majoritarian in nature, and there is no assurance that mainstream interests will not dominate in those decisions' (Rickard, 1994, p. 154, discussed in Shuibhne, 2002, pp. 194–5). Consequently, advocates suggest, majorities need to be checked by law:

> In democracies, founded by definition on the presupposed majority consensus, law acts as an intervenor, capable eventually of counterbalancing the tendencies of majorities to impose their hegemony in political and institutional spaces. (Martel, 1999, p. 74)

The language rights literature often expresses sympathies with alternative models of democracy, which limit the scope of majorities in determining political outcomes. A long-standing alternative proposed is the consociational model, which institutionalises ethnic rights and representation (Lijphart, 1977; Rannut, 1999, p. 109). More recently, Rawlsian-inspired 'diversity management' models have been favoured in the literature (Grin, 2003b; p. 178). Such ideals are evident in international linguistic rights advocacy, seeking equality between languages and equality of outcomes, not only equality of opportunity (Phillipson, 1998, p. 110; Skutnabb-Kangas, 1998, p. 22). Whatever the model, a perceived need to regulate majorities and informal relations is evident in European and international human rights processes. In the meantime, 'judicial activism' has been important in language rights developments (Shuibhne, 2002, p. 220).

It is highly ironic that language rights advocates should be wary of the political sphere, when language concerns communication, and the political sphere is above all the public space for speech and contestation of ideas (Arendt, 1998, [1958], pp. 26–7). Codification of advocacy concerns as fundamental rights, beyond the political sphere, suggests that people cannot really be trusted to determine competing ideas of justice and make ethical choices. Maximising the free political contestation of ideas is associated with undesirable outcomes. Certainly, politics might not endorse the policies human rights advocates wish to secure, but this does not necessarily mean that outcomes are unjust, merely that they embody different visions of justice (Laitin and Reich, 2003). So, while linguistic human rights advocacy condemns monolinguism and champions linguistic diversity, it appears less comfortable living with the indeterminacy of both the political and the private spheres. Advocacy for third-generation cultural rights implies revising first-generation civil and political rights, not simply supplementing them, through proposals such as recognising a firm duty to maintain one's mother tongue (Skutnabb-Kangas, 1998, p. 21). That the contemporary global human rights models support diversity of forms, but increasingly imply conformity of political and social content, is perhaps clearest in ecolinguistic advocacy, discussed in Chapter 9.

Evolving liberal theories of rights and justice

To better understand the growing importance of legal regulation and minority rights to effect social justice, it is useful to consider evolving liberal theories of rights and justice. Here I draw on Kevin Yuill's compelling analysis of US liberalism and race politics (Yuill, 2006). The post-war economic boom, expanding employment and rising living standards experienced by western states seemed to offer the possibilities of social justice overcoming systemic tensions between democratic ideals of equality and socio-economic inequalities (Yuill, 2006; pp. 17–18). Western European post-war democracies had been ready to use state intervention in their Keynesian economic and welfare models. Conversely, US Cold War anti-communism politics made US liberalism more hostile towards social engineering solutions, including legal regulation (Yuill, 2006, pp. 26–7). Policies emphasised economic expansion to overcome social divisions, including racial divisions.

Policy-makers followed Swedish sociologist and international development adviser Gunnar Myrdal's *An American Dilemma* (1944), which argued that equal opportunities, civic institutions and integration would overcome racial or ethnic prejudices (Myrdal, 1944, discussed in Yuill, 2006, pp. 20–5). Myrdal's approach did not believe in fostering group rights, which he saw as being at variance with the rights of the individual (Myrdal, 1944, p. 336; Yuill, 2006, p. 22). US policy opposition to using law for social engineering was paralleled internationally. US foreign policy, having initiated the UN Declaration on Human Rights 1948, did not seek to treat international human rights documents as law in this period (Evans, 1996; Sellars, 2000). Furthermore, minority rights had been discredited internationally during the Second World War through Nazi use (Arendt, 1968, pp. 267–302).

However, reliance on economic growth strategies to address social legitimacy and justice concerns was brought into question by slower economic growth (Habermas, 1976; Wolfe, 1977; Yuill, 2006, pp. 71–92). The evident social alienation and conflict manifested in civil and political violence (race riots, campus unrest, political assassinations), civil rights and anti-war movements, and the national moral and physical defeats in Vietnam created a legitimacy crisis which compelled the US government to become more interventionist from the 1970s, including using law to effect social and political change (Habermas, 1976; Yuill, 2006, pp. 84–7).

The changing economic, social, political, philosophical and legal assumptions of post-war liberalism may be illustrated in the evolving theories of the influential liberal philosopher John Rawls (Rawls, 1958; 1973; Yuill, 2006, pp. 196–208). Rawlsian models influence language rights approaches (Grin, 2003a; Réaume, 2003). Crucially, Rawls' model of justice, as it matured, shifted from assumptions of political, social and economic freedoms and informal regulation to administrative intervention and formal regulation. Rawls' 1958 article 'Justice as Fairness', paralleling the context of post-war growth liberalism, presumes that representative citizens will believe in the principle that unequal distribution works to their advantage (Rawls, 1958; Yuill, 2006, p. 198). However, his seminal work *A Theory of Justice* (1973) is sceptical about economic growth realising social justice, and suggests problems legitimising the system from the perspectives of the less advantaged (Rawls, 1973; Yuill, 2006, pp. 198–9). Rawls' revisions reflect the context of civil and political violence and economic slowdown. They seek to address legitimacy problems in conditions of moderate scarcity. His revised liberal principles shift from 'acceptability' to representative citizens to the 'greatest benefit' to the least advantaged (Rawls, 1973, pp. 95–8). The revised ideals are not merely supplementary, but involve profound shifts in liberal thinking: first, the implied comprehensive interventions to modify equality of opportunity and manage social and economic inequalities; second, the implied re-conception of citizens' rights, and a move from the former liberal ideal of rational, autonomous, moral self-determining individuals (Yuill, 2006, pp. 199–203).

Rawls' original model of justice saw political consensus achieved through citizens as active knowing political subjects in the public realm, who could represent universal interests (Rawls, 1958). But Rawls' revisions impose a so-called veil of ignorance on individuals, which effectively strips citizens of their individuality (Rawls, 1973, pp. 136–42). Instead, citizens are treated as fragmented, isolated subjects, who are guided by expert knowledge and excluded from the free exercise of public reason (Sandel, 1982; Yuill, 2006, p. 207, note 61). Rawls' model determines principles and regulatory norms in advance of citizens' participation. Citizens' rights of self-determination and exercise of public reason are significantly circumscribed (Habermas, 1995; Yuill, 2006, p. 202). For Rawls excludes political or social views, departing from the assumptions of his model:

> The intense convictions of the majority, if they are indeed mere preferences without any foundation in the principles of justice antecedently established, have no weight to begin with...To have a complaint against the conduct and belief of others we must show that their actions injure us, or that the institutions that authorize what they do treat us unjustly. (Rawls, 1973, p. 450, in Yuill, 2006, p. 203)

Rawls effectively removes problems of equality from democratic political determination to administrative determination (Yuill, 2006, p. 202). And again we see suspicion of the majority, and concern to limit its political power (Rawls, 1973, pp. 228–30). Rawls' *Theory of Justice* involves a fundamental revision of the relationship between the citizen and government, and between the legal subject and their civil and political rights, at the expense of both the public and the private sphere (Habermas, 1995; Yuill, 2006, pp. 199–203). Rawls' model retreats from seeing citizens as the authors of law. Instead, they become its recipients in Rawls' concept of law as 'a coercive order of public rules addressed to rational persons for the purpose of regulating their conduct and providing the framework for social cooperation' (Rawls, 1973, p. 235). Individuals become bystanders to the organisation of society by third-party advocates, acting in the name of the least advantaged. Rawls effectively asserts expert privilege against the equality of speech between citizens implied in the democratic political sphere, where citizens come together to speak with their peers (Arendt, 1968, pp. 9–13; 1998, [1958], pp. 3–4, 26–32, p. 41). Consequently, Rawls circumscribes the meaning of liberty and freedom of speech, even if he formally gives them priority (Rawls, 1973, p. 223, p. 235, pp. 243–50). Rawlsian-type concerns over public discourse have been invoked against free speech for speech regulation, to protect the vulnerable, in works such as Stanley Fish's *There's No Such Thing as Free Speech, and It's a Good Thing Too* (Fish, 1994, pp. 102–19).

Juridification and the subject of human rights

The limits on democratic politics are justified as correctives to the imbalance of power between marginal groups and the majority of the population. However, it is only by a sleight of hand that the problem of the powerlessness and representation of marginal groups is resolved in the human rights model. There are several aspects to this problem, which need to be disentangled, but essentially at issue is the problem of the moral agent of human rights. The idea of rights based on the incapacity of the rights holder presupposes the existence of third-party arbiters. The classic rights model does not pose this conceptual problem, because it presupposes that the rights-holder and the moral agent of rights are one, that is, rights-holders have the capacity to determine and guarantee their own rights.

But who can claim to act on behalf of the human rights-holder? Who can claim to determine what fundamental human rights are? Who is entitled to represent the interests of particular human rights-holders? Who determines what interests are paramount? Who determines their implementation? Who determines what claims are to be prioritised in the allocation of resources? How are human rights-holders able to hold the third-party advocate to account for how their interests are represented? Who, indeed, determines what voices are deserving and heard? As Shuibhne asks, 'Ultimately, who should decide which interests should take precedence?' (Shuibhne, 2002, p. 189).

Questions concerning third-party advocacy are left unanswered in most human rights literature, if asked at all. This omission is all the more striking given how keen literature is to demonstrate how politics is open to abuse. A disinterested world of human rights professionals is assumed, seemingly above the temptations of the tainted world of politics. Human rights advocacy is profoundly sceptical of third-party representation, when it concerns democratic majorities representing the interests of minorities, but remarkably unreflective about the problem of third-party representation inherent in its own model. Indeed, the very concept of empowerment embodies this hubris. Effectively, while democratic representation is treated as prone to abuse, the legitimacy of representation by self-appointed guardians is taken for granted. There are occasional warnings of the undemocratic nature of expert-made policy, but warnings against democratic politics loom larger in the literature. Pennycook, for example, is ambivalent about imposing human rights codes onto non-western societies, but his lack of belief in people's capacity to resist discourse leads him back to strategies promoting professionals as mediators of knowledge, speech and consciousness (Pennycook, 1994; 1998b, p. 86; discussed in Holborow, 1999, pp. 81–6). Consequently, mistrust of democratic accountability leads to preference for supranational law over national law, and experts, rather than the people, as the final arbiters.

There are tensions in juridification, or the growth of formal legal processes to address social problems (Clark and Wedderburn, 1987, p. 165; Habermas, 1987, p. 357). Juridification of social problems tends to emphasise procedural justice, target setting, auditing mechanisms and policies. But emphasis on regulatory processes may lead to political and civil freedoms, and questions of substantive transformation, becoming secondary (Habermas, 1987, p. 368). Multicultural approaches, which linguistic human rights advocates favour, represent a retreat from socio-economic and political transformation and eradicating social inequalities through promoting universal prosperity. Indicatively, linguistic human rights advocacy, like Rawlsian theories and other prevailing international policy approaches, addresses global justice in terms of distribution, not production (Kymlicka and Patten, 2003; Rawls, 1973; Sen, 2001; Shapiro, 1986, p. 250; Skutnabb-Kangas, 1999; Yuill, 2006, pp. 196–203, 207). Codification of detailed positive rights as fundamental rights privileges particular justice models and assumes that how we conceive of justice and injustice is static. But justice and injustice, social problems and social solutions are politically contested and can change. Legal models entrenching positive claims as fundamental rights become inflexible in conserving earlier claims and policy responses (Laitin and Reich, 2003). Codification of positive identity rights also involves predetermining social identities, for all the literature's reference to the constructed nature of social identities. Past, justified claims may become unjustified privileges under changed social circumstances, social problems or conceptions of justice. Notably, particular models of justice may produce unintended social ramifications that were not anticipated at the time of their codification.

The thickening global human rights regimes, including linguistic rights, embody a shift from politics to administration of justice. They parallel the shift from earlier international development aspirations to more limited bureaucratic social goals and targets as reflected in the Millennium Development Goals (MDGs) and Poverty Reduction Strategy Papers (PRSPs), which have replaced the older structural adjustment programmes (Duffield, 2007; Harrison, 2004; Pender, 2002; Pupavac, 2005; 2010). Simultaneously, opposition is excluded from national poverty reduction strategy papers, which are drawn up by states in collaboration with global institutions and donor states. The global MDGs and PRSPs' strategies, like Rawlsian theories of justice, address distribution norms, not production (Shapiro, 1986, p. 250; Yuill, 2006, p. 207). Nevertheless, the bureaucratic social goals and targets are attractive in giving the illusion of some progress to elites in an era of circumscribed economic and social progress. Global governance assumes that populations will only seek basic needs, just as Rawls assumes that individuals will not seek more than minimum basic entitlements or pursue maximum gains, and risk everything important to them (Rawls, 1973, pp. 143–4, p. 154; Yuill, 2006, p. 201). However, modern ethnic conflicts, or peasant violence historically, suggest that some individuals or groups are prepared to take risks to secure their material advantages.

Multicultural approaches legitimise differential treatment under law to overcome social injustice (Fish, 1994; MacKinnon, 1987; 1993; Sandel, 1982; Taylor, 1994). But recognition of differential treatment under law is a double-edged sword, which may actually jeopardise legal protections.

The principle of common standards acts as a check against discrimination, because it demands equal treatment, whereas the codification of difference relativises justice, and may unwittingly legitimise unequal treatment. More fundamentally, third-generation identity rights may weaken the rule of law itself by eroding the unity of law. The tendency to fragment law militates against law acting as a bulwark against oppression and discrimination.

Undermining the character of modern law

When contemporary human rights advocacy reverses the relationship between law and politics, it also changes the character of law. Instead of being derived from the will of the people, law becomes derived from transcendent norms or external grants. Accordingly, law is external to people, not the embodiment of their will. So, although the human rights model is consciously championed as a progressive innovation, it actually represents a retreat from democratic law-making to elite law-making by self-elected experts. Laws created externally, or against the popular will, may have the form of law, but lack its substance, because they are not created through the subjective engagement of citizens. At the same time, such elite law-making creates a moral hierarchy between the disinterested (human rights) legislator and the irrational, untrustworthy masses. The resulting legislation has the character of decrees and is more likely to rely on external policing than self-policing. Where such instances are the exception, they are not fatal to the rule of law, but too much legislation bypassing the moral, political and legal agency of citizens weakens their identification with the law in general, not just specific laws. There is a growing sense that law is distant from social life, especially international human rights law, which epitomises trends towards law-making beyond the national political community (Griffiths, 2001, p. 104). If people no longer identify with law as theirs, then compliance through the internalisation of norms is also weakened and cannot be taken for granted. This in turn encourages the resort to more authoritarian methods of compliance. Yet, it has been recognised that the use of law to realise language rights, even if successful, may exacerbate ethnic divisions (Martel, 1999, p. 51, p. 76).

Contemporary human rights advocacy breaks the correspondence between law and the people in its efforts to create law external to the political will of the majority. Human rights law instead engages the *demos* post factum. The people are thereby not treated as creators of law, but as objects of regulation. Law-making bypassing the *demos* denies the moral, political and legal agency of the people, and in doing so undermines the democratic character of law, and infantilises citizens. The post factum engagement of the *demos*, through human rights education and other measures, is no substitute. Nor are the self-esteem components, flattering citizens in social programmes, any substitute. So, even if human rights documents are recognised as law, they actually depart from democratic law, creating a distance between the law and the people. It is ironic that language rights proponents should endorse an expert-made law, circumventing the voice of the *demos* in law-making, and attenuating the relationship between people and the law, so that the communication of law becomes one-way, down to the people.

Human rights advocacy is sensitive to the distance between people and law (for example, Phillipson, 1998, p. 111), although its approach is premised on that distance. Third-generation rights are linked with this sensitivity. Cultural rights are not simply a response to the demands of minority groups, but have been cultivated as official policies to make institutions closer to people, by recognising people's cultural identities; that is, cultural rights are driven from above, not simply from below. The European Union project exemplifies efforts to enhance the legitimacy of its institutions through official recognition of cultural difference. However, flattering people's identities is no substitute for the democratic deficit that haunts the European Union (Menendez, 2004).

Furthermore, formal recognition of our identities involves regulation of our subjectivity, departing from earlier liberal ideals of individual autonomy. The fate of individual rights is problematic under proposals such as the Universal Declaration of Linguistic Rights 1996. Likewise, the UN Declaration on the Rights of Indigenous Peoples 2007 states: 'Indigenous peoples have the right to determine the responsibilities of individuals to their communities' (article 35). In turn, relations within communities are subject to external governance through other international provisions, which undermine the autonomy of communities, and therefore also meaningful recognition and rights (Berlin, 1969, pp. 154–62). So, while the Declaration and other proposals commonly contain safeguards concerning democratic processes, welfare and non-discrimination, they do, nevertheless, undermine the substantive meaning of principles of freedom and self-determination. And, under revised Rawlsian liberal theories, they should have no cause to object if they are being treated fairly according to the human rights codes.

Fragmenting international law

The claim of human rights to empower those who lack rights is deeply attractive. Much of human rights advocacy in the 1990s was internationally directed to empowering marginal groups in oppressive states, or fostering the rule of law in weak or post-conflict states. Language rights advocates have sought the international community to take responsibility for people's security against failing governments (Skutnabb-Kangas, 1999, pp. 197–8). They support the UN having a stronger enforcement role, and the EU having a more active foreign policy on minority rights (Shuibhne, 2002, p. 223; p. 321; Skutnabb-Kangas and Dunbar, 2010).

The 1990s challenged the traditional realist model of international relations, along with its principles of national sovereignty and non-interference in the internal affairs of states. The imperatives of human suffering around the globe encouraged the belief that international human rights law should take precedence over national law. International organisations began to treat international human rights regimes as directly applicable, irrespective of whether states had ratified treaties, although ratification was more forthcoming than previously, as states were keen to put themselves on the respectable side of international morality.

International law was assigned new significance in enabling international peace and security role in the 1990s, but it has not been sufficiently recognised how legal principles, and ultimately the rule of law, were challenged in this decade. These developments were mystifying, because the erosion of law and rights was conducted in the very name of expanding the rule of law and rights. The 1990s are now looked back on nostalgically as an interregnum, a decade when power politics seemed to be in retreat. Conversely, the past decade has been viewed as witnessing the return of power politics with a vengeance, following the World Trade Center bombing of 2001, and reversing the development of global norms against traditional state-centric power politics. However, this reading of the 1990s fails to take into account the contradictions of the expansion of international law in the decade, and how it was consistent with international power politics. There have been strong post-Iraq critiques of the degradation of international law (Bowring, 2008; Sands, 2005). But its degradation in the 1990s has not received the same critical attention. Unfortunately, power relations were not suspended in this decade, but informed the development of international human rights regimes, and their challenge to the principles of sovereignty and non-interference in the internal affairs of states, expressed in international documents such as the State Responsibility and Responsibility to Protect (ICISS, 2001). The elevation of human rights over claims to sovereignty, however well intended, failed to counter the problem of power and powerlessness, and ended up compounding the problems of international inequalities and lawlessness. Not least, the very concept of the international community, which assumes for itself the role of interpreter and enforcer of international law, embodies a western coalition of approved states and non-state actors. The division of international society into an elect of civilised, responsible states, who interpret and enforce the law against the rest undermines the principle of sovereign equality. Thus, the human rights challenge to sovereignty represents a challenge to the principle of sovereign equality, not sovereignty *per se*, and actually enhances the sovereignty of the Great Powers in relation to weaker states.

Ironically, the evolving human rights system complements a changing balance of power in the international system, and legitimises the right of powerful states to impose their will on weaker states (Chandler, 2002;

Chomsky, 1999). Military enforcement has not been explicitly supported by language rights advocates, although it is implicit in demands to treat language violations as crimes against humanity, and demands for stronger enforcement means (Skutnabb-Kangas and Dunbar, 2010). Key human rights organisations such as Human Rights Watch and advocates like Michael Ignatieff, involved in the International Commission on Intervention and State Sovereignty (ICISS, 2001), and other minority rights advocates in conflict management have lobbied for military humanitarian intervention. Moreover, the new paradigm of human rights does not imply that state sovereignty gives way to the sovereignty of man, as was presumed by the eminent international lawyer Hersch Lauterpacht (Lauterpacht, 1950, p. 70). For the human rights model, doubting the moral capacity of citizens for self-determination, involves expanding governance of individuals as well as states.

Global human rights superseding national law is envisaged as promoting universalism, by overcoming the particularism of rights being realised through the nation state, but the development denotes a retreat from universalism, both conceptually and in its practice. Such international law is not derived from the universalist principle that the subjects of law are its creators. Instead, international law becomes determined by a non-universal, self-declared international community of responsible states, who enforce the law against those states deemed in violation, but without being accountable to the populations themselves. A higher non-territorially and non-politically contingent law denies the universal and democratic authority of law as deriving from the general will of the people. Equally, the demise of sovereign equality reverses universalist principles, and further allows the law to be differentially, rather than universally, applied. The consequence of these developments is that law becomes authoritarian, particular and arbitrary, and therefore lawless in Diceyan terms, even where the intent is not to oppress (Cosgrove, 1980, p. 79; Dicey, 1959, [1889], p. 188).

Strikingly, linguistic imperialism critiques do not engage with critical legal studies, which have explored global human rights governance as forms of legal imperialism (Douzinas, 2000; Fitzpatrick, 2001). Language advocates denounce claims for the neutrality of English, and may speak disparagingly of 'power politics' determining language rights (Réaume, 1991, p. 57), but they assume the neutrality of international or regional human rights regimes, whether domestic judicial activism or global governance over populations. Simultaneously, language rights advocates assume a positive identity and role for the international community (Skutnabb-Kangas, 1999, p. 198), and do not seriously explore how the concept of the international community relates to global power relations. Again, linguistic imperialism studies attack linguistic homogenisation (Skutnabb-Kangas, 2009), but do not address legal homogenisation. So, while linguistic imperialism critiques attack global English for 'destroying interdependent self-directed societies' (Pattanayak, in Phillipson, 1992, p. 276), they do not address the anti-democratic implications of global human rights governance (Chandler, 2002; 2004; Chomsky, 1999; 2000; Duffield, 2001; 2007; Lewis, 1998; Mieville, 2005; Sellars, 2002). Advocates assume that law supports diversity, but what we have is officially sanctioned and restricted forms of diversity, as opposed to political freedom and freedom of cultural expression. Advocates' attempts to bridge the gap between their ideals and existing conditions through pre-emptive legal decrees have authoritarian political and social implications. Essentially, the international human rights governance strategies favoured by key advocates may be analysed as forms of anti-democratic politics or legal imperialism (Chandler, 1999; 2002; 2004; Chomsky, 1999; 2000; Fitzpatrick, 1995; 2001; Fitzpatrick and Tuitt, 2004; Lewis, 1998).

Linguistic imperialism studies cite Galtung's attack on global English (Galtung, 1985; Phillipson, 1992, pp. 51–6; Pennycook, 1994, pp. 48–51), but have been slow to pick up on his long scepticism towards the European Community as a political and law-making superpower, embodying the interests of global capitalism (Galtung, 1973; 1989, pp. 35–6). Language rights literature has generally favoured the European Union as a form of 'suprastate democracy' over national politics (De Varennes, 1996; Ives, 2004c; Shuibhne, 2002). Belatedly, the language rights advocacy literature raises the problem of the European Union's 'democratic deficit' and the 'gap between elites and citizens' along with concerns over its language rights policies (Phillipson, 2009b, p. 91). But advocates do not consider how expanding human rights regimes are part of the expanding democratic deficit in regional or global governance, or how identity recognition represents a substitute for proper democratic accountability. Similarly, language rights advocates have been supportive of the OSCE (Skutnabb-Kangas, 2009, p. 44), but have not explored the non-democratic implications of the OSCE's expanding role, or that of similar regional or international organisations, as an aspect of external post-liberal governance.

Language advocates also tend to assume that the international rise of NGOs, or 'NGO-isation', is a neutral or positive development (Norgaard, 2001, p. 536). Studies do not engage with the critical NGO-isation debates of the last two decades concerned with the sector's relation to global governance and containment of political activism (Chandler, 2004; Duffield, 2001; 2007; Sogge, 1996). Ironically, critiques of global English may be extended towards global human rights regimes as 'made in English', which have reinforced the imperative to know English in national politics, bureaucracies and NGO sectors. The expanding international NGO sector by its very presence has promoted global English and English-speaking elite policy-making circles, marginalising the broader non-English-speaking population from authorship of their own laws and policies.

Western abuse of human rights is noted, but not followed up (Skutnabb-Kangas, 1999, p. 201). Human rights as *lingua bellica* today are neglected in international language advocacy. Thus, linguistic imperialism critics attack western wars in the Middle East (Phillipson, 2009b, p. 93), but do not address the Kosovo War or other military humanitarian interventions, or how the Iraqi and Afghan wars were fought in the name of human rights, not simply western security interests. Furthermore, international human rights advocates have been tempted to appeal to security imperatives, militarising and short-circuiting democratic politics and international UN processes and restraints. Language rights advocates and linguistic imperialism critics have directly appealed to international humanitarian law and the laws of war to enforce language protection.

Genocide and crimes against humanity

A growing number of linguistic human rights advocates, most prominently Tove Skutnabb-Kangass, want language death to be treated as 'linguicide' or linguistic genocide (Skutnabb-Kangas, 2001, p. 400). The 1948 Genocide Convention does not specifically include an article on linguistic genocide. However, an earlier draft did contain an article on cultural genocide with a clause related to language:

> prohibiting the use of the language of the group in daily intercourse or in schools, or the printing and circulation of publications in the language of the group. (In Abtahi and Webb, 2008, p. 1009, pp. 1061–3)

Advocates want this clause to be restored, or similar provisions to be recognised. Linguistic genocide would encompass acts of commission or omission '(actively) "to kill a language" and (without killing its speakers as in physical genocide) or (through passivity) "to let a language die"' (Skutnabb-Kangas, 1998, p. 13). Furthermore, leading advocacy in this area would interpret prohibition as encompassing indirect actions, such as not using bilingual teachers, or non-mother tongue education, or not making the minority language the main medium of instruction, as subtractive education amounting to linguistic or cultural genocide (Dunbar and Skutnabb-Kangas, 2010; Skutnabb-Kangas, 1998, pp. 12–13; 2009, p. 40). Opposing universal mother tongue education or other language maintenance policies is seen as complicity in genocide or crimes against humanity (Skutnabb-Kangas, 2009, p. 55). Simultaneously, advocacy demands for linguistic genocide to be recognised slide into claimed statements of law and calls for the UN to take action against violating states. So far, linguistic genocide recognition debates are primarily conducted in select advocacy literature or specialist blogs. Nevertheless, the idea is beginning to be invoked by politicians. MEP Sogor Casaba, for example, claimed: 'There is linguistic genocide in the European Union' in a European Parliament debate on minority language rights in 2009 (Casaba, 2009).

When linguistic human rights advocates propose to make the intentional failure to provide non-mother tongue education a crime against humanity, if not genocide, they have not thought through the power relations of international criminal processes and the implications of criminalising states. The studies seeking to have language rights violations potentially recognised as genocide, or a crime against humanity, only superficially address international criminal law itself. They do not understand what is implied by their demands for enforceable rights, or the politics of international war crimes. Their demands assume the neutrality of international criminal law, just as they accuse other linguists of assuming the neutrality of global English.

In seeking to link positive language rights to genocide and crimes against humanity, advocates are effectively legitimising expanding the grounds of military intervention of powerful states with the greatest military capacity. If we look at the jurisprudence of international ad hoc tribunals, or the International Criminal Court, it is evident that some states, politicians and military are more equal than others (Laughland, 2002; 2008; Zolo, 2009). Crucially, the developments in international criminal law since the end of the Cold War have loosened the *jus ad bellum* constraints limiting the right to go to war, and focused on *jus in bello*, limiting how war is conducted in particular areas. The expansion of the international criminal justice system has taken place in the name of the victims, but its evolving jurisprudence shows reluctance to speak truth to power, and preference for indictments and victims favoured by the dominant western powers. Overall, it has allowed the expansion of western liberal military interventions while supporting a flexible foreign policy tool to criminalise the conduct of war by weaker states or non-state parties.

The international criminal law developments have helped legitimise the erosion of defendants or suspects' rights in the name of victims, which has subsequently become a matter of human rights concern in the war on terror. These erosions include long detention prior to trial, circumscribed rights of self-defence, the use of anonymous witnesses, hearsay evidence and evidence obtained through inhumane treatment (Holbrook, 2002; Laughland, 2002; 2008). Moreover, language rights advocates have not even thought through the implications of expanding international criminal law and the language question. The international tribunals do recognise the language rights of defendants and witnesses. However, there are civil and political implications for defendants and witnesses testifying in translation about events within a national, political and social context before foreign judges. So, while contemporary translation studies has promoted the idea of the impossibility, or violence, of translation, little has been written from this perspective about international tribunals, or other aspects of global governance under which national policies are increasingly determined by or with international officials through global English and its translation. Ironically, international criminal processes accelerate the expanding status and use of global English as against smaller languages. If the expansion of global English represents a form of linguistic imperialism, does not the expansion of international courts and tribunals, whose jurisprudence has been dominated by western powers, and the English or French languages, represent a form of legal linguistic imperialism?

The undemocratic relationship between the legislator and society is exemplified in the de facto international protectorates in post-conflict states such as Bosnia, where the country's laws are effectively drafted by international officials (Chandler, 1999; Knaus and Martin, 2003). International officials have sought to enhance the legitimacy of their state-building efforts and help people identify with the new state's institutions through granting extensive formal recognition of cultural rights. But championing cultural rights is a poor substitute for the political self-determination that internationalists previously aspired to realise. Policies of cultural recognition have not overcome the distance of people from the internationally sponsored institutions and laws, but require continuing intense micromanagement (ICG, 2011). Unsurprisingly, too, the sharper disjuncture between international law-making and populations has magnified the willingness among international policy-makers to resort to coercive measures. Thus, international legal advocacy, which began with a wish to assert international law against the violence of a world of states, ironically ends up endorsing the Great Powers having expanded powers for the use of force against weaker states. As such, Shelley's description of, 'Golden and sanguine laws which tempt and slay', seems apt (Shelley, 1998, [1819], p. 333, line 10). The implications of elevating law over politics, and international law over national law, in a world of unequal states remain unaddressed in the linguistic human rights literature, despite its concern to highlight problems of cultural imperialism. Moreover, its approach to law and legal codification of difference risks eroding the capacity of law to protect vulnerable groups. At the same time, identity rights embody a degraded form of subjectivity, which questions, rather than affirms, people's integrity as moral beings. The next chapter traces back contentions over language rights as freedom or culture to Enlightenment and Romantic debates.

3
From Enlightenment Speech to Romantic National Languages

Introduction

Linguistic human rights advocates believe it is important to retain minority languages, because language embodies our identity, and each language involves a unique way of looking at the world. These ideas may be traced back through the Boasian anthropological tradition to the Romantic view of language and nation, and the ideas of the German philosophers Johann Hamann and Johann Herder. This chapter examines Enlightenment concern with language as communication, and Romantic concern with language as culture, and how their ideas anticipate contemporary language rights debates.

Enlightenment exploration of language as communication addresses the everyday view of language. Treating language as communication is an inadequate account of language. After all, most language is never spoken or communicated to others, but remains a dialogue in one's head. But the focus has important merits, which tend to be discounted in contemporary language rights advocacy – not least beliefs in expanding freedom of speech and expression. Romantic thinking developed more sophisticated historical accounts of language, which understood how language did not simply reflect reality, but involved relations to the world. Nevertheless, Herderian Romantic and post-Romantic approaches end up with their own reductive accounts of language, questioning human subjectivity and linguistic creativity.

The clear distinctions I present here between Enlightenment and Romantic thinkers involve obvious generalisations. Individual writings may span Enlightenment and Romantic ideas. Herder's philosophy of language may be understood as that of a child of the Enlightenment, and a parent of Romantic thinking on language (Malik, 1996, pp. 78–9). Enlightenment and Romantic themes on language were already being raised in the works of seventeenth-century philosophers such as Vico and Leibniz (Berlin, 2000; Steiner, 1998, [1975], pp. 76–9). Moreover, the differences between

Enlightenment and Romantic interpretations are not necessarily always the most salient differences: radical or conservative streams of thought may be more significant in understanding different language philosophies (Israel, 2002, pp. 97–141, pp. 259–94; Malik, 2008, pp. 87–95). Mainstream Enlightenment figures such as the philosopher Immanuel Kant (1724–1804) who influences contemporary human rights, retreated to unenlightened positions when writing on socially unequal groups (Kant, 1974, [1798]; 1997, [1775]); while Romantic figures like Coleridge, Wordsworth and Wagner were inspired by radical thought in their youth, but adopted conservative political positions in later life (Malik, 2008, pp. 117–19; Thompson, 1997). Nevertheless, the generalisations are characteristic of the different eras, and anticipate today's opposing themes.

Enlightenment humanism and sociability

The Enlightenment has few supporters and many detractors in contemporary critical thinking. The field of linguistic human rights advocacy is no exception. Key contributors are hostile towards Enlightenment thinking and define their approaches against its perceived wrongs. The Enlightenment is now condemned for modern horrors from the Holocaust to colonialism , totalitarianism and soulless materialism (Bauman, 1989; Horkheimer and Adorno, 1997, [1944]). It no longer conjures up images of light and air, but of oppression. If the associations are not the death factories, then it is Mr Gradgrind drilling barren facts into hapless children (Dickens, 1985, [1854]). But to suggest a clear line from the Enlightenment to the death camps distorts Enlightenment thinking beyond recognition, and ironically reproduces a mechanistic, teleological account of history that critics often attribute to Enlightenment thinking. The common stereotype takes one theme in Enlightenment debates – a mechanistic model of the universe – out of the historical context of the nascent sciences, trying to assert themselves against privilege and church authority, and conflates it with the idea of treating people as machines (Tawney, 1921, pp. 19–20). Key thinkers such as Descartes specifically argue for creative language use against mechanistic understandings of human language (Chomsky, 2002, pp. 51–62), whereas some critics, particularly in the field of ecolinguistics, ironically develop rather deterministic accounts of language, refuting human sociability and linguistic creativity.

Defending the Enlightenment does not necessarily mean romanticising the Enlightenment era or overlooking contradictions in Enlightenment thought, as key contributors made clear. Kant's famous *What is Enlightenment?* speaks of his times as 'not an enlightened age', but an age of Enlightenment seeking more rational understanding (Kant, 2001, [1784]), while Voltaire specially attacks Panglossian thinking and complacency about contemporary society as the best of all possible worlds (Voltaire, 2006, [1759]). Negative stereotypes of the Enlightenment as totalitarianism-in-waiting have to shut their eyes to the iconoclastic enlightened spirit: its questioning of received wisdom, and demands for greater freedom and knowledge. Condemnations commonly conflate Enlightenment ideas with counter-Enlightenment developments. Kant described Enlightenment as 'emergence' from 'self-imposed immaturity' and summed up Enlightenment philosophy as 'Dare to Know', exhorting people to have the courage to think for themselves (Kant, 2001, [1784]). Truth was not given from above, but worked out by people reasoning and experimenting for themselves. Indeed Adorno and Horkheimer's well-known critique *Dialectics of Enlightenment* sought to make their readers think for themselves towards revitalising Enlightenment thinking, having torn down modern society's pretensions to Enlightenment in the aftermath of the Holocaust (Adorno and Horkheimer, 1997, [1944]). Efforts at Enlightenment were fuelled in an irreverent atmosphere of rowdy boisterous disputation, high passions, partisanship, idiosyncratic enthusiasms, eclecticism and devil-may-care experimentation. Enlightenment was above all sociable and cosmopolitan, and attached to the coffee house, the club, the salon and the expanding press (Porter, 2000). Such an atmosphere fostered free-thinking figures like Thomas Paine, or lesser-known figures like the brothers Charles and Robert Pigott, who upheld radical views on political rights and freedom of speech (Pigott, 1795; 2004). Conservatives, like the writers Jonathan Swift and Samuel Johnson, also contributed to an iconoclastic spirit in their parodying of the new philosophical ideas, enthusiasms and progressive schemes like Swift's labour-saving mechanical invention for speculative learning (Swift, 2001, [1726], pp. 170–1). Against stereotypes of its arid character, Enlightenment iconoclasm encouraged the satirising of its own ideals, follies and passions (or attempts to deny passion). Satire flourished from Moliere's *Bourgeois Gentilhomme* (Molière, 2000, [1670], pp. 198–203), Swift's Yahoos and Houyhnhnms (Swift, 2001, [1726]), to Hogarth's Rake's Progress or Charles Pigott's *Jockey Club* (Pigott, 1792; 1794).

Humans were inherently sociable creatures with strong social affections, it was argued, but could be more sociable (Arendt, 1992, p. 40; Kant, 1952, [1790], section 60, p. 226; Paine, 1996, [1791], p. 121). These ideas informed approaches towards language:

> humanity signifies, on the one hand, the universal feeling of sympathy, and, on the other, the faculty of being able to communicate universally one's inmost self – properties constituting in conjunction the befitting social spirit of mankind, in contradiction to the narrow life of the lower animals. (Kant, 1952, [1790], section, 60, p. 226)

Sociability was important for cultivating reason, as well as moral sensibility. In the words of Kant, 'Reason is not made "to isolate itself but to get into community with others"' (Kant in Arendt, 1992, p. 40). For Kant, thinking is not simply a solitary activity, a dialogue with oneself, but is also sociable and dependent on its public use. Without '"the test of free and open examination", no thinking and no opinion formation are possible' (Arendt, 1992, p. 40). The ability to imagine different standpoints is needed to enlarge our understanding and develop our judgements (Kant, 1952, [1790], section 40, p. 151; Kant, 1968, [1771], p. 108 in Arendt, 1992, pp. 42–3). Enlarged thought does not mean simply empathising with others, or exchanging our prejudices with theirs; instead, we strive to develop 'a general standpoint' (Arendt, 1992, p. 43). Enlightenment cannot, therefore, be confined to an elite, but requires a public to flourish (Kant, 1998, [1781], B884, in Arendt, 1992, p. 38, Arendt's translation). Enlightenment thinking aspires that the 'narrow footpath for the few would become a high-road' [for all] (Kant, 1998, [1781], B884, Arendt, 1992, p. 38, Arendt's translation). Kant's own understanding of public and private freedom of speech was heavily circumscribed. Nevertheless, enlightenment belief in 'emergence' from a 'self-imposed immaturity' holds possibilities for subordinated social groups. The philosopher Mary Wollstonecraft's *A Vindication of the Rights of Women* (1992) [1792] directly addresses the subjugation and infantilisation of women. Tellingly, the novel, expressing new individual and social consciousness, became dominated by women novelists, despite the era's continuing prejudices against women (Porter, 2000, p. 327).

Freedoms of speech and publication were core concerns of the age. The political radical Paine approvingly cites the French Declaration of the Rights of Man and Citizens, which declares:

> The unrestrained communication of thoughts and opinions being one of the most precious Rights of Man, every citizen may speak, write, and publish freely provided he is responsible for the abuse of this liberty, in cases determined by the law. (in Paine, 1996, [1791], p. 73)

Paine's work embodies a passion to communicate and popularise radical ideas using plain language, accessible to the mass of ordinary people. Paine speaks of how 'A single expression, boldly conceived and uttered, will sometimes put a whole company into their proper feelings' (Paine, 1996, [1791], p. 188). Paine's own writings reached a wide audience – *Rights of Man* sold between 100,000 and 200,000 copies – while other publications such as the popular satirical paper *Pigs' Meat; or, Lessons for the Swinish Multitude* sought to disseminate ideas among ordinary people, and staunchly supported freedom of speech. The paper appropriated the term 'swinish multitude' for its title from Burke's derogatory characterization of the people and their demands for political rights, thereby specifically ridiculing and attacking Burkean conservatism (Burke, 1986, [1790], p. 173). 'Without freedom of thought,' the paper proclaims, 'there can be no such thing as wisdom; and no such thing as public liberty without freedom of speech' (*Pig's Meat*, 1795, p. 3). The publication links thinking, feeling and freedom of speech: 'To forbid...people to speak is to forbid them to feel' (*Pig's Meat*, 1795, p. 68). Their defence of enlightened reason is infused with passion, irrelevance and sensibility, illustrating how Enlightenment thinking was not cut off from feelings as its detractors accuse.

Common humanity and common rights

Too often accounts of language politics and language standardisation overlook the radical Enlightenment tradition (Crowley, 1991; 2003; Pennycook, 1994; Phillipson, 1992). But grammars and dictionaries were compiled and contested as part of 'struggles in the cause of freedom', as Holborow outlines in her critical analysis of the politics of standard English (Cobbett in Holborow, 1999, p. 163). Radicals like the satirist and dictionary compiler Charles Pigott (died 1794), imprisoned for his writings, struggled for citizens' rights and a freer, more just, rational society (Pigott, 1795; Rix, 2004, pp. xv–xix).

Pigott's *Political Dictionary* (1795) asserts the central Enlightenment demands for freedoms of knowledge, speech and association. Pigott denounces governments 'where the noble and investigating mind of man dares not promulgate known truths, where the scrutinizing eye of the philosopher has penetrated, but where that eye dares only see in secret' (Pigott, 1795, p. 180). His definitions rage against social injustices of the day, from war to the emerging capitalist economy, and the appalling treatment of slaves or workers with starvation wages as mechanical hands (Pigott, 1795, p. 150, p. 171). Pigott condemns how 'In England, we protest to love freedom, and yet we are the chief agents of wickedness in the infernal traffic of human flesh!' (Pigott, 1795, p. 152). His definitions outline the humanity of black slaves and their suffering:

> In the West-Indies, is a human being, who is marked upon the back with the initials of his Christian master's name. He is torn from his native country, from his friends and connections, from the arms of an aged parent; a beloved wife, or his dear children, never to behold them more. (Pigott, 1795, p. 152)

Pigott satirises denial of slaves' humanity, defining the black slave as 'a biped, but clearly not a human being, as he is neither a Christian, nor can he talk English' (Pigott, 1795, p. 100), while wryly observing how 'Many princes desire...that their subjects might be all blacks, because they would sell them' (Pigott, 1795, p. 152). His dictionary condemns Britain's overseas expansion in definitions like 'Company (East India). Chartered robbers, licensed murderers, finding out military ruffians to conquer, plunder, and desolate the remotest countries' (Pigott, 1795, p. 13), while his definition of famine challenges Malthusian explanations, and anticipates Amartya Sen's socio-political explanations of famine (Pigott, 1795, p. 35; Sen, 1981).

The Enlightenment, if not an enlightened age, supported developments towards a dynamic secular public sphere, constituted by self-determining citizens. Reason needed to be emancipated from unreason, custom and particularity (Gellner, 1992, p. 1–3; Tallis, 1999, pp. 18–24). Enlightenment thought celebrated universalism and a common human race, and aspired to transcend differences through progress. Intellectual exchanges were maintained across Europe and the Atlantic, notwithstanding the decline of Latin as the universal European language of scholarship and the rise of the vernaculars, circumscribing French as the new *lingua franca*. In this spirit, radicals like Paine or Robert Pigott, brother of the dictionary compiler, were involved in Parisian radical circles (Rix, 2004, p. xv).

Belief in a common humanity encouraged the idea of common rights. If human beings were essentially the same everywhere, with the same essential needs, then every person should have the same natural rights. Paine argues for 'the unity of man;...that men are all of one degree, and consequently that all men are born equal, and with equal natural rights' (Paine, 1996, [1791], p. 32). Enlightenment cosmopolitanism leant towards understanding the nation as a political concept, associated with a political system, embodying the will of the people, not just the nobility or the church. The nation meant citizens of a state, rather than a fixed ethnic group: that is, an expanded polity. The English Republicans Paine and Joseph Priestly could become French citizens, and elected to the French parliament, notwithstanding Paine's professed lack of aptitude for foreign languages (Malik, 1996, p. 134). Nationalism in this sense was associated with internationalism, and championing political freedoms, rather than chauvinism (Malik, 1996, pp. 133–8). Differences would be overcome in union under the rights of man (Paine, 1996, [1791], p. 109, p. 124). More fixed definitions of the nation invoked suspicion. Pigott, for one, sees Burkean invocation of the nation as a cover for narrower interests:

> A collective term, arbitrarily used for a small number of people who against the consent of a large number, agree to submit themselves and their posterity for ever, to the unlimited and uncontrolled tyranny of one man. (Pigott, 1795, p. 96)

Pigott attacks national prejudice as undermining truth and justice (Pigott, 1795, p. 123). Accordingly, Pigott criticises the division of the world into separate nations and traditions as inhibiting Enlightenment, and allowing truth to have an arbitrary character under the rule of 'the rack and the wheel' (Pigott, 1795, p. 197).

Enlightenment thinking, believing in a common humanity and questioning tradition, became interested in understanding other societies with a new openness, beyond simply recording exotic differences. Enlightenment defiance of the biblical injunction against eating from the tree of knowledge supported efforts to develop universal knowledge, language, encyclopaedias and libraries (Israel, 2002, pp. 119–41). Universalist perspectives and a new openness helped foster more tolerance towards different societies, as studies sought to discover what was common to humanity, and were more ready to see cultural differences as arising from different environments.

However, tensions existed in the age's attitudes towards non-European societies (Malik, 1996, pp. 38–70; Porter, 2000). Belief in a common humanity and the rights of man fostered arguments against national prejudice and slavery. Thinkers such as Rousseau extolled the virtues of the noble savage, uncorrupted by civilisation, to indict what was rotten in modern society – an attitude taken up in Romantic thought and familiar in anthropology. But the rights of slaves to freedom were counterposed to the property rights of slave-owners (James, 2001, [1938]; Malik, 1996, pp. 61–8). Further, philosophers like Kant were tempted to contrast their Enlightenment with its absence among others, whether women, the lower classes, or non-European populations, and condemn them as stagnant, backward, lacking industry and corrupt (Kant, 1974, [1798]; 1997, [1775]; Malik, 2008, pp. 106–7). They fell back on prejudices and failed to follow through their calls for more enlightened understanding. Nevertheless, Enlightenment ideals demand more universalism, more reason and critical judgement, not less (Arendt, 1992, pp. 42–4; Paine, 1996, [1791], pp. 164–5). Haitian slaves did not dismiss Enlightenment thinking on the rights of man, but forcefully invoked Enlightenment logic against the social and political limits of the age (James, 2001, [1938]; L'Ouverture, 2008, [1793–1802]).

Enlightened reformers and radicals believed that contemporary society was rotten, because there was too much attachment to the old beliefs and customs, and not enough enlightened reason and social change. Reactionary narrowing of Enlightenment to a select group in society, a position antithetical to an enlightened spirit, was encouraged by the contradictions between Enlightenment ideals and the difficulties of their realisation in the existing conditions. These contradictions informed the later usurpation of Enlightenment ideas to support specific nationalist projects, whose particularist readings helped to reconcile the Enlightenment to notions of racial superiority (Malik, 1996, pp. 130–3; Todorov, 1993, pp. 140–6; 156–7, p. 226). We see this in Ernest Renan's appropriation of the Enlightenment to the French national identity at the end of the nineteenth century (ibid.). Ironically, particularist readings of the Enlightenment are reinforced in common critiques. I will return to the limitations of cultural critiques of racism in the next chapter.

Universal language and enlightened language reform

Enlightenment imperatives to communicate, reason, understand and debate fostered interest in language. European curiosity grew about languages and societies, ancient and contemporary. The philosopher John Locke's *An Essay concerning Human Understanding* devotes much space to language, 'speech being the great bond that holds society together' (Locke, 2001, [1690], Book III, chapter 10, p. 420). Similarly, the famous dictionary compiler Samuel Johnson stresses how 'Society is held together by communication and information' (in Porter, 2000, p. 72). Enlightenment concerns draw on philosophers like Gottfried Liebniz. Leibniz's project for a universal language aspired to foster international peace and understanding by making language a better tool for reason, and facilitating communication between peoples. Leibniz wanted to prevent miscommunications and abuses of words, which manipulated ordinary people and confounded justice and religion (Leibniz, 1981, [1704], pp. 340–351). Leibniz explored mathematical language and Chinese writing towards creating a universal pictorial dictionary, widening knowledge to the less literate (Leibniz, 1981, 1981, [1704], p. 354).

Locke's *An Essay Concerning Human Understanding* follows Leibniz, outlining comprehension as the ends of language:

> First to make known one man's thought or ideas to another; Secondly, to do it with as much ease and quickness as possible and: Thirdly, thereby to convey the knowledge of things. (Locke, 2001, [1690], Book III, chapter 10, p. 409)

In a section entitled 'Of the Abuse of Words', Locke condemns how language abuse allows abuse of people's rights, whereas unambiguous language helps people settle their rights:

> that the use of words were made plain and direct; and that the language, which was given us for the improvement of knowledge and bond of society, should not be employed to darken truth, and unsettle people's rights; to raise mists, and render unintelligible both morality and religion. (Locke, 2001, [1690], Book III, chapter 10, paragraph 13, p. 409)

In turn, Locke's belief in improving communication informs Enlightenment writings on language (Johnson, 1792, p. 3; Monboddo, 1774, volume, 2, p. 1; Tooke, 1786, p. 23, p. 37, p. 44). Political radicals like Priestly, Thomas Spence and Horne Tooke took up language reform and standardisation as part of attacking privilege and defending citizens' rights (Tooke, 1786). Clear language demystified power relations. Accordingly, works such as Priestly's *The Rudiments of English Grammar* (1784) and Spence's *Grand Repository of the English Language* (1775) relate to egalitarian ideas (Porter, 2000, p. 214), as opposed to later post-Enlightenment elitist language policies (Crowley, 2003). Transparent rational rules of speech would be open to anyone to learn, minimising miscommunication, clearing away mystification and prejudice, and furthering equality between people (Spence, 1796).

Indicatively, reformers based the standard on the more egalitarian source of ordinary people's language, rather the more privileged source of the written language. Priestly argues that 'the custom of speaking, is the original, and only just standard of any language' (Priestly, 1784, p. ix). Land reformer Spence calls for the written form to be based both on ordinary speech, and the 'egalitarian principle' of one letter for each sound, making reading more accessible to the poor (Porter, 2000, p. 460). General practice, rather than arbitrary rules, should guide the standard (Priestly, 1784, p. xvii). Tooke highlights how abstract words derive from ordinary human actions, while Pigott attacks aristocratic language norms (Porter, 2000, pp. 460–1). Tellingly, the aristocrat Lord Monboddo, author of the six-volume *Of the Origin and Progress of Language* (1773–1992), disagrees with the spoken word founding the standard. Yet Monboddo views foreign language borrowings positively, as, 'plentiful nourishment to a meagre body' (Monboddo, 1774, p. xviii). Enlightenment cosmopolitanism encouraged grammatical comparisons with neighbouring modern languages, against the grammatical authority of Latin (Priestly, 1784, p. xvii). Studies by Leibniz, Monboddo and others undermined prejudices that the speech of other peoples was jabbering, although chauvinistic language attitudes could be exhibited (for example, Johnson, 1792, p. 9).

Even if Enlightenment thinkers did not individually live up to their ideals of clarity, or enlightened thought free from prejudice, their work could be judged by the ideals. Tooke, for one, struggled to practise what he preached on linguistic clarity, while Kant apologises that his *Critique of Pure Reason* is awkwardly written, and blames his impatience to complete the work (Arendt, 1992, pp. 38–9). Kant sees making ideas clear to a reading public vital for their intellectual rigour, cautioning: 'every philosophical work must be susceptible of popularity; if not, it probably conceals nonsense beneath a fog of seeming sophistication' (Kant, 1967, [1783], p. 101, in Arendt, 1992, p. 39, Arendt's translation).

Enlightenment thinkers were optimistic about human invention and perfectibility in their practical attitudes towards language and tradition. Enlightenment thought envisaged cultural differences eroding as societies converged on rational principles (Paine, 1996, [1791], p. 109, p. 124). Enlightenment interest in languages did not, therefore, mean interest in preserving languages as living languages. The overriding concern was developing common human understanding and culture through furthering rational communication between people. Language differences could hamper communication, and enlightened cosmopolitanism aspired to transcend traditional loyalties, atavistic customs and language differences, which it saw as hampering communication. Meanwhile, social thirst for linguistic perfection, knowledge and classification are parodied in works like Moliere's *Bourgeois Gentilhomme*, in which the hero is instructed on how to pronounce his basic letters, something he has evidently been doing all his life (Molière, 2000, [1670], pp. 198–203). Swift's *Gulliver's Travels* satirises language reformers in his grand Academy of Lagodo, developing a scheme to dispense with the imperfections of language and use things, although its proponents end up weighed down by the objects needed to express themselves (Swift, 2001, [1726], pp. 172–4).

The paramountcy of communication informs later liberal and left-wing politics of the nineteenth and twentieth centuries, which could be scathing about minority languages. The liberal philosopher Mill famously argues that people's wish to be integrated into the modern state would be greater than their attachment to minority languages (Mill, 1991, [1861], p. 314); while the Marxist Friedrich Engels predicts the demise of various Slavic languages in his analysis of the 1848 revolutions, ranging particular Slav nations with counter-revolutionary forces (Engels, 1849a; 1849b). Progressives broadly assumed that people would favour speaking extensively spoken languages, rather than less widely spoken languages, to participate in wider society and communicate with as many people as possible. To cling to a minority language was to side with reactionary forces and condemn oneself to political, social and cultural isolation, counter to personal fulfilment. Such ideas have become suspect in today's identity politics and ethics of difference. These ethics may be traced back to earlier Romantic challenges to Enlightenment thinking on language.

Romantic national attachments

We have seen how the Enlightenment approach towards language was influenced by its perception of humanity; so, too, was Romantic thinking. Critics like Edmund Burke argued that asserting universal reason against culture neglected how people valued tradition (Burke, 1986, [1790]). A counter-Enlightenment tradition traceable back to the pre-Enlightenment Italian thinker Vico has been outlined by the philosopher Isaiah Berlin, which challenges negative associations of culture with unreason (Berlin, 2000; Tallis, 1999, p. 19). Vico questions historical progress, arguing that each culture has its values and masterpieces, which live and die with that culture (Berlin, 2000; Tallis, 1999, p. 19). Vico's ideas on national cultures resonated with German thinkers concerned about French cultural dominance and its determination of Enlightenment ideals of universal mankind and reason (Hamann, 2007, [1760], pp. 9–32; Haynes, 2007, p. xxii; Tallis, 1999, pp. 22–3). Calls to break French cultural hegemony and promote German culture were fuelled by political aspirations to unite German-speaking lands, and by the wider European reaction to the French Revolution and its universalist ideals. External fears over social radicalism and violence displaced initial enthusiasm for the French Revolution, and encouraged mainstream thinking to censure attacks on tradition. Burke's conservative critique exemplified reaction against the Enlightenment (Burke, 1986, [1790]). Ironically, however, it was one of the more egalitarian eighteenth-century thinkers, Herder, whose writings helped forge the narrower Romantic concepts of political community, as I will discuss below.

Romantic thinkers like Hegel and Humboldt develop more sophisticated philosophies of history and language. Romantic thinking suggests a historically changing human nature against static views of human nature, posited in much Enlightenment thought. Yet, despite its sensitivity to historical change, Romantic thinking also develops more fatalistic, naturalised models of social change invoking notions of birth and decay. Romantic fatalism is underpinned by social fears and political disappointments, which fostered more pessimistic conservative politics against earlier radical Enlightenment and Romantic strands (Malik, 2008, pp. 110–132; Thompson, 1997). Indicatively, Romantic writing often invokes anxious metaphors of impurity, disease and contamination, rather than the more sanguine clockwork metaphors of Enlightenment writing. Confronting dramatic social upheavals, Romantic thinking defensively seeks refuge in nature against society, feeling against reason, tradition against revolution, the cultural against the political, and the inner world against the social world.

Romantic thinking asserts the uniqueness of the individual soul, each people and its traditions, against the soullessness and cruelties of early mass industrialisation, and against the ramifications of the French Revolution and Napoleonic Wars. In essence, Romantic thought defines the nation organically, as a specifically named people or race, whose identity has been forged through historical and geographic bonds, counter to the more civic models in Enlightenment thought. Political principles are subsumed into national identifications. So struggles for national recognition become the motivating force in history, and Enlightenment reason becomes subsumed into national identifications. Romantic writings on language are preoccupied with the fate of distinct national language traditions and national rights, as against Enlightenment interest in linguistic clarity and language rights as freedoms of communication.

Hamann and Herder

Berlin's counter-Enlightenment tradition singles out two eighteenth-century German thinkers, Hamann (1730–1788) and Herder (1744–1803), as anticipating and influencing the shift from Enlightenment ideas to Romantic ideas (Berlin, 2000; Malik, 2008, pp. 123–7). Herder, in particular, contributed to thinking on pluralism, expressionism and popularism (Berlin, 2000, p. 176). But first I want to discuss Herder's less well-known friend Hamann, and his philosophical break with Enlightenment thinking.

Hamann believes reason and consciousness are mediated through particular languages and cultures, and are therefore fallible. 'Not only the entire ability to think rests on language,' Hamann argues, 'but language is also the centerpoint of reason's misunderstanding with itself' (Hamann, 2007, [1784], p. 211; Tallis, 1999, pp. 23–4). In short, 'Reason is language,' Hamann declares to Herder (Hamann in Haynes, 2007, p. xiv). Hamann questions both Leibniz's belief in a universal language and Kantian attempts to outline universal laws, translatable across languages and cultures (Berlin, 2000, p. 319). Instead, every language is associated with particular ways of life and patterns of experience, which are only really comprehensible to themselves (Berlin, 2000, pp. 359–61). Simultaneously, Hamann sees language in sacred communal terms, and opposes treating language as primarily serving communicative functions (Haynes, 2007, pp. xiv–xxv). He sees translating or using foreign languages as inauthentic (Berlin, 2000, pp. 326–7). For Hamann, language is a gift of God, revealing God's purposes (Berlin, 2000, pp. 319–20). Accordingly, Hamann interprets the Tower of Babel as an alien construction, an unfeeling edifice of abstract reason against God's purposes, in attempting to eradicate divinely given linguistic and cultural differences (Berlin, 2000, pp. 319–20). Similarly, Hamann opposes certain orthographic reforms, simplifying the written language, arguing to retain 'h' as a letter embodying God's breath (Hamann, 2007, [1773], pp. 146–63; Haynes, 2007, p. xxiii). Hamann satirically refutes Herder's secular account of the origins of language (Herder, 1966, [1772]). Instead, his defence of religion attacks the Enlightenment for having its own mysticisms and prejudices (Hamann, 2007, [1772], pp. 96–110; [1784], pp. 205–18; Haynes, 2007, pp. xvii–xxii). He invokes human embodiedness against Enlightenment abstractness, and obscure language against false clarity (Hamann, 2007, [1772], pp. 102–3; [1784], pp. 212–15; Haynes, 2007, pp. x–xiii), strategies adopted in later critiques of modernity (Adorno and Horkheimer, 1997, pp. xiv–xv).

Hamann is anti-authoritarian in his pointed satires against the powerful. He opposes philosopher-kings, dictating abstract universal laws, uninformed by everyday life, and imposing them on citizens (Hamann, 2007, [1772], p. 102; Haynes, 2007, pp. viii–xvi). Instead, Hamann draws faith from the masses in a non-liberal populist political vision (Berlin, 2000, pp. 341–2). But Hamann overlooks the social injustices of the traditional order in his defence of custom against reformers (Berlin, 2000, pp. 356–7).

Herder remains more an Enlightenment child, believing in a common human nature (Herder, 1969, [1780], pp. 266–9; Herder, 2002, [1772], p. 159). Herder declares, 'Each human being has…all the abilities that his whole species has, and each nation the abilities that all nations have' (Herder, 2002, [1772], p. 159). Herder shares belief in the natural sciences and secular ideas (Berlin, 2000, p. 173), although he deplores how a mechanistic outlook encourages overly abstract thinking, detached from people's lived experiences. Herder seeks to illuminate 'the different minds of the peoples based on their circles of sensation and of life' (Herder, 2002, [1767–1768], p. 50).

Herder's scepticism towards Enlightenment abstraction is against imposing uniform laws onto people's diverse lives and relations (Herder, 1969, [1774], pp. 196–202). Here Herder anticipates critiques of modern social engineering and global governance creating uniform subjectivities albeit it with a multicultural face:

> This is a time when the art of legislation is considered the sole method of civilizing nations. Yet this method has been employed in the strangest fashion to produce mostly general philosophies of the human race, rational axioms of human behaviour ... maxims of philanthropy and wisdom, views of all times and peoples for all times and peoples. For all times and peoples? That means, alas, precisely not for the very people whom the particular code of law was meant to fit like clothing. (Herder, 1969, [1774], p. 203)

Herder rails against a superficial 'paper-culture' of philosophical and philanthropic generalities, concealing the actual oppressive conditions of civilised society (Herder, 1969, [1774], p. 205, pp. 212–20). His *Dissertation on the Reciprocal Influence of Government and the Sciences* (Herder, 1969, [1780], pp. 225–52) supports freedom of speech and expression in pursuit of truth and authenticity:

> All inquisition is prejudicial to the republic of learning. A book which must first be passed by ten censors before it reaches the light of day is no longer a book but the hackwork of the Holy Inquisition, a mutilated thing, scourged with rods, a muzzled wretch and always a slave. (Herder, 1969, [1780], p. 245)

Herder insists on respect for national self-determination and condemns overseas expansion:

> we should wish that no foreign power interfere in the free experiment of an independent nation which undertakes this experiment on itself or disturb this experiment through premature wisdom and interloping. (Herder, 2002, [1774], p. 320)

For Herder, distinct national souls with different qualities make distinct contributions towards humanity: 'Perhaps the sum is equal – only in different proportions and compensations' (Herder, 2002, [1793–1797], p. 395). Herder has some wry comments on enlightened missionary endeavours treating people as blank canvases. He ridicules attempts to change ideas and beliefs in other societies, without relating to their existing ideas and beliefs, and without expanding their 'circles of sensation and of life' (Herder, 2002, [1778], p. 220). His insights on missionaries are relevant to aspects of human rights advocacy, seeking to codify global social laws without transforming people's ways of life:

> What an abyss there is between even the finest general truth and the least of its applications to a given sphere, to a particular purpose and in any one specific manner! (Herder, 1969, [1774], p. 203)

Herder often judges enlightened civilised society as worse than savage or barbaric peoples, without the state or law (Herder, 2002, [1774], pp. 307–17). Herder challenges prejudices towards non-Europeans and contests the idea of dividing humanity into races (Herder, 1969, [1784–1791], p. 284). Instead, he invites his contemporaries to imagine themselves from the perspectives of other societies, 'The Negro has as much right to consider the white man a degenerate, a born albino freak, as when the white man considers him a beast, a black animal' (Herder, 2002, [1793–1797], pp. 394–5; Berlin, 2000, p. 223; Malik, 2008, pp. 123–6). Herder warns against assuming the superiority of Europeans over non-Europeans as a 'presumptuous, covetous conceit', asserting that groups called 'savage or barbaric' are essentially more humane than European societies (Herder, 2002, [1793–1797], pp. 385–6). Herder condemns prejudices against other peoples as a cloak for evils like slavery (Herder, 2002, [1793–1797], p. 394). 'Let one not put into the hands of any people on earth on ground of "innate superiority" the sceptre over other peoples – much less the sword and the slave whip', Herder demands against racial thinking (Herder, 2002, [1793–1797], p. 394). Allowing slavery against any members of humanity destroys humanity's humanity (Herder, 2002, [1793–1797], p. 394).

Herder's work demonstrates sensitivity to how historical differences are reflected in the human mind. Herder satirises Enlightenment cosmopolitanism as promoting abstract love of humanity and French cultural hegemony:

> We are all philanthropic citizens of the world. The princes speak French, and soon everybody will follow their example; and then, behold, perfect bliss: the golden age, when all the world will speak one tongue, one universal language, is dawning again! (Herder, 1969, [1774], p. 209)

Against this vision, Herder cries out, 'National cultures, where are you?' (ibid.). Herder's historical consciousness breaks with Enlightenment philosophy, and projects the awakening German national consciousness onto human history (Malik, 2008, pp. 123–6). Simultaneously, Herder's and Hamann's attacks on French Enlightenment abstraction claim a more vital ancient Germanic tradition (Tallis, 1999, pp. 18–24). Accordingly, Herder calls for plain speech against the French language of *politesse* and its artifices (Herder, 1969, [1769], pp. 106–13).

While Herder condemns 'despotic hereditary government' and traditional social ranks as against nature, he naturalises the idea of hereditary nations and condemns states' 'wild mixing of various races and nationalities' (Herder, 1969, [1784–1791], pp. 324–5). For Herder, 'the formulation and progressive formation of a nation is never anything but a work of fate' (Herder, 2002, [1774], p. 320). Herder's political thought does not take into account the American War of Independence, and the possibilities of consciously constituting a nation, which roused republicans such as Paine. National cultural identity becomes the core organising principle of all human societies: 'Each nation has its center of happiness in itself', writes Herder (Herder, 2002, [1774], p. 297 in Berlin, 2000, p. 211). Herder's historical fatalism narrows political and social horizons to the nation, and legitimises a rather conservative political outlook in which people's identifications are given by birth, rather than potentially consciously created. National cultural determination trumps alternative political visions, making description of national cultural differences become prescriptive. Herder neglects alternative collective identifications, such as republicanism, which appealed to Enlightenment thinkers.

Ironically, Herder ends up legitimising national prejudice, for all his enlightened views on non-European societies (Malik, 2008, pp. 124–5). Moreover, he legitimises national prejudice precisely through his desire not to be prejudiced. Herder repeatedly condemns European negative judgements of other societies, invoking the failings of European societies:

> Least of all ... can our European culture be the measure of universal human goodness and human value; it is no yardstick or a false one. ... there are so many shortcomings and weaknesses, so many twistings and horrors, bound up with it that only an unkind being could make these occasions of higher culture into a collective condition of our whole species. (Herder, 2002, [1793–1797], p. 396)

Herder believes it is hypocritical for European societies to judge other societies, and retorts that 'Each nation must ... be considered solely in its place with everything that it is and has' (Herder, 2002, [1793–1797], p. 395). Enlightened thinkers would agree with Herder on their own societies' hypocrisies. Herder's reasoning, however, becomes ensnared when he argues that societies should be judged in their own terms. Crucially, Herder questions the possibility of comparing societies, and transcending the values of one's own culture:

> What is a measuring of all peoples by the measure of us Europeans supposed to be at all? Where is the means of comparison? ... let each of us beat his own breast and look for the beam in his own brain. (Herder, 2002, [1793–1797], p. 386)

Herder's rejection of judging falls into the trap that Kant's plea for critical judgement warns us against (Arendt, 1992, pp. 42–4). Herder demonstrates 'an enormously enlarged empathy' towards other societies, as Kant calls for, but Herder's empathy becomes passive acceptance of other standpoints (Kant in Arendt, 1992, p. 43). Herder's empathy for other people's viewpoints effectively invites us to accept each other's prejudices, and does not imagine people transcending their own limited personal experiences, and consciously coming together to formulate common judgements and aspirations. Herder's relativism contradicts his stated cosmopolitanism and beliefs in freedom of speech and expression, and becomes a recipe for abandoning thinking and resigning ourselves to social stasis. The best of Enlightenment thought condemns existing European societies as unjust and seeks more enlightened thinking and action. But Herder's abandonment of external (critical) judgement legitimises national myth-making, which refuses to evaluate its own history. The refusal of external judgement, self-absorption and elevation of inner qualities, rather than acting as a bulwark against racism, may allow the racist imagination free flow, unhindered by the nation's real existence (Arendt, 1968, p. 227). Thus, there are potentially greater dangers in the national mystique invoked in Herder's philosophy than national chauvinism, which at least logically invites comparison and measurement against a common humanity (Arendt, 1968, p. 227). Conversely, appeals to a people's uniqueness and intangible inner qualities, which deny the possibility of comparison with other peoples, logically deny a common humanity (ibid.). In claiming 'its people to be unique, individual, incompatible with all others', Arendt warns, a Romantic national mystique 'denies theoretically the very possibility of a common mankind long before it is used to destroy the humanity of man' (Arendt, 1968, p. 227).

Some Romantic ideas did evolve into racial thinking and asserted hierarchical racial differences between people (Malik, 1996, pp. 73–84; 2008, pp. 110–32). Herder's cultural relativist position, of biological universalism and cultural difference, informs twentieth-century anthropology and linguistic human rights advocacy. Yet problems exist in the cultural relativist position as a strategy for overcoming ethnic conflict, racism and social inequality, as I will begin to discuss below. Not least, the emphasis on cultural difference erodes a sense of what humanity shares in common. So, while Herder's cultural analysis demonstrates the historically contingent character of the human mind and human creativity, his approach ends up legitimising their constraint. These problems are evident in Herder's account of language and the Romantic bonds between a nation, its language and history.

Language as culture

Enlightenment writers were aware of the political character of language, and how language could mean different things to different people, creating misunderstandings and allowing manipulation. Linguistic meaning is politicised by the reformist or radical politics expressed in dictionaries and grammars. Nevertheless, Enlightenment philosophies tend to treat language as merely descriptive of the world, equating words with objects, in the image of the biblical Adam naming creatures, rivers and mountains (Condillac, 2001, [1746]; Forster, 2002, p. xv; Taylor, 1985, pp. 226–8). Herder's *Treatise on the Origin of Language* and other works develop a more sophisticated expressive or interpretative account of language (Berlin, 2000, pp. 189–97; Forster, 2002, pp. xiv–xvi; Taylor, 1985, pp. 226–34). Herder emphasises language as embodying the 'consciousness of living people' (Herder, 1969, [1769], p. 107). Since language expresses the particular perspectives of a nation or an individual, and different societies and individuals have different experiences and develop different understandings of the world, then linguistic meaning cannot be fixed and guaranteed. Instead, words involve background meanings, provided by the overall speech or text, and the world view of the speaker. Herder, therefore, rejects Enlightenment optimism over perfecting language, and suggests that the problem of interpretation is inherent in language.

Herder's linguistic philosophy challenges the limitations of Enlightenment linguistic philosophies, yet his account becomes straitjacketed into linguistic determinism against human creativity, when he suggests that each national language embodies and determines the scope of a people's understanding: 'each nation speaks in accordance with its thought and thinks in accordance with its speech' (Herder, 2002, [1767–1768], p. 50). Herder's linguistic analysis, like his historical analysis, becomes fatalistic, as it fastens exclusively onto national ethnic consciousness. His belief that national language determines thought does not account for the historical development of the human consciousness and languages. Instead, Herder treats the existence of particular national languages and cultures as self-evident. So, while Herder's relativism suggests the need to take into account different cultural perspectives, it also narrows cosmopolitan possibilities of mutual communication and cross-cultural influences. Different languages may evolve their own associations of meaning dependent on their distinct histories. However, shared historical experiences foster shared perceptions of the world, and therefore shared meanings across languages. Thus, different languages do not necessarily involve significant cultural differences and concepts of knowledge, beauty and morality. Indeed, Herder's concept of the nation reflects particular historical experiences shared across Europe, which allowed the term to acquire similar connotations among contemporaries across European languages.

Herder's philosophy anticipates the Romantic concern with language expressing the nation's soul (Berlin, 2000, p. 182–9, pp. 204–5). As such, the national language is to be treated as a sacred heritage, whose purity the people have a duty to revere and preserve from external incursions. For Herder, nation and language are bound together, and a nation deprived of its language is alienated from its essence. He decries people not speaking their mother tongue as profane, and denies that they can express themselves authentically in a foreign language: 'I am able to stammer with intense effort in the words of a foreign language; its spirit will evade me' (Herder in Malik, 1996, p. 79). Against the Enlightenment cosmopolitanism and disregard for particular languages, Herder asserts: 'Has a nation anything more precious than the language of its fathers?' because 'In it dwell its entire world of tradition, history, religion, principles of existence; its whole heart and soul' (Herder in Berlin, 2000, p. 189; in Malik, 1996, pp. 78–9).

Herder's discussion of language is steeped in religious terms of heresy and sacrilege, despite his secular treatment of the origins of language and sacred texts (Herder, 1966, [1772]). His idea of the sacredness of the mother tongue repeats (in a secular national form) theological perspectives on the word as divine revelation, and translation taking humanity away from God's word. In this vein, Herder's interpretation of the Babel story echoes Hamann in affirming religious authority over humanity:

> The diversity of languages, ethics, inclinations, and ways of life was destined to become a bar against the presumptuous linking together of the peoples, a dam against foreign inundations – for the steward of the world was concerned that for the security of the whole each people and race preserved its impress, its character; peoples should live beside each other, not mixed up with and on top of each other oppressing each other. (Herder, 2002, [1793–1797], p. 385)

Thus, we see how expressive models of language, as Tallis outlines, tend to oppose linguistic assimilation, whereas representational accounts offer hope of advancing 'a *characteristica universalis* and transparency between languages' (email to author dated 29 June 2010). Indicatively, Herder talks of 'the presumptuous linking together of the peoples', but the development is only presumptuous here if one opposes its challenge to divine power and custom. Herder's treatment of humanity as distinct races who should not mix effectively retreats from Enlightenment belief in our common humanity. As such, his reading of the Babel story represents a conservative agenda, constraining secular power, along with human union and human creativity.

Romantic expressive ideas of language legitimised the concept of linguistic races, and undermined the Enlightenment idea of the nation as a fluid political concept (Malik, 1996, pp. 141–2; Kedourie, 1960; Todorov, 1993, pp. 140–6). The Napoleonic Wars, and post-revolutionary retrenchment, encouraged British writing on language to narrow to the unfolding of the national language (Crowley, 2003; Pennycook, 1994, p. 115). Similarly, on the continent, belief in linguistic races influenced Fichte's *Addresses to the*

German Nation (1807–1808), Arndt's poem *The German Fatherland* (1813), and Renan's writings on language and nation (Kedourie, 1960, pp. 62–72; Todorov, 1993, pp. 140–6). In Renan's words, 'language is, for a race, the very form of its thought' (Renan in Todorov, 1993, p. 144).

Herderian ideas of each nation having its own natural language and concerns for linguistic purity against national degeneration unwittingly fed into ideas of racial purity (Kedourie, 1960, 59–72; Malik, 2000b, pp. 123–6). Thus, linguistic nationalism came to overlap with racial nationalism (Gellner, 1998, pp. 21–5; Kedourie, 1960, pp. 71–3). Biological racism was discredited after the Nazi experience, and displaced by ideas of cultural difference. Yet approaches seeking to preserve cultural difference implicitly reintroduce ideas of racial difference (Kuper, 2000, pp. 236–41; Malik, 1996, pp. 141–177; Malik, 2008, pp. 154–189, pp. 282–88; Todorov, 1993, pp. 156–7). Crucially, models of cultural difference provide more acceptable ways to understand inequalities between people, and are therefore weak defences against racial thinking. Yet there are some obvious problems with the Romantic identification of nation, culture and language.

Determining national language and culture

Romantic accounts overlook the question of whether the national language is the product of nationalism, or the nation the product of national language (Malik, 1996, pp. 139–40). Linguistic and territorial boundaries do not necessarily conform to Romantic ideals. Huge regional linguistic variation existed within territories, especially prior to the modern state. The idea of unique languages and cultures assumes it is easy to delineate where one language begins and another ends. The languages spoken across many rural regions of Europe, prior to national state-building projects, were not sharply delineated, but progressively distinguished themselves village by village. Distinct languages were determined through the accumulated differences, and strong national language distinctions often followed from official standardisation of the language, rather than from prior linguistic conditions. Tellingly, linguistic histories and ethnographic studies commonly accompanied official national standardisation strategies, demonstrating how particular dialects belonged to the national language, and thereby supporting national claims against rival territorial claims (Gellner, 1998, pp. 131–2).

At what point on the map, for example, could one distinguish where the Bulgarian language ended and the Serbian or Macedonian languages began, when the languages shaded into one another? The language in parts of southern Serbia was closer to the western dialects of Bulgaria than the language of northern Serbia. Dialects across borders were typically closer to each other than the speech of their respective capitals. The choice of the standard language during the nation-building era involved important political decisions over which regional dialect would form the standard. The chosen standard needed to help form a coherent sense of nationhood, and to distinguish itself from the standard language of neighbouring states. Consider the choice of an eastern dialect, rather than a western dialect, as the basis of the modern Bulgarian standard language. This choice made the standard more distinct from the language spoken in southern Serbia, and also facilitated the latter's potential to be codified into a distinct Macedonian language, when Macedonia was created as a political unit within post-1945 Yugoslavia.

Romantic thinkers, in their identification of nation, language and state, further overlooked how sovereign rulers historically often spoke a different language from their populations. The English monarchy, for example, spoke a different language from the population in various historical periods: Norman French in the early medieval period; German in the eighteenth century. Equally, if we take Geoffrey Chaucer, who has been named the father of English literature, can we say that Chaucer spoke English? The Norman rulers had essentially been assimilated by the time of Chaucer and increasingly spoke English as their primary tongue rather than Norman French, but to what extent was their or Chaucer's English English? Their language is very different from both the language spoken in England prior to the Norman conquest and the language of Elizabethan English just a couple of centuries later. Scholars have referred to the language in Chaucer's time as French English rather than English (Horobin, 2007; Rothwell, 2004). Yet Herderian thinkers assume historical continuities of a national language and territory, and underestimate temporal discontinuities within a national language, including the rapid changes occurring within their own times. Interestingly, studies have noted how Herder's late eighteenth-century German differs considerably from the German of writers 'less than a generation' later (Steiner, 1998, [1975], p. 20).

Histories of individual languages question the polarity of peoples, and reveal their cross-linguistic influences, including grammar, vocabulary and script. Deciphered ancient scripts uncover shared cultural and linguistic roots, including common myths or bilingual texts. Philological research reveals, for example, the shared East Mediterranean culture of the ancient Greeks and Hebrews, their interaction with ancient Egypt, and its borrowing of the Greek script in late antiquity (Gordon, 1971, p. 33). The historical use of particular languages for transnational communication further undermines the idea of languages as cultural islands – whether Akkadian, Babylonian, Greek, and Latin in the ancient world, or French and English in the modern period (Gordon, 1971, p. 89). Latin influenced the codification of European languages – although Slavonic languages have taken fewer words with Latin roots than Romance languages, their case systems illustrate Latin influence. Modern German found its voice, it has been argued, through its achievements in translating and appropriating Shakespeare (Steiner, 1998,

[1975], pp. 400–2). Indeed Herder invoked Shakespeare as an exemplar for German art and culture against French neoclassicism (Herder, 2008, [1773]). Meanwhile, historical influences may remain in certain dialects even if they have been lost from or are marginal to the standard language. Consider the Cumbrian dialect's Norse roots and links with modern Norwegian (Thorson, 1936) in phrases such as 'there's some barrens laiken ovver theer' (Butler, 2005, p. 15). The familiar differences between American and British English standards may be smaller than the dialect variations within their respective standards.

Moreover, the content of speech is not determined within a given language, even assuming grammatical conservatism. A common language, or even shared dialect, obviously does not guarantee a shared world view, as political divisions or civil wars demonstrate. Claims for the uniqueness of each language, and its embodiment of a particular culture, assume a homogeneous community and its beliefs. Romantic ideas on language and identity overestimate cultural homogeneity between speakers of the same language, and underestimate internal indifference or dissent, or tend only to see it in alternative minority linguistic identities. Contemporary language rights advocates may see ethnic identities as historically constructed, but their arguments for language rights as cultural protection also risk essentialising people and languages. Minority language groups may be presented as culturally homogeneous, even as advocates vigorously argue for the diversity of societies more generally, and rail against the prevailing standard majority language as culturally oppressive.

Mere communication?

The Romantic view of language as the expression of identity prevails in language rights advocacy, which explicitly or implicitly questions the view of language as communication (Ives, 2005, p. 460; Phillipson, 1992, pp. 271–88). The idea of language as communication is an inadequate account of language, but is not a reason to dismiss its claims. The political and ethical aspects of Enlightenment emphasis on language as communication tend to be discounted today. Yet communication rights, freedoms of speech, and public contestation of ideas have underpinned progressive political struggles, from the eighteenth-century political demands against feudal privilege to the twentieth-century political demands for equality. The imperative to speak out, communicate and clarify ideas with others has historically been integral to challenging privilege and oppression. Against this experience, influential critical approaches today question both the possibility of communication and its ethical and political value. The practical Enlightenment emphasis on language as a means of communication is commonly disparaged as merely instrumental, overlooking how identity was instrumentalised in colonial anthropology (Malinowski, 1945) and is instrumentalised in contemporary global governance.

The influence of Romantic ideas on language rights advocacy follows its influence on other fields, notably anthropology and post-colonial studies. Nevertheless, while critics attack language rights approaches as exuding 'Romantic despair' (Davies, 1996, p. 486), language advocates, linguistic imperialism theorists and ecolinguists retreat from Romantic beliefs in human subjectivity and linguistic creativity. The next chapter considers the shift from Romantic ideas of human subjectivity and linguistic creativity to linguistic anthropological ideas of linguistic adaptation, which influence contemporary language rights advocacy.

4
From Romantic Subjectivity to Post-Romantic Cultural Identities and Linguistic Adaptation

Romantic subjectivity to linguistic adaptation

Contemporary language rights advocacy seeking linguistic cultural recognition follows Romantic ideas against Enlightenment universalism. Advocates' scepticism towards modernity and yearning for an unpolluted natural life are quintessentially Romantic themes. Nevertheless, language advocacy approaches differ from earlier Romantic thinking in key respects. This chapter compares Romantic linguistic philosophy with later linguistic anthropological understandings, which influence today's advocacy. Both Romantic national building and Romantic revolt exude a strong sense of subjectivity. If Romantic writing elevates the nation, it also fiercely asserts the individual, whether the individual genius against the mediocrity of conventional society, or the individual soul, particularly the artistic soul, against mass industrial society. Romanticism expresses 'a belief in human potential taken beyond ordinary limits' (Wordsworth and Wordsworth, 2003, p. xxiii). Conversely, contemporary language advocacy is sceptical towards human subjectivity and linguistic creativity.

Language and modern nation state-building

Romanticism encompasses diverse conservative, radical and aesthetic approaches, commonly critical of modernity in the name of earlier values (Sayre and Löwy, 1984). Nevertheless, Romantic ideas supported modern state-building projects against multi-ethnic empires, or divided city states and principalities. Nationalists have claimed the ancient origins of their nation and language, but subsequent historiography shows their modernity. Indeed one of the paradoxes of modern ethnic nationalism has been how leading proponents of national cultural identity have typically been among those most distant from traditional culture (Gellner, 1998, pp. 21–9).

Influential studies like Benedict Anderson's *Imagined Communities* or Eric Hobsbawm and Terence Ranger's *The Invention of Tradition* emphasise how the nation was constructed. Anderson's seminal work explores how the development of modern nation states and national languages was linked to print-capitalism (Anderson, 1991). Anderson praises earlier historians who discuss the history of language (Seton-Watson, 1977) alongside the national political, social and economic history (Anderson, 1991, p. 71). Anderson puts language at the centre of his account of the modern nation state. He gives three core reasons for language's development of an imagined community. First, a shared language among politically significant elites, with territorial or vernacular ties, facilitates identifications, which may become the basis of a modern nation. Second, the shared language becomes solidified through administration and print media. Third, the elite administrative language becomes universalised through the expanding public administration in citizens' lives and public education (Anderson, 1991, pp. 46–9). Or, as Anderson summarises, 'Print-language is what invents nationalism, not a language per se' (Anderson, 1991, p. 134).

Anderson distinguishes pre-modern and modern understandings of language, identity and power, and traces the rise of national languages from informal developments to conscious policies. Anderson contrasts the earlier rise of administrative vernaculars as 'a gradual, unself-conscious, pragmatic, not to say haphazard development' with the later 'self-conscious language policies pursued by nineteenth-century dynasts confronted with the rise of popular linguistic nationalisms' (Anderson, 1991, p. 42). He observes that 'The pre-bourgeois ruling classes generated their cohesions in some sense outside language, or at least outside print-language' (Anderson, 1991, p. 76). For Anderson, print-capitalism changes the significance of linguistic diversity within a territory:

> print-capitalism created languages of power of a kind different from the older vernaculars. Certain dialects inevitably were 'closer' to each print-language and dominated their final forms. (Anderson, 1991, p. 45)

Common national languages were forged from the diverse dialects or languages of the ruling classes and the populace (Anderson, 1991, p. 80). Post-1848 states had to take into account the masses as political forces, and communicate more widely with them through language they understood. Simultaneously, the modern state and its languages-of-state created new linguistic requirements on populations (Anderson, p. 80, pp. 135–8).

Anderson, drawing on Seton-Watson (1977), describes nineteenth-century Europe as 'a golden age of vernacularizing lexicographers, grammarians, philologists and litterateurs' (Anderson, 1991, p. 71). Romantic national interest fostered histories of the national language, along with comparative philology and folklore, collected by nineteenth-century writers such as the Brothers Grimm (Grimm and Grimm, 2002 [1857]) or Vuk Karadžić (Karadžić, 1992; 1997). Anderson's account outlines a progressive expansion, drawing in the populace into national linguistic communities:

> Monolingual dictionaries were vast compendia of each language's print-treasury, portable (if sometimes barely so) from shop to school, office to residence. Bilingual dictionaries made visible an approaching egalitarianism among languages – whatever the political realities outside, within the covers of the Czech-German / German-Czech dictionary the paired language had a common status. (Anderson, 1991, p. 171)

Such efforts were not simply descriptive, but normative, supporting the construction of unified national languages as part of nation-building projects (Gellner, 1998, pp. 131–2; Kedourie, 1960, pp. 59–72). Illustrating the invention of national state languages, Hobsbawm argues that the French language was spoken by only 50 per cent of the population in 1789, while the Italian language was spoken by a mere 2½ per cent of the population at the time of Italian unification (Hobsbawm, 1990, p. 60, p. 38).

Other studies have contested the degree to which nations and their national languages were invented. Anthony Smith has emphasised the ethnic roots of modern national identities against the invention school in a series of works, including *The Ethnic Origins of Nations* (1986), *National Identity* (1991) and *The Antiquity of Nations* (2004). Smith argues that key national languages show continuity amid change, notwithstanding regional differences (Smith, 2004, p. 73). Even if distinct regional dialects have persisted in the Italian state (Ruzzo, 2000; Steiner, 1998, [1975], p. 32), to what extent are they not Italian, either at the time of unification or today? They may differ markedly from the standard language, but still be a recognisably Italian variant.

Whereas Smith stresses the ethnic roots of modern nations, studies over the last two decades have increasingly invoked ethnic identities against nations to demonstrate the artificiality or illegitimacy of national modernising projects (May, 2003; Nettle and Romaine, 2002, p. 22). Contemporary language rights advocates share scepticism towards earlier nation-building with western foreign policy advisers, who favoured the break-up of the Russian Federation and Yugoslavia at the end of the Cold War. Conversely, an earlier era opposed the division of states, as codified under the 1945 UN Charter. They study national language standardisation as elitist oppressive homogenising processes disciplining both the language and the population, and punishing those not following the imposed official linguistic norms (Crowley, 2003; Nettle and Romaine, 2000, pp. 139–41). Their studies further explore how the standardisation of European national languages was accelerated by colonialism and the colonial civil service examinations system. Fascinatingly, Nebrija's *Gramatica Castellana* was printed in 1492 as Christopher Columbus sailed to discover the new world (Illich, 1981a; 1981b; Pennycook, 1994, p. 111). Nebrija petitioned for support from the Spanish monarch by representing his grammar as a 'tool to colonize the language spoken by her own subjects' (Illich, 1981b in Pennycook, 1994, p. 111).

Changing character of critical accounts

Studies have long shown how linguistics has been political, not neutral in its prescriptions. However whereas Anderson documents tensions between elite and popular elements in the making of the modern nation and language (Anderson, 1991), sociolinguistic accounts today ironically affirm elite accounts of a language's history, when they do not discuss alternative radical, progressive attempts to standardise language. Different political imperatives drove standardisation historically, as we saw in the last chapter. Seventeenth and eighteenth-century aspirations to standardise the language were linked to efforts to address arbitrary rule and legal abuses. Egalitarian moves to expand communication, and encourage common access to the public sphere, contrast with nationalist concerns over linguistic purity, or elite-driven exclusionary prescriptions, reinforcing differential access to polite society. Codification of English Received Pronouncement (RP) in the late nineteenth century represented an exclusionary project for the British national and colonial elite, diametrically opposed to the spirit of eighteenth-century radical grammars (Holborow, 1999). Yet again the eighteenth-century ideas of polite society, and its refined feminised discourse, had egalitarian as well as anti-egalitarian tendencies – namely, elevating the status of (middle-class) women in the domestic sphere against masculine, aristocratic norms.

Anderson and other earlier studies are more sanguine about the overall impact of language standardisation:

> Language is not an instrument of exclusion in principle, anyone can learn any language. On the contrary, it is fundamentally inclusive, limited by the fatality of Babel: no one lives long enough to learn *all* languages. (Anderson, 1991, p. 134)

Symbolically, Anderson describes 'visionary drudges' toiling to produce their grammars and dictionaries (Anderson, 1991, p. 71), whereas contemporary advocates often depict grammarians as linguistically disciplining populations. Anderson suggests that language standardisation is not necessarily oppressive, and prescriptive grammars may complement emancipatory politics. Gramsci's support for a prescriptive Italian grammar against the fascist government's opposition is an obvious example (Forgas and Nowell-Smith in Gramsci, 1985, p. 166; Gramsci, 1971, p. 41), as I discuss in Chapter 6. Anderson is further open to the possibilities of foreign languages becoming languages of anti-colonial nationalism, radicalism and revolt:

> Much the most important thing about language is its capacity for generating imagined communities, building in effect *particular solidarities*. After all, imperial languages are still *vernaculars*. (Anderson, 1991, p. 133)
>
> Nothing suggests that Ghanaian nationalism is any less real than Indonesian simply because its national language is English rather than Ashanti. (Anderson, 1991, p. 133)

Anderson sees no problems with 'radical Mozambique' using the former colonial language of Portuguese (Anderson, 1991, p. 134). He also exudes confidence, or perhaps indifference, towards the survival of dialects or languages (Anderson, 1991, pp. 146–8). Anderson's study belongs to a left-wing tradition, following Enlightenment thinking on language, knowledge and social progress. The invention school, although critical of nationalist politics and elite mobilisation, implicitly affirms human imagination and the possibilities of political invention and re-invention. Their critical histories of nationalism seek alternative political mobilisations. Accordingly, earlier leftwing historiography such as CLR James *The Black Jacobins* and E. P. Thompson's *The Making of the English Working Class*, do not see the people as given, but politically and socially created through their own actions within particular historical circumstances (James, 2001, p. 20; Thompson, 1964).

Against the earlier invention school, language rights advocates follow Herderian concerns for linguistic identity and authenticity. They are deeply sceptical towards modern nation state-building, including post-colonial nation-building projects, as I explore in later chapters. Their advocacy has a more fatalistic view of the origin and character of the people. Advocates tend to represent national identities as artificial, but naturalise ethnic or indigenous linguistic communities, even if they acknowledge the social constructions of identities. Anderson and Hobsbawm remained sceptical towards identity politics, although they were, ironically, associated with the journal *New Left Review*, which helped re-orientate British left-wing thinking from social–economic to cultural critique (Heartfield, 2009; Hobsbawm, 1996; Thompson, 2007).

Humboldt and linguistic subjectivity

The Romantic era fostered major breakthroughs in the philosophy of language, notwithstanding Romanticism's descent into narrow reactionary ideas. The philosopher and educationalist Wilhelm von Humboldt (1767–1835) made important contributions to linguistic philosophy. Humboldt was immersed in both French and German intellectual circles, and synthesises humanist strands of Enlightenment and Romantic thinking in his philosophy. His contributions belong to a liberal moment, when the nascent German state embraced political reform, liberalising the press and lifting discriminatory laws against Jews. Humboldt's writings helped develop modern linguistics, notably influencing Saussure's systemic analysis of language and Chomsky's theories on linguistic creativity and critique of behavioural linguistics (Chomsky, 1959; 2002; Losonsky, 1999, pp. xxviii–xxxii; Saussure, 1974, [1916]; Tallis, 1999, pp. 272–89). Humboldt's writings exude belief in human subjectivity, linguistic creativity, sociability, universality and individuality (Humboldt, 1999, [1841], pp. 26–9). They illustrate how the sharp distinctions between Enlightenment and Romantic ideas may be less meaningful than those between radical or progressive, and conservative thought. Here I follow Losonsky's excellent introduction to Humboldt's philosophy of language (Losonsky, 1999).

Words, Humboldt argues, 'emerge from the totality of speech' against understanding language as a heap of words (Humboldt in Losonsky, 1999, p. xix; Humboldt, 1999, [1841], pp. 58–9, p. 70). Humboldt knew Herder, and follows Herder's linguistic philosophy, in believing each language has its distinct 'standpoint' and 'characteristic world-view' (Humboldt, 1999, [1841], p. 60; in Losonsky, 1999, p. xvii):

> The spiritual traits and the structure of the language of a people are so intimately blended that, given either of the two, one should be able to derive the other from it to the fullest extent.... Language is the outward manifestation of the spirit of the people: their language is their spirit, and their spirit is their language; it is difficult to imagine any two things more identical. (Humboldt in Salzmann, 1998, p. 39)

Humboldt's statements on national culture have been used to support Whorfian ideas of linguistic determinism, discussed below (Sapir, 1921; 1929; Whorf, 1940a; 1940b). An unbroken line, 'from Herder and Humboldt to...Whorf', is commonly described (Steiner, 1998, [1975], p. 98; Taylor, 1985, pp. 255–6). Even critics of Whorfian ideas have attributed linguistic determinist models to Humboldt (Penn, 1972, p. 22). But Humboldt avoids Herder's impasse, or the impasses of subsequent post-Romantic interpreters. Humboldt's belief in the distinctive character of national languages does not preclude belief in the core commonality of languages, or the individuality of individuals' speech (Humboldt, 1999, [1841], p. 47; Losonsky, 1999, p. xii). Languages, although *'the work of nations', 'still remain the self-creations of individuals, in that they can be produced solely in each individual'* (Humboldt, 1999, [1841], p. 44; Losonsky, 1999, p. xxiii, italics in the original). Humboldt stresses the 'principle of *freedom*' in language and the language making faculties of peoples and individuals. Different languages express different national paths and have different degrees of refinement, but no language is 'an absolute restraint' on individual speakers (Losonsky, 1999, pp. xxii–xxiii). Their diversity arises from human originality, individuality and imagination, which may foster new linguistic development within and across languages (Humboldt, 1999, [1841], p. 26; Losonsky, 1999, pp. xiv–xvi).

Humboldt puts forward a dynamic dialectic or triadic philosophy of language, which explores how linguistic acts involve interactions between the individual speaker, a community of speakers, general and specific language forms, and linguistic and non-linguistic objects (Losonsky, 1999, p. xviii–xix). Similar dialectic or triadic philosophies of language underpin later linguistic studies such as Vygotsky's *Thought and Language* (Vygotsky, 1986, [1934]) and Tallis' *Not Saussure* (Tallis, 1988). Humboldt's linguistic philosophy, paralleling Hegelian historical philosophy, proposes that a human 'can project nothing from himself that does not at once become a thing that reacts upon him and conditions his further creation' (Humboldt, 1999, [1841], p. 214; discussed in Losonsky, 1999, p. xviii). Humboldt, like Vygotsky, believes thought is distinct from language, although their development is bound to each other (Vygotsky, 1986, [1934]). Language imposes itself on thought, but equally thought imposes itself on language (Humboldt, 1999, [1841], pp. 91–2). No concepts exist without language, and language is needed for human cognition of the world (Humboldt, 1999, [1841], p. 27; Losonsky, 1999, p. xi).

Humboldt stresses an active creative view of language. Language, for Humboldt, is 'no product (*ergon*), but an activity (*energia*)' (Humboldt, 1999, [1841], p. 49 in Losonsky, p. 1999, p. xi). Humboldt emphasises the synthesis of the individual and systemic in language. Accordingly, Humboldt criticises the Enlightenment philosopher Condillac for analysing language abstractly, without considering how language arises from 'the activity of the "I"' (Humboldt in Losonsky, 1999, p. xxvi). The mental power to speak is innately human, and in that sense involuntary, but individual speech acts are unpredictable, creative, autonomous acts, and break 'quasi-mechanical' activities or natural laws (Humboldt, 1999, [1841], p. 26; Losonsky, 1999, p. xii). Humboldt asserts the importance of the individual speaker: 'Only in the individual does language receive its ultimate determinacy' (Humboldt, 1999, [1841], p. 63). Humboldt's emphasis on the 'I' of speech contrasts with post-Saussurean treatment of 'I' as a fiction (Barthes, 1967, 1977; Derrida, 1973, pp. 94–5, pp. 145–6; Derrida, 1976, pp. 7–8, p. 166; Milanović, 1992, p. 7; discussed in Tallis, 1988, pp. 179–89 and Tallis, 1999, pp. 276–88, pp. 461–6). However small '*the power of the individual*' is against the inherited language, language depends upon living users, not 'its dead heritage' (Humboldt, 1999, [1841], p. 63, italics in the original). Humboldt emphasises both the primacy of speech in linguistic development and the people as the vital creators of language (Humboldt, 1999, [1841], pp. 148–50).

> Without being an act of immediate consciousness, indeed of instant spontaneity and freedom, [language] can still belong only to a being endowed with *consciousness* and *freedom*, and proceeds...from the unfathomable depth of his *individuality*, and from the *activity* of forces within him. (Humboldt, 1999, [1841], p. 214, italics in the original)

Grammarians make conscious a language's general systematic character, but have a limited refining role (Humboldt, 1999, [1841], p. 150).

The external world and the specific system of language shape human consciousness, freedom and creativity in language, but do not refute their exercise or development (Humboldt, 1999, [1841], pp. 214–15). Humboldt challenges the idea that human thought is imprisoned in language:

> the nature of man has intimations of a region that transcends language, and is actually constricted by language; but that language in turn is the only means of exploring and fertilizing this region, and that precisely by technical and sensuous improvement it is capable of assimilating an ever larger proportion thereof to itself. (Humboldt, 1999, [1841], p. 157)

Crucially, Humboldt's confidence in individual human subjectivity springs from his sense of a common humanity. For Humboldt, '*the unity of human nature*' and language as its 'joint possession' is the solution to the idea that language is alien to the individual (Humboldt, 1999, [1841], p. 62, italics in the original):

> Language belongs to me, because I bring it forth as I do; and since the ground of this lies at once in the speaking and having-spoken of every generation of men...that...which limits and determines me has arrived there from a human nature intimately allied to my own, and its alien element is therefore alien only for my transitory individual nature, not for my original and true one. (Humboldt, 1999, [1841], p. 63)

Humboldt anticipates and counters post-Saussurean anxieties over language imprisoning humanity and alienating humanity from the world (Barthes, 1967, p. 68; 1977; Derrida, 1973, pp. 94–5, pp. 145–6; Derrida, 1976, pp. 7–8, p. 166; discussed in Tallis, 1988, pp. 179–89; Tallis, 1999, pp. 276–89, pp. 461–6). Individuals' active speech acts prevent them from being imprisoned by language: 'The soul must treat the word more as a resting-place for its inner activity, rather than let itself be imprisoned within verbal limits' (Humboldt, 1999, [1841], p. 92).

Humboldt celebrates how 'language unites' the 'opposition' between human commonality and individuality (Humboldt, 1999, [1841], p. 151). Language needs freedom to develop but also regularity to develop shared meanings (Humboldt, 1999, [1841], p. 144). He refutes claims that 'language, as a universal medium' reduces individual differences 'to a common level'. Rather, language builds 'bridges from one individuality to another, and is a means of mutual understanding' and 'enlarges the difference itself...' (Humboldt, 1999, [1841], p. 151). In other words, we simultaneously develop our sociability and our individuality through language. 'How differently each man takes and uses the same mother-tongue...' Humboldt exclaims (Humboldt, 1999, [1841], p. 151). Humboldt concludes how language allows 'individualization within a general conformity' and in that sense 'the whole human species has but one language, and that every man has one of his own' (Humboldt, 1999, [1841], p, 53).

Humboldt sees language use as involving 'infinite employment of finite means' (Humboldt, 1999, [1841], p. 91 in Losonsky, 1999, p. xxxii). Moreover, the finite means of each language, its 'regulated freedom' (Humboldt, 1999, [1841], p. 144) or 'rule-governed creativity' (Chomsky, 2002, p. 68), are influx, and ever modified through individual speech acts (Tallis, 1999, p. 289). (Losonsky outlines distinctions between Humboldt's and Chomsky's understandings here, but suggests their general compatibility though a different focus.) Humboldt's emphasis on human imagination, creativity and freedom is in tune with Romantic critiques of Enlightenment reason and the limits to scientific evaluation of language (Losonsky, 1999, p. xii). But Humboldt also upholds the Enlightenment ideals of expanding universal human knowledge. Humboldt warns that a language decays if it lacks 'an ardour directed to the enlargement of its own culture' (Humboldt, 1999, [1841], p. 175). He seeks an authentic spirit of linguistic and cultural striving.

Simultaneously, Humboldtian linguistic philosophy is positive about non-European languages and their creative potential, arguing: 'Even the languages of so-called savages... exhibit... a wealth and multiplicity of expressions that everywhere exceeds what is required' (Humboldt, 1999, [1841], p. 60). Humboldt explicitly affirms universal linguistic capacity for abstract thought and metaphors (Humboldt, 1999, [1841], p. 33, p. 218), against later theories such as Malinowski's functionalist linguistics (Langendoen, 1968, pp. 3–29; Malinowski, 1923).

Humboldt links language differences to human individuality and creativity, not just different circumstances (Humboldt, 1999, [1841], p. 29, p. 42, p. 215). He suggests that circumstances may favour, or stifle, linguistic creativity, but no language is an 'absolute restraint' to developing thought (Humboldt, 1999, [1841], p. 29; Losonsky, 1999, p. xxiii). Accordingly, Humboldt argues, 'Even in his earlier circumstances, man transcends the present moment' (Humboldt, 1999, [1841], p. 30). Romantics in the Humboldtian tradition are cosmopolitan in their outlook, and open to what other societies could contribute to broader human understanding. In this spirit, learning foreign languages frees our thought and understanding from national linguistic boundaries (Schopenhauer, 1992, [1851], p. 7).

Humboldt's ideas of linguistic creativity and imagination are shared with other Romantic writers such as Goethe or Coleridge. For Coleridge, imagination 'is essentially vital, even as all objects (as objects) are essentially fixed and dead' (Coleridge, 2001, [1817], volume I, p. 272). Simultaneously, Coleridge associates our imagination with the transcendent capacity to seek human similarities, whereas reason observes our differences (Coleridge, 2001, [1817], volume I, p. 272; Shelley, 1998, [1821], p. 363), a reversal of today's assumptions associating Romanticism with the affirmation of difference. The imagination transcends existing ideas, conditions and associations, and is utopian in conceiving 'the nowhere'. Thus his contemporary Shelley emphasises the importance of imagination in historical struggles for freedom and the accumulated 'power of communicating and receiving intense and impassioned conceptions of man and nature' (Shelley, 1998, [1821], pp. 365–6). Romanticism's bold account of (thwarted) human possibility and imagination contrasts with more pessimistic views of humanity, which developed in Boasian anthropology, discussed below.

Coleridge distinguishes imagination from fancy, defined as a more limited faculty, dependent on existing ideas, objects and associations:

> FANCY, on the contrary, has no other counters to play with, but fixities and definites. The fancy is indeed no other than a mode of memory emancipated from the order of time and space; while it is blended with, and modified by that empirical phenomenon of the will, which we express by the word Choice. But equally with the ordinary memory the Fancy must receive all its materials ready made from the law of association. (Coleridge, 2001, [1817], volume I, p. 272)

Romantic imagination effectively recedes to the lesser faculty of fancy in Boasian anthropological models of adaptation, linguistic determinism and learned patterns of behaviour. More fatalistic notions of culture, language and identity come through changing cultural and linguistic primordialism.

Romance of nature

Political philosophers have long been drawn to the leitmotif of the primitive to indict modern society (Mill, 1962, [1859], p. 400; Rousseau, 1968, [1762], p. 127, p. 149; Rousseau, 1984, [1755], p. 144). In this vein, Herder invokes the natural savage against the 'cultivated shadow' of the 'idle cosmopolite' (Herder in Kedourie, 1960, p. 57). Contemporary language rights advocacy is influenced by the long strand of the western philosophical tradition, which seeks spiritual renewal for a tired civilisation in primordial culture. Language advocates identify with naturalised indigenous communities against inauthentic mass culture and globalisation. Their idealised accounts of indigenous communities may be compared to Oliver Goldsmith's much-cited elegy on *The Deserted Village*, which gives us honest rustics and innocent maidens in a bountiful rural Eden against the 'poor exiles' and 'thin mankind' of the greedy immoral city (Goldsmith, 1910, [1770], pp. 23–4).

There are important distinctions in how nature has been invoked philosophically and politically. Enlightenment thinking attacks feudal privilege and despotisms of custom as opposing natural law (Taylor, 1989, pp. 327–30). In listening to nature, humans are listening to their essential nature. The natural goodness of an undistorted human nature would support general benevolence, the alleviation of suffering, and an enlightened pursuit of human happiness. These themes are continued in radical Romantic thinking. Shelley's 1813 poem *Queen Mab* invokes natural virtue against 'precedent and custom': 'Nature rejects the monarch, not the man;/The subject, not the citizen' (Shelley, 1822, p. 29). Later Enlightenment and Romantic thinking is troubled by earlier mechanical accounts of nature, and believes reason is an inadequate foundation for moral development. They look to ground moral sensibility in an expanded account of human nature that encompasses both reason and feeling (Taylor, 1989, pp. 343–7). Effectively, nature represents our inner conscience and our true feelings (Taylor, 1989, pp. 383–4).

Romantic arguments rhetorically lean towards cultural primitivism. However, the Romantic reconnection to nature is not simply a primordial return to nature, although Romantic writing is primordialist at times, or interpreted as primordialist (Taylor, 1989, pp. 383–6). Rather, Romantic thinking elevates humanity to a new level of dignity, in which humanity is understood as being both of nature and above nature. Nature is awesome but blind. Humanity's appearance makes nature conscious, expressive and meaningful. The sublime in nature inspires awe at the miracle of humans as uniquely conscious, thinking, speaking, creative beings, as Byron's *Childe Harold III* and other Romantic poetry expresses (Byron, 1816, verse 75, lines 667–8 in Wordsworth and Wordsworth, 2003, p. 305; Keats, 1970, [1816], p. 38; Wordsworth, 1995, [1850], Book One, line 414; Wordsworth, 1998b, [1798], pp. 70–3). Humanity's capacity to imagine geological time, or time outside its own existence, suggests an immortal character to human imagination beyond mortality, and reinforces human dignity (Taylor, 1989, p. 350). The Romantic movement fiercely asserts the individual's importance, whether the individual genius against the mediocrity of conventional society or the uniqueness of the individual soul, particularly the artistic soul, against mass industrial society.

Romanticism aspires to a transcendent reconciliation with nature as opposed to adaptation (Goethe, 1932). Schiller, Goethe, Hegel, Marx and others elaborated a dialectical view of history and humanity's relationship to nature (Lukács, 1968). Romantic dialectical thinking is opposed to simple 'oneness with nature', or 'mere sunkenness in nature', as Hegel disparagingly dismissed (Hegel, 2004, [1842], p. 55). In dialectical understanding, severing reason from nature has been historically necessary for humanity to develop its powers of reason. This development assured, it is possible to return to nature 'at a higher level' synthesising reason and feeling (Taylor, 1989, p. 386). Enlightenment naturalism and radical Romanticism therefore affirm humanity, human creativity and humanism in their relationship to nature, as against contemporary accounts invoking nature to indict humanity.

If radical Romanticism identifies untamed nature with political and spiritual freedom, conservative Romanticism identifies nature with a paternalistic rural feudal order (Thompson, 1997). Romantic nationalism transmuted into racial thinking during the nineteenth century, when nature was invoked to support belief in a hierarchy of civilised and uncivilised races, and further legitimised the treatment of particular groups as sub-human. Moreover, the naturalising of human groups could legitimise their denial of rights and extermination (Arendt, 1968, [1951], pp. 191–3, 397–402). Yet European racial thinking also expressed elements of primordialism amid its racial hierarchies. Namely, European racial thinking expressed fears that the white race was degenerating, seduced by the comforts of modern urban life, and displayed sneaking admiration for tough tribal peoples, especially the Zulus (Haggard, 2002, [1885]). Intellectual disdain for the urban masses, fed on tinned food, is a common theme in European nineteenth and twentieth-century literature (Carey, 1992). Historical moments appear when the urban 'labouring multitude' is not disdained (Wordsworth, 1995, [1850], Book Ninth, p. 374, lines 503–34, and Book Eleventh, pp. 434–44, lines 568–756). But even sympathetic advocacy seems compelled to re-impose pastoral ideals onto people as innocent children of nature, but denies them as real political subjects outside the pastoral imaginary (Carey, 1992, p. 45; Césaire, 1972, pp. 38–9; Fanon, 2008, [1952], p. 2; Sardar, 2008, p. xiv). Romantic sentimentalism indicts industrial conditions, yet also legitimises ambivalent social responses, pathologising and criminalising the urban working classes (Cox, 1996; Parton, 1985). Cultural primordialism in language rights advocacy is politically ambivalent too.

Linguistic primordialism

The cause of indigenous languages rebukes modern civilisation and modern standard languages. The idea of retrieving purer natural language has long antecedents, although the motives may diverge historically. Language's power in the past, and its exhaustion in modern civilisation, is an old theme (Gustafson, 1992, pp. 185–7; Murdoch, 1989, pp. 64–80; Steiner, 1998, [1975], pp. 180–6). These are not only Romantic themes, but were also Enlightenment preoccupations. Seventeenth-century philosophers like

Leibniz were concerned that civilised languages had become corrupted, and distanced humanity from nature, and from each other (Leibniz, 1981, [1704]). Empiricism, for example, sought to overcome linguistic confusion through direct observation of nature. Humanity, divided by languages, could be reconciled through nature and the natural sciences (Gustafson, 1992, p. 154). Thus, linguistic primordialism could be associated with pro-Enlightenment, pro-science, universalist positions concerned about the confusion of languages (Gustafson, 1992, pp. 144–54). For figures such as Leibniz, the study of ancient languages and the languages of primitive peoples could aid endeavours to perfect language and represent nature's essence (Gustafson, 1992, p. 187). Poets and writers, too, looked to a fresh and sublime language in ancient and primitive languages.

The early Enlightenment scholarship was primarily concerned with language's inexactness and irrationality. Later Enlightenment and Romantic thinking shared concern over language's inability to convey emotion, lamenting that language was overly exact and rational. Both Herder and Rousseau's essays 'On the Origin of Language' complain that civilised languages lack passion and feeling (Herder, 1966, [1772]; Rousseau, 1966, [1781]). They suggested that primitive people express through their language more feeling for their fellow creatures. Romanticism deplored the sterility of refined language, and sought language's renewal in the language of ordinary people (Wordsworth, 1998a, [1842]).

The Romantic cultural movement in Europe created fascination with its oral tradition, from the folk stories collected by the Brothers Grimm (Grimm and Grimm, 2002, [1857]) to the South Slav oral poetry collected by the language reformer Vuk Karadžić (Karadžić, 1992, [1824]; 1997, [1814–1833]). Interest in documenting folklore, and the language of the people, was entangled with growing national movements. Simultaneously, ideas of linguistic races and natural linguistic ties were invoked as the basis for political national boundaries (Kedourie, 1960, pp. 62–73). Romantic ideas of linguistic races informed racial nationalism and suggested that each race had its own natural language, whose linguistic purity needed protecting against national degeneration (Kedourie, 1960, 59–72; Malik, 1996, pp. 141–3).

Ideas of linguistic authenticity could involve other politically ambivalent impulses. Indicatively, the Romantic search for renewed language spurned the urban poor. Wordsworth's *Lyrical Ballads* (1998a, [1802]) appeal to the simpler language of the rustic peasants, as opposed to the speech of the growing industrial populations (Crowley, 2003, pp. 120–1; Gustafson, 1992, pp. 184–7; Hoggart, 1958, pp. 24–9; Williams, 1973). Overwhelmingly, the European literary tradition suggests that urbanisation harms language and morals (Gustafson, 1992, pp. 184–7; Williams, 1963, p. 48; 1973, pp. 197–214; Wordsworth, 1998a, [1802]), with a few exceptions (Gaskell, 1970a, [1850]; 1970b, [1855]). Rural dialects are commonly associated with innocent expressive children of nature, and urban speech with corrupted fallen figures (for example, Hardy, 1978, [1891], discussed in Crowley, 2003, pp. 135–6). So language rights and linguistic imperialism literature, condemning the rise of global English and globalisation, follow abiding themes in European writing, invoking ideals of natural communities against inauthentic modern industrial living, and natural speech against degenerate speech (for example, Betjemen, 1970, pp. 22–4; Leavis, 1962). Language advocacy is influenced by Boasian anthropology and its theories of cultural and linguistic adaptation.

Boasian cultural determinism against racial anthropology

Franz Boas (1858–1942) dominated western anthropology from the late nineteenth century to the mid-twentieth century, directly influencing several generations of anthropologists, including figures such as Alfred Kroeber, Edward Sapir, Ruth Benedict and Margaret Mead, who established what became known as the Culture and Personality School based at Columbia University (Salzmann, 1998, pp. 1–2). Boas challenged theories of racial hierarchy, and their determination of language and culture, in studies such as *The Mind of Primitive Man, Race, Language and Culture* or *Handbook of American Indian Languages* (Boas, 1963, [1911], pp. 1–9). Herder influences Boasian anthropology and its cultural theories against biological determinism, essentially identified with custom and tradition (Boas, 1940, pp. 8–13; Kuper, 1988, pp. 140–1, pp. 150–1; Penn, 1972, pp. 19–32, pp. 48–54; Tallis, 1999, pp. 22–4). Boas questions belief in the advancement of human civilisation and hierarchical classifications of historical evolution (Kuper, 1988, p. 131, p. 142; 2000, p. 172). His thinking, fusing Herderian culturalism and positivism, recognises a plurality of cultures as legitimate to themselves. In a sense, Boasian anthropology follows a 'Godless social theology', seeing each culture having evolved to its part in a harmonious whole, whose harmony is threatened by change (Malik, 2000b, p. 145).

Boas' cultural relativism is informed by disillusion with modern society, a perspective shared across western elites (Bookchin, 1995, pp. 172–80; Kuper, 2000, pp. 33–8, pp. 64–6; Malik, 2000b, pp. 142–3; Tallis, 1999, pp. 186–211). Boas follows Romantic ideas of cultural diversity, but without its belief in national historical destiny. Boas notes the 'positive, creative side of nationalism': 'widening the field of individual activity', 'setting definite ideals to large cooperating masses', bringing together larger groups under law (Boas, 1962, [1928], p. 96). However, Boas believes earlier positive aspects are overshadowed by aggressive nationalism (Boas, 1962, [1928], pp. 96–7). Boas' political pessimism is accompanied by circumscribed views of humanity as habitual and adaptive, rather than imaginative, inventive or creative (Malik, 2000b, p. 145). Kroeber takes Boas' ideas to outline an anthropological concept of culture as the 'superorganic' determining individuals' development (Kroeber, 1917; Malik, 2000b, p. 145). While Benedict's

Patterns of Culture sees human nature as plastic, and cultural custom shaping individuals' thoughts and actions (Benedict, 1961, [1934], p. 183; Malik, 2000b, p. 139). Boasian anthropology sees 'historically founded' cultural diversity as a bulwark against modern mass politics (Boas, 1962, [1928], pp. 199–200). British anthropology developed similar cultural functionalist models under Bronislaw Malinowski, and shows similar influences of East European Romanticism, positivism and scepticism towards western civilization (Gellner, 1998, pp. 123–37; Malinowski, 1945).

Herderian and functionalist ideas shape Boasian linguistic anthropology's primary concern with 'the interrelation between language and culture', although Boas also declares interest in language 'as a means of communication' (Boas, 1962, [1928], p. 15). Boasian linguistics is commonly described as following Humboldt, even by critics (Penn, 1972, pp. 19–32; Steiner, 1998, [1975], p. 98). Certainly, Boas follows Humboldt's systemic view of language, and anticipates that comparative analysis of languages will show 'the unit of human speech as we know…is the sentence, not the word' (Boas, 1940, p. 208). But Boas' interpretation of linguistic determinism and linguistic relativism is closer to Herder and Hamann than Humboldt, when he proposes that 'Language sways the forms of our thought' (Boas, 1962, [1928], p. 152). Just as culture under Boasian anthropology is no longer a conscious human creation (Malik, 2000b, pp. 145–6), Boasian linguistic anthropology retreats from Humboldt's model of conscious linguistic creation (Humboldt, 1999, [1841]; Losonsky, 1999). Boasian models emphasise culture and language over people, and linguistic habitual use over linguistic creativity (Boas, 1962, [1928], p. 139, pp. 149–53). Human subjectivity is downgraded under the weight of culture and language, whereby *'culture determines language'* (Boas, 1962, [1928], p. 150, emphasis in the original) or 'when new cultural needs arise' language 'will supply the forms that express them' (Boas, 1962, [1928], p. 149).

Yet Boas does not make language paramount in group identity as contemporary language advocacy does. Nineteenth-century European national aspirations were linked to language, whether Italian or German unification or national independence in the Balkans (Boas, 1962, [1928], p. 91). But Boas contends it is 'not very long that the bonds of language have been felt so intensely' (Boas, 1962, [1928], p. 91). He observes:

> In small, tribal communities sameness of race, language and culture does not form a uniting tie. Each small social unit looks with suspicion, if not enmity, upon its neighbours. (Boas, 1962, [1928], p. 95)

He concludes that:

> Unity of language is more an ideal than a real bond; not only that divergence of dialects makes communication difficult, but community of

> thought among the members of different social classes is also so slight that no communication of deeper thought and feeling is possible. (Boas, 1962, [1928], p. 92)

The Sapir–Whorf hypothesis suggests a stronger 'community of thought' within a linguistic community, and resurrects ideas of spiritual essence, as do strands of contemporary language rights advocacy.

Sapir–Whorf hypothesis

The famous Sapir–Whorf hypothesis was developed by Boas' student Edward Sapir (1884–1939) and Sapir's student Benjamin Lee Whorf (1897–1941). The Sapir–Whorf hypothesis involves the double principles of linguistic determinism (a language determines how we think) and linguistic relativity (language differences embody different world views) (Salzmann, 1998, p. 42). Sapir proposes that language conditions thinking, and I quote his much-cited words:

> In a sense, the network of cultural patterns of a civilization is indexed in the language which expresses that civilization... Language is a guide to 'social reality.'... it powerfully conditions all our thinking about social problems and processes. Human beings do not live in the objective world alone, not alone in the world of social activity as ordinarily understood, but are very much at the mercy of the particular language which has become the medium of expression for their society... The fact of the matter is that the 'real world' is to a large extent unconsciously built up on the language habits of the group. No two languages are ever sufficiently similar to be considered as representing the same social reality. The worlds in which different societies live are distinct worlds, not merely the same world with different labels attached. (Sapir, 1929, p. 209; 1949, pp. 161–2).

Sapir suggests language and thinking are synonymous: 'language and our thought-grooves are inextricably interwoven' and 'are, in a sense, one and the same' (Sapir, 1921, p. 228, p. 232, in Salzmann, 1998, p. 40). Whorf expanded and popularised these ideas to a broader audience. These famous passages illustrate the popular hypothesis:

> the background linguistic system (in other words, the grammar) of each language is not merely a reproducing instrument for voicing ideas but rather is itself the shaper of ideas... We dissect nature along lines laid down by our native languages... organize it into concepts, and ascribe significances as we do, largely because we are parties to an agreement to organize it in this way – an agreement that holds throughout our speech community and is codified in the patterns of our language... [Not] all

> observers are…led by the same physical evidence to the same picture of the universe, unless their linguistic backgrounds are similar. (Whorf, 1940a, p. 231)

Whorf proposes that different grammars lead to different comprehension of the world:

> users of markedly different grammars are pointed by their grammars toward different types of observations…and hence are not equivalent as observers but must arrive at somewhat different views of the world. (Whorf, 1940b, p. 61)

Sapir and Whorf follow Boasian anthropology in their linguistic anthropology, and similarly assert cultural differences against theories of innate racial characteristics (Sapir, 1949, p. 311; Mandelbaum in Sapir, 1949, pp. 305–7). Their approach to culture stresses the spiritual dimension of language and linguistic identity, following the Herderian Romantic tradition (Berlin, 2000; Hamann, 2007, [1759–1786]; Herder, 1800; 2002, [1765–1797]). Their spiritual approach to culture is exemplified in Sapir's essay 'Culture, Genuine and Spurious' (Sapir, 1949, pp. 308–31; Kuper, 2000, pp. 61–4). Sapir's essay outlines three approaches to culture. First, culture is understood as the 'socially inherited element in the life of man, material and spiritual' prevailing in Boasian anthropology (Sapir, 1949, p. 309). Second, culture is 'individual refinement' or civilization in the Arnold tradition (Arnold, 1960). Third, culture is the 'spiritual possessions of the group', and 'nearly synonymous with the "spirit" or "genius" of a people' (Sapir, 1949, pp. 310–11). Sapir follows the latter spiritual Herderian notion of a culture's soul, and its implied distinctions between authentic and false culture (Sapir, 1949). He distinguishes harmonious authentic cultures having a strong spiritual dimension, and criticises industrial scientific-driven cultures as lacking harmony, or strong spiritual dimensions, and fragmenting communal life through their separate functions. Sapir implicitly criticises Boasian approaches for treating culture overly functionally, without evaluating a community's spiritual quality of life. Sapir's belief in a group's *geist*, or spiritual soul, suggests culture as inherited and an innate characteristic, though he is critical of collective personality models (Sapir, 1949, p. 310–11). Both Sapir and Whorf believe separation from one's birth culture damages the personality (Kuper, 2000, pp. 62–8). Here their cultural anthropological concerns overlap with Anglo-American social psychology (Sapir, 1949, pp. 507–90). Their spiritual concept of culture associates a language's decline with spiritual decline and psychological pathology.

Contesting Sapir–Whorf

Boasian anthropological linguistics suggests that languages could differ radically and unpredictably from each other (Sapir, 1929; Whorf, 1940b). The idea of radical linguistic difference is taken up in the science fiction writer Ursula le Guin's *Changing Planes: armchair travel for the mind* (2005, pp. 144–56). Le Guin's family were anthropologists, and anthropological ideas are imaginatively experimented with in her writing. Le Guin's Nna Mmoy language puts forward the idea of a language in which words have no denotation, only 'a nucleus of potential connotations', and whose written form is not linear, but 'radial' or 'polydirectional' (Le Guin, 2002, p. 145). Nna Mmoy is a language that is so radically different from any other it is impossible for foreigners to learn, and translation is meaningless, for its words lack clear denotations (Le Guin, 2002, pp. 144–53). China Mieville's *Embassytown* (2011) also imagines a radically different language whose speakers are unable to lie. However, he suggests that its radical difference and incomprehension is only maintained though elite gate-keeping. Nothing approaching the radical linguistic difference of the fictional language has been discovered, although the potential enchants linguistic anthropology. Sapir and Whorf's ideas continue to fascinate and inform popular academic works, such as Guy Deutscher's *Through the Language Glass: How Words Colour Your World* (2010). Periodic excitement and debate are generated over languages with unusual features (for example, Boettcher, 2010; Everett, 2005; Nevins *et al.*, 2009a; 2009b).

Despite their abiding appeal, claims of fundamental differences have been contested, including the popular themes of colour, numbers, time and gender. Studies have observed that the spectrum of colour classifications across languages shows eleven basic core colour classifications, and, if fewer, then a general sequence of expanding colour classifications across languages (Berlin and Kay, 1969; Penn, 1972, pp. 36–7; Salzmann, 1998, pp. 45–6; see also Tallis, 1988, pp. 51–2, pp. 80–1). (Here I follow Salzmann's textbook to give a sense of how the debates are commonly presented to sociolinguistic students.) Likewise, strong Sapir–Whorf representations of isolated linguistic communities without number concepts have been contested. Boas earlier observed the challenge of learning alien number systems (Boas, 1962, [1928], pp. 151–2). Confronted by unfamiliar number concepts, we might initially react blankly like Baldrick, even when our language has developed mathematical terminology (BBC *Blackadder*, 1986). Different grammar patterns are not serious obstacles to a shared world of mathematics as implied under the Sapir–Whorf hypothesis, although everyday use or educational opportunities would affect mathematical understanding (Salzmann, 1998, p. 51).

Similarly, Whorf's claims over the Hopi language containing 'no reference to TIME, either explicit or implicit' have been contested (Whorf, 1936, p. 67). A language might not express time through tenses, but use time words like 'today' or 'tomorrow' (Voegelin and Voegelin, 1957, p. 24 in Salzmann, 1998, p. 64). Again, social patterns of gender discrimination do not follow grammar gender distinctions (Salzmann, 1998, pp. 49–51). Importantly, linguistic gender distinctions, as linguistic forms in general, may reflect past cultural norms, and lose their former meanings. We may linguistically over-interpret terms when we study a foreign language. Consider how the words sunset, bonfire, breakfast, disaster and spinster do not determine or reveal contemporary cultural understandings (Gramsci, 1971, p. 450; Jakobson, 1992, [1959], pp. 146–7; Ortega, 1992, [1937]; Salzmann, 1998, p. 47), as I will explore in the next chapter. Against strong Sapir–Whorf claims, different societies are not divisible simply through different languages, but through social class, and different language codes are significant in such affiliations, as Boas acknowledged (Boas, 1940, p. 92; Hymes, 1974; Salzmann, 1998, pp. 168–9).

Strong linguistic determinist interpretations have been refuted by subsequent research (Berlin and Kay, 1969; Hymes, 1968; Salzmann, 1998, pp. 45–64). Indeed, the anthropologist's implicit cosmopolitan standpoint, and assumed capacity to represent other cultures and languages, question strong anthropological cultural relativist claims. But modified cultural and linguistic relativist theories remain popular (Carroll, 1963; Deutscher, 2010). Accordingly, Guy Deutscher's popular *Through the Language Glass: how Words Colour your World* (2010) presents a modified linguistic relativist position, notwithstanding its bold linguistic determinist title. Salzmann's textbook concludes: 'differences in thought that are responsive to differences in grammatical structure exist, but tend to be superficial' (Salzmann, 1998, p. 56).

Against such conclusions, the twin ideas of linguistic relativism and linguistic determinism influence linguistic human rights advocacy. The broader Herderian belief that each language embeds a unique view of the world inspires imperatives to preserve all languages and support declining linguistic communities. The idea that grammar influences cultural norms informs ecolinguistic arguments that the grammar of indigenous languages encourages ecological thinking, while that of modern European languages encourages negative attitudes. Yet Herderian–Boasian cultural approaches are ambivalent towards progressive anti-racist politics and addressing inequalities internationally and nationally.

UNESCO's cultural critique of race

Romantic ideas of the cultural nation and linguistic races helped shape later racial thinking (Kedourie, 1969, pp. 62–70; Malik, 1996; 2008; Todorov, 1993). Race was important in underpinning nineteenth-century European imperialism and its framing of the international order (Grovogui, 1996). But the international racial framework became problematic to western powers in the twentieth century with the rise of national anti-colonial movements (Furedi, 1998; Wolton, 2000). Fears of a potential future race war, worse than the two world wars, compelled urgency for international action to address the race question (Comas, 1956, pp. 26–7; Furedi, 1998, pp. 160–92; Little, 1956, p. 213). Western elites were conscious of how the Soviet bloc could use the issue of racial inequality, and how they needed to establish alternative approaches to the Marxist ideas prevailing in international anti-racist political circles (Furedi, 1998, pp. 192–201, pp. 212–17; Grovogui, 1996, pp. 168–170; King, 2004, pp. 21–37; pp. 215–38). These political imperatives influenced the establishment of UNESCO.

UNESCO's Constitution declares the organisation's purpose: 'to contribute to peace and security...through education, science and culture' and to further 'universal respect for justice, for the rule of law and for the human rights and fundamental freedoms...without distinction of race, sex, language or religion' (UNESCO, 1948, article 1, section 1). UNESCO's constitution invokes universalist humanist Enlightenment beliefs in advancing knowledge and freedom: 'in the unrestricted pursuit of objective truth', and 'the free exchange of ideas and knowledge' (UNESCO, 1948, preamble). The Constitution supports mass communication and 'the free flow of ideas by word and image' (article 1, section 2(a)). Nevertheless, UNESCO is strongly influenced by Boasian anthropology and cultural relativism.

UNESCO's approach to race follows western anthropological and social psychology approaches in associating the causes of conflict with cultural and racial prejudice and emphasising their management through education (for example, Dewey, 1916; 1940). Anthropologists distanced themselves from the UN Universal Declaration on Human Rights (Barnett, 1948; Steward, 1948; Washburn, 1987; Wilson, 1997, pp. 2–5), but were closely involved in developing UNESCO's position on race (Malik, 2000b, pp. 134–47). Anthropologist Ashley Montagu chaired UNESCO's original committee on race, which was overwhelmingly made up of cultural anthropologists and sociologists, although biologists were later added (ibid.). UNESCO's statements on race refute racial explanations for group differences, and instead proclaim different 'cultural experience' to be the key (UNESCO, 1952, section 6). In summary, UNESCO sees humanity as 'biologically singular but culturally plural' (Malik, 2000b, p. 140). UNESCO follows a form of 'pedagogical anthropology', which advocates advancing social progress, through changing individual attitudes and patterns of culture (Leiris, 1956, pp. 99–106; pp. 115–16; Modell, 1984, p. 208; Montagu, 1963, p. 67).

Countering cultural prejudice involves learning to appreciate cultural difference under the Boasian cultural 'theology', seeing each culture having its part in a harmonious whole (Malik, 2000b, p. 145). Accordingly, Montagu refers to differences between individuals being qualities 'to be cherished and cultivated' (Montagu, 1963, p. vi). As a start, UNESCO recommended that the term 'race' be dropped and replaced with 'ethnic groups' (UNESCO, 1950, section 6; Montagu, 1963, pp. 61–71).

Anthropological model of international cultural diversity

The anthropologist Claude Lévi-Strauss (1908–2009) made an influential contribution to UNESCO's *The Race Question in Modern Science* (1956). Lévi-Strauss highlights how earlier linguistic race theorists believed that peoples 'differed in their special aptitudes rather than in their absolute value' (Lévi-Strauss, 1956, pp. 123–4). Lévi-Strauss also believes in essential differences between people – originality for Lévi-Strauss relates to 'ultimate essence' rather than creativity (Lévi-Strauss, 1956, p. 158). He fears that, where our differences erode, so too does our essential humanity (Malik, 2000b, p. 142).

Lévi-Strauss treats cultures as different trains, moving in different directions, at different speeds, with different reference systems, with no common measurement (Lévi-Strauss, 1956, pp. 140–1; Malik, 2000b, p. 141). He suggests that we cannot judge other cultures from the window of our cultural train:

> Whenever we go, we are bound to carry this system of criteria with us, and external cultural phenomena can be observed only through the distorting glass it interposes, even when it does not prevent us from seeing anything at all. (Lévi-Strauss, 1956, p. 140)

Lévi-Strauss calls for respect towards the cultural difference of other cultures, even if their 'ultimate essence' eludes us and we can 'reach no more than an imperfect understanding of them' (Lévi-Strauss, 1956, p. 158).

Lévi-Strauss questions ideas of human invention and progress, along with ideas of western superiority (Lévi-Strauss, 1956, pp. 136–7, pp. 142–7). Instead, he suggests, 'the originality of each culture consists rather in its individual way of solving problems' (Lévi-Strauss, 1956, p. 144):

> the true contribution of a culture consists, not in the list of inventions which it has personally produced, but in its difference from others. (Lévi-Strauss, 1956, p. 158)

Lévi-Strauss' international vision is of 'a world-wide coalition of cultures, each of which would preserve its own originality' and exhibit 'the maximum possible diversities' (Lévi-Strauss, 1956, p. 158). Development takes the form of adaptation, rather than transformation. For Lévi-Strauss, 'all cultural progress depends on a coalition of cultures', and 'the greater the diversity between the cultures concerned, the more fruitful such a coalition will be' (Lévi-Strauss, 1956, p. 159). Simultaneously, however, Lévi-Strauss problematises greater global communication and interaction (Malik, 1996, pp. 168–9). For Lévi-Strauss, the desired cooperation between cultures tends to foster cultural convergence and undermine the cultural diversity, and the pool of culturally diverse approaches to problems, he sees necessary for 'the biological and cultural survival of mankind' (Lévi-Strauss, 1956, pp. 159–60). Progress was driven in the past through contact with new peoples, or the pressures of social inequalities, but international collaboration and social improvements iron out these sources of diversity (Lévi-Strauss, 1956, pp. 159–61). Lévi-Strauss notes a third potential of source of diversity in 'antagonistic political and social systems' (Lévi-Strauss, 1956, p. 161). He prefers cultural diversity to political contestation. Nevertheless, he fears cultural traditions ossifying, and is even prepared to tolerate offensive forms of self-expression to foster dynamic diversity (Lévi-Strauss, 1956, pp. 159–62). But anti-dynamism is inherent in Lévi-Strauss' model of social policies, circumscribed by adaptation to cultural tradition. Such cultural approaches are criticised by the anti-colonial writer Frantz Fanon as mummifying cultures (Fanon, 1967). For Fanon, culture is inherently linked to political freedoms, without which cultural life withers (Fanon, 1967, p. 189).

Essentialising cultural difference

Lévi-Strauss, like Boasian anthropology, fears that cultural change damages individuals and the harmonious whole of cultures (Boas, 1904, p. 253; Malik, 2000b, pp. 142–5). Sapir deplores how the American Indian has 'slipped out of the warm embrace of a culture into the cold air of a fragmentary existence' (Sapir, 1949, p. 318 in Kuper, 2000, p. 240). But here Sapir, and the cultural relativist critique of race, ironically give cultural difference a permanence akin to biological difference, albeit without the previous hierarchical scale (Kuper, 2000; Malik, 1996). On Sapir's understanding of culture, Walter Michaels observes:

> If the Indian's culture were simply identical to his behavior and in no way related to his race, then he could never slip out of its warm embrace. In order for a culture to be lost, then, it must be separable from one's actual behavior, and in order for it to be separable from one's actual behaviour, it must be anchorable in race. Sapir's critique of race by culture is actually the continuation of race through culture. (Michaels, 1995, pp. 120–1 in Kuper, 2000, p. 240)

Consequently, Boasian concepts of culture re-legitimise differences (and potentially inequalities) in a culturally different form, despite their crucial contribution to undermining western scientific racism theories (Eriksen, 2001; Kuper, 2000; Malik, 2000b, pp. 142–3; Michaels, 1995). Culture is given a seemingly innate inherited quality, even as biological racism is discredited (Kuper, 2000, p. 14).

Boasian egalitarianism, arising out of disillusion with progress, contrasts with both Enlightenment egalitarianism, believing all people could progress and become more civilised, and nineteenth-century racial thinking, believing only some races were capable of advancement (Malik, 2000b, pp. 142–3). Boasian cultural relativist critiques do not address important evolving dimensions of European imperialism – crucially, colonial rule in the interwar period was increasingly justified in cultural relativist terms (Furedi, 1998). Colonial anthropology and Boasian anthropology share preoccupations with pathological 'deracinated' or de-cultured subjects (Furedi, 1998, pp. 132–60). Further parallels exist between British colonial rule, seeking to promote cultural determination against political self-determination, and Boasian anthropology, seeking cultural diversity within larger federal political units (Boas, 1962, [1928], p. 103). Accordingly, Boas regretted the division of the Austro-Hungarian Empire into separate nation states (Boas, 1962, [1928], p. 100). Malinowski similarly saw the Austro-Hungarian and the British imperial forms as models for the League of Nations (Gellner, 1998; Malinowski, 1945). Nor do contemporary cultural relativist critiques address important dimensions of today's power politics, whether the institutionalising of difference under global governance, or governments using relativist arguments against human rights, and political and civic freedoms.

Here we may compare how Lévi-Strauss' model of cultural diversity and cultural adaptation downplays human originality and individuality against their reassertion in Arendt's political philosophy (Arendt, 1998, [1958], pp. 246–7). Arendt's *The Human Condition*, too, contemplates the expanding homogenising governance of people's lives in mass society. However, Arendt reasserts the fact of human individuality against humanity as species. And, because humans are individuals, not merely members of a species, the potential for new thinking and action is ever present (Arendt, 1998, [1958], pp. 176–9, p. 184). So, whereas Arendt's ideas affirm political action and speech, Boasian anthropological ideas suggest adaptation to the existing range of customs and traditions. UNESCO's Constitution envisages diversity being preserved politically through the diversity of independent national states:

> With a view to preserving the independence, integrity and fruitful diversity of the cultures and educational systems of the States Members of the Organization, the Organization is prohibited from intervening in matters which are essentially within their domestic jurisdiction. (article 1, section 3)

Back in 1945, the principles of national sovereignty and non-interference were considered integral to maintaining international diversity. However, global governance challenges the political diversity of independent states, even as it seeks to preserve cultural diversity. Whereas the earlier ideal was a more politically open-ended notion of diversity, subsequent notions of cultural diversity are more ossified. Political freedom, with its diversity of potential ends, is secondary to cultural maintenance in contemporary advocacy. Its Whorfian-inspired models fix people into different linguistic and cultural identities, even though advocates may recognise identities as constructed, and specifically warn against essentialising differences (Pennycook, 1994, pp. 64–5).

Advocates share the tensions of UNESCO's cultural relativism. On the one hand, their cultural relativism seeks to maintain indigenous cultures and is ambivalent towards the modern state (Eriksen, 2001, p. 130). On the other hand, their educational and rights policies assume the development of modern states. Advocates simultaneously maintain Romantic visions of linguistic communities opposed to modernity and see identity as dependent on institutional recognition and elaborating comprehensive material demands of the modern state.

Beyond noble primitives?

The anti-colonial writings of Amie Césaire, Fanon, James and others attack ideals of noble primitives for their paternalistic assumptions, legitimising traditional hierarchies, and denying political subjectivity and change (Césaire, 1972, pp. 38–9; Fanon, 1967, [1961], pp. 251–5; 2008, [1952], pp. 91–8; Gramsci, 1985, p. 202; King, 2004, pp. 123–50, pp. 199–238, pp. 239–65; Wright, 1964, p. 2, pp. 12–13, p. 59; 1994, [1956], p. 199). Richard Wright's *White Man, Listen* (1964) expresses anti-colonial suspicion of western Romantic celebrations of indigenous cultures:

> I suspect any white man who loves to dote upon those 'naked nobles' who wants to leave them as they are, who finds them 'primitive and pure,' for such mystical hankering is, in my opinion, the last refuge of reactionary racists and psychological cripples tired of their own civilization. (Wright, 1964, p. 2)

Western support for indigenous cultures was, and is, compatible with subordinating non-western societies and maintaining international inequalities (Wright, 1964, p. 59).

Linguistic imperialism studies have been criticised for tending towards Romantic stereotypes of noble primitives, and reading off people's politics from their (linguistic) identity (Davies, 1996). Their critiques commonly associate Enlightenment universalism with colonial or neocolonial relations, and overlook how key anti-colonial writers continued to identify themselves with the radical Enlightenment ideas, notwithstanding their condemnation of western civilization (Fanon, 1967, [1961]; 1980, [1959]; James, 2001, [1938]; Wright, 1964, pp. 44–53). Linguistic advocates' antipathy towards universalism and universal language (Pennycook, 1998a, pp. 213–14), contrasts with the earlier idealised association, made by progressives like Martin Luther King (Sunnemark, 2003, p. 53). Equally, Said, whose orientalism thesis is often invoked in linguistic imperialism studies or ecolinguistics to refute universalism and humanism, is critical of Romantic essentialising of difference (Said, 1994b, pp. xiii–xiv, p. 59; p. 88; 2003). Said's vision of the intellectual questions the cultural relativism and linguistic determinism implied in the Sapir–Whorf hypothesis:

> Is the intellectual galvanized into intellectual action by primordial, local, instinctive loyalties – one's race, or people, or religion – or is there some more universal and rational set of principles that can and perhaps do govern how one speaks and writes? (Said, 1994b, p. 88)

The next chapter explores the problem of Babel, and how ideas of linguistic creativity or linguistic difference impact on translation theories. Romantic beliefs in human subjectivity and imagination suggest translation's creative possibilities. Conversely, contemporary theories influenced by Whorfian concerns problematise both the possibilities and the ethics of translation. The following chapters explore the limits of cultural relativist critiques of colonial and post-colonial relations, and how they legitimise new forms of global governance, circumscribing political subjectivity and freedom of expression.

5

Righting Babel? Translation as Cultural Transfusion or Cultural Violence

Problem of Babel: translation or anti-translation?

The Babel myth opens with a vision that 'the whole earth was of one language, and of one speech' (Genesis, chapter 11, verse 1). The people decide to build 'a city, with a tower that reaches to the heavens, so that we may make a name for ourselves; otherwise we will be scattered over the face of the whole earth' (Genesis, chapter 11, verse 5). However, God sees the tower people are building and says: 'If as one people speaking the same language, they have begun to do this, then nothing they plan to do will be impossible for them.' So God decides to intervene and 'confuse their language so they will not understand each other' (Genesis, chapter 11, verse 7). The myth associates a common human language with human ambition and challenge to God's authority, and humanity's linguistic division with humility and submission to God's authority. The biblical story could represent the original imperial divide and rule! Yet contemporary language advocacy and translation ethics, like Hamann and Herder, appear to side with God against humanity, and seek its re-submission to sacred or quasi-sacred cultural injunctions.

Language advocates seek to enforce global language identity rights to protect languages against globalisation and global English. Global human rights governance, however, implies increased cross-language communication. Whorfian concerns to maintain linguistic diversity make translation crucial, but are also ambivalent about it, for translation may disturb the harmony of cultural and linguistic adaptation under the Boasian secular theology. This chapter examines debates in translation studies. Debates over Babel reflect tensions between universalism, emphasising our common humanity, and relativism, emphasising our cultural linguistic differences. Chomskian and Whorfian themes are evident in translation theories, which have shifted towards cultural relativist positions against universalism, following broader intellectual and political trends. The translator James Holmes has described the Sapir–Whorf thesis as hindering translation theories, and Chomskian universal grammar theories as not helping much (Holmes, 1994, p. 104). Universal grammar theories do not give us norms for translating between languages, as they address language at the sub-cultural level (Chomsky, 1965, p. 30, pp. 201–2; Steiner, 1998, [1975], p. 111). The theories, although founded as a critique of behaviouralism's neglect of human meaning (Chomsky, 1959), focus on linguistic structures, rather than linguistic–cultural meaning (Steiner, 1998, [1975], p. 114; Tallis, 1988, pp. 72–3; 1999, p. 293, p. 343). Nevertheless, universal grammar's foundation in a common humanity affirms endeavours to translate. Conversely, Whorfian theories, while sensitive to linguistic difference, tend to problematise translation ethically for destabilising cultural and linguistic identities.

Discussion of translation over the centuries shows certain recurring themes. The reoccurrence has led Steiner's seminal *After Babel* to question how many genuinely original contributions have been made to the subject (Steiner, 1998, [1975], p. 283). But, even if many theoretical concerns are perennial themes, it is possible to identify trends in translation studies. While Steiner believes that translation is both 'desirable and possible' (Steiner, 1998, [1975], p. 266), key translation theories today suggest that translation is both impossible and ethically questionable. The chapter begins with trust in communication, and ends on the contemporary ideas of communication's violence and its implications for language rights advocacy. Effectively, key translation theories support linguistic identity protection against freedom of translation.

Trust in communication

Translation debates are primarily focused on the problems of communicating between different languages and cultures. Translation theories, informed largely by the ideals of literary translation, are often counsels of perfection leading to despair. Yet translation between different languages and cultures simply makes explicit the problem of translation, which is present in all human communication (Steiner, 1998, [1975], p. xii). The universal need for translation arises from humanity's separation from nature, and 'man from man' (Paz, 1992, [1971], p. 153). Humans think and act as individuals, not simply as a species (Arendt, 1998, [1958]). As Ortega y Gasset's essay on 'The Misery and Splendour of Translation' argues, translation is premised on two utopias: humanity as utopian beings, and language and translation as utopian activities (Ortega y Gasset, 1992, [1937]). Communication in a mother tongue is itself a utopian act, even before the utopian experiment of translation (ibid.). First, we have the miracle of the appearance of humans as conscious beings, who do not just follow the possible, but strive for the impossible, against the givens of nature. Then we have the related miracle of human speech, and the translation of experiences and thoughts into words (Paz, 1992, [1971], p. 154). To deny the possibilities of translation between languages would be to deny the possibilities of language itself, and the translation of thought into word (Vygotsky, 1986, [1934], pp. 210–56).

Basic human sociability, evident in speech, suggests an instinct to communicate and to understand against despairing translation theories. Cries of translation's impossibility fly in the face of everyday experience (Steiner, 1998, [1975], p. 264). Translation happens between individuals in ordinary conversations, with their web of interpretations of the world (Paz, 1992, [1971], pp. 152–4). Just as translation in ordinary communication is possible, so translation between languages is possible, even if perfect unmodified communication is not possible, because we do not think or feel as a species, but as individuals with different individual and social experiences of the world (Steiner, 1998, [1975], p. 264).

For Steiner, translation begins with the translator's trust in the coherence of the world and trust that meaning is to be found in and across languages, and that efforts will uncover meaning (Steiner, 1998, [1975], pp. 312–13). Even in unpromising circumstances in which people have few words of each other's language, they may communicate adequately with each other when they want to be understood. Readiness to understand allows ideas to be communicated between individuals, or translated between languages, although the ideas conveyed may only be rough approximations of the original, or require circumlocution or the coining of new words. After all, the link between sound and word in language is arbitrary, save for words attempting to imitate sounds, and therefore not fatal to conveying meaning across languages. In its approximations, translation mirrors the rough and ready character of ordinary human communication. Everyday speech and interaction invariably involve approximations and elisions, reflecting how ordinary life is not conducted with clinical exactness. Reception of ideas in everyday encounters is not guaranteed, and is merely more obvious in translation across languages. Just as our speech embodies our experience and interpretation of the world, equally, our reception of ideas depends on our experience and interpretation of the world. We do not absorb information as empty vessels, or blank sheets in the Lockean image, but bring our own ideas to the ideas conveyed to us. A word may have additional connotations in one language that it does not have in another, or what Chomsky has called 'accessory ideas'; that is, 'a word excites in our minds, besides the principal idea which we regard as the proper meaning of the word, other ideas' (Chomsky, 2002, p. 131). Certain contexts are consciously wary of accessory meanings (legal contracts) or consciously embrace them (word play) (Beano, 2001). In practice, the speaker's position or context will help screen off many accessory meanings in both the original and the translation (Holmes, 1994, pp. 9–10).

Moreover, the translation of thought into word is more complex than that between languages, because of their qualitatively different character.

Communication of thought, as the Russian psychologist Vygotsky explores, involves more than 'merely vocalizing silent speech', as thought involves sense without being directly tied to words (Vygotsky, 1986, [1934], p. 248). The words spoken by individuals are only the tip of the verbalised and unverbalised thoughts swimming in our heads. Attempts to translate our thoughts or feelings into words are not always successful. 'A thought once uttered is untrue,' the Russian poet Fyodor Tyutchev despairingly declared in his poem *Silentium*. Tyutchev's poem is not alone in calling for silence in face of the disjuncture between thoughts and words, and the difficulty of expressing oneself. Steiner's *Language and Silence* discusses how silence was advocated as an ethical position after the Holocaust (Steiner, 1969). The ethics of speech or non-speech recur in post-structuralist and ecolinguistic theories over language and power.

The fact that thoughts are not the same as words is only too apparent to those of us who struggle to articulate our thoughts. Writers' block is testimony to the distinction between thoughts and words (Vygotsky, 1986, [1934], pp. 249–50). Tellingly, authors suffering from writers' block sometimes turn to translation as an activity, illustrating how translation between languages may feel more realisable than the intimate translation of one's thoughts into words.

Yet the difficulty of translating thought into speech should not be exaggerated. Conviction helps communication. The American Romantic thinker Henry Thoreau's *Walden* advocates silence in his vision of the simple natural contemplative life (Thoreau, 1986, [1854]). But Thoreau abandoned silence when convinced of slavery's injustice; his newfound conviction gave him the moral courage to speak out publicly against its injustices. The imperatives of circumstance may galvanise thought and speech: the striking outpouring of writing (and reading) at times of historical turbulence testifies to how anxieties over translating one's ideas into speech or writing suddenly become irrelevant. James' *The Black Jacobins* suggests the ease of writing when one has clear political positions:

> in the hour of danger Toussaint, uninstructed as he was, could find the language and accent of Diderot, Rousseau and Raynal, of Mirabeau, Robespierre and Danton. And in one respect he excelled them all. For even these masters of the spoken and written word, owing to the class complications of their society, too often had to pause, to hesitate, to qualify, Toussaint could defend the freedom of the blacks without reservation, and this gave a strength and single-mindedness rare in the great documents of the time. (James, 2001, [1938], p. 161)

Consider, too, how the threatened Jewish radical Abram Leon rapidly analysed *The Jewish Question* (1970, [1950]) during wartime, against the postwar counsels of silence (Steiner, 1969). Conversely, difficulty articulating one's thoughts may point to intellectual confusion, doubt, social anxiety, or simply absence of anything compelling to say. Think of the everyday stumbling over taboo topics or words.

Where cross-communication is rare or relations are fraught, the possibilities of misinterpretation are greater. One translation attempt may not communicate ideas well; another translation may convey ideas better. If equivalence is impossible, correspondence may be found (Holmes, 1994, p. 101). Translation of ideas from one language to another is unlikely to be limited to a one-off event. The repeated experience of translating from one language to another will help individual translations (Holmes, 1994, p. 12), although perfect accord between the original and the translation is not reached. Indicatively, belief in correspondence appears more common among those who are primarily practising translators than those who are primarily theorists.

Conservative Romantic and Whorfian approaches focus on discontinuities in meaning between languages, downplaying how languages evolve in contact with other languages and may share similar roots. Simultaneously, they suggest stability of meaning within a language. But barriers between languages are not static, because meaning is not permanently fastened in language. The associations a particular word might have in one language, or one era as opposed to another, shift. The general meaning of a word, translated across different languages, may be closer in meaning than the same word historically within a particular language. Even if a language is dominated by a particular worldview, that language and world view are likely to have shifted considerably over the course of time (Humboldt, 1999, [1841], p. 43, p. 182, pp. 208–11).

English speakers today read classic texts such as Chaucer's *Canterbury Tales* or *Beowulf* with great difficulty. We need translations or very detailed commentaries to understand early English texts, because we experience the language as foreign. Meanwhile, Dutch students find it relatively easier to read *Beowulf*, or other early English texts, than native English speakers, because modern Dutch is closer to old English. Nevertheless, Chaucer is arguably closer to us today than in previous centuries, and even part of the traditional canon that teenage students find most accessible! Conversely, the seventeenth-century poet John Dryden's contemporaries were unenthusiastic about Chaucer's work, even with translation into modern English. According to Dryden, they considered Chaucer 'a dry, old-fashioned wit, not worth reviving' (Dryden, 1992, [1680], p. 26). So language barriers should not be equated with communication barriers. If Chaucer's stories communicate better to us than yesteryear, we are more estranged from certain Victorian poetry, even if we formally understand it. Pre-Raphaelite poetry does not communicate well to contemporary culture, and feels more alien to us than Chaucer or post-colonial writing, despite their temporal, geographical or linguistic distance (Steiner, 1998, [1975], p. 15).

Universality of spirit

Belief in translation finding corresponding meaning has been underpinned by belief in the 'universality of spirit' (Paz, 1992, [1971], p. 152). Leibniz's idea of a universal language sought to overcome miscommunication, arising from words having different associations, and divergent meanings. Leibniz overlooked the problem of his speakers bringing accessory ideas from their own experiences, the very problem his project was supposed to solve (Toulmin, 1992, p. 103). The creation of a universal language cannot guarantee that people understand experiences or concepts in the same way. Nevertheless, shared meaning is fostered through shared experiences, interests and empathy. So, even if Leibniz's ideal is impossible, the sentiments he brought to his project foster communication between peoples. Romantic thought developed more sophisticated understanding of language difference than earlier Enlightenment thinkers like Leibniz. Yet many Romantic thinkers also believed in the 'universality of spirit' or 'world spirit' realisable through history.

Goethe, whose language philosophy resonates with German idealism and Hegelian dialectics (Hegel, 2004, [1842]), believed in a universal, paradisal language and a 'hidden grammar' shared between languages (Goethe, 1998, [1819–1827], p. 457). Translation theories inspired by Goethe's ideals (1992, [1819]) see translation's ultimate purpose as metamorphosis advancing the human spirit (Benjamin, 1992, [1923]; 1999, [1923]; Ortega y Gasset, 1992, [1937]). They affirm human creativity linguistic experimentation, and utopian strivings in translation, even if our achievements only approximate our ideals. At the same time, they believe translation should transform the consciousness of the translator, and the receiving language and society (ibid.). As such, translation theories help in understanding the divisions between subject and object, or word and world, and potentially overcoming alienating conditions (Ives, 2004a, pp. 127–33). Translation is, therefore, for humanity, to advance human culture in the broadest sense, not only a particular culture. Hence they suggest that translation should transcend the original, seeking a higher synthesis (Benjamin, 1992, [1923]; 1999 [1923]; Ortega y Gasset, 1992, [1937]). In this universalist spirit, Goethe champions the concept of world literature, which represents a synthesis of human creative achievement and reveals the essential unity of humanity (Steiner, 1996, pp. 145–7).

Inspired translation by Goethe and others spurred national literary creativity, and a new literary German language. Goethe's *West-Eastern Divan* collection expresses his aspiration 'to restore through poetry the unity of the two separated hemispheres of Orient and Occident' (Goethe, 1998, [1819–1827], pp. viii–ix). Goethe's poem cycle identifies with the fourteenth-century Persian poet Hafiz as his twin ideal poet (Goethe, 1998,

[1819–1827], p. 63). The Divan cycle was originally criticised by Said as Orientalist (Said, 1991, [1978], pp. 154–5, pp. 167–8), but Said later honoured Goethe's work through the Divan Orchestra initiative, collaborating with Daniel Barenboim, and seeking to transcend East–West divisions (http://www.west-eastern-divan.org/).

Today it is commonly argued that poetry is 'lost in translation' (Frost in Satterlee, 1996). Dramatically, the writer and translator Vladimir Nabokov's 'On Translating Eugene Onegin' characterises translation as butchering:

> What is translation? On a platter
> A poet's pale and glaring head,
> A parrot's screech, a monkey's chatter,
> And profanation of the dead.
>
> (Nabokov, 1992, [1965])

Nabokov's much-cited poem condemns poetic translation as a travesty of the original. For poetry involves not just ideas, but the attachment of ideas to particular sounds and rhythms, which reinforces mood, atmosphere and judgement at a more subconscious level. As such, Whorfian identification of form and content has some credence for poetry (Holmes, 1994, p. 18).

Yet Vico calls poetry 'the first common language of all the ancient nations', against ideas of poetry's untranslatability (Vico, 2002, [1725], p. 151). Equally Hamann and Herder, also cultural relativist philosophers, similarly describe poetry as 'the mother tongue of humanity' (in Moore, 2008, p. xx). Similarly, Hegel declares that poetry is the most universal of the arts (Hegel, 2004, [1842], pp. 95–7). In this tradition, T.S. Eliot argues that 'Genuine poetry can communicate before it is understood' (Eliot, 1965, p. 8). The best poetry transcends translation, and communicates beyond the immediate language of the poem. Poetry's capacity, like that of music, to communicate meaning beyond words returns us to the distinction between thought, word and sense, and the idea of translation as liberating human thought from particular words (Schopenhauer, 1992, [1851]).

Poetry has been exalted as embodying the human spirit, and addressing people deontologically, beyond their particular social identities. Goethe argues that speaking out 'subjective feelings' does not make a poet. Only when a writer knows how to 'express the world' is 'he…a poet' (Goethe in Eckermann, 1883, pp. 166–7). Similarly, Wordsworth declares poetry's object to be 'truth, not individual and local':

> In spite of difference of soil and climate, of language and manners, of laws and customs: in spite of things silently gone out of mind, and things violently destroyed; the Poet binds together by passion and knowledge

> the vast empire of human society, as it is spread over the whole earth, and over all time. (Wordsworth, 1998a, [1802], p. 91; discussed in Williams, 1963, p. 58)

The radical Romantic imagination sought a transcendent universalism, reconciling people at a higher cultural synthesis (Coleridge, 2001, [1817], p. 272; Shelley, 1998, [1821], p. 363). It is in this sense that Shelley's *Defence of Poetry* suggests poets as the legislators of the world (Shelley, 1998, [1821], p. 366). Accordingly, Shelley's *Ode to the West Wind* sees a poet's thoughts rekindling human consciousness, and rekindled through their dissemination across the world. So, while Shelley refers scathingly to the 'vanity of translation', he also argues that 'grammatical forms ... are convertible with respect to the highest poetry without injuring it as poetry' (Shelley, 1998, [1821], pp. 344–5). Translators draw on the broader translation role of the poet, who, according to Wordsworth, 'does not scruple to substitute excellencies of another kind for those which are unattainable by him' (Wordsworth, 1998a, [1802], p. 90).

Goethe's dialectical understanding of translation parallels Romantic beliefs in the imagination and transcendent synthesis (Coleridge, 2001, [1817], p. 272; Humboldt, 1999, [1841], p. 157). Subsequent Romantic thought, and post-Romantic thought, retreat from Goethe's translation ideals. Tensions appear between Romantic ideals of transcendence and authenticity. Schopenhauer disparages translation as 'chicory for coffee', although he welcomes learning new concepts through translation (Schopenhauer, 1992, [1851], p. 34–5). Instead of translation, Schopenhauer advocates polyglotism, which he sees as increasing flexibility of thinking, since concepts become separated from specific words (Schopenhauer, 1992, pp. 34–5). Similarly, Schleiermacher's interpretation of Goethe is more prosaic and less utopian. Schleiermacher still emphasises human linguistic creativity, and sees translation as broadening one's horizons (Schleiermacher, 1992, [1813]). However, Schopenhauer and Schleiermacher's linguistic philosophical ideals narrowed to a scholarly cultural elite and a universal spirit realisable at the level of the individual scholar, rather than universally.

Universalist humanist ideals suggest that translation gives the original new life, and potential immortality (Benjamin, 1992, [1923]; 1999, [1923]). Accordingly, Keats' sonnet on *On First Looking into Chapman's Homer* celebrates translation as revitalising the original, and expanding human knowledge:

> Oft of one wide expanse had I been told
> That deep-browed Homer rules as his demesne;
> Yet did I never breathe its pure serene
> Till I heard Chapman speak out loud and bold!
>
> (Keats, 1970, [1816], p. 38, lines 5–8).

Keats compares reading Chapman's translation of Homer to Cortez exploring America:

> Or like stout Cortez when with eagle eyes
> He stared at the Pacific – and all his men
> Looked at each other with a wild surmise,
> Silent, upon a peak in Darien.
> (Keats, 1970, [1816], p. 38, lines 11–14).

These humanist ideals support translation across national, political or cultural divisions as acts of solidarity between people against power interests. In this spirit, writers such as the Russian poet Yevgeny Yevtushenko or the American writer Arthur Miller invited translations of their work towards recognising a common humanity against international political barriers. Thus, Miller's production of *Death of the Salesman* in China aspired to illustrate one humanity, beyond the confusion of languages (Miller, 1991). Similarly, Yevtushenko appealed to fellow poets across the Cold War divide to translate each other's work:

> if we poets of this world won't lend one another a hand, what then will befall the rest of mankind? In return for your help I give my solemn word to 'take revenge' and translate several of your own poems which you might choose for me. I grant you, of course, full freedom in your work, for I know well from my own experience that only a free and unrestricted translation can in any way claim to be poetry. (Yevtushenko, 1972, p. xxiv)

Yevtushenko depicts translation as a lifeline, against Nabokov's depiction of translation as murder:

> The translation of various literatures from language to language is a mysteriously powerful mutual transfusion of blood between the sliced-up pieces of the single body of mankind. (Yevtushenko, 1979, p. xiii)

Yevtushenko honours his translators as both his allies and his rivals, whose activities are mutually 'life-enhancing' (Kahn, 1972, p. xxiv). Each translator given free rein by Yevtushenko creates a new poem based on a personal reading of Yevtushenko, while translation's immortalising role elevates the translator's creative role. For Yevtushenko or Miller there is no sense of translation's violence , but of cultural understanding, rapprochement and aesthetic appreciation.

However, as utopian and universalist ideals have waned, so translation theories increasingly propose 'the irreconcilability of differences', as opposed to commonalities within difference (Paz, 1992, [1971], p. 153). Beliefs in the 'universality of spirit' have eroded with declining humanism and belief in humanity (Bookchin, 1995; Tallis, 1999). Cultural linguistic barriers against translation loom larger as utopian hopes of transcendence have receded. Simultaneously, the unequal relations between cultures and languages have prompted scrutiny of the ethics of translation, and parallel the imperatives of language advocacy and official multiculturalism, institutionalising formal identity rights against the indeterminacy of democratic politics and unregulated multicultural relations. Ethical concerns over translation come out more sharply in comprehension as an aggressive act (Steiner, 1998, [1975], p. 312).

Comprehension as aggression

The idea of comprehension as aggression is an old metaphor, which we see in the commonplace expressions of grasping and mastering ideas. There is a long philosophical tradition seeing language, knowledge and judgement as violent for initiating action and breaking natural determinism (Derrida, 1992, pp. 33–5; 2007, [1985]; Fitzpatrick, 2001, pp. 78–81). The purpose of translation in classical thought was to add to the stock of human knowledge by taking knowledge developed in other societies, that is, content-driven translation. Reverence towards aesthetic or cultural expression was not a primary motivation, at least among the Romans. St Jerome famously writes of the translator capturing meaning 'just like prisoners, by right of conquest' (Steiner, 1998, [1975], p. 281). Against the ancient metaphor, the European biblical translation tradition developed theories of fidelity to the original (Arnold, 1862; Dryden, 1992, [1680]; Humboldt, 1992, [1816]; Steiner, 1998, [1975]). Yet metaphors of violence and mastery persist, dramatising the pursuit of knowledge and expressing theories of history's advance through clashes of ideas. In this tradition, translation, even mistranslation, develops human thought and creativity to a higher plane. So, while key contemporary theories see the violence metaphor as compromising translation, the metaphor has been associated with radical movements linking comprehension of oppression and its eradication, including in anti-colonial writings (Césaire, 1995, [1939]).

Simultaneously, the violence metaphor also reflects how translation may threaten the existing cultural or religious order, and its monopoly of truth. Indicatively, St Jerome, known as the patron saint of translators, was periodically threatened by religious persecution for his translation of ancient Greek and Roman classical texts (Manguel, 2007, pp. 60–3). Equally, the act of translation and comprehension, even good translation, may corrode the original in the sense of demystifying the original as an object of awe (Steiner, 1998, [1975], p. 314). As such, translation is not faithful, but sacrilegious. In secular terms, a good translation may eclipse the original and thereby betray the author; hence the popular Italian aphorism *Traduttore, traditore* associating translation with betrayal (Steiner, 1998, [1975], p. 314). But superior translation only betrays the original from the narrower perspective of two competing entities. If translation is understood from a universalist perspective, as an act advancing humanity's knowledge and culture, not just for a particular individual or culture, then translation's possible superiority is unproblematic. Belief in fidelity to the original raises questions over whether translation should be faithful to extra-textual beliefs. Religious objections to translation are shrewd in understanding translation's assault on sacred distance. Indicatively, the pioneering and commonly persecuted, vernacular bible translators, such as John Wycliffe, Martin Luther and William Tyndale, sought to challenge existing church authority, while the official King James bible translation sought to re-establish it (Nicolson, 2004). Extra-textual concerns have returned under the influence of Boasian culturalism and identity politics, and inform the rise of translation ethics and renewed concerns with cultural or linguistic defilement.

Not taking language seriously

Concerns over sacrilegious or unethical translation tend to assume identity of language and culture. But, as Ortega y Gasset observes, 'We don't speak seriously' (Ortega y Gasset, 1992, [1937], p. 104). We say that the sun is coming out, although we do not believe the sun has agency (ibid.). Even if, theoretically, 'each language imposes a circumscribed table of categories', in practice 'the tables devised by each language no longer have validity, ... we use them conventionally and jokingly' (Ortega y Gasset, 1992, [1937], pp. 104–8). On the one hand, our thoughts are articulated in language; on the other, our understanding is not contained by language, and we use language ironically. We happily use the words 'sunrise' and 'sunset' without believing the sun revolves around the earth, or the word 'disaster' without believing in astrology (Gramsci, 1971, p. 450; Jakobson, 1992, [1959], pp. 146–7; Salzmann, 1998, p. 47). A language may involve finite standard grammatical forms within a given time and place, but neither a language, nor its use, is finite, or inherently tied to a particular world view (Chomsky, 2002, pp. 51–71; Humboldt, 1999, [1841], pp. 29–30, p. 53; Tallis, 1988, pp. 51–2, pp. 80–1). Meanings can shift, even without wide lexical and grammatical innovation. As Dryden explains:

> Words are not like landmarks so sacred as never to be removed; customs are changed, and even statutes are silently repealed, when the reason ceases for which they were enacted. (Dryden, 1992, [1680], p. 28)

The pitfall of linguistic literalism is a well-known problem. The freshness of foreign words experienced by the anthropologist or the translator may lead to over-interpretation, which the familiarity of the words lacks to the native speaker. Too often the etymology of words has been cited as proof of present beliefs, when etymology may merely reveal traces of past belief systems. If English speakers use the words 'sunrise' and 'sunset' without attaching a literal cosmic meaning, so too may speakers of other languages.

A linguistic situation is not given and is open to historical change. Greek and Latin obviously did not begin as languages with developed scientific concepts, but only became so. Much scientific writing in Western Europe during the medieval period was in Latin, when science was still dominated by Greek scientific discoveries and theories inherited via the Romans. Latin was displaced as the language of science by the national vernaculars in Europe when European scientific advancements superseded the science of the ancient world – Vico's use of Italian, Leibniz's use of German and so on (Koestler, 1964). Previously the European vernaculars were not generally considered suitable for scholarship, but they became so through scientific activity. New concepts may tap into the existing lexicon. Whorf, for instance, famously argued, against his own emphasis on linguistic–cultural immutability, that the native American Hopi language was better suited to wave particle physics in its ability to convey the idea of dynamic motionless (Whorf, 1936, pp. 130–1; discussed in Salzmann, 1998, pp. 42–7; Steiner, 1998, [1975], p. 93). Modern standard English might not neatly convey the idea of dynamic motionless, yet wave particle physics developed in English, irrespective of any linguistic inadequacies. Equally, much past language advocacy, against Whorfian ideals of linguistic difference, has sought to support national and minority languages, developing their academic and scientific lexicons against adopting English in secondary and higher education.

Emphasis on the difficulty of conveying meaning out of context across cultures underestimates novel expression in everyday life, and how novel expressions are conveyed linguistically (Chomsky, 2002, p. 112). Just as the individual can absorb new words and ideas, so too can individual languages (Mc Gilvray, 2002, p. 20). The universal human capacity for imagination and metaphor, translating ideas from one context to another, underpins the possibility of translation from one language to another. Human understanding has developed precisely from human capacity to convey meaning out of context. Abstract concepts have developed from metaphors, borrowed from ordinary activities (Arendt, 1977b, pp. 104–5). The vitality of a language, and a culture, has, accordingly, been linked to its receptivity to metaphor (Steiner, 1998, [1975], p. 24). Moreover, translation between different languages liberates concepts from specific words, increasing the flexibility of our thinking and expanding our minds and cultural ideas (Schopenhauer, 1992, [1851]).

However, contemporary translation theories are ambivalent about translation's destabilising cultural impact (Steiner, 1998, [1975], p. xvi). Discussion of cultural incorporation may invoke religious ideas of 'sacramental intake' or defilement, and express cultural fears of being devoured, against Goethe's embrace of metamorphosis (Steiner, 1998, [1975], p. 315). Anxieties over cultural appropriation or eclipse lead translation theorists like Steiner to endorse a more conservative translation model, suggesting the need for a restorative act, which essentially seeks to restore the status quo between cultures:

> translations which restore, which achieve an equilibrium and poise of radical equity between two works, two languages, two communities of historical experience and contemporary feeling. (Steiner, 1998, [1975], p. 429)

We may compare the aspiration of Goethe's dialectical model that translation should transcend existing cultural positions (1992, [1819]) and advance creative fusion on a higher cultural plane. Conversely, Steiner's equilibrium model seeks cultural exchange rather than synthesis, whereby distinct cultural identities are preserved but enhanced by their contact and the continuing balance between them. Steiner, indicatively coming from comparative literature rather than Goethe's world literature, gives us a modified view of universal knowledge and culture, not as synthesis, but as the sum of different cultures. A modest vision of cultural evolution is implied within existing cultural identities, interestingly paralleling global sustainable development models.

Steiner's ethical doubts are magnified in structuralist and post-structuralist critiques of translation. Steiner is no naïve proponent of equilibrium, and recognises sociolinguistic inequalities (Steiner, 1998, [1975], pp. 33–5), but his equilibrium model is unconvincing to key strands of translation theory today. Not least, its accounting analogy of book-keeping and balance sheets is unappealing as an aesthetic and political image, and raises more doubts than it allays. Steiner's economic accountancy metaphors continue in post-modern translation theories, but debt and insolvency are the tropes (Derrida, 2007, [1985] p. 199). The equilibrium model, to borrow from Marx, only addresses the arena of individual exchange between the original and translation, not the overall unequal relations of translation production. As such, it may even help legitimise those unequal global cultural, language and translation relations, as critical linguistic imperialism literature explores (Ives, 2006; 2010; Pennycook, 1994; Phillipson, 1992; 2009). However, the linguistic imperialism literature, rather than following Marxist or anti-colonial critiques of international relations, essentially follows more conservative critiques of modernity and Whorfian language and cultural models. Structuralist approaches have been accused of reaching a [Whorfian] intellectual and political impasse (Pennycook, 1994, pp. 26–5, pp. 56–7), but major post-structuralist approaches also face this problem (Holborow, 1999, pp. 81–6).

Translation as violence

Post-modern theories, which attack translation as violence, are exemplified in Derrida's essay on the Tower of Babel (Derrida, 2007, [1985]). Derrida's language theories influence contemporary translation theories, notably through the theorist Gayatri Spivak, whose writings and translation of Derrida's key work into English brought his work to a wider international audience, including post-colonial studies. Derrida's interpretation of the Babel story echoes Hamann's and Herder's views on Babel (Berlin, 2000, pp. 319–20; Herder, 1969, [1769], p. 107; Herder, 2002, [1793–1797], p. 385). Simultaneously, Derrida follows European intellectual concerns over the sickness and failures of language (Murdoch, 1968, pp. 64–80; Steiner, 1969; 1998, [1975], pp. 184–95), as opposed to humanist or utopian translation theories (Benjamin, 1992 [1923]; Ortega y Gasset, 1992, [1937]).

Derrida questions not only utopian strivings for translation between languages, but meaning-making in language (Derrida, 1976). For Derrida, the Babel story tells 'of the inadequation of one tongue to another... of language to itself and to meaning...' (Derrida, 2007, [1985] p. 191). Cultural pessimism underpins post-modern theories, which question conscious human agency and conscious speech against subconscious secondary associations (Eagleton, 1996, pp. 96–100; Heartfield, 2002). If translation is premised on trust in the world's meaning and coherence (Steiner, 1998, [1975], p. 312), such assumptions are in crisis (Bracken, 2002; Laïdi, 1998). Tellingly, Babel's own meaning is lost in its shift from the tower of God to the tower of confusion (Derrida, 2007, [1985], pp. 197–8). As contemporary societies have become more atomised and people feel increasingly estranged from each other, mistrust pervades interpersonal and intercultural communication. Echoing experience of social estrangement, post-modern linguistic theories suggest that sound and meaning do not meet in language (Derrida, 1976, pp. 50–1; Tallis, 1988, pp. 79–95; 1999, pp. 462–3). Overall, they are fatalistic, suggesting that meaning is arbitrary and established through force, deterring trust in speech and its translation (Derrida, 1973, pp. 77–82, pp. 94–5, pp. 145–16; 1976, pp. 7–8, p. 166; 1982; 2007, [1985]). The very structure of language is attacked as being premised on binary discriminations (Barthes, 1967; 1977; Derrida, 1976; Spivak, 1976). Conscious human subjectivity is marred by historical associations of the word 'subject' with subjugation (Heartfield, 2002, pp. 15–21, pp. 41–3). Assertions of subjectivity become a will to subject another. Etymology thereby becomes destiny, as language is marked by original sin, while conscious action becomes effectively reduced to the temporary release of the carnival, or word play.

Derrida follows the philosophical tradition seeing language, knowledge and judgement as violent for initiating action and breaking natural determinism (Derrida, 1992, pp. 33–5; 2007, [1985]; Fitzpatrick, 2001, p. 78–81). However, his and other post-modern approaches invoke the metaphor to emphasise translation's destructive, rather than creative, aspects (Steiner, 1998, [1975], p. 313). Nabokov, we have seen, condemns bad translation as offering up the severed head of the poet (Nabokov, 1992, [1965]). Contemporary translation theories go further in condemning translation for violating, not simply an individual writer, but a people's cultural identity and tradition. Derrida's discussion of language relations stresses the empirical violence of humanity. His Babel-makers are imperialists engaged in colonial violence and linguistic imperialism (Derrida, 2007, [1985], p. 193). Against linguistic imperialism, Derrida proposes an anti-translation position of 'not to communicate' as a form of resistance (Derrida, 2007, [1985], p. 204).

Babel's linguistic imperialism and cultural power relations are developed in the Translation as Violence and Translation as Manipulation schools (Bassnett, 2002; Bassnett and Lefevere, 1998; Hermans, 1985; 2006; 2007; Lefevere, 1992a; 1992b; Venuti, 1992; 1993; 1995; 1998a; 1998b; 2004). The translation theorist Lawrence Venuti is a key proponent of the violence thesis within translation studies. Venuti's much cited 'Translation as Cultural Politics' declares that 'the violence of translation resides in its very purpose and activity' (Venuti, 1993, p. 209). Not only is bad translation indicted, but translation itself. The very action of making 'another culture comprehensible' is tarred with violence (Dingwaney, 1995, p. 4). Translation is condemned as 'the *forcible* replacement of the linguistic and cultural difference of the foreign text with a text that will be intelligible to the target-language reader' (Venuti, 1993, p. 209, emphasis added). As such, violence becomes translation's central defining feature, while its creative features are degraded. Negative views of translation are mainstream in translation studies, even if they do not go as far as equating translation with the use of force.

Should we treat St Jerome's metaphor as evidence of translation's will to power and domination? Earlier ideals saw different cultures meeting and affirming their common humanity through translation, and fostering a higher shared culture. 'Translation as violence' theories follow the broad questioning of universalism, humanism, secularism and the pursuit of knowledge (Bookchin, 1995; Tallis, 1999). Their ethics oppose ideas of mastering nature, and seek to minimise the human footprint on the world. Cultural relativist scepticism links the pursuit of knowledge with imperialism, and gives paramountcy to cultural respect and the preservation of cultural tradition. Translation's erosion of cultural and linguistic difference therefore becomes perceived as causing cultural and linguistic harm. Non-communication, withholding translation, eschewing fluency, aspiring to 'radical inaccessibility' (Dingwaney, 1995, p. 5) and textual opaqueness (Karamcheti, 1995, p. 193), are variously proposed as strategies following Derrida to resist power.

Anxieties over translation as violence inform the rise of translation ethics as a field. The central ethic of translation has previously been to represent the truth of a text, an uncensored representation, which is not subordinated to extra-textual cultural sensitivities, whether of the source text or the translated text. However, appropriateness is increasingly proposed as an alternative goal of translation; that is, translation should represent the cultural sensitivities of the society in which the original text was created (Dingwaney, 1995, p. 5). In asking that translation be appropriate, the standard is not one of striving for accuracy, or the universal truth of a piece, transcending one's own standpoint, but conformity to specific group cultural values. So, while post-modern translation studies has celebrated multiple readings and is critical of translation etiquette associated with conformity to the cultural sensitivities of the receiving society – it is very scornful of nineteenth-century European and North American translation prudery – it is demanding translation etiquette, conforming to the cultural sensitivities of the source society.

But, in demanding conformity to cultural norms, post-modern translation etiquette is potentially taking its cue from the most conservative members of community, or imputing to a community particular cultural sensitivities which may actually be its own. In either case, translation etiquette is subordinating the truth of a text to conformity to what are deemed appropriate attitudes. But where do notions of cultural appropriateness leave the cultural rebels, those whose writings are a counter-statement to their world? Do, or how do, such approaches defend the translators and translations of Salman Rushdie's *Satanic Verses*? For Rushdie, his publishers and his translators have endured very real intimidation and violence, including the killing of his Japanese translator (Malik, 2009, pp. 1–16). Policies putting cultural respect before access to knowledge are actually being adopted across western public institutions, but they have negative consequences for any cultural dissidents whose voices become stifled under the officially protected cultural identities. (Jenkins, 2010; Malik, 2008, pp. 204–18).

The core concerns of translation studies in recent decades have related to cultural protection, rather than freedom of translation. Is the original text to be treated as a sacred cultural relic, which foreigners or non-believers are not entitled to see, or interpret, in case their unbelieving breath defiles its sacredness? Such approaches imply restricting freedom of interpretation and freedom of experimentation in the name of cultural affirmation. But without these freedoms creativity is stifled and cultures become ossified and mummified, as Fanon warns (Fanon, 1967, [1961], p. 180). Contemporary translation studies have contradictory positions on cultural identity. They commonly condemn cultural essentialism along with universalism (Spivak, 1992, p. 187) but then put forward ideas suggesting essentialist positions such as 'white theory' (Spivak, 1992, p. 192). Treating cultures as discrete entities, incomprehensible to outsiders or at risk of cultural contamination, is profoundly conservative, and ironically echoes racist ideas of cultural linguistic purity against miscegenation. Furthermore, the insistence on indigenous cultural tradition was adopted by the dominant British colonial power to counter anti-colonial opposition. Conversely, translation facilitated the dissemination of anti-colonial ideas. So it is ironic that post-colonial translation theories are adopting positions echoing British colonial cultural concerns, as the next chapter discusses.

Anti-translation strategies reverse earlier liberal or emancipatory strategies premised on advancing knowledge and spreading ideas (Gustafson, 1992, pp. 1–13; Locke, 2001, [1690], Book III, chapter X, paragraph 13, p. 409). Abolitionist campaigns wanted to name slavery 'slavery' and bring to light its inequity (Gustafson, 1992, pp. 386), while anti-colonial writers wanted to appropriate the language of power to challenge colonialism and racism. In Wright's words, 'We stole words from the grudging lips of the Lords of the Land, who did not want us to know too many of them or their meaning' (Wright in Gustafston, 1992, p. 256).

Demands to make the text opaque coincide with demands to make the translator or translation practice visible (Maier, 1995, p. 31). But there is a narcissistic aspect to the refusal of the translator, or rather the translation theorist, to translate for others. Such strategies risk 'self-aggrandisement' at the expense of translation (Dingwaney and Maier, 1995, p. 316). In various ways, contemporary translation approaches put the translation theorist into the limelight, and obscure the translated text. Unsurprisingly, translation practitioners express impatience with anti-translation translation theories. The gulf between translation practice and translation studies has led to accusations of 'armchair theorizing' (Holmes, 1994, p. 96) and demands to leave 'ideological reductionism and intellectual snobbery' and consider how theory may aid practice (Rosenstein, 2002).

Seemingly, radical non-translation positions in translation studies echo elitist prescriptions that works should be read in the original, even though this would restrict access to those able to understand them. As Steiner writes, when the translator has understood the original there is no need for the translator to go ahead with the translation (Steiner, 1998, [1975], p. 312). That the translator does translate represents a democratic act, in the sense that it is undertaken, not for the benefit of the translator, but for those who do not have access to the language of the original. (The act's altruism is underscored by the historically poor rates of pay for most literary and non-literary translation! The rates for translators in Croatia, for example, are comparable to those of cleaners, whose pay is notoriously low (*Slobodna Dalmacija*, September 2010). The actual dangers and violence faced by interpreters working in conflict zones have only gained academic attention in recent years (Baker, 2006; Baker, 2010; Inghilleri and Harding, 2010). Organisations like the International Association of Interpreters, the International Federation of Translators, InZone: the Center for Interpreting in Conflict Zones, and Red T have been developing international codes of practice and field guides to protect these interpreters, often employed casually in very dangerous environments. (See also the Arts and Humanities

Research Council (AHRC) Languages at War Project conducted by the Universities of Southampton and Reading with the Imperial War Museum, and the AHRC Language and International NGOs (LINGOs) Project 2012 conducted by the Universities of Reading and Nottingham.)

Overall, contemporary translation theories profoundly question trust in translation and the translator, paralleling the erosion of trust elsewhere. We see parallel soul-searching and doubts in the western humanitarian sector over their mediating role (Vaux, 2001), and in language rights advocacy, concerned over linguistic imperialism and seeking human rights governance over national polities (Pennycook, 1998a; 1998b; Phillipson, 1992; 2009a and 2009b). Unsurprisingly, the translator's identity, and whose voices he/she represents, are questioned under the rubric of cultural linguistic protection and appropriateness.

Anti-translation and governance of communication

Derrida's interpretation of the Tower of Babel takes up the violence metaphor to suggest the linguistic imperialism of the Babel-builders:

> when God imposes and opposes his name, he ruptures the rational transparency but also interrupts the colonial violence or the linguistic imperialism. (Derrida, 2007, [1985], p. 199)

His more literal historical reading may appear at first sight to be more politically radical than a mythological reading, but actually leads to a reactionary anti-humanist position, denying human emancipation. For Derrida's despair of language and translation ironically ends up identifying with a jealous, deconstructive God, who destroys Babel, crushing not only colonial violence and its linguistic imperialism but also independent human action:

> for having wanted thus to make a name for themselves, to give themselves the name, to construct for and by themselves their own name. (Derrida, 2007, [1985], p. 195)

Derrida implies that it is illegitimate to seek recognition from one's own actions. Instead, Derrida suggests, recognition should only come from God, or, in secular terms, from an external authority. Simultaneously, Derrida may be read as condemning not only colonial violence, but also independence movements seeking to construct their own polities. For Derrida, God embodies universal reason, whereas human universalism and reason are condemned as imperialist. (Human desire for peaceful transparency, though highlighted by Derrida, is sidelined in his interpretation.) Derrida is effectively calling for an external authority to rule over a perpetually divided humanity and mediate their relationships. As such, Derrida's theories anticipate western critiques of national sovereignty and assumptions of global governance in the last two decades, as espoused by politicians such as Tony Blair, Bill Clinton and Bernard Kouchner.

Simultaneously, Derrida's deconstructivist God identifies God with deconstruction, and Derrida the deconstructivist with God. His interpretation echoes Hamann, who sees language in sacred communal terms (Hamann, 2007, [1772], pp. 96–110, pp. 146–63; Haynes, 2007, pp. xiv–xxv). For Hamann, the Tower of Babel is a sacrilegious edifice of abstract human reason against God's truth (Berlin, 2000, pp. 319–20). So Derrida's deconstruction returns us to a traditional, authoritarian, theological order under a jealous God. And, if this reading of Derrida seems unjust, in drawing out its authoritarian violence, it may be recalled that Derrida's own readings sought to uncover the hidden violence of others' texts. His identification with the destructive avenging God of the Old Testament contrasts with earlier Romantic identifications with a tragic Satan, rebelling against patriarchal authority (Milton, 2003, [1667]; Shelley, 1998, [1821]). Again, his misanthropic account of translation as violence and mutilation opposes Yevtushenko's belief in translation as life-transfusing (Yevtushenko, 1979, p. xiii).

Derrida's interpretation of the Babel myth concludes in an anti-translation impasse, demanding that language be un-reconciled. Derrida's conclusions may be contrasted with Benjamin's inspiring vision of translation, transcending Babel and pointing towards 'the central reciprocal relationship between languages' and their 'reconciliation and fulfilment' (Benjamin, 1992, [1923], p. 74, p. 76; 1999, [1923], p. 73, p. 76). Benjamin suggests that, even if there is no synthesis at the level of individual sentences and texts, an underlying reconciliation of humanity and synthesis of languages are achieved in the yearning to translate and the striving for truth (Benjamin, 1992, [1923], p. 78; 1999, [1923], pp. 75–7). Against Benjamin's revelatory and liberatory vision of cultural linguistic creativity, Derrida offers a misanthropic account, which denies the possibilities of human emancipation. Indeed, retreat from transcendent ideals to more 'banal' positions is admitted by Spivak (Spivak, 2001, note 1, p. 21).

Despite theoretical scepticism, translation ideals of overcoming barriers between people and spreading shared understanding are still expressed, though more among novelists or practising translators. The novelist and translator Rosario Ferré speaks passionately of translators as people:

> dedicated to the pursuit of communication, of that universal understanding of original meaning which may one day perhaps make possible the harmony of the world. They struggle to bring together different cultures,

> striding over the barriers of those prejudices and misunderstandings which are the result of diverse ways of thinking and of cultural mores. (Ferré, 1995, p. 41)

Ferré subscribes to this ideal, but it is less prominent among fellow translation theorists. Practising translators continually testify to possibilities of communicating and transcending difference. Anti-translation theoretical positions underplay the continuing creative efforts to translate.

Norms of inappropriateness and inaccessibility represent elitist gate-keeping. The thrust of theoretical conclusions implicitly elevates translation theorists' status as cultural mediators, as against translation practitioners' and ordinary people's everyday cross-cultural encounters. If translation is problematic, if cross-cultural communication is difficult, then specialist culturally sensitive mediators are required to manage relations appropriately. Discourse theories of language and agency, Habermasian theories of communication or post-structuralist theories of the incommunicable and untranslatable all tend towards strategies promoting third-party mediation of interpersonal communication. Yet, ironically, language rights advocacy, although inclined towards Whorfian ideas of linguistic difference and untranslatability, assumes the universal translatability of law under global human rights governance. The translation power relations under global governance implied by global human rights regimes, poverty reduction strategy papers or international criminal tribunals have been neglected in linguistic rights advocacy literature. Overall, for all the seeming radicalism, anti-translation theories along with language rights advocacy end up endorsing mainstream conservative, bureaucratic views of identity and psychosocial management. Similar tendencies are evident in linguistic imperialism critiques and their human rights governance strategies, discussed in the next chapters.

Steiner's metaphor of being consumed is apt today: translation studies has incorporated so many anti-translation ideas from other fields, it risks becoming consumed. Tellingly, the rise of academic translation studies in the 1980s paralleled the decline of modern foreign languages, or their restructuring as cultural and theoretical studies. Translation practice has declined as a core aspect of British school language exams and university language degrees over recent decades. Students may increasingly take language degrees without having to sit specific translation exams. Equally, translation practice has been downgraded intellectually in academic work fostered by bureaucratic research evaluation regimes. The earlier UK Research Assessment Exercises, introduced in the 1990s, marginalised translations from their evaluations of academic scholarship, thereby discouraging translation practice in these managerial target-driven times. Nevertheless, translation studies has been revitalised in recent years against anti-translation impasses by interpreting studies and their particular interest in formal and informal interpretation experiences across language barriers. Here we could single out research into the practices of interpreting in violent conflict situations conducted by Barabar Moser-Mercer and her colleagues at InZone and academics elsewhere (Baker, 2006; Baker, 2010; Inghilleri and Harding (2010); InZone; Visoka, 2012).

However, translation studies as a field, lacking secure foundations in flourishing academic translation practice and modern languages departments, remains institutionally insecure. Meanwhile, interpreters working in conflict zones continue to risk their lives as mediators between international and local forces with little substantial protection or recognition, although a few among them may rise to influential public office within their societies as key mediators of global governance (Visoka, 2012).

6
Linguistic Imperialism, Global English and Modernity

Robinson Crusoe's linguistic imperialism

'I likewise taught him to say Master; and then let him know that was to be my name,' the shipwrecked Robinson Crusoe narrates (Defoe, 2001, [1719], p. 163). In Daniel Defoe's *The Life and Adventures of Robinson Crusoe*, teaching English defines and subordinates the other. The stranger is treated as a nameless empty vessel, without language, knowledge, history or community, until the hero inscribes a language and identity on him. The stranger is named Friday, symbolising how he only assumes an identity through that encounter. Thus begins Friday's life of relentless servitude, not equality, under Crusoe's claimed civilising education, which makes Friday an instrument to accumulate his wealth. For Marx, Crusoe is the ideal bourgeois capitalist subject (Marx, 1976, [1867], pp. 169–71). For James Joyce, Crusoe 'is the true prototype of the British colonialist, as Friday... is the symbol of the subject races' (Joyce, 1964, p. 24).

Linguistic imperialism studies examine Defoe's *Robinson Crusoe* as epitomising colonial and post-colonial English language hierarchies (Pennycook, 1994; 1998a; Phillipson, 1992). Teaching *Robinson Crusoe* is analysed as lessons in cultural imperialism, legitimising the 'racial structure of western society at the heyday of slavery' (Phillipson, 1992, p. 109). Indeed, simplified abridged versions of Robinson Crusoe were a staple of the colonial English literature curriculum (Pennycook, 1994, pp. 319–21; 1998, pp. 10–16; Phillipson, 1992, p. 109). Linguistic imperialism critiques join a longer tradition of critical readings of Crusoe as colonial mythology (Watt, 1987; 1997). Yet Defoe was also among the early writers to attack expanding British overseas power and slave trade (Defoe, 1702).

This chapter considers linguistic imperialism critiques of the English language as complicit in colonial and neo-colonial relations: 'English is both the language that will bestow civilization, knowledge and wealth on people and at the same time is the language in which they are racially defined' (Pennycook, 1998a, p. 4). We have already seen how Derrida's essay on the

Tower of Babel associates universal communication with colonial linguistic violence (Derrida, 2007, [1985]). The 'leitmotiv' of linguistic imperialism studies is 'the dominance of English as serving Western imperialist interests' (Skutnabb-Kangas *et al.*, 2009a, p. 327). However, there are flaws in linguistic imperialism critiques, which ironically echo colonial concerns.

Challenging global English

Phillipson's influential book *Linguistic Imperialism* (1992) identifies key linguistic imperialist assumptions, underpinning policies promoting English as the dominant world language:

- capacities: English-intrinsic arguments, what English is
- resources: English-extrinsic arguments, what English has
- uses: English-functional arguments, what English does (Phillipson, 1992, p. 271)

English-intrinsic arguments suggest the language's superiority in advancing modern culture, science and security. English, it is argued, has attained a neutral universal character, transcending particular national ties (and prejudices), and its spread as a shared world language contributes to international peace and stability (Phillipson, 1992, p. 275). Linguistic imperialism studies note the contradictory claims of the language's neutrality against Anglo-American foreign policy aspirations to promote the English language in their national interests (Phillipson, 1992, p. 276). Phillipson pointedly observes: 'Apologists for English are inconsistent here: arguments for the non-ethnic nature of English rub shoulders with the "opportunity" or "responsibility" of the British to meet the demand for English' (Phillipson, 1992, p. 276). Against celebratory accounts, linguistic imperialism studies see the English language supporting colonial and neo-colonial power relations, following studies suggesting the German language's complicity with Nazism (Pennycook, 1994; 1998a, pp. 3–4; Steiner, 1969, pp. 136–51). Linguistic imperialism critiques draw on post-modern and post-colonial interest in language, discourse and power. Studies commonly cite Fanon's statement on how speaking a language means 'to assume a culture, to support the weight of a civilization' (Fanon, 2008, [1952], p. 8, in Dingwaney, 1995, p. 3; Pennycook, 1994, p. 25, pp. 32–3).

English-extrinsic arguments believe in promoting English because of the access to resources it brings. Post-independence support for English language planning is linked to nationalists' desire for rapid industrialisation (Phillipson, 1992, p. 278). Linguistic imperialism critiques see the language's resources reflecting unequal power relations. Phillipson borrows from underdevelopment theories to criticise how 'the present-day imperialist structure... perpetuates the development of English and the underdevelopment of other languages' (Phillipson, 1992, p. 279). Resource arguments are attacked for creating a vicious circle, leading to the English language accumulating disproportionate resources at the expense of resources available to other languages (Phillipson, 1992, p. 279). Phillipson condemns British and US investment in English language publishing directed towards developing countries for undermining African publishing (Phillipson, 1992, p. 279).

Furthermore, the literature questions how global policies determine what are considered useful resources, reflecting western interests against weaker groups. Phillipson questions the appropriateness of textbooks in English for pupils whose mother tongue is not English. This critique is extended into criticisms over what constitutes legitimate knowledge resources, based on modern rational scientific knowledge as opposed to traditional concepts of knowledge. Ecolinguistics, discussed in Chapter 9, demands more space to be devoted to indigenous knowledge in policymaking and the curriculum.

The third category of arguments concerns the use of English as a language of wider national and international communication, and claims for English as advancing political security and economic prosperity. Advocates for English as a world language believe that, if people speak a common language, then this will foster social bonds and help prevent war. These ideas echo Leibniz's speculations on a universal language. Linguistic imperialism theories question whether a common language is any guarantee against social divisions or war, citing conflict in Northern Ireland and numerous other examples of civil or international wars between people speaking the same language. Phillipson states: '"National unity" is not something that any language can guarantee, just as proclaiming a single official language cannot wish away a multilingual reality' (Phillipson, 1992, p. 283). Linguistic imperialism critiques argue that global English embodies particular power interests, which jeopardise the security of minority and indigenous peoples and the planet. Critics observe that knowledge of English is no guarantee of prosperity, whether individually or nationally, invoking the economic insecurities of English-speaking countries like Jamaica or Kenya. Instead, the use of English is linked to furthering exploitative international economic policies, and fostering an elite which is socially, economically, culturally and politically separate from the rest of the population and identifies with international/foreign interests.

Against pro-English arguments, Phillipson stresses what the language lacks: 'those who represent English linguistic hegemony do *not* come with arguments which stress what English *is not*, does *not have* and does *not do*' (Phillipson, 1992, pp. 285–6). In his list of what English lacks, Phillipson emphasises how English does not support people's cultural identity: for those 'whose mother tongue is not English, English is *not* the language of their cultural heritage, *not* the language of intense personal feeling and the community' (Phillipson, 1992, pp. 285–6, emphasis in the original). Adopting English involves surrendering one's cultural identity and becoming subjected to an alien hegemonic culture. 'Resistance to the use of mother tongues is an expression of a colonized consciousness' (Phillipson, 1992, p. 297). Linguistic imperialism critiques stress language as identity against functionalist language as communication arguments. English is criticised as having negative materialist values and lacking spiritual values. Minority language advocates argue against global English that indigenous languages offer cultural identity, precious indigenous knowledge, alternative values, and ways of life opposed to globalisation and modern materialism.

Linguistic imperialism as cultural imperialism

We have seen how Derrida's article 'Des Tours de Babel' accuses the Babel architects of 'linguistic imperialism' (Derrida, 2007, [1985], p. 199). Linguistic imperialism has been defined by Phillipson's seminal study *Linguistic Imperialism* (1992) as follows:

> *the dominance of English is asserted and maintained by the establishment and continuous reconstitution of structural and cultural inequalities between English and other languages.* Here *structural* refers broadly to material properties (for example, institutions, financial allocations) and *cultural* to immaterial or ideological properties (for example, attitudes, pedagogic principles). (Phillipson, 1992, p. 47, emphasis in the original)

Linguistic imperialism is further seen as a form of *linguicism*, defined by Phillipson as follows:

> ideologies, structures, and practices which are used to legitimate, effectuate, and reproduce an unequal division of power and resources (both material and immaterial) between groups which are defined on the basis of language. (Phillipson, 1992, p. 47)

Studies are alarmed by how English has become a *lingua franca, lingua economica, lingua emotiva, lingua academica, lingua cultura* and *lingua bellica*, and compare linguistic imperialism to imperialism in other spheres (Phillipson, 1992, p. 305; 2009b, p. 92; Skutnabb-Kangas, 2009, p. 37). Linguistic imperialism critiques draw on the concept of cultural imperialism, which emerged from the 1960s (Tomlinson, 1991, p. 2). Cultural imperialism studies shift from Marxist to post-Marxist approaches, and from the economic, social and political spheres to cultural production, especially the media (Tomlinson, 1991, pp. 25–6). Said's *Orientalism* (1991, [1978]) and *Culture and Imperialism* (1994) inform thinking on cultural imperialism, and influence linguistic imperialism studies (Pennycook, 1994; 1998a).

Cultural imperialism is now a key concept in the humanities and social sciences, as Raymond Williams' *Keywords* outlines (Williams, 1988, pp. 87–93;

Tomlinson, 1991, pp. 4–6). So how is it defined? Studies like John Tomlinson's *Cultural Imperialism* (1991) are reluctant to give hard definitions against foreclosing debates, and refer to cultural imperialism discourse. Problems of defining cultural imperialism are linked to problems of defining culture. Nevertheless, cultural imperialism discourse leans towards relativist understandings of culture, as against universalist or classical understandings of culture as human perfection or the best of human civilisation (Arnold, 1960, [1869]). Essentially, the literature understands culture as a particular way of life, traditions and customs, that is, ethnicity (Smith, 1991, p. 21). The pluralist understanding of culture owes much to Boasian anthropology, although identity's socially constructed character is recognised. Tomlinson's *Cultural Imperialism* outlines four key clusters of approaches to cultural imperialism as 'media imperialism', 'discourse of nationality', 'critique of global capitalism' and 'critique of modernity' (Tomlinson, 1991, pp. 19–28). Linguistic imperialism theories follow the latter cultural imperialism concerns over authentic, traditional cultures threatened by homogenising western (especially American) consumer cultures (Tunstall, 1977, p. 57; Tomlinson, 1991, p. 8; pp. 140–72).

Applied linguistics has described studies like Phillipson's *Linguistic Imperialism* (Phillipson, 1992) as a 'hard-edged Marxian, if not Marxist, response' (Bolton, 2006, p. 384). Certainly, Marxist and structuralist critiques of imperialism are drawn on in various studies (Phillipson, 1992; Holborow, 1999; 2006; Ives, 2004a; 2004b; 2005). Phillipson's *Linguistic Imperialism* (1992) refers to Marxist and structuralist writings, notably by Johan Galtung (Galtung, 1971), but also by Gramsci (Gramsci, 1971 [1929–1935]; 1985 [1913–1935]) and Lenin (Lenin, 1996 [1916]; Phillipson, 1992, pp. 51–77). Marnie Holborow explores the Marxist linguistic theories of Vološinov and Vygotsky (Holborow, 1999; 2006), while Peter Ives develops Gramscian theories on globalisation and language (Ives, 2004a; 2004b; 2004c; 2004d; 2010). References to Marx have re-emerged more widely following the global economic crisis in 2008 (for example, Skutnabb-Kangas, 2009, p. 36). However, Holborow criticises linguistic imperialism approaches for neglecting the international political economy (Holborow, 1999, p. 78). Their analysis and advocacy strategies effectively reject imperialism theories in the Marxist tradition, whether implicitly (Phillipson, 1992) or explicitly (Pennycook, 1994, pp. 30–4, p. 37, pp. 55–6).

Linguistic imperialism critiques follow recurring Romantic critiques, mediated through anthropology and post-colonial studies, which essentially represent 'opposition to capitalism in the name of pre-capitalist values' (Sayre and Löwy, 1984). Common Romantic themes involve nostalgia for a pre-industrial past, longing for unity with nature, society's corruption and search for more natural, authentic communities outside consumer society. Accordingly, interpretations of earlier theorists, if not rejected, marginalise their enthusiasm for the possibilities of modern life and industrial production. The growing field of ecolinguistics, combining ideas of linguistic and ecological imperialism, demonstrates ecology displacing Marxism in linguistic imperialism critiques (Mühlhäusler, 1996). Ecolinguistics, discussed in Chapter 9, opposes global English for having an anti-ecological character, alienated from nature, whose discourse threatens the planet's global ecology (Fill and Mühlhäusler, 2001).

Linguistic imperialism studies follow the concerns of post-colonial studies over the former colonial language (Pennycook, 1998a, p. 213). English language teaching is described as 'a process almost of brutalization' with people having 'a difficult and sometimes almost violent relationship to English' (Pennycook, 1998a, pp. 208–13). Linguistic imperialism studies see global English as supporting neo-colonial power relations between and within states. Studies criticise mainstream linguistics for analysing English abstractly, as a neutral form of communication (Pennycook, 1994, p. 16; Phillipson, 1992, pp. 173–270; 2009a, pp. 147–76). Diverse Englishes are celebrated against prescriptive grammars, a homogenised standard and monolingual norms (Bolton and Kachru, 2006; Crowley, 2003; Kirkpatrick, 2007; Pennycook, 1994). Studies draw on dependency theories, and explore global English as the international language of authority, through which an Anglo-American metropolitan centre prescribes linguistic and cultural norms to peripheral states (Galtung, 1971; 1985; Phillipson, 1992, p. 279). Global English is accused of globalising a homogenised alienated consumer culture, and threatening the survival of cultures (Pennycook, 1994; Phillipson, 2009a, pp. 45–9, 59–64). Simultaneously, global English media are accused of promoting narrow western interests and stereotypes of non-western countries (Pennycook, 1994, pp. 50–3; Galtung, 1985; Phillipson, 2009a, pp. 152–3). Above all, linguistic imperialism studies are alarmed over global English threatening cultures and languages, and seek to protect minority and indigenous languages from extinction (Mühlhäusler, 1996). Critics oppose languages being deposed from public use and relegated to the private informal sphere, thereby marginalising non-English speakers (Pennycook, 1994, p. 17; Phillipson, 2003; 2009a, pp. 82–102).

Linguistic imperialism studies have analysed official colonial language policies, and their continuities in post-independence language policies (Pennycook, 1994; 1998a; Phillipson, 1992, pp. 109–35). Structuralist accounts have emphasised expansionist colonial and post-colonial linguistic policies (Phillipson, 1992, pp. 109–35). Phillipson explores the British Council's cultural and linguistic role in promoting British national political and economic interests abroad (Phillipson, 1992, pp. 136–72). Post-structuralist accounts like those of Pennycook (1994; 1998a) draw on Said's concept of orientalism to analyse British colonial officials' ambivalence towards promoting English language learning (Pennycook, 1994, p. 74). Said's concept of orientalism refers to western constructions of non-western societies, which essentialise and pathologise non-western cultures and support western dominance. In Said's words, 'Orientalism is a style of thought based upon an ontological and epistemological distinction made between "the Orient" and (most of the time) "the Occident" (Said, 1991, [1978], p. 2), which legitimises 'dominating, restructuring, and having authority over the Orient' (Said, 1991, [1978], p. 3). Linguistic imperialism studies have taken up orientalist ideas of 'the European identity as a superior one', including a 'linguistic Orient' to deconstruct the claims made of global English (Said, 1991, [1978], p. 7, p. 22). Said's *Orientalism* highlights how philology and anthropology intertwined to construct the Orient (Said, 1991, [1978], pp. 297–99). Pennycook develops a dualist anglicist and orientalist model of British colonial language policies (Pennycook, 1994, pp. 73–106; Pennycook, 1998a). Previous structuralist studies like Phillipson's *Linguistic Imperialism* (1992) address the anglicism of British colonial language policies promoting English (Phillipson, 1992, pp. 109–35). But they neglect its orientalist policies, seeking to maintain the vernaculars and traditional cultures, while denying people's capacity for self-determination (Pennycook, 1998a, pp. 80–1).

Marxist and Gramscian approaches explore how international political economic relations, rather than official compulsion, compel people to learn English (Brutt-Griffler, 2002; Holborow, 1999; Ives, 2004a, 2006, 2010). Discourse studies also analyse language in use, rather than official language planning (Brutt-Griffler, 2002; Pennycook, 1994, pp. 68–9, p. 74; 1998a, pp. 26–30). Together they highlight how approaches seeing global English as structurally bound to the modern capitalist system may overlook the language as a potential site for counter-hegemonic articulations, and end up in a political impasse (Brutt-Griffler, 2000; Holborow, 1999; Ives, 2004a; 2004b; 2004c; 2004d; Pennycook, 1994, pp. 325–6). Holborow warns against counter-strategies adopting linguistic determinist positions, assuming that promoting indigenous languages challenges international political inequalities (Holborow, 1999, p. 80, p. 92, pp. 97–148, pp. 192–3). Overall, critiques of global English are inclined towards liberal multiculturalism, or the Herderian language and culture tradition (Kymlicka, 1995; Taylor, 1994), rather than Gramsci's revolutionary aspirations supporting development of a common world language (Gramsci, 1971; 1985), as I discuss below.

Holborow questions how linguistic imperialism studies understand contemporary international politics, and suggests that critics end up supporting the international nation state system (Holborow, 1999, pp. 76–96). She condemns models locking 'into an anti-imperialist strategy of nationalism and the promotion of national languages' (Holborow, 1999, p. 77), observing that such strategies 'have neither broken with the world order nor necessarily encouraged linguistic rights' (Holborow, 1999, p. 80). Holborow's scepticism towards nationalism reflects how post-independence states became incorporated into existing international politics and lost their potential transformative role (Holborow, 1999, pp. 76–8). As Holborow outlines, 'national languages do not necessarily lead in emancipatory directions', and may legitimise more conservative politics (Holborow, 1999, pp. 92–4). The official promotion of Irish in the twentieth century, for example, was associated with retreat from anti-colonial politics and social transformation (ibid.). Ethnic nationalist politics and bureaucratic claim-making have informed language rights debates in Europe. Simple centre–periphery models are therefore inadequate as critiques of international politics (Holborow, 1999, p. 96). Nevertheless, critiques of nationalism are also inadequate today because of the way they have legitimised the erosion of sovereign equality, and the external governance of weaker states, as Chapter 8 explores.

Key linguistic human rights advocates, such as Phillipson, explicitly seek to transcend national sovereignty through international human rights law (Phillipson, 1998). They are concerned to promote local minority languages, and are wary of official standard national languages being promoted against minority languages. Phillipson outlines how he advocates 'the rights of all languages' and is 'suspicious of domination by speakers of any languages' (Phillipson, 1996, p. 163). Their minority language advocacy has made them ambivalent towards the nation state. However, their global human rights strategies legitimise the modified post-1989 international order and the expanding global governance of non-western societies. Nevertheless, linguistic human rights advocacy remains tied to the nation state by its language rights strategies, which are dependent on states maintaining languages. Overall, the prevailing strategies of linguistic imperialism critiques are problematic for emancipatory politics, and commonly end up seeking solutions, which may be criticised as forms of human rights imperialism. Indicatively, linguistic imperialism critiques omit legal imperialism from their list of imperialisms (Phillipson, 1992, p. 305; 2009b, p. 92; Skutnabb-Kangas, 2009, p. 37), although critical legal studies has explored expanding international law as neo-imperialism, legitimising international inequalities and the authority of western states over weaker states (Douzinas, 2000; Fitzpatrick, 2001; Mieville, 2005). Linguistic imperialism studies, like linguistic human rights advocacy, have not drawn on fellow linguist Chomsky's critical writings on international politics, and his critiques of human rights imperialism, and militarised humanitarianism, as noted in Chapter 2. For the linguistic imperialism critiques and linguistic human rights advocacy are wary of Chomsky's universal grammar theories.

Pennycook's post-structuralist critique of global English, as we have seen, is ambivalent about human rights codes as disciplinary regimes. Pennycook provides a more nuanced historical overview of colonial language policies (Pennycook, 1994; 1998a). But his idealist account of linguistic imperialism struggles is in tension with his Foucauldian critique and rejection of grand narratives of liberal humanism (and Marxism) (Pennycook, 1990), as Holborow has perceptively analysed (Holborow, 1999, pp. 81–7). His deconstruction of global English ends up in a linguistic determinist impasse, suggesting that people are victims of hegemonic language. His solutions, having written out people's historical role, become focused on psychological change facilitated by professional empowerment (Holborow, 1999, pp. 84–6), or a form of post-liberalism without the liberal subject (Eagleton, 1996, pp. 96–100). Here Pennycook echoes western humanitarianism of the 1990s, which has sought expanding global therapeutic governance (Pupavac, 2004).

I now want to compare Gramsci's earlier critical writings on language and power. Gramsci's linguistic and cultural studies bridge classical Marxist approaches to imperialism, and anticipate contemporary debates on globalisation and cultural imperialism (Gramsci, 1971, pp. 277–318). For Gramsci, language reflects real social relations, and language questions are 'an aspect of political struggle' (Gramsci, 1985, pp. 27–30; p. 187). Gramscian theories have therefore been attractive to those developing critiques of global English.

Gramsci's politics of linguistic revolution

Gramsci's language theories draw on Croce's romantic ideas of language as expression, and socio-linguistic ideas linking language and social relations (Forgacs and Nowell-Smith in Gramsci, 1985, pp. 87–91). Gramsci writes against language merely being about communication (Gramsci, 1985, pp. 26–31; Ives, 2004a; 2010). '[L]anguage in and for itself is an expression of beauty more than a means of communication,' Gramsci argues (Gramsci, 1985, p. 27). Equally, Gramsci associates language, culture and consciousness, suggesting that languages embody particular world views. Gramsci's belief in language's expressive role criticises Esperanto as an artificially created ahistorical language, against languages derived from historical social interactions (Gramsci, 1985, pp. 26–31). He also argues that Esperanto has not socially developed to communicate as well as existing national languages, and its use 'would fetter thought' (Gramsci, 1985, p. 29). Gramsci criticises purist arguments, propounding 'the ideal of a definite language', proposing that 'the beauty of a language is not fixed in time and space; it does not even exist' (Gramsci, 1985, p. 28). Rather, the beauty consists in a language adequately expressing our feelings and concerns (Gramsci, 1985, p. 28).

Many linguistic imperialist critics, or minority rights advocates, would probably agree thus far. However, most part company with Gramsci's further arguments, which are not for language maintenance, but linguistic revolution (Gramsci, 1985, pp. 188–91). A strong pro-modernising and industrialising thread runs through Marxism, including that of Gramsci (Gramsci, 1985, pp. 41–3, pp. 50–1, p. 390; Lenin, 1965, [1924], p. 47; Marx, 2002, [1948]; Trotsky, 1927; 1934). Gramsci sides with world history, world culture and modernity, not particular traditions (Gramsci, 1985, p. 181). He sees a revolutionary political role for the peasantry, but judges traditional peasant culture itself as patriarchal and socially limited, and favours modernising production and culture (Gramsci, 1971, p. 96; 1985, pp. 41–3). Similar political beliefs are shared by anti-colonial writers like Césaire, Fanon and James, explored in the next chapter (Césaire, 1971, p. 25; Fanon, 1967, pp. 251–5; 1980, [1959], p. 83, p. 123; 2008, [1952], pp. 91–8; James, 2001, [1938]). Gramsci aspires to build a mass popular collective movement, and a proletarian alliance with peasants, clashing with Romantic linguistic critiques seeking to maintain traditional peasant life (Forgas and Nowell-Smith, 1985, pp. 196–8; Gramsci, 1971, p. 132; 1985, pp. 41–3, pp. 246–7). Gramsci polemicises against folkloric paternalism and 'the disenchanted cosmopolitan spirit of tourists in search of strong and original raw sensations' (Gramsci, 1985, p. 202). Essentially, Gramsci wants to counter capitalist hegemony with proletarian hegemony towards building socialism internationally. To this end he propounds a 'conquering spirit' or 'spirit of scission' against the forces of nature as well as capitalism and the coloniser's language (Gramsci, 1985, p. 42, p. 390). Conversely, linguistic imperialism critics seek to promote minority communities and rein in human development against nature.

Consequently, Gramsci would oppose global English insofar as it embodies reactionary political forces (Ives, 2004a; 2004b; 2006; 2010). But, following Lenin (Lenin, 1972a, [1913]; 1972b, [1914]; 1977 [1913]), he does not oppose certain languages displacing others where their adoption is voluntary, linked to progressive forces:

> When the International is formed, it is possible that the increased contacts between peoples, the methodical and regular integration of large masses of workers, will slowly bring about a reciprocal adjustment between the Aryo-European languages and will probably extend them throughout the world, because of the influence the new civilization will exert. (Gramsci, 1985, p. 30)

He anticipates that the language of 'the first country to found socialism' could displace others internationally (Gramsci, 1985, p. 30). People across different countries would identify with this language politically and socially, and want to learn and use it. Ives, who has written key studies of Gramsci's politics of language, therefore warns opponents of global English that relying on Gramsci is 'problematic' for their arguments (Ives, 2010, p. 529).

Contemporary language advocacy would further struggle to agree with Gramsci's attitudes towards dialects. While Gramsci opposes Esperanto, and affirms the spontaneous grammar of dialects, he suggests that modern standard national languages are superior to local dialects in encompassing the richness of world culture (Gramsci, 1971, p. 325). Here Gramsci echoes the Romanticism of Goethe or Humboldt, whose aspirations for the national language were linked to universalist ideals (Gramsci, 1985, pp. 181–2). For Gramsci, those who only speak dialects have 'necessarily...an intuition of the world which is more or less limited and provincial,...fossilised and anachronistic', leading to their interests being 'more or less corporate or economistic, not universal' (Gramsci, 1971, p. 325). Gramsci affirms the historical subjectivity of a national language created through popular mobilisation as against dialect: 'between the dialect and the national-literary language something changes: precisely the cultural, politico-moral-emotional environment' (Gramsci, 1985, p. 177). His editors outline how he assumes 'a necessary elevation out of the dialects into a common monolingualism' (Forgas and Nowell-Smith, in Gramsci, 1985, p. 167). Modern standard languages are associated with progress, and dialects with subaltern political fragmentation and subordination to conservative tradition (Forgas and Nowell-Smith, in Gramsci, 1985, p. 167; Ives, 2010, p. 529). Gramsci's judgements, therefore, contravene contemporary language advocacy, whose sympathies follow the recurring ideals of rural local dialects as superior to the exhausted or corrupted urban dialects of civilisation. Nevertheless, Gramsci argues against imposing a standard language by coercive decree, which he sees as counterproductive to assimilation and the creation of collective political unity.

Linguistic imperialism critiques appear closer to Croce than Gramsci and anti-colonial writers. Gramsci, although drawing on Croce's linguistic theories, criticises Croce's Romantic view of language and politics, and his emphasis on ethnic language (Forgas and Nowell-Smith, in Gramsci, 1985, pp. 88–90, pp. 164–7; Gramsci, 1985, pp. 103–7, p. 177). Conversely, Gramsci is not interested in maintaining language as an expression of particular ethnic identities. Instead, he wants to forge new subjectivities and language as living expression, transcending particular local identities.

Differences between Gramsci and Croce are reflected in Gramsci's opposition to the Italian 1923 Education Act, which eschewed prescriptive grammar in schools (Forgas and Nowell-Smith, in Gramsci, 1985, p. 166). Today prescriptive grammar is associated with conservative politics, and socially stigmatising. However, Gramsci supported working-class and peasant children being taught the modern standard Italian language, and saw prescriptive grammar as politically progressive and its removal as reactionary. Conversely, it was the education minister Giovanni Gentile, a key philosopher of fascism, who opposed prescriptive grammar (Forgas and Nowell-Smith, in Gramsci, 1985, p. 166). Gramsci believed that Gentile's education policy, of not teaching children a national standard language and grammar, perpetuated class inequalities: 'Thus we are going back to a division into juridically fixed and crystallized estates rather than moving towards the transcendence of class divisions' (Gramsci, 1971, p. 41).

Linguistic imperialism accounts note Gramsci's linguistic politics (for example, Pennycook, 1998a, pp. 126–7), but overall they favour language conservation and reject Gramscian aspirations for linguistic revolution. Ironically, linguistic conservatism in international language advocacy echoes British colonial language concerns.

Linguistic imperialism critiques of British colonialism

I now turn to British colonial concerns over maintaining vernaculars against destabilising European influences. Cultural traditions have not necessarily been suppressed, but permitted by ruling powers as a way of mediating their rule, such as the millet system under the Ottoman empire, or native administration under the British empire. British colonial approaches were more pervasive in European colonial governance than French colonial doctrine, since Britain governed larger territories and populations (Hobsbawm, 1994, pp. 56–83). British colonial caution over modernity's impact on cultural tradition also anticipates contemporary global concerns, and has left traces on present global advocacy through European and American anthropology, UNESCO, and western development cooperation (Lee, 1967, pp. 246–8; Malinowski, 1945).

Major studies of global English, like Phillipson's influential *Linguistic Imperialism* (1992), associate colonial language politics with imposing their language onto colonial subjects, and anti-colonial resistance with defending indigenous languages and culture (Phillipson, 1992, pp. 109–35). Lord Macaulay's infamous 1835 *Minute on Indian Education* proclaims the superiority of the English language and European civilisation over Indian languages and cultural traditions. These extracts give a flavour of the Minute:

> We must at present do our best to form a class who may be interpreters between us and the millions whom we govern, – a class of persons Indian in blood and colour, but English in tastes, in opinions, in morals and in intellect. (Macaulay, 1935, [1835], p. 359)
>
> To that class we may leave it to refine the vernacular dialects of the country, to enrich those dialects with terms of science borrowed from the Western nomenclature, and to render them by degrees fit vehicles for conveying knowledge to the great mass of the population. (Macaulay, 1935, [1835], p. 359)
>
> [T]he dialects commonly spoken among the natives of this part of India contain neither literary nor scientific information, and are moreover so poor and rude that, until they are enriched from some other quarter, it will not be easy to translate any valuable work into them. (Macaulay, 1935, [1835], p. 348)

Macaulay's Minute exudes mid-Victorian confidence in Europe's civilising mission and is seen as epitomising British cultural and linguistic imperialism (Said, 1991, [1978], p. 152). Yet neither British colonial practice, nor even the more assimilatory official French colonialism, were characterised by universalising assimilatory policies (Hobsbawm, 1994, pp. 56–83). Certainly, the ideals of post-revolutionary France were universalist, but assimilatory policies were only formally adopted in a minority of its colonial possessions, such as Senegal's four designated communes (Betts, 2005; Crowder, 1964). French imperial expansion, and racist colonial discriminations, circumscribed universalist ideals under a modified doctrine of association. This doctrine declared colonial territories like Algeria to be French, but many colonial subjects were under distinct military regimes, governed through local chiefs, and effectively excluded from French education and rights (Heartfield, 2002, pp. 111–28).

Key to understanding British colonial policies is how the colonial elite projected traditional British hierarchies onto the colonies (Cannadine, 2002; Dirks, 2001). Colonial development thinking, like that of many an anthropologist, was often inspired by 'a romantic revolt against industrial society' (Lee, 1967, p. 73), creating an 'unholy alliance' between anthropologists and conservative colonial administrative officers (Cannadine, 2002, pp. 59–67, p. 126, pp. 141–38; Lee, 1967, p. 40; Misra, 2008). European elites, uncomfortable with modernity, might seek cultural vitality in a romance of non-European cultures (Cannadine, 2002, pp. 66–7, pp. 72–8). They could imagine themselves as saviours of innocent infantilised primitives from cruel barbarians (Duffield, 1996). Such dualistic representations appear in Kipling's *White Man's Burden* (1899), which sees colonial subjects as 'half savage, half child'. Identification with colonial subjects as noble primitives created disquiet over the harm caused by Europeans to indigenous life, but legitimised colonial rule itself (Furedi, 1998).

The Romantic anti-modernising strands of linguistic imperialism critiques have discouraged critical examination of parallels between their human rights advocacy and the Romantic anti-modernising aspects of colonial governance. Against this neglect, Pennycook has explored the ambivalence of British colonial language policies through a dualist anglicist–orientalist frame (Pennycook, 1994, pp. 73–106; 1998a). Anglicism disparages the culture of colonial subjects, but implicitly affirms their intellectual, political and moral capacities as comparable to those of Europeans, whereas orientalist celebration of their cultures may deny their capacity for political self-determination. As such, orientalism may involve worse racist assumptions than anglicism (Pennycook, 1998a, pp. 80–1).

Taking the popular theme of Defoe's *Robinson Crusoe*, various linguistic imperialism studies read back modern racism into Defoe's account (Phillipson, 1992, p. 109). However, Defoe's Crusoe regards the 'savages' he encounters as belonging to the same human race, and having the same capacities and feeling, but with different conditions leading to different customs. Defoe's Crusoe recognises them as equally human, with:

> the same Powers, the same Reason, the same Affections, the same Sentiments of Kindness and Obligation, the same Passions, and Resentments of Wrongs, the same Sense of Gratitude, Sincerity, Fidelity, and all the capacities of doing Good, and receiving Good, that he has given us. (Defoe, 2001, [1719], p. 165; discussed in Malik, 2008, pp. 86–7)

Defoe's hero attributes the differences between them to fate, rather than race. He reflects that these 'savages' would make better use of 'these powers enlighten'd by the great lamp of instruction, the spirit of God, and by the knowledge of his Word' than civilised society (Defoe, 2001, [1719], p. 165). Equally, Macaulay's 1835 Minute, while disparaging Oriental culture, affirms their intellectual capacity, unlike later European racial theories (Macaulay, 1935, [1835]; Pennycook, 1998a, p. 80, p. 93; Wolton, 2000, pp. 7–8). On the very subject of Indian education, Macaulay observes how:

> I have heard the very question on which I am now writing discussed by native gentlemen with a liberality and an intelligence which would do credit to any member of the Committee of Public Instruction. Indeed it is unusual to find, even in the literary circles of the Continent, any foreigner who can express himself in English with so much facility and correctness as we find in many Hindoos. (Macaulay, 1935, [1835], p. 358)

If Macaulay believes in a European civilising mission, Defoe suggests the destructive logic of the political economy as 'a secret overruling Decree that hurries us on to be Instruments of our own Destruction' (Defoe, 2001, [1719], pp. 13–14). Defoe's satirical poem *The Reformation of Manners* (1702) attacks brutal European mercantilism and enslavement of 'harmless Natives'. Defoe condemns the British as worse than the Dutch and Spanish in their cruel bartering of 'Baubles for the *Souls of Men*' and forced transportation to 'Christian Climes...To serve worse Heathens than they did before' (Defoe, 1702). Ironically, British imperial expansion, and consolidation of colonial rule, became justified in terms of defending native rights and eradicating slavery, reconstructed as a practice of foreigners (Heartfield, 2011).

Britain's anglicising doctrine, embodied in Macaulay's 1835 Minute, was significant in galvanising a domestic audience around imperial ideals, rather than representing general colonial policy and practice (Pennycook, 1998a, pp. 93–4; Wolton, 2000, pp. 7–8). Macaulay's statement does not envisage the vast majority of colonial subjects being taught English – after all, there was not yet political consensus on universal education at home. English, even in India, the prized 'jewel in the colonial crown', was only aimed at a minority of Indians needed for colonial civil service. Instead, the

British colonial authorities trained their officers in a composite standard Hindustani language for communication with the mass of their Indian colonial subjects (Barkawi, forthcoming; Cohn, 1996, pp. 16–56; Gilchrist, 1787; Shakespear, 1817; Monier-Williams, 1858; Tisdall, 1911). Consequently, it is better to understand the imperatives to learn English as deriving from colonial rule itself – the need to speak to power (Pennycook, 1994, pp. 77–9) – rather than due to colonial languages policies actively imposing the English language on populations.

British imperialism developed policies of 'race pragmatism', representing more circumscribed colonial ideals based on cultural pluralism, which envisaged separate development and equality of opportunity for people, within their own unequal potential for development (Furedi, 1998). Lord Lugard, architect of the British colonial model of native administration, sets out how:

> complete uniformity in ideals, absolute equality in the paths of knowledge and culture, equal opportunity for those who strive, equal admiration for those who achieve; in matters social and racial a separate path each pursuing his own inherited traditions, preserving his own racial purity and race pride; equality in things spiritual; agreed divergence in the physical and material. (Lugard, 1926, p. 213, in Furedi, 1998, p. 92)

Lugard's concept of *The Dual Mandate* is grounded in traditional native authorities, not the increasingly radicalised urban centres (Lugard, 1926). British colonial rule legitimised itself as trustee, respecting the cultural traditions of colonial subjects (Westermann, 1934, pp. 8–15; pp. 279–91) – ideas echoed in contemporary global governance. Preparation for self-government through native administration under the 'sympathetic supervision of British officers' is discussed as an aspect of colonial trusteeship, but training was conceived as taking 'generations or even centuries', the British Governor of Nigeria suggested (Wallbank, 1935, p. 239). Colonial constitutional planning, as developed in J.S. Furnivall, *Colonial Policy and Practice* (1948), sought to codify a plural society and communal representation. Simultaneously, British colonial policies illustrate how policies of cultural recognition may limit political and personal freedoms.

British colonial development concerns

The British colonial authorities outlined colonial development strategies against competing pressures. A key push for the creation of formal colonies was European rivalry and fear of protectionism. Colonies like Egypt were arguably formalised more as a means for securing the route to India than necessarily of interest in their own right. The British government wanted the colonies to pay for themselves. Hopes of the colonies becoming new overseas markets intertwined with hopes of alleviating the social pressures of poor, crowded, industrial populations through colonial settlement (Nasson, 2004, p. 133). But the colonial powers were always ambivalent about industrialising their colonies. Industries and workers in Britain were opposed to developing competing industries in the colonies (Hobsbawm, 1994, p. 65). European commercial interests fostered extract industries and exploitation of colonial labour, but did not drive broad industrialisation. The authorities wanted to make European raw material industries in the colonies more efficient. But they feared that European interests and influences would disturb traditional ways of life, undermining colonial stability and fuelling nationalist opposition (Malinowski, 1945). Long-term political concerns over British national security and potential decline made colonial policy wary of creating an imperial economy in which productive labour would shift to the colonies (Hobsbawm, 1994, pp. 82–3), while white settlers opposed assimilatory policies and were jealous of their privileges. Hence, there were divergent interests between the British government, British society, colonial officials and white settlers.

British colonial development evolved policies to address the social consequences of European industries for the traditional subsistence economies, rather than an industrialising programme (Lee, 1967, p. 87). In the words of one colonial official, policies had to address 'the social cohesion of African society in contact with European culture, taking as the starting-point ... the economic changes resulting from that contact' (in Lee, 1967, p. 81). Colonial officials, anthropologists and missionaries raised alarm over urbanisation and industrialisation causing social maladjustment, crime and immorality (Davis, 1967; Furedi, 1998, p. 143; Malinowski, 1945, p. 2, pp. 71–2, pp. 79–80; Westermann, 1934, pp. 279–91). The 'worker in the mines, the plantation hand, or the urbanized Native' was seen as socially dysfunctional (Malinowski, 1945, pp. 79–80). A major preoccupation was the regulation of labour migration resulting from European primary industries, especially in the copper belt, and whether to stabilise that migration (Davis, 1967). But, while colonial development policies sought to contain migration and maintain traditional subsistence farming communities, the monetary system of taxation encouraged involvement in trade or wage labour (Nasson, 2004, pp. 144–5). (Similarly, international sustainable development today seeks to maintain traditional farming communities, but taxation, education, health and other social charges necessitate trade or wage labour.)

Colonial ideas of organic society overlapped with anthropological models of holism, and saw each group having its place and function, in which disturbing one element disturbed the whole (Smuts, 1927). Indigenous culture was regarded as a tool for social cohesion and stable colonial rule (Lee, 1967, p. 88). Even missionaries' efforts were castigated among colonial policymakers for destabilising traditional cultures. Instead, official thinking advocated fostering local cultures in the colonies, despite regarding local cultures as inferior. Consider the following editorial comment in the *Journal of the Royal African Society*:

> We wish to create or maintain in the African a pride in his own proper culture; but in comparison with our own the African's culture is greatly inferior. The African knows it, and his first impulse is to cast aside his own and to adopt European ways. (*Journal of the Royal African Society*, 1927, p. 78)

The editorial comment is revealingly cynical in wanting to use culture to contain nationalist aspirations. But advocacy for traditional cultures could be sincere, based on distaste towards modern European societies and their urban masses. Colonial development thinking was influenced by the British upper classes' nostalgia for a pre-industrial order (Cannadine, 2002, pp. 59–67, pp. 72–8, pp. 138–41; Lee, 1967, p. 84). On the eve of decolonisation, colonial development thinking remained reluctant to plan national industrial development goals, and instead focused on rural development, education and social welfare (Lee, 1967).

Cultural tradition against the deracinated

Colonial development thinking was influenced by the functionalist school of anthropology led by Malinowski (1884–1942), who dominated British mid-century anthropology (Lee, 1967, p. 81). Malinowski's cultural theories draw on both East European Romanticism and positivism, and parallel those of the Boasian culture and personality school (Gellner, 1998, pp. 123–39; Malinowski, 1945, p. 8). Malinowski is sceptical towards romantic accounts of culture (Malinowski, 1945, pp. 27–8). Nevertheless, he is ready to foster Romantic myths of cultural identity towards developing a model of functional cultural governance (Gellner, 1998, p. 185; Malinowski, 1935, p. 481).

Malinowski directly addresses colonial concerns in *The Dynamics of Culture Change: An Inquiry into Race Relations in Africa* (1945). Malinowski describes European contact as a 'malediction, blight' on native communities (Malinowski, 1945, p. 68). Malinowski fears that European education deprives colonial subjects of pride in their cultural inheritance and produces 'educated Africans who have no place in either the tribal world or the European community' (Malinowski, 1945, p. 8, p. 60, p. 67). '[M]aladjustment and neuroses' are seen as inevitable consequences of wanting to modernise traditional societies (Neisser, 1955, p. 364). Colonial concerns reflect broader western concerns over the social impact of modernity, expressed in studies such as Everitt Stonequist's *The Marginal Man: A Study in Personality and Culture Conflict* (1961) (discussed in Furedi, 1998, pp. 138–49). Time and time again, British colonial officials, anthropologists, missionaries and other writers invoke the spectre of rootless, maladjusted, deracinated natives. Lugard attacks the 'deraciné and pseudo-European' Africans, whose education has made them discontented, bitter and disloyal (Lugard, 1926, pp. 80–2, p. 429; 1933, p. 8).

Exposure to European society, and an individualising education, are blamed for undermining communal bonds and making colonial subjects susceptible to political agitation (Furedi, 1998, pp. 140–1; Malinowski, 1945, p. 135). Colonial advisers and anthropologists alike accuse European education for fostering African demagogues (Malinowski, 1945, p. 11, p. 141), and promoting 'racial or national jingoism' as anti-colonial sentiment was negatively described (Schmidt, 1930, p. 142). Studies express anxieties over the 'new class of intellectuals', unable to integrate and fulfil their ambitions, joining 'the ranks of radical nationalists' (Neisser, 1955, p. 364). The higher-educated African is accused of 'belonging to the ilk readiest to appropriate whatever European culture offers of factors which can be most successfully used against the European themselves' (Schmidt, 1930, p. 142). Solutions look to fostering a functional 'selective conservatism' organised around 'new tribalisms' (Malinowski, 1945, pp. 60–3).

The colonial authorities sought to govern through traditional village chiefs against younger, radicalised urban workers. Colonial rural development schemes wanted to temper urban growth and avoid creating rootless individuals susceptible to political radicalism. As one writer on community development outlines:

> One of the major aims in rural development schemes has been the revitalizing of village life in order to stop this suicidal migration of detribalised individuals to the cities. (Neisser, 1955, p. 365)

The author's use of the term 'suicidal' transposes colonial fears about social instability onto migrants.

Education was designated a key role in helping the African adapt to the 'maelstrom' of change (East Africa Commission, 1925, p. 21). Reports such as *Education Policy in British Tropical Africa* (1925) criticised academic curricula and favoured basic literacy, technical, moral and social instruction. Colonial educational trusteeship should:

> eschew the so-called 'literary' education and give the *average* African a training which consists, primarily, of work in the field and shop preparing him to carry on efficiently in his probably future status as peasant or craftsman. Instruction in general science, a reading and writing knowledge of the vernacular and perhaps the *lingua franca* of the region, the inculcation of the basic laws of health ... and impartation of knowledge concerning sound ideals of character and the proper use of leisure. (Wallbank, 1935, p. 233)

However, young urban colonial subjects, it was admitted elsewhere, saw adopting English and other aspects of European culture 'as an instrument for freeing themselves from tribal control and tradition' (*Journal of the Royal African Society*, 1927, p. 78). Official and academic writings had to grapple with ambitions outstripping the colonial vision of traditional culture. Native administration was attacked for pushing Africans 'back into effete tribalism under reactionary chiefs' (Macmillan, 1934a, p. 137), and 'chieftainship' as 'the arch-ally of white administration' (Matthews, 1937, p. 434). Against the limits in the colonial model for Africa, critics observed 'the African himself wants a fuller life' (Macmillan, 1934b, p. 427). Young male migrant labourers resented their limited opportunities under native administration based on traditional authorities (Lee, 1967, pp. 177–87). Ironically, Jomo Kenyatta, Malinowski's former student and later leader of post-independence Kenya, was seen as personifying Marginal Man (Furedi, 1998, p. 141). Kenyatta was attracted to cultural tradition and ambivalent about modernity (Berman, 1996), but was not satisfied with political organisation under native administration. Kenyatta and other nationalist leaders sought the nation state, and contested its being reserved for white nations (Derrick, 2008).

Colonial development thinking appears more preoccupied with cultural contact and loss than with poverty, economic exploitation or political rights (Lee, 1967, p. 91). Its development studies were weak on economic analysis – economists were not attracted to colonial economies – and were dominated by anthropological research, including linguistic studies (Lee, 1967, pp. 93–4). Social anthropological research, like Malinowski's *The Dynamics of Culture Change* (1945), often represents an anti-development plea (Lee, 1967, p. 99), similarly to sustainable development and linguistic imperialism studies today. While Malinowski declares himself 'a Native advocate', he does not mean an advocate of African nationalism and political rights of independence (Malinowski, 1945, p. 9, p. 41, p. 61, p. 161). Malinowski does not seek to criticise British colonialism, but to improve colonial governance, when he highlights racial and socio-economic discrimination against colonial populations (Malinowski, 1945, p. 41, p. 60). Malinowski's proposals for expanded international governance under the League of Nations draw on the Habsburg Empire and British indirect rule (Gellner, 1998, pp. 142–3). Malinowski envisages an international system limiting state sovereignty, but fostering cultural traditions (Gellner, 1998, p. 187). Malinowski echoes Boas and other western theorists of nationalism of the mid-twentieth century, seeking to circumscribe sovereignty and promote cultural determination under international institutions (Pupavac, 1998).

Colonial language policies

British colonial concerns over cultural maintenance are reflected in interwar language policy debates. Against assumptions of anglicising missions, evolving British colonial language strategies sought to promote demands for vernacular language education and resist those for English language education (Adejunmobi, 2004, pp. 1–23; Cohn, 1996; Lee, 1967, p. 79). The colonial policy lessons following the Indian Mutiny were that other colonies should restrain English education (Barkawi, forthcoming; Cohn, 1996, pp. 16–56; Rai, 1984; Singh, 1998). Lugard, as chief architect of native administration, supported vernacular languages, while the influential linguist Diedrich Westermann, director of the International Institute of African Languages and Cultures, supported Lugard's model. Their accord is illustrated by how Westermann's widely reviewed *The African Today* has a preface by Lugard (Westermann, 1934). Colonial language planning, influenced by anthropological linguistics, saw language as key to supporting cultural tradition (Lee, 1967, p. 87).

British anthropological linguistics shares Boasian ideas on language and culture (Langendoen, 1968, pp. 3–36). Malinowski's linguistic theories retreat significantly from Humboldt's belief in linguistic creativity, and suggest finite possibilities of expression, dependent on direct experiences (Langendoen, 1968, pp. 3–29; Malinowski, 1923). Language is treated as encompassing a whole way of life, not simply an open-ended means of communication (Langendoen, 1968, pp. 7–8, p. 20; Malinowski, 1922, p. 309; 1938). According to Malinowski, 'Each primitive or barbarous tribe, as well as each type of civilization has its world of meanings and the whole linguistic apparatus of this people' (Malinowski, 1922, p. 309 in Langendoen, 1968, p. 20). Malinowki's studies simultaneously argue for the need to respect vernacular language use, and not extend English language instruction, and suggest that African languages are weaker at handling abstract concepts (Langendeon, 1968; Lee, 1967, p. 79; Malinowski, 1923).

British colonial language thinking followed relativist perspectives on language identity: each people had its own culture or way of life; language expressed the soul of a people and its culture; colonial peoples needed to retain their vernacular languages because these reflected their way of life. The English language, belonging to another people and way of life, was not considered an appropriate medium for most colonial peoples with different cultural traditions. Its widespread adoption would alienate people from their cultural traditions. There was broad consensus among colonial officials, academics and missionaries for an adapted curriculum, synthesising the old and the new, that respected local cultures and languages and did not tear young Africans away from their old traditional ties (Oldham and Gibson, 1931). The model Achimota College in Accra was praised for taking 'Special care ... not to alienate the African from the praiseworthy features in his own tribal heritage', and promoting 'Gold Coast history, tribal drumming, native vernaculars, and indigenous music' (Wallbank, 1935, p. 245). Colonial advisers constantly raised concerns over education in the colonies not being sufficiently culturally adapted, although they admitted that African criticism was the reverse (Wallbank, 1935, p. 245).

Overwhelmingly, colonial language policy papers associate English language instruction with fostering instability, and vernacular instruction with fostering stability. The 'political situation will be considerably aggravated in those situations where the Europeans have actively discouraged the native language', advised an article on 'The teaching of African Languages in African Schools' (Elliott, 1938, p. 76). Colonial officials complained of English-speaking colonial subjects being a nuisance, even though colonial administration and trade inevitably promoted the need for English. Too many English-speaking Africans, they criticised, were without work because they saw themselves as '"too good" for manual work' (Smith, 1932, p. 436). Vernacular vocational education was advocated to exorcise 'the fanatical spirit' and discourage ambitions centred on government service (Lord Lloyd in Currie, 1935, p. 41). White settlers were particularly suspicious of English-speaking Africans because of the social threat their knowledge represented. They objected to Africans receiving English instruction in the Christian missionary schools, which were the main providers of schooling in the colonies (West, 2002, p. 20; Whitehead, 2003, p. 20). Missionaries helped codify vernacular languages as part of their evangelising mission, and often sought to support vernacular instruction and traditional cultures against Europeanisation. But they found that their schools often had to offer English education to attract pupils.

Vernacular instruction was seen as important for the psychological stability of individuals. Arguments emphased linguistic emotional needs: 'For emotional thought in particular an imported language of totally foreign structure can be no substitute for the mother tongue, or an allied vernacular' (Elliott, 1938, p. 75). Even where it was impractical to provide instruction in every mother tongue, it was considered more appropriate for children to be taught in a native vernacular for their cultural affinities (Hussey, 1932, p. 174; Schmidt, 1930, pp. 139–43). In the words of Westermann, 'it is flesh of his own flesh, it is an expression of his own material and mental world' (Westermann, 1929, p. 346). Instruction in the vernacular complemented education, 'to train and fit them, not for the life in big centres, but in their own small communities' (Westermann, 1929, p. 350).

Conversely, European education led Africans to disparage a rural way of life, and fostered a disaffected intelligentsia (Pickard-Cambridge, 1940, pp. 147–52). Only a minority of colonial subjects involved in colonial administration or trade required European languages, but their education in the vernacular could not be neglected without grave social risks (Schmidt, 1930, pp. 139–43). Neglect of the vernacular and too much instruction in European languages risked making Africans 'conceited' and receptive to 'pretentious, radical and revolutionary' ideas (Schmidt, 1930, p. 140). Colonial policy literature even invoked how the Soviet Union had secured 'the added loyalty of its various peoples, by assuring them of the security of their own language in the new order' (Sauer, 1943, p. 183).

However, a gap between colonial vernacular policies and educational practice was frequently observed. Furnivall, advocate of the colonial idea of plural society and a supporter of vernacular education, states how:

> The policy has been to exercise restraint over the growth of western education and to encourage vernacular education. Yet everywhere western schools are vigorous and have multiplied even to excess. (Furnivall, 1948, p. 374)

Furthermore, Furnivall observed, this was not simply a question of provision: 'it has often been easier to provide vernacular schools than to get children to fill them' (Furnivall, 1948, p. 374). His findings repeat earlier observations that it was 'impossible to refuse the demand for the thorough teaching of English' (Laughton, 1938, p. 222). The language policy papers constantly deplore how colonial subjects do not want vernacular education (Broomfield, 1930; Elliott, 1938, p. 77), echoing Macaulay's earlier complaint that students needed incentives for vernacular education over English education, despite declamations 'about the love and reverence of the natives for their sacred dialects' (Macaulay, 1935, [1835], p. 353). Advisers complained of English having 'a sort of magic' attraction as 'the easy road to civilization and wealth' (Sauer, 1943, p. 183).

Neither African teachers nor parents were enthusiastic about instruction in vernacular languages. Westermann and other supporters of vernacular languages acknowledged that English instruction was 'ardently desired by the people – there will always be plenty of children in a school which promises English' (Westermann, 1929, p. 349). Conversely, it was observed, 'insistence upon teaching in the vernacular would, in some regions drive pupils from the schools' (*Journal of the Royal African Society*, 1927, p. 78). The aspirant African middle classes objected to receiving a dumbed-down curriculum inculcating menial skills and being expected to speak simplified 'kitchen kaffir' English as opposed to literary English (Whitehead, 2003, p. 20). So, while post-colonial writers spoke movingly of being forced to learn English (Ngũgĩ, 1986, pp. 10–12), their English education was secured by local pressure against official colonial education thinking. English education was officially recommended for only a minority of colonial subjects (East Africa Commission, 1925).

Attempts to impose a non-European curriculum in the vernacular were perceived 'as an attempt to keep the African down or to treat him as in someway inferior' (Elliott, 1938, p. 147). The African Teachers Association in Rhodesia attacked separate native education in vernacular languages and demanded a universal education system (West, 2002, p. 54). Equally, the Gold Coast Teachers' Union called for English to become a *lingua franca*

(James, 1977, p. 62). Such was the importance attached to having an academic education equal to Europeans that Latin was insisted on at Achimota College by Africans, against the judgement of colonial advisers (Wallbank, 1935, p. 240). Some advice recommended ignoring local demands for English: 'It would be undesirable to comply with any unwise wishes the natives themselves may express in favour of adding European languages' (Schmidt, 1930, p. 139). However, attempts to impose vernacular education and indigenous exams were met with anti-colonial agitation, because of their association with colonial efforts to promote conservative tribal authorities against the growing anti-colonial politics (Ruxton, 1930, p. 10).

In this situation, experts advised that Europeans would need to take the initiative to sponsor vernacular languages and publish vernacular literature (East, 1936; Elliott, 1938, p. 78; Smith, 1932, p. 438). For example, the International Institute of African Languages and Cultures introduced a vernacular writing competition. Cooperation with Africans was recommended to counter suspicions over vernacular language being introduced to limit advancement (Mayhew, 1933, p. 181). But colonial language policies struggled to follow vernacular language education. In practice, the colonial authorities were unable to resist demands for English medium education, because colonial relations made knowing English important to colonial subjects trying to secure their position under colonial rule.

Apartheid and anti-Apartheid language politics

Apartheid South Africa pursued British colonial policies of cultural racial recognition against political self-determination, but more systematically. Pierre Van de Berghe's pioneering study of Afrikaner nationalism analyses its Romantic beliefs in language and culture, and antipathy towards modernity, even as it exploited Black labour in its industries. Van de Berghe documents: 'Afrikaner identity includes, "anticapitalist agrarianism", fear of "cultural assimilation" "ethnocentrism", "narrow provincialism" as well as racism, xenophobia' (Van den Berghe, 1970, p. 248). Its Romantic ideas of language and nation were projected onto Apartheid's model of separate development (Van den Berghe, 1970, p. 253). Apartheid helped control the expanding Black urban masses through the repressive population policies of Bantu reservations, which operated in the interests of the Apartheid regime and economy (Mbeki, 1964; Wolpe, 1990). Conversely, anti-Apartheid opposition was influenced by universalist ideals of equality (Hirson, 1981; Van den Berghe, 1970, p. 251). Black South Africans were becoming linguistically more assimilated, despite the Apartheid regime's 'retribalising' language policies:

> To the extent that Africans of various language groups have intermixed, intermarried, learned each other's tongues, and lived and worked side by

> side in the cities under identical conditions of oppression and destitution, they have developed a common consciousness which transcends ethnicity. The government policy of 'retribalization' is in part a conscious effort to counteract these universalist trends and to isolate each ethnic group in a cultural and political desert. (Van den Berghe, 1970, p. 252)

Denial of English was associated with denial of political and employment equality and the suppression of political dissent. The Apartheid Bantu language education policies insisted on mother-tongue instruction, and resisted demands for education in English:

> the entire educational system for Africans has been 'tribalized' by the Bantu Education Department. Mother-tongue instruction is stressed at all levels of schooling despite overwhelming opposition of Africans who would prefer to be taught in English, at least beyond the lower grades. (Van den Berghe, 1970, p. 253)

The Bantu education system kept English out of primary school education and only introduced education in English (and Afrikaans) in secondary school when the vast majority of Blacks were denied the possibility of secondary education. Repeatedly, Black Bantu school governing boards, teacher associations and parents demanded more teaching in English (Brooks and Brickhill, 1980, pp. 33–55). Official measures to restrict teaching in English and expand Afrikaans, along with other grievances, sparked the Soweto school strikes, exam boycotts and riots of 1975–1976, and propelled the mass anti-Apartheid struggle (Brooks and Brickhill, 1980, pp. 33–55).

Anti-Apartheid language politics illustrates the primacy of struggles for rights of political freedom and equality in the mass twentieth-century political movements against official politics of racial or cultural difference. So, while anti-Apartheid resistance took some inspiration from negritude ideas, as did anti-colonialism, its struggles were overwhelmingly informed by universalist politics rather than cultural relativist politics. Linguistic imperialism critiques, therefore, depart from earlier political struggles, and are, ironically, closer to colonial thinking in their Whorfian cultural–linguistic concerns and Romantic anti-modernising ideas (Lee, 1967, p. 40, p. 73; Cannadine, 2002, pp. 59–67, pp. 72–8, pp. 141–38; Van den Berghe, 1970, pp. 248–53). Conversely, anti-colonial thinking saw cultural tradition as ultimately limited in challenging the colonial authorities. The next chapter explores anti-colonial and post-independence language politics, from aspirations to limits.

7

Anti-Colonial and Post-Independence Language Politics: From Emancipatory Aspirations to Limits

Changing language politics

'[T]he majority of children start school using a foreign language', a 2010 education report on African education observes (Ouane and Glanz, 2010, p. 4). The UN designated 2006 the Year of African Languages, and the Organisation of African Unity (OAU) agreed a new Plan of Action for African Languages to address the continent's language situation, in which 'Most African countries continue to use the former colonial language as the primary language of instruction and governance' (Ouane and Glanz, 2010, p. 4). Twenty years earlier the OAU had drafted a similar Plan of Action, seeking to overcome the continent's reliance on former colonial languages. The same year, Ngũgĩ wa Thiong'o published *Decolonising the Mind: The Politics of Language in African Literature* (1986), which condemned Africa's failure to embrace its own languages and free itself from linguistic dependency (Ngũgĩ, 1986, p. 4).

This chapter considers language politics, from the aspirations of anti-colonial opposition to the problems of post-independence states. Post-independence nation-building was initiated with high expectations of national transformation and justice. But progressive nation-building was frustrated. Post-independence states became characterised by repressive politics and ethnicised particularist interests. Declining national and international emancipatory political forces struggled to maintain progressive universalist ideals, and became orientated around more defensive conservative models of development and justice.

Anti-colonial language politics believed in human potentiality, creativity and emancipation. Yet, as Ngũgĩ wa Thiong outlines, 'Even at their most radical and pro-African position...they still took it as axiomatic that the renaissance of African cultures lay in the languages of Europe' (Ngũgĩ, 1986, p. 5). Anti-colonial approaches to language questions in national liberation struggles differ significantly from those of post-colonial studies or linguistic imperialism critiques inclined towards cultural relativism (Sharpe, 2000). Major anti-colonial writings identified with radical universalist humanist ideals (Fanon, 1967, [1961], pp. 251–5; 2008, [1952], pp. 178–81; James, 1977, p. 21; 2001, [1938]; Wright, 1964, p. 63). They condemned how European politics was failing progressive humanist ideals, and hoped that anti-colonial struggle would forge a more enlightened humanism (Césaire, 1995, [1939], p. 125; Fanon, 1967, [1961], pp. 253–5). Key anti-colonial intellectuals identified themselves as black Europeans or Westerners, and contested the idea of returning to non-European roots (James, 2001, [1938]; Wright, 1964, pp. 44–7).

Anti-colonialism and negritude debates

To understand anti-colonial positions on culture and language, it is useful to consider negritude debates, developed against the experience of racism, and the contradictions of French colonial assimilatory or associational policies. Two core strands of negritude have been identified: one developed by Senegalese academic and politician Léopold Sédar Senghor (1906–2001), and the other by Martinique poet and politician Amié Césaire (1913–2008).

Senghor's concept of negritude involves 'cultural métissage' against assimilation to the colonial culture (Bernsconi and Cook, 2003, p. 4). Senghor was from Senegalese territories subject to stronger assimilatory policies than other French colonies. He received a French education, and trained as a linguist studying under Lilias Homburger, whose works include *The Negro African Languages* (Homburger, 1949). Senghor's thinking on negritude and opposition to assimilation draws on European Romantic and anthropological theories, suggesting that each linguistic race has its own specific part in human culture. 'Emotion is Negro, as reason is Hellenic,' Senghor controversially argues in his essay on 'What the Black Man Contributes' (Senghor, 2003, [1939], p. 288). Senghor enthuses about European anthropological studies like Leo Frobenius writing on African history and culture (Frobenius, 2007, Senghor, 2007), Placide Tempel's *Bantu Philosophy* (Tempel, 1959), and Diedrich Westermann's *The African Today* (1934) (Marchand, 1997). Most controversially, Gobineau's 'Essay on the Inequality of the Human Races' influences Senghor's thinking on linguistic races, and negritude as an inherited identity (Bernasconi and Cook, 2003, p. 4). These writings encourage Senghor to link African languages and culture, identifying key African linguistic features with negritude's emotionality or sense of divine difference (Senghor, 1971, pp. 79–80; Writh, 2003, p. 278).

Senghor shares European Romantic and anthropological concerns over a 'crisis in civilization' and a vision of communal pluralism against modern mass society and individualism (Marchand, 1997; Senghor, 2003, [1939], p. 294). Senghor envisages:

> It is at the level of the tribe, rather than the kingdom, that one can most clearly grasp the solution that the Negro has provided for social and political problems. (Senghor, 2003, [1939]; p. 292)

Senghor's strand of negritude, therefore, supports cultural relativist values against assimilation under modernity.

The alternative concept of negritude developed by Césaire takes a different political direction (Césaire, 1995, [1939]; James, 2001, [1938], pp. 239–50). Césaire has been described as 'perhaps the greatest poet of the anti-colonial movement' (Malik, 2010b). Césaire was inspired by Senghor's writings on negritude, but rejects his European romantic and anthropological concept of negritude (Césaire, 1972, pp. 69–70). Césaire defines negritude in the commonality of suffering as opposed to a particularist inherited identity. Césaire's *Notebook of a Return to My Native Land* declares:

> As there are hyena-men and panther-men, I shall be a Jew-man
> a kaffir-man
> a Hindu-from-Calcutta-man
> a man-from-Harlem-who does-not vote. (Césaire, 1995, [1939], p. 85)

For Césaire, negritude represents a struggle for political emancipation, rather than a movement for cultural identity recognition. Accordingly, Césaire sees negritude standing up for its own humanity in the Haitian Revolution, when slaves rebelled and created an independent nation (Césaire, 1971, pp. 72–8; 1995, [1939], p. 91, p. 125).

The writings of Fanon (1925–1961) hugely influenced anti-colonial thinking. Fanon's *Black Skin, White Masks* follows Césaire's understanding of negritude as an emancipatory political movement against racial oppression (Fanon, 2008, [1952]; pp. 86–7). Fanon's concept of negritude is influenced by Marxist dialectical understandings of history and his critical engagement with Sartre's writings. Sartre's *Black Orpheus* (1964–1965) and *Anti-Semitism and the Jew* (1995) [1946] read negritude dialectically as an antithetical phase of political struggle against colonial capitalism towards a higher synthesis transcending racial difference. Fanon contests Sartre's treatment of negritude as a minor transitory phase, for both undermining its antithetical force and overlooking its universalist content (Fanon, 2008, [1952], p. 103, pp. 143–4). But, while Fanon affirms negritude as resistance, he distinguishes between its revolutionary and regressive aspects (Fanon,

2008, [1952], p. 6). Fanon warns against negritude becoming complicit in its oppression and a safe release for colonialism's frustrations and aggressions (Fanon, 1967, [1961], pp. 170–89; 2008, [1952], pp. 93–105).

Fanon's *Wretched of the Earth* sees cultural opposition as limited in challenging colonialism, 'You will never make colonialism blush for shame by spreading out little-known cultural treasures under its eyes'. (Fanon, 1967, [1961], p. 179). Fanon wants to expand human freedom, not preserve cultural identities, arguing, 'In the absolute, the black is no more to be loved than the Czech, and truly what is to be done is to set man free' (Fanon, 2008, [1952], p. 2). Instead Fanon identifies liberating and regressive elements in indigenous cultures.

National struggles for freedom awaken local cultural expression, which goes through different stages of consciousness: first, internalisation of colonial contempt for native culture; second, native art and craft becoming defensive and formalistic as a clandestine culture; and, third, formalism shattering, and the imagination renewing and creating new forms of expression (Fanon, 1967, [1961], pp. 190–9). Conversely, colonialists, Fanon argues, become defenders of traditional native customs (Fanon, 1967, [1961], p. 195). However, for Fanon, custom represents 'the deterioration of culture' and its democratic character (Fanon, 1967, [1961], p. 180). Fanon's ideal of culture is dynamic and universalist, driven by popular struggle, not folklore (Fanon, 1967, [1961], pp. 187–8). As such, Fanon would have been sceptical towards cultural identity rights as encasing humanity in a 'stock of particularisms' (Fanon, 2008, [1952], p. 180).

Césaire and Fanon have been subsequently criticised for not recognising a Creole identity. But their understanding of negritude is political, not particularist, towards building international anti-colonial struggle. They oppose promoting a Creole identity, which they link to nestling racisms supporting colonial power whereby colonial subjects define themselves in terms of western or colonial racial-cultural divisions, including Creole against African (Fanon, 2008, [1952], p. 16, pp. 76–7, p. 118). Fanon's *Wretched of the Earth* strongly warns against anti-colonial politics becoming ethnicised and reduced to 'replace the foreigner' (Fanon, 1967, [1961], pp. 125–8, p. 131).

Anti-colonial scepticism towards cultural strategies was fuelled by colonial policies, promoting cultural self-determination as a substitute for national political self-determination (Pupavac, 1998). Influential British academics and policy-makers during the interwar and war periods questioned national self-determination as political sovereignty, and wanted to promote cultural self-determination as a viable substitute for the risks of political sovereignty (Carr, 1942; Hayes, 1968; Macartney, 1934; Zimmern, 1927). British colonial authorities, having ultimately failed to contain nationalist pressures through cultural tradition, then sought to determine the post-independence constitutional arrangements and institutionalise cultural pluralism and communal representation, retaining a European political presence (Lee, 1967, pp. 240–50).

Conversely, nationalists campaigned for universal suffrage against proposals for communal representation. Universal suffrage was associated with accelerating the transfer of power, and minority rights with attempts to delay or limit the transfer of power (Lee, 1967, pp. 215–19). Nationalists feared communal representation entrenched communal interests and discouraged national unity (Lee, 1967, p. 191, pp. 240–50). Minority rights and pluralist arrangements were critically regarded as checks on black majority power and attempts to retain the power of the white European minority, which could be exercised against the majority black populations (Lee, 1967, p. 219; Nasson, 2004, p. 174). In short, 'Did "plural society" mean anything more than the existence of vociferous Europeans?' (Lee, 1967, p. 219).

Colonial uses of cultural tradition led customary chiefs to be viewed as colonial collaborators (Césaire, 1971, p. 24; Fanon, 1967, p. 74; King, 2004, pp. 212–14; Wright, 1964, p. 1). Philosophies of African spiritualism and non-materialism (Tempels, 1959) could legitimise colonial exploitation, while respect for traditional elders and ancestor-worship could legitimise colonial hierarchies (Césaire, 1971, pp. 38–9; Wright, 1964, p. 1). In this vein, Fanon saw 'the liquidation of regionalism and of tribalism' as necessary to the anti-colonial struggle (Fanon, 1967, p. 74). Yet Césaire's and Fanon's writings are commonly invoked in post-colonial studies to support Romantic critiques and cultural identity rights, while overlooking their beliefs in revolutionary historical change against cultural traditions (King, 2004, pp. 239–65; Rosello, 1995, pp. 9–64; Sardar, 2008, p. xviii; Sharpe, 2000, p. 114). Fanon's anti-colonial cry to 'show no pity at all toward the caids and the customary chiefs. Their liquidation is the preliminary to the unification of the people' (Fanon, 1967, p. 74) hardly supports cultural relativist ideals. But such passages of Fanon are either not known, or not alluded to, in linguistic imperialism and language rights advocacy literature. (Discussion of Fanon's attitudes towards violence is beyond the scope of this book. Mahatma Gandhi famously espoused non-violent resistance, along with support for traditional customs, identities and spiritual values. However, anti-colonial writings, overall, saw the use of force as necessary to resist colonialism, but opposed and warned against a politics of revenge. See, for example, James (2001) [1938] and King (2004).) Divergent spiritual culturalist and secular modernising strands were documented by Wright among the new post-independence leaders (Wright, 1994, [1956], p. 205). Overall, Césaire's and Fanon's politics came down to a modernising politics, as did Wright's own:

> Today, as never before, it can be seen that the future of national cultures will reside in the willingness of nations to take up modern ideas and live out their logic. (Wright, 1994, [1956], p. 199)

Nevertheless, in siding with modernising politics, anti-colonial writers were conscious of modernity's traumas (King, 2004).

Césaire and Fanon's anti-colonial development writings

Anti-colonial writers wrote passionately of the spiritual void caused by the colonial destruction of African cultures. Césaire outlines in a much-cited passage:

> natural *economies* that have been disrupted – harmonious and viable *economies* adapted to the indigenous populations – about food crops destroyed, malnutrition permanently introduced, agricultural development oriented solely toward the benefit of the metropolitan countries, about the looting of products, the looting of raw materials. (Césaire, 1971, p. 22)

Romantic critiques of colonialism and capitalism, as critiques in the name of earlier forms of life, are attractive because '*ante*-capitalism' represents pre-colonialism (Césaire, 1971, pp. 22–3). But Césaire was no 'prophet of the return to the ante-European past' (Césaire, 1971, p. 23), although he is sometimes cited as such (for example, Pennycook, 1998a, p. 44). Nor did Fanon believe in the past as a 'patent for humanity' (Fanon, 2008, [1952], p. 175). Repeatedly, anti-colonial writings mocked western attraction towards primitivism, and rejected a return to an idealised past (Césaire, 1971, pp. 38–9; Fanon, 1967, pp. 251–5; 2008, [1952], pp. 91–8; James in Said, 1994a, p. 300; King, 2004, pp. 123–50, pp. 199–238, pp. 239–265; Wright, 1964, p. 2, pp. 12–13; 1994, [1956], p. 199). Fanon considered that colonials' own feelings of alienation were expressed in their ideal of colonial populations as non-political idyllic primordial subjects:

> The presence of the Negroes beside the whites is in a way an insurance policy on humanness. When the whites feel that they have become too mechanized, they turn to the men of color and ask them for a little human substance. (Fanon, 2008, [1952], p. 98)

Indigenous cultures represented a refuge for alienated westerners, countering 'their excess of boredom' (Césaire, 1995, [1939], p. 103). For these anti-colonial writers, European exoticism or 'Europe, mistress of rites' (Césaire, 1971, p. 53) was as problematic as European racism in supporting colonial or neo-colonial relations (Césaire, 1971, p. 53). They suggested colonial rule 'artificially' perpetuated the tyranny of 'local feudal lords' and 'the survival of local pasts in their most pernicious aspects' (Césaire, 1971, p. 24). Significantly, representations of idealised, Romanticised natives may pathologise or deny real subjects (Arendt, 1968, [1951], pp. 191–3, pp. 397–402;

Carey, 1992; Fanon, 2008, [1952], pp. 98–101; Sardar, 2008, p. xiv). In short, real subjects become 'No person' (Sardar, 2008, p. xiv).

National anti-colonial struggles were conceived not as preserving cultural tradition, but as struggles for freedom, seeking a 'fundamentally different set of relations' (Fanon, 1967, pp. 197–9). Against European colonial preoccupations over preserving cultural tradition, Césaire observes:

> it is the African who is asking for ports and roads, and colonialist Europe which is niggardly on this score; that it is the colonized man who wants to move forwards, and the colonizer who holds things back. (Césaire, 1971, p. 25)

Reversing colonial dependency models, Césaire claims his part in building modernity:

> And I tell myself Bordeaux and Nantes and Liverpool and New York and San Francisco
> not a piece of this world that does not bear my fingerprint
> and my calcaneus on the backs of skyscrapers and my filth
> in the glitter of gems! (Césaire, 1995, [1939], p. 91)

Anti-colonial writers identified with universalist movements, bringing together people and forging world time (Fanon, 1967, p. 156). Their thinking was influenced by Marxist political economy, although they were profoundly sceptical of official communist dogmas (King, 2004, p. 204; pp. 244–6; Rosello, 1995, p. 35). They sought to 'stretch' Marxism to take into account the colonial and neo-colonial conditions (Fanon, 1967, p. 31; also Césaire, 1971, pp. 69–70; King, 2004, pp. 215–29). Thus, their attacks on economic exploitation represent attacks on western capitalism, and not attacks on modernising or globalising politics *per se*. And their attacks on colonial oppression indict, not the European or the white man *per se*, but rather particular social classes, notably the bourgeoisie and their '*progressive dehumanization*' (Césaire, 1971, p. 49, Italics in original).

Fanon's writings increasingly focused on the problems of post-independence states (Fanon, 1967). He argued for developing productive forces by the people, for the people (Fanon, 1967, pp. 150–7). But Fanon feared that the national elites had succumbed to European stasis, and failed to show the initial inventive adventurous progressive character of western middle classes. Instead, they only showed their moribund side (Fanon, 1967, pp. 140–1):

> It is already senile before it has come to know the petulance, the fearlessness or the will to succeed of youth. (Fanon, 1967, p. 123)

Fanon questioned whether the national elites have the capacity to develop productive industries and mechanise agriculture. Fanon deplored how the experiences of national elites had given them the psychology of 'the businessman, not that of a captain of industry', leading them to emphasise trade and small business, not industrial investment (Fanon, 1967, p. 120). Consequently, national economies would remain tied to economic patterns of production characteristic of the colonial era: namely, an economy exporting raw materials, instead of finished products, coexisting alongside a local peasant economy (Fanon, 1967, pp. 120–5). Meanwhile, the national middle classes will carve out parasitical unproductive decadent roles replacing the colonials. Fanon describes a 'tribal' 'dictatorship of civil servants' whose parasitical and nepotistic nature furthered an ethnic politics of 'replace the foreigner' at all levels of society, supported by the artisan classes and traditional rural authorities (Fanon, 1967, pp. 145–8).

Against the elite's ethnicised politics, Fanon placed his hopes in mobilising peasants and workers in defence of democratic politics. Fanon wanted to expand people's political and social consciousness, and secure spaces for speech where people debated vital issues, instead of being reduced to an audience for political speeches (Fanon, 1967, pp. 157–63). Simultaneously, he aspired to expand the connections between the 'mass of humanity' and escape local particularisms towards a humanist politics (Fanon, 1967, p. 253). Fanon's aspirations to further national and international communications lead on to anti-colonial language politics.

Césaire and Fanon's anti-colonial language politics

Anti-colonial writings address the problem of developing a political voice under colonial conditions. Césaire's poetry is explicitly political: 'My mouth will be the mouth of those griefs which have no mouth, my voice, the freedom of those that collapse in the dungeon of despair,' Césaire declares (Césaire, 1995, [1939], p. 89). Writings explore the inferiority complex that leads educated colonial subjects to distance themselves from their vernacular and adopt the colonialiser's language and culture (Fanon, 2008, [1952], pp. 13–14). Fanon observes: 'To speak a language is to take on a world, a culture' (Fanon, 2008, [1952], p. 25). This quote is commonly cited in post-colonial or linguistic imperialism studies to support language identity rights. However, anti-colonial language politics did not simply follow Whorfian ideas, associating loss of one's language and culture of birth with psychological harm and incapacity (Sapir, 1949; Whorf, 1940a; 1940b). Rather, they wanted to break down language divisions, and communication barriers, and expand political and social consciousness. In Fanon's words, 'new men, and with it a new language and a new humanity' (Fanon, 1967, p. 152).

Thus, when Wright describes nationalist elites as 'Men without Language', he refers to their having 'no vocabulary of history'. And he goes on to argue for radical transformation: 'Only a complete reversal of the economic and political situation can enable him to speak, to allow him to grasp a language, a vocabulary, that he can feel is his own' (Wright, 1964, pp. 37–8). Wright emphasises not a given language, but how people make language their own through their conscious action. Similarly, Césaire seeks revolutionary political language, challenging existing orders and borders:

> Words? As we handle quarters of the world, as we marry delirious continents, as we break down steaming doors, words, oh yes, words! But words of fresh blood, words which are tidal waves and erysipelas and malarias and lavas and bush-fires, blazes of flesh, and blazes of cities...(Césaire, 1995, [1939], p. 99)

Anti-colonial writings suggest that loss of tradition is politically and personally liberating (Fanon, 1967, p. 180; 2008, [1952], pp. 175–80; Wright, 1964, p. 23, pp. 59–60; 1994, [1956], p. 200). Fanon contends: 'I am not a prisoner of history. I should not seek there for the meaning of my destiny' (Fanon, 2008, p. 179). In this vein, James observes how West Indians, having 'no native culture, no native language, no native religion...raised entirely in the British tradition', found it easier to forge links with international anti-colonial political circles (James, 1977, p. 76). Their emancipatory politics focused on expanding international communication rather than cultural preservation. The dominant colonial languages are treated as a potential medium to communicate subversive ideas, rather than having fixed colonial or neo-colonial identities. The English language is to be actively appropriated as a *lingua franca* for international anti-colonial politics in Africa, Asia and the West Indies (James, 1977, p. 76; Mazrui, 1966; Windmiller, 1954).

Anti-colonial accounts illustrate how the identity of European colonial languages with colonial interests could be destabilised in the course of political struggle, even where the colonial language was closely associated by the population with colonial oppression. Fanon's essay 'This is the Voice of Algeria' in *A Dying Colonialism* describes how the identity of the French colonial language was destabilised and appropriated by Algerian colonial subjects (Fanon, 1980, [1959], pp. 47–75). Algerians went from viewing the French language and the radio as instruments of the colonial oppressor to seeing them as media for broadcasting their anti-colonial struggle:

> The French language, language of occupation, a vehicle of the oppressing power, seemed doomed for eternity to judge the Algerian in a pejorative way. Every French expression referring to the Algerian had a humiliating content. Every French speech heard was an order,

> a threat, or an insult.... The broadcasting in French of the programs of Fighting Algeria was to liberate the enemy language from its historical meanings. The same message transmitted in three different languages unified the experience and gave it a universal dimension. The French language lost its accused character, revealing itself to be capable also of transmitting, for the benefit of the nation, the messages of truth that the latter awaited. Paradoxically as it may appear, it is the Algerian Revolution, it is the struggle of the Algerian people, that is facilitating the spreading of the French language in the nation. (Fanon, 1980, [1959], p. 68)

The meaning of French, Fanon argues, was also destabilised for the colonial, making him 'realize the relative character of his signs' (Fanon, 1980, [1959], p. 68). And broadcasting the same messages in Arabic, or other local languages, questioned prejudices about their capacity for abstract thinking (Fanon, 1980, [1959], p. 69). So the anti-colonial struggle challenged the mystiques around language, 'stripped the Arabic language of its sacred character, and the French language of its negative connotations' (Fanon, 1980, [1959], p. 70). The nation witnessed how it was not imprisoned in one language or medium, but could appropriate and represent itself in different languages and technologies. The new nation and 'the new language of the nation' could make itself 'known through multiple meaningful channels' (Fanon, 1980, [1959], p. 70). While the radio before 1954 had 'meant allowing the colonizer's language to filter into the very heart of the home', after 1954 it meant 'entering into communication with the Revolution' (Fanon, 1980, [1959], p. 61) and 'hearing the first words of the nation' (Fanon, 1980, [1959], pp. 70–1).

Appropriation of the colonisers' language to express anti-colonial interests demonstrated that no nation could claim a monopoly on a language, or solely determine its use. English and French became the languages of Pan-Africanism, politically and culturally, and a medium of revolutionary ideas (Mazrui, 1966). Ironically, anti-imperial struggles and the agency of non-mother tongue speakers thereby helped the rise of World English (Brutt-Griffler, 2002). However, since anti-colonial politics took active views of language and culture against colonial culturalism, this was not necessarily negative. In Fanon's words, anti-colonial struggle fuelled language's creative force: 'The nation's speech, the nation's spoken words shape the world while at the same time renewing it' (Fanon, 1980, [1959], p. 73).

Post-colonial studies have criticised earlier anti-colonial politics for supporting the continued use of European colonial languages, linking language, identity and culture (Nandy, 1983; Ngũgĩ, 1986, p. 5, pp. 15–16). Césaire, for example, has been attacked for supporting assimilation to France, politically and culturally, including maintaining French language education in Martinique and not developing Creole (Rosello, 1995, pp. 18–20, pp. 44–52).

Ngũgĩ argues against the colonial language in a widely quoted essay on African literature and language politics:

> language was the most important vehicle through which [colonial] power fascinated and held the soul prisoner. The bullet was the means of physical subjugation. Language was the means of spiritual subjugation. (Ngũgĩ, 1986, p. 9)

The paramountcy of language's expressive and spiritual role for Ngũgĩ has strong echoes of Herder and Sapir. Ngũgĩ describes the trauma of being forced to discard his mother tongue and use English at school (Ngũgĩ, 1986, pp. 10–12). As a writer, he later rejected English for Gikuyu and Swahili, and has criticised those who prefer writing in English. The latter tend to see language, culture and identity as more fluid (Bisong, 1995). The writer Chinua Achebe concludes in his essay on 'The African Writer and the English Language' that:

> I feel that the English language will be able to carry the weight of my African experience. But it will have to be a new English, still in full communion with its ancestral home but altered to suit its new African surroundings (Achebe, 1975, p. 103, cited in Bisong, 1995, p. 129 and Ngũgĩ, 1986, p. 8).

Writers' individual decisions are given cultural and political significance in post-colonial studies (Ngũgĩ, 1986, p. 4), as post-independence countries have struggled to realise emancipatory progressive nationalist ideals. Already we have seen how anti-colonial writings like Fanon's *Wretched of the Earth* (1967) were anticipating the problems of post-independence states. To Fanon's prophetic work we may add both historical and fictional works: James' historical study *Black Jacobins* and Césaire's drama *The Tragedy of King Christopher* on Haiti, James' *Nkrumah and the Ghana revolution* (1977), Césaire's *A Season in Congo* (1966), and Achebe's *A Man of the People* (2001) [1966] on Africa.

Post-independence national development

National independence struggles won the right to be politically self-governing, and demonstrated their national political will. The nation state had been born, but a common national life had to be developed. James described the situation of newly independent states as analogous to Russia in 1917 – populations mobilised into political struggle against predominantly traditional peasant conditions, whose core organisations reflected communal tribal or ethnic identities (James, 1977, p. 189, pp. 209–10). Many African nationalists were attracted towards socialism, including in Ghana,

Kenya and Tanzania (Kenyatta, 1965; James, 1977; Nyerere, 1968; Pratt, 1999). But they lacked a substantial social basis in a small urban middle and working class. The potential for realising socialism was limited where organised labour was in a minority (James, 1977, pp. 16–17). Wider national and international consciousness was fostered through the struggle against colonialism. But national government could seem remote once independence was gained, and a sense of national identity tenuous among populations where the national infrastructure, institutions and services were rudimentary, and had little influence on people's everyday lives. If key nationalist leaders like Nkrumah sought to engage their populations in emancipatory nation-building, they tended to have a weak relation to and grasp of their traditional peasant ways of life (James, 1977, p. 62). Objective problems and political weaknesses encouraged leaders to rely on the state to impose their visions on the population (James, 1977,p. 22). So even politically conscious leaders like Nkrumah became tempted into repressive decisions, silencing and punishing dissent. James observed that their actions against dissenting individuals, 'dismiss us, all of us', and betrayed their own principles (James, 1977,p. 181). The failure to build on people's raised political consciousness displayed in anti-colonial struggles, and engage them in development, fostering alternative organisational forms, meant that the majority remained organised around communal tribal and ethnic links (James, 1977, p. 22).

The newly independent nation states needed to establish themselves and secure their position of influence in the international system against the historical dominance of the European powers. International ambitions for developing the Third World soared during the 1950s and early 1960s, during the high point of Third World nationalist movements, and the most intensive period of decolonisation. (Most decolonisation of British African colonies took place in a very concentrated period between 1959 and 1964.) Their high aspirations were expressed at the seminal 1955 Bandung conference, as documented in Wright's *The Color Curtain: A Report of the Bandung Conference* (1994) [1956]. Symbolically, Bandung brought together the newly independent states without the (white) western powers, and demonstrated the Third World as a new third force in international politics (Furedi, 1998, pp. 206–8; Wright, 1994, [1956]).

Nation-building ambitions to catch up with western powers envisaged modern national economies, infrastructures, welfare systems, communications and media. Rapid industrialisation was a key theme among nationalists, who sought to forge an alternative modernity, and new national cultures that appropriated modern science and industrial means, even as they were inspired to explore past African or Asian languages and cultures (Prashad, 2008; Robeson, 1955; Wright, (1994), [1956]). Belief in industrialisation was tantamount to a new religion among new states, who opposed western calls for more gradualist approaches towards development, especially as the colonial powers were still calling for gradualist approaches towards independence (Wright, 1994, [1956], p. 74, p. 163). Progressive nationalist leaders like Nkrumah warned that neo-colonialism was more insidious and worse than colonialism for confusing power relations (Nkrumah, 1970, p. 102). They were suspicious of allowing an unequal international division of labour in which developing countries would remain weak, poor, primarily agricultural producers (Mahalanobis, 1959).

Wright's report on the Bandung conference of non-white nations envisages economic development overcoming East–West divisions:

> When the day comes that Asian and African raw materials are processed in Asia and Africa by labor whose needs are not as inflated as those of Western laborers, the supremacy of the Western world, economic, cultural and political, will have been broken once and for all on this earth and a de-Occidentalization of mankind will have definitely set in. (Thus, in time, the whole world will be de-Occidentalized, for there will be no East or West!) (Wright, 1994, [1956], p. 203)

Western powers were ambivalent towards developing countries' industrialisation, but their doubts were marginalised in the Cold War competition over the hearts and minds of the Third World. Cold War security concerns over nationalists' attraction towards socialism galvanised a western modernisation vision, as set out in Walt Rostow's *Stages of Economic Growth* (1971) [1960]. However, industrialisation strategies held more significance as a political idea, and were not pursued comprehensively by international organisations in practice. Only a few states considered of strategic importance, such as South Korea, enjoyed significant industrial investment. Most newly independent countries experienced less than a decade of international industrialisation goals. Without comprehensive transformative investment, their position in the international political economy persisted as subsistence agricultural economies with narrow export sectors. Rapid industrialisation strategies in international development were already being shelved by the late 1960s. Some countries, such as Angola and Mozambique, did not become independent until the mid-1970s, when donor states had already abandoned industrialisation as a goal for developing countries.

Various Third World-sponsored UN declarations showed continuing national aspirations. In 1974, the UN Declaration on a New International Economic Order called for international aid for Third World industrialisation. But such declarations, vocalised against waning Third World nationalism, did not determine the retrenched international development agenda. Progressive leaders sought to re-engage their populations in a struggle against bureaucracy for more human-centred development and emancipatory socialist politics: for example, Julius Nyerere of Tanzania and Kenneth Kaunda of Zambia in the 1960s and 1970s (James, 1977, pp. 212–21). But their efforts to forge progressive national development floundered, as Nkrumah's had earlier. National elites retreated from radical nationalism towards narrower technocratic state-building approaches, marginalising the political role of their working classes and peasantry (James, 1977; Prashad, 2008). Prestige projects were undertaken, representing symbols of modernity, rather than comprehensive strategies, just as Fanon had warned (Fanon, 1967). Bandung modernisation became characterised by technocratic state-building, accompanied by more authoritarian, if not outright, military rule. This pattern encouraged scepticism towards economic development as reflecting neo-colonial elite interests. As James observed, 'The harder you drive for westernisation, modernisation, the more you create these conflicting forces' (James, 1977, p. 185). Dependency theories attacked modernisation theories as reflecting western interests and perpetuating the underdevelopment of non-western states and repressive politics (Amin, 1976; Frank, 1971).

The stalled nation-building projects undermined progressive national language policies and the development of national languages. However, I want to discuss nationalist aspirations over national languages at the time of independence, before indicating their problems. Linguistic imperialism literature suggests the functionalist neo-colonial character of promoting the English language or other European languages in post-independence states as languages of wider communication. Nevertheless, models from either Cold War bloc also potentially supported policies recognising plural language rights, supplementing the designated official national language or languages. UNESCO's cultural pluralist approaches (UNESCO, 1953), Stalin's minority language approaches, and former colonial and US anthropological approaches all favoured cultural recognition against language planning for rapid assimilation. However, languages policies, whether linguistic assimilation or multilingual recognition, faced problems over available resources and competing resource priorities.

Language planning under modernisation

From Africa to Asia, nation-building projects typically envisaged developing a shared national language in what were predominantly multilingual countries. 'The first and last need of India at the present moment is that it should be a nation,' proclaimed a 1948 Constituent Assembly Report on the language question. 'Everything which helps the growth of nationalism has to go forward, and everything which throws obstacles in its way has to be rejected,' the report contended (Linguistic Provinces Commission, 1948 in Windmiller, 1954, p. 298).

Language planning emphasised developing national communication for a modern national economy and civil service. Assimilation was not viewed negatively under nationalist ideals of people coming together to forge the nation. However, it was not straightforward to create an official common national language in the prevailing multilingual situations. Political controversies existed over whose language should become the national language. Ideally, the nation-builders wanted the national language to be based on an indigenous language, and replace the former colonial language as the language of national communication. However, a linguistic group would enjoy obvious advantages if its language were chosen, and others would have obvious disadvantages.

One suggestion was that the official language should be the former colonial language. Colonial languages were commonly the *lingua franca* among the urban educated classes, and an important medium in nationalist movements. The imperatives of national development could support arguments for retaining the former colonial language as an international language, where it was felt state-aided education in vernacular languages would divert resources away from economic development priorities (Lee, 1967, pp. 190–1). So some nationalists were receptive to making the former colonial language the official language.

Others opposed recognising a non-native language as the official language in newly independent states (Asamoa, 1955; Owiredu, 1957). Critics argued that the new nations would never escape their former colonial dependency and achieve real self-determination if they continued to use the colonial language. Echoing Herder, the vernacular language, it was argued, expressed the soul of a nation (Asamoa, 1955, p. 67). An individual's personality was bound up with his or her language. Making the colonial language the national language, not an indigenous language, compromised a nation's cultural identity: 'Sole adoption of English will lead to cultural subordination which is detrimental psychologically to the national health of the people' (Owiredu, 1957, p. 296). Africans (or Asians) could successfully imitate other countries in a foreign language, but, critics argued, how inventive could they be?

> A nation cannot make any essential contribution of knowledge or culture to the world through a foreign language. She would not only lose her identity in the process, but what she produced would be second-rate and inadequate. (Asamoa, 1955, p. 67)
>
> If a distinctive African contribution is to be made to the world, it must be based on the African's love and respect for the mental inheritance of his people, and much of this is enshrined in language. (Owiredu, 1957, p. 296)

In advocating a vernacular language for the national language on psychological grounds, these authors ironically concurred with colonial vernacular language advisers, some of whom became international advisers. Indeed, some arguments in favour of a vernacular would directly cite the writing of colonial vernacular advisers. The authors above cite the same passage from Westermann's *The African Today and Tomorrow* on language and spiritual heritage being bound together (Asamoa, 1955, p. 61; Owiredu, 1957, p. 295).

The importance these critics give to the vernacular did not mean that they supported recognising every mother tongue within their country. They argued that linguistic recognition of several indigenous languages was only an interim measure until one language emerged as the national language (Asamoa, 1955, p. 69). In the case of Ghana, it was argued, 'about five such languages should be preserved for the time being until one of these emerges as the national language of the whole country' (Owiredu, 1957, p. 298). The language differences in many post-colonial countries, it was observed, were exaggerated by treating dialects as distinct languages. The presence of dialects was 'universal', and national standardisation was compatible with the existence of diverse dialects (Owiredu, 1957, p. 297). The historical example of medieval England's distinct dialects was cited as having been no barrier to developing a standard English language. It was hoped a generous attitude, rather than 'tribal jealousies', would prevail (Owiredu, 1957, p. 298). Out of decolonisation, 'with the birth of nation, there comes to life a desire for unity which is stronger than local rivalries' (Asamoa, 1955, p. 75). So, even among those who emphasised language's role in people's self-identity, not simply its communicative function, language differences were ultimately to be transcended, rather than cultivated, in the modern nation state. Against universal language recognition, it was argued: 'If we attempt to save all vernaculars, then we shall save none' (Owiredu, 1957, p. 298). So their visions are distinct from today's ecolinguistics and language rights advocacy preserving linguistic diversity against language death.

If a decision could not be reached as to one national language, then an alternative compromise was to recognise the former colonial language as the official language, along with various indigenous languages – in many respects a concession to the status quo, in that the language was already the language of widest communication among the post-independence political classes (Windmiller, 1954, p. 314). The compromise was politically acceptable at the time, because the colonial language was also the language of anti-colonial nationalism. This was the route that many African countries took. Most former British colonies in Africa recognised English as the official language; most former French colonies recognised French. Swahili as a language of wider regional communication in East Africa was recognised as the national language in Tanzania, and achieved an official status in Kenya along with English. But attempts to promote Swahili as an *African* language of pan-African communication faltered, with Uganda, for example, wavering between its Luganda language and Swahili, allowing English to remain the key official language. Thus, a common post-independence compromise was bilingualism in a standardised indigenous national language and the former colonial language as an international language. Ideally, language planning aspired to deal with language difference through bilingual education, in which early schooling would be in the mother tongue as far as possible, and pupils would only progressively be introduced to instruction in the common national language, which would prevail in secondary and higher education.

Policy emphasis was on creating a wider sense of national belonging. Assimilation, following universalist ideals, was viewed positively against the experience of colonial attempts to entrench European power through communal representation and minority rights. Furthermore, international communication remained a concern of the newly independent states, which saw their interests lying with international co-operation. Even Ethiopia, having made Amharic the national language, also recognised English, although it had not been a British colony with an established English-speaking colonial civil service. Post-colonial critiques condemn decisions to recognise European colonial languages as motivated by economic growth ambitions. However, such condemnations overlook how nationalist development ideals were linked to aspirations for international equality and prosperity, although policies came to embody narrower economic interests. As a language of international communication, the former colonial language could be appropriated as a medium for progressive internationalism and used by the Non-Aligned Movement.

Such possibilities are expressed in Wright's report on the Bandung conference, which celebrates 'mankind negatively freed from its traditions and customs' and 'the first attempt in history on the part of man and man to organize himself' (Wright, 1994, [1956], p. 206). Wright notes the irony of how 'The Western world was at Bandung in a way that could not be denied; it was on everybody's tongue, for the English language was the dominant language of the Conference' (Wright, 1994, [1956], p. 199). Yet the English language expressed anti-colonial nationalist ideals: 'the strident moral strictures against the Western world preached at Bandung were uttered in the language of the cultures that the delegates were denouncing!' (Wright, 1994, [1956], p. 200). For Wright, Bandung's use of English politically and morally enhanced the language:

> I felt that there was something just and proper about it; by this means English was coming to contain a new extension of feeling, of moral knowledge. (Wright, 1994, [1956], p. 200)

In short, the English language was not inherently the language of linguistic imperialism, but could be appropriated to the cause of anti-imperialism.

Illustrating post-independence language politics

A key aspect of building a national culture related to the language question, so to what extent were shared national languages developed under states willing to pursue modernising politics? Indian language debates in the early post-independence period indicate some of the tensions.

Mahatma Gandhi had favoured India developing a vernacular national language against colonial English. Calls to 'Boycott British English' complemented boycotts of British goods. But many nationalist leaders had received an anglicised education, and English was a *lingua franca* among the Indian elites across the country's diverse languages (Ramanathan, 2005, p. 39). Gandhi proposed developing Hindustani as the national language, assimilating elements from the Hindi and Urdu languages, and symbolically assimilating the Hindu and Islamic populations as language communities (Windmiller, 1954, p. 313). Gandhi's proposal regarding Hindustani is particularly striking, given the colonial promotion of a composite Hindustani for its colonial officers to communicate with the population (Barkawi, forthcoming; Cohn, 1996, pp. 16–56; Gilchrist, 1787). Nevertheless, anti-colonial nationalists saw the potential of its appropriation for the post-independence state. In the name of nation-building, India's 1948 Report on language did not want to support each province having its own official language: 'We have applied this test to linguistic provinces ... and judged by this test ... they fail and cannot be supported' (Constituent Assembly, 1948 in Windmiller, 1954, p. 298).

Gandhi's optimistic proposal to create Hindustani as the national language became politically frustrated with the bitter war over Pakistan's secession. Hindu nationalists, who followed, sought Hindi as the national language, instead of developing a common Hindustani language incorporating shared influences transcending ethnic–religious political divisions. However, Hindi, although the most widely spoken Indian language, was not spoken by the majority of Indians. As Nehru observed, 'Hindi is also a foreign language to most Indians and ... their fears of a Hindi-speaking elite are frequently greater than the abhorrence of English' (in Windmiller, 1954, p. 315). Non-Hindi-speaking states were not ready to give up their languages. Thus it was proposed in 1950 that English should be the official language for fifteen years, in a compromise over linguistic contestation (Windmiller, 1954, p. 314). Sixty years later, English still pervades Indian public life.

Studies have documented India's official language policies, and problems over establishing a national language, and its social and ethnic dimensions (Chatterjee, 1992, pp.194–220; Ramanathan, 2005, pp. 125–6). Indian language politics are vividly captured in Vikram Seth's *A Suitable Boy* (1993), a novel that explores post-partition India's ethnic and social divisions. Seth outlines different positions on the language question, prompted by the recognition of Hindi in the Devanagari script as the official language. Immediate problems were experienced by Muslims, who could not compete for public service employment (Seth, 1993, p. 1107). But Hindu nationalist politics, seeking to create an authentically pure standard Hindi language, resurrecting archaisms and purging Urdu words, could make the language hard to understand for Muslims and Hindus alike (Seth, 1993, p. 1107). Seth's novel documents how nationalists, brought up in a broader cultural heritage, struggled with a heavily Sanskritised Hindi and the Devanagari script, where they had been brought up to read and write the Urdu – or Arabic – script (Seth, 1993, pp. 353–4). The official language was being codified in a way which denied India's shared cultural heritage. Urdu had been used by Hindu writers in the past, and there were many Urdu words in modern Hindi. Seth shows Urdu becoming deviant in the post-partition India – symbolically, the rajah's son Maan in his novel learns Urdu merely to advance his illicit affair, and has no interest in its wider public use.

Seth also shows defence of official policies, first, on functional grounds: 'duplication of all government work in two languages, two scripts, is utterly impracticable and unworkable' (Seth, 1993, p. 1105). Second, official policies are defended on the basis of fears over the new state fragmenting further: 'You are asking for a two-language theory now, you will be asking for a two-nation theory tomorrow' (Seth, 1993, p. 1105). Yet again the argument is made that the real problem is dealing with the continuing dominance of the former colonial language, English: 'It is English that we should be working to displace, not each other's languages' (Seth, 1993, p. 1105).

Seth subtly indicates how language is a key indicator of ethnic or social differences, or anxieties. English is deployed to maintain social hierarchies, assert social superiority and social ambition. Thus, the grandmother is told by her socially ambitious daughter-in-law that her grandchild should call her 'Grandma' in English, not in Hindi, and that Bengali, not Hindi, was 'the only truly civilised language in India' (Seth, 1993, p. 334). Here we see how an elite aversion to popular Hindu nationalism and tradition is asserted through language. However, not any English is acceptable to the daughter-in-law – she scorns the fluent Midlands-accented English of Haresh, the shoemaker and eventual suitable boy of the novel. While Seth illustrates the multiple ways language is used to exclude, rather than to communicate, his hopes, for reconciliation across social, ethnic and linguistic divides, echo earlier reform writers' ideals (Gaskell, 1970b, [1855]).

The themes explored by Seth persist today, including the social capital of speaking English. English may be used to reinforce class authority over ordinary people, alongside India's retention of caste and class system, a traditional peasant economy, and land tenure patterns. The importance of English in Indian public life means that the language is a potent obstacle to social mobility for many poorer Indians, and may be used against them to assert social superiority (Chatterjee, 1992; Ramanathan, 2005). However, a provincial state's decision to promote an official state vernacular against English could disadvantage those seeking employment in the wider national Indian state. Gandhi's home state of Gujarat has reflected his views and emphasised the vernacular against making English the dominant language

(Ramanathan, 2005, pp. 27–36). But Gujarat's promotion of the vernacular has had implications for people from the state in national institutions, where English continues to be important for success in civil service exams (ibid.).

International language declarations

Aspirations to establish a shared national language became politically and practically difficult to realise in many countries, but illustrate the high nation-building ideals of the immediate post-independence period. Radical nationalism's demise and the prevailing narrower elite politics impacted on language politics in many former colonies, which, like India, showed persistent socio-linguistic inequalities and divisions. Post-independence language politics, therefore, witnessed pragmatic accommodation to existing local and international relations. Notably, Tanzania has had success promoting Swahili (Mazrui, 2004, pp. 45–7), but efforts to make Swahili a language of transnational communication in Africa waned with Pan-Africanism's decline. In Kenya, for example, Kenyatta's rule became dominated by his ethnic group, the Kikuyu, which encouraged the promotion of the Kikuyu language in competition with Swahili. But, since the Kikuyu language was not favoured by other ethnic groups, English continued as the key language of official public discourse, especially with Kenya's shift from Soviet influences to western ties in the Cold War.

UNESCO observes how conferences and declarations on African languages since the 1960s have restated the need to support vernacular languages against the dominance of the former colonial languages in African governance and education. These themes recur in the 1975 Intergovernmental Conference on Cultural Policies in Africa, the 1976 Cultural Charter for Africa, the 1986 OAU Language Plan of Action for Africa, the 1997 Harare Declaration on Language Policies in Africa, and the UN Year of African Languages 2006 (UNESCO, 2006, p. 61). Along with these initiatives, others like the UNESCO Universal Declaration on Cultural Diversity (2002), the Charter of the African Cultural Renaissance (2006) and the Bamako Commitment on Universal Multilingualism (2009) support African languages as communication, and languages as 'carriers of cultural inheritance' (UNESCO, 2006, p. 61).

Reports repeat earlier colonial language concerns over negative attitudes towards vernacular education. Experts observe that parents and teachers are reluctant to support mother tongue education over education in the official language or languages, unless there are interventions to encourage them to do so (Ouane and Glanz, 2010). Vernacular language advocates fear that the status of former colonial languages as official languages has created dependency and is 'disempowering' (Ouane and Glanz, 2010, p. 16; Mazrui,

1990; 2004). Some writings are more optimistic about the language picture, and do not see education in the medium of English as necessitating cultural homogenisation or loss of vernaculars (Bisong, 1995). However, international language policy thinking over the last decade has become more anxious over cultural diversity, linked to sustainable development and pluralist political models (UNESCO, 2006, p. 20; 2010). Echoing Lévi-Strauss, UNESCO envisages:

> peaceful coexistence of people in a society where pluralism does not entail replacement of one language or identity by another, but instead promotes complementarity of functions as well as co-operation and a sense of common destiny. (UNESCO, 2006, p. 74)

Lévi-Strauss' ideas run through other reports, which do not just seek for the rights of languages to be spoken, but propose the need to develop them (Ouane and Glanz, 2010, pp. 6–8).

Nevertheless, there are tensions in thinking on international multilingual language policies. Intergovernmental initiatives link indigenous language policies to supporting modernisation and independence (UNESCO, 2006, p. 13), whereas international linguistic rights advocacy, especially ecolinguistics, is influenced by Romantic critiques of modernity. UNESCO and the World Bank have historically had distinct positions on language (Mazrui, 1997; 2004, pp. 44–6). The World Bank's association with modernisation and UNESCO's with anthropological cultural relativism echo the dualism of post-colonial economies and continue the dualism of colonial economies. But the picture is more intertwined. If the literature notes tensions between UNESCO's modernising and culturalist strands, it overlooks how the World Bank has become more influenced by Romantic critiques of the global economy.

The World Bank shows growing receptivity to supporting vernaculars in reports such as *In Their Own Language...Education for All* (World Bank, 2005) or *Mother Tongue as Bridge Language of Instruction* (Kosonen and Young, 2009), but is criticised for remaining within modernisation or globalisation paradigms (Mazrui, 1997; Phillipson, 2009a, p. 41, pp. 57–8). However, the World Bank is modifying its position, linked to its own retreat from modernisation strategies. The World Bank's seminal *Voices of the Poor* report (Narayan et al., 2000) elaborates a retrenched development vision for the poor, and their governance in the counter-culture language of well-being and empowerment against wealth (Pender, 2002). Essentially, contemporary international development strategies, whose aims are set out in the Millennium Development Goals, are based on helping the poor realise their own livelihoods and welfare through petty trade or farming, and do not envisage significant material transformation of their lives (Abrahamsen, 2000; Duffield, 2007; Pupavac, 2010). So, while critics have contrasted the

World Bank's and UNESCO's development, there has been some convergence around a vision:

> where development is not construed in narrow economic goals but instead in terms of a culturally valued way of living together; and within a broader context of justice, fairness and equity for all; respect for linguistic rights as human rights, including those of minorities. (UNESCO, 2006, p. 74)

Politically, the vision legitimises the retreat from significant material transformation, and more intervention in countries, communities and households in the name of cultural and human rights governance.

Limits of anti-linguistic imperialism strategies under TINA

Linguistic imperialism studies draw on a large literature on imperialism, colonialism and post-colonialism, but their critiques suffer the problem of trying to develop counter-strategies in an age which has witnessed the decline of mass political movements, and significant political transformation no longer seems possible (Jacoby, 1999; Laïdi, 1998). A mood of liberal triumph in 'the end of history' following the demise of communism and Apartheid (Fukuyama, 1992) was quickly displaced by a sense of political, social and economic limits. The words of Prime Minister Margaret Thatcher, 'there is no alternative to the market' (TINA), encapsulated the sense of limited possibilities. Thus, Michael Hardt and Antonio Negri's *Empire* makes profound attacks on contemporary global politics, but ultimately suggests a rather modest international reform agenda with aspirations concerning global citizenship, basic income, and access to new communications technology like the internet (Hardt and Negri, 2000; Harvey, 2003, pp. 167–9; Žižek, 2001): sound and fury echoing mainstream international discourse. Indicatively, their concept of multitude is fused with Romantic cultural and religious longing and tropes re-invoking spontaneous children of nature (Hardt and Negri, 2000, pp. 392–413).

We may compare how, in a different historical era, anti-imperialist theories related to building mass popular–national majorities (Gramsci, 1985, p. 332, pp. 344–5; Marx, 2007, [1852–4]; Marx and Engels, 2002, [1848]). If Hardt and Negri's concept of multitude resurrects a Romantic ante-capitalist ideal of the masses (Hardt and Negri, 2000, p. 413), linguistic human rights strategies address minorities, and their marginalisation in conditions assuming TINA. In important respects, the cultural identity concerns of linguistic imperialism studies follow wider trends in western societies, rather than opposing them. Identity politics arose out of the fragmentation of left-wing political movements in the late 1960s, following the failures of radical politics to mobilise the working classes to a universalist project. Instead, political activity has become concentrated on narrower groups in society, and mobilising their identities. This pattern spans politicians, so-called warlords, international officials, international minority rights advocates and radicals. The culturalist approach has been criticised as divisive. Indeed, while anti-linguistic imperialism studies invoke Said, Said himself became increasingly sceptical towards post-colonial politics organised towards cultural difference, and looked again at more universalist forms of oppositional politics (Said, 1994a, p. 276; 1994b). Said attacks nativist projects as 'hardly what great resistance movements had imagined as their goals', and suggests they follow the logic of colonialism, rather than opposing it (Said, 1994a, p. 276).

Linguistic imperialism critiques rail against capitalism, but their socio-economic strategies revolve around 'correctives to free market' (Skutnabb-Kangas, 1999, p. 197; Skutnabb-Kangas *et al.*, 2009, p. 358). In effect, they follow the contemporary mainstream development thinking of Rawlsian liberalism (Rawls, 1973) and Sen's human development thinking (Sen, 1981; 2001), advocating fairer, more inclusive, regulated operation of the market, which reflects loss of faith in growth liberalism and the market, but an inability to imagine strategies going beyond the market. Thus, Sen's entitlement critique of famine politics demonstrates the failures of the market to realise human security, while his capabilities development approach seeks an enabling international community of state and non-state actors to empower people in the market (Pupavac, 2010; Sen, 1981; 2001). Such ideas inform documents like UNESCO's *Why Language Matters for the Millennium Development Goals* (UNESCO, 2012).

The collapse of belief in future-orientated politics and political movements has fostered attraction towards *ante*-capitalist solutions. Accordingly, they seek to limit the impact of modernity and sustain or revitalise minority communities (especially indigenous peoples) against modern society's homogenising tendencies. Nevertheless, their solutions actually assume the role of the modern state going against counter-culture ideals: its legal regulation and resources providing language education and community support. Romantic antipathy towards material growth appears at odds with advocacy making comprehensive institutional language resource demands of the state. Their language maintenance rights strategies, and concerns over funding allocation decisions, assume states acting as comprehensive welfare distributors and education providers (Skutnabb-Kangas, 2009, pp. 53–4). As such, they assume the establishment of developed modern welfare states and an international community of developed states with ample surplus resources to meet their comprehensive demands. Simultaneously, their strategies assume an enhanced role for the state in society, notwithstanding their attacks on the modern state. Advocates refer to the 'duty of government' and the 'duty of international community' to act (Skutnabb-Kangas, 1999, p. 198). Furthermore, their strategies seek for their policies to be institutionalised legally as mandatory rights. So their strategies depend on the modern state, and all its legal apparatus, notwithstanding their critiques of modernity and the state.

The state's centrality in language rights advocacy strategies belies counter-cultural stances in linguistic imperialism critiques. Here we may contrast the views of Illich, commonly cited in linguistic imperialism critiques. Illich was not only opposed to the modern state's military and economic policies; he also opposed state welfarism, which he saw as having 'regressive', 'destructive' consequences (Illich, 1973a, p. 149). Underdevelopment, for Illich, 'implies the surrender of social consciousness to prepackaged solutions' (Illich, 1973a, p. 137). Illich believed the 'social imagination' was being 'destroyed by its fixation on these [welfare] institutions' (Illich, 1973a, p. 139). In this vein, he called for an education philosophy separate from institutional schooling (Illich, 1973a, pp. 136–9; Illich and Verne, 1976). Emphasis on official recognition of languages and official language maintenance is therefore antithetical to Illich-inspired counter-culture critiques, opposing 'salesmen of schools' or other institutional solutions (Illich, 1973a, pp. 136–7). Illich counterposed the cultural revolutionary to the 'political magician', who behaved 'as if the noble savage could either be restored to the throne or the Third World transformed into a reservation for him', and the 'institutional revolutionary', who sought 'to reshape the design and distribution of the product' (Illich, 1973a, p. 150). International language rights advocates display both political magician and institutional bureaucratic tendencies in their attempts to realise global socio-linguistic justice through international human rights decrees. Here they repeat the pattern of post-independence leaders, believing they could achieve national development through government decrees (James, 1977, pp. 182–3, p. 186). Furthermore, cultural and linguistic identities become changed under bureaucratic global governance. Rather than cultural rights transcending Marcuse's modern one-dimensional man (Marcuse, 1964), culture becomes appropriated as correctives or supplements to the post-industrial consumer identity (Žižek, 1997; 1999a).

Language politics in an age of limits

Linguistic imperialism critiques oppose modernising economic growth models, but their strategies depend materially upon modern economies with the capacity to sustain their vision of global language rights governance. A material gap exists, therefore, between their critiques of modernity and their strategies presuming expanded roles for international and national institutions in the governance of identity, diversity and provision of welfare, while a political gap exists between their strategies appealing for tighter global governance regimes and their critiques appealing to counter-culture philosophies. Today's advocates seek institutional recognition as necessary to constitute identity and selfhood, whereas counter-cultural philosophers saw authentic selfhood as realised outside of modern institutions. Linguistic human rights strategies are essentially bureaucratic institutionalising solutions. Human rights advocacy over the decades has become significant in condemning oppressive governments globally, but the incorporation of human rights into international relations has involved a shift from activism to global governance, elaborating universal enforceable normative regimes to address state failures and social injustice. The postcolonial theorist Gayatri Spivak's essay on 'Does the Subaltern speak?' (1988) raises pertinent questions for human rights advocacy claiming to speak on behalf of others. However, her ideas of 'strategic essentialism' are problematic as a form of resistance where identity recognition is a core aspect of contemporary global governance.

At the same time, the gap between human rights norms and social conditions has been marked by increased readiness to support disciplinary approaches, circumscribing political self-determination. The next chapter discusses the former Yugoslavia's ethnic language politics and rights, and global conflict management approaches which show functional recognition of cultural and linguistic identity rights. Multicultural global governance echoes earlier colonial governance in its cultural recognition and its mistrust of political self-determination.

8

Language Rights Politics in the Former Yugoslavia and International Therapeutic Governance in Bosnia

Herderian ideas on a nation's soul and language have had a strong resonance in European national movements, including the Balkans. Not only have language developments been influenced by nationalism, but language politics has played a significant role in nationalist politics. Namely, the rise and fall of a common official Serbo-Croatian language has paralleled political aspirations and developments in the Balkans. The importance of language in nationalist movements has long been recognised. More recently, language rights have been taken up in international conflict management. Affirming linguistic identity is seen as enhancing the sense of group security and social stability. The OSCE envisages a 'pluralist, multicultural model of societal organisation', where rights protection supports '"integrating diversity", that is the simultaneous maintenance of different identities and the promotion of social integration' (Holt and Packer, 2001, p. 102).

International language rights require states to promote linguistic identities and linguistic communities on their territories, not simply to refrain from discrimination. The international provisions have tended to treat the existence, or not, of a language and its recognition as unproblematic, based on a group declaring itself a language community. Nevertheless, the issue of 'when is a language?' can be highly contentious, most notably in conflict situations. As socio-linguistics has analysed, questions over what is a language, and who belongs to a particular language community, involve political and subjective issues, not simply objective linguistic criteria. Crucially, subjectively defined linguistic difference may legitimise denial of communication.

Marginalised groups may demand identity rights, but they may represent claims to general rights, especially when groups astutely anticipate that contemporary policy responses favour identity claims, rather than general claim-making. As Christina Paulston pointedly observes, 'What looks on the surface like linguistic rights may indeed rather be human rights'

(Paulston, 1997, p. 189), or the rights, freedoms and social goods enjoyed by other citizens. Tackling social problems by valorising difference and special claim-making risks encouraging a cacophony of competing victim statuses, championed by identity representatives, whose elevated status inside and outside their community depends on the maintenance of the group's marginalised condition. At the same time, the institutionalisation of identity facilitates social problems being understood in terms of difference, and exacerbating inter-ethnic antagonisms. This was precisely the experience of Yugoslavia, which international governance has repeated in Bosnia.

This chapter examines language rights politics in the former Yugoslavia and in Bosnia under international conflict management. The chapter begins by outlining international conflict management approaches as a form of therapeutic governance. The chapter then discusses post-war Yugoslavia socialist approaches to language rights, before discussing international therapeutic governance and language rights policies in Bosnia.

International conflict management approaches

Language rights advocates see language recognition as integral to a secure personal and communal identity, and economic, political and social well-being (Skutnabb-Kangas, 1998, p. 20; Skutnabb-Kangas and Phillipson, 1994, p. 102). The linguistic repertoire to be protected is not just language acquisition, but specific linguistic identification. Identification with a mother tongue is regarded as a universal fundamental need by advocates (Phillipson *et al.*, 1994, p. 9), although the notion that self-identity necessarily involves identification with a mother tongue has been contested by cross-cultural research (Gupta, 1997). Nevertheless, advocates believe that identification with a mother tongue is crucial to self-identity, and should be fostered. Consequently, language rights as fundamental human rights are proposed to support individuals to 'identify positively with their mother tongue, and to have that identification respected by others' (Phillipson *et al.*, 1994, p. 2). Such concerns have influenced international language policy papers of the last two decades. The Harare intergovernmental report of 2006 links indigenous language recognition with securing a functional identity and personality (UNESCO, 2006, p. 31).

The significance given to linguistic identification in international language policy-making may be traced back to the psychoanalyst Erik Erikson's influential identification theory, which has been summarised as 'no identity, breakdown' (Bloom, 1990, p. 140). A sense of well-being is regarded by Erikson as 'a symptom' of an increasing sense of identity (Erikson, 1959, p. 118). The atomised and mobile character of modern society poses challenges to the narrative of the self, not posed by pre-modern societies organised around status and tradition (Sennett, 1998). Nevertheless, earlier writing on the subject was relatively sanguine about individuals developing a sense of identity and meaning under modern conditions. This optimism was expressed in the post-war popularity of existentialist philosophy, as espoused in works like Sartre's *Existentialism and Humanism*, which embraces the individual freedom and responsibility of making ourselves and our ethics through our chosen actions (Sartre, 1948). The need for a narrative of the self is not in itself controversial, although the contemporary perceived need for official recognition to achieve self-actualisation is (Furedi, 2003, pp. 162–74; Macintyre, 1985). Official identity recognition intertwines with official governance of cultural identities and intercultural relations. Both involve doubts over individuals' functionality, and their capacity to live with diversity, along with anxieties over modernity destabilising communities and fostering rootless, alienated individuals. Official multiculturalism's governance of difference therefore needs to be distinguished from multiculturalism as a lived experience (Malik, 2008; Žižek, 1999b).

UNESCO has been important in promoting cultural pluralism and cultural models of conflict in international policy. UNESCO's Universal Declaration on Cultural Diversity affirms its cultural pluralist approach, stating:

> culture should be regarded as a set of distinctive spiritual, material, intellectual and emotional features of society or a social group and that it encompasses, in addition to art and literature, lifestyles, ways of living together, value systems, traditions and beliefs (UNESCO, 2002).

The Declaration seeks to build social stability on the basis of recognising cultural difference: 'Aspiring to greater solidarity on the basis of recognition of cultural diversity, of awareness of the unity of humankind, and of the development of intercultural exchanges' (UNESCO, 2002). Cultural prejudice is treated as a key cause of war. As UNESCO's constitution states:

> ignorance of each other's way and lives has been a common cause...of that suspicion and mistrust between the peoples of the world through which their differences have all too often broken into war. (UNESCO, 1948, preamble)

These ideas are reiterated in UNESCO's initiatives over the last two decades, from its Culture of Peace Programme to its projects under the 2010 International Year for the Rapprochement of Cultures (UNESCO, 2010).

Language rights advocacy follows UNESCO in seeing the denial of linguistic and cultural identity rights as promoting ethnic conflict and violence, and their recognition as resolving conflict (Ouane and Glanz, 2010, p. 8; Skutnabb-Kangas, 1998, p. 19). Opposition to comprehensive multilingual recognition is ascribed to myths, prejudices and unfounded fears that it may lead to conflict or the fragmentation of states (Ouane and Glanz, 2010, p. 8; Skutnabb-Kangas, 1998, p. 19; UNESCO, 2006, p. 20). In this vein, it is contended:

> cultural identity was not the cause of these conflicts. Cultural identities were used to fuel them; causes are usually economic inequalities and struggle over power. (Ouane and Glanz, 2010, p. 8)

Language rights advocacy does not really address why a country which arguably had one of the most comprehensive systems of ethnic cultural recognition internationally should have collapsed into ethnic conflict. If sceptical attitudes towards multicultural or multilingual identity recognition are influenced by myths, prejudices or unfounded fears, they are myths, prejudices and fears given political force in the demise of SFR Yugoslavia. Its institutionalised, cultural ethnic identities encouraged political grievances to follow ethnicised lines (Hayden, 1999; Woodward, 1995). Nevertheless, the prevailing international conflict management approaches continue to attribute problems to the character of specific cultures, rather than their models of cultural identity recognition. They share beliefs that the nation state has 'probably outlived itself' and states should be treated as negotiable entities (Skutnabb-Kangas, 1998, p. 19). Extensive intervention into states and communities is therefore accepted against previous international norms of non-interference.

War as cultures of violence

International conflict models, intertwining anthropological and behaviouralist theories, see culture as a *learned* system of meaning and behaviour, and therefore as a system of meaning and behaviour that can be (re)taught, leading to the idea of specific programmes to create new patterns of thought and action. In her seminal *Patterns of Culture,* Benedict speaks of human nature as plastic, but shaped by a particular culture's patterns of thoughts and actions (Benedict, 1961, [1934], p. 183). The very plasticity of human nature implies here susceptibility to cultural conditioning, whereby individuals are cast negatively as malleable, rather than positively as creative. But, if violent conflict is a culturally acquired trait (Benedict, 1961, [1934], p. 180), then positive cultural conditioning could promote benign cultural traits, including non-violent ways of resolving problems (Benedict, 1961, [1934], pp. 22–3).

Conflict management approaches see identity as a fundamental psychological human need and cultural recognition as vital for the stability of societies. So their interventions seek to modify the content of cultural identities, while still respecting them. The social psychologist Herbert Kelman describes conflict programmes as creating a new shared culture between former adversaries, without requiring the parties to give up their own culture:

> the goal of conflict resolution is to shape new political and social arrangements that will empower the parties, meet their vital needs for identity and security, and lay the foundation for a stable, cooperative relationship consistent with the welfare and development of each party. Such changes imply some redistribution of power, as well as the gradual creation of a new culture shared by the former adversaries (without of course abandoning their separate cultures). (Kelman, 1993, p. xi)

Cultural causes of war became more significant at the end of the Cold War, evident in the rise of constructivist theories of international relations, emphasising the constructed nature of social identities and norms. The constructionist approach has been neatly outlined by Tarja Väyrynen in her book on *Culture and International Conflict Resolution* (2001):

> Culture is constitutive of human reality. Culture offers a grammar for acting in and interpreting the world, and it refers to widely shared practices and to commonly held assumptions and presuppositions that individuals and groups hold about the world. It involves the social structuring of both the world outside the self and the internal world. According to this view, since culture produces understandings of conflict and conflict resolution, the study of these is an important element of any meaningful analysis of conflict. In other words, international conflict analysis should be a form of cultural analysis. (Väyrynen, 2001, p. 3)

Constructivist theories share a belief in the importance of culture and the plasticity of human nature, whose plasticity is associated with vulnerability and the need for external support. Recognising the constructed nature of social identities and norms, proposals seek to recreate tolerant, non-violent ethnic traditions and inclusive multi-ethnic communities (for example, Broome, 1993, p. 104; Wachtel, 1998, pp. 2–3).

International policy-making in the 1990s adopted models attributing war to violent culture (UNESCO, 1998a, para. 2). Such goals inform UNESCO's Culture of Peace Programme, which was set up in 1994, prompted by the intrastate character of wars in the post-Cold War era. UNESCO characterises these wars as 'largely originating in the exploitation of lack of knowledge of others, and of other beliefs, values and perceptions, and ignorance and violation of fundamental human rights' (UNESCO, 1998b, para. 11). Its programme aspires to transform a 'culture of violence and war' into a 'culture of peace and non-violence' (UNESCO, 1998a, para. 2). Its Declaration on a Culture of Peace outlines 'a process of individual, collective and institutional transformation' (article 2), 'transforming values, attitudes and behaviours to those which promote a culture of peace and non-violence' (article 3), including respect for cultural identity and diversity. International conflict management advocates envisage a radical transformation of cultural norms through interventions at all levels of society, involving indigenous institutions, and devising programmes in accordance with local cultures and traditions. Nevertheless, they have profound ramifications for cultural self-determination. The anthropologist Thomas Eriksen has wryly commented: 'in order to save "a culture" one must lose it!' (Eriksen, 1993, p. 129). Functional or instrumental use of the expressive is evident in former Yugoslavia and Bosnia under international governance.

Ethnic key and ethnic rights politics in post-war Yugoslavia

Multiculturalism, multilingualism and identity recognition are core to international conflict management and language rights advocacy. Yet the international identity recognition models, in important respects, repeat post-war Yugoslavia's own multi-ethnic rights approach. Far from insensitivity towards ethnic identification, the constitutional arrangements of SFR Yugoslavia revolved around the principle of multi-ethnicity or the ethnic key. As Zoran Pajić, formerly professor of law at the University of Sarajevo, has commented:

> The constitutional guarantees for the safeguarding of minority identity were substantial and comprehensive. The protection of the native language groups in the former Yugoslavia will remain unrivalled in constitutional practice for a long time. (Pajić, 1994, p. 62)

Yugoslavia's federal constitution and ethnic rights provisions were of interest to UNESCO as a potential model for newly independent states in Africa and Asia (Campbell, 1997). Yugoslavia's popular international political standing was promoted in the developing world as the only white state in the Non-Aligned Movement. Various reports were written by Yugoslav experts for UNESCO on its constitutional provisions and cultural, social and educational policies (*International Social Science Journal*, 1961; Majstorović, 1980), for socialist Yugoslavia's ideals of 'national and cultural pluralism' and 'participative federalism' lent themselves to UNESCO's own ideals (Majstorović, 1980, p. 17). On the eve of war in 1990, the Minority Rights Group's World Directory of Minorities praised Yugoslavia's minority rights protection. Its report states, inter alia, that its handling of its minorities in the province of Vojvodina was 'highly creditable', citing its recognition of no fewer than five official languages in the province (MRG, 1990, p. 124).

The experiences of the Second World War in the region, which witnessed ethnic killings and persecution, made post-war Yugoslavia acutely conscious of the dangers of ethnic nationalism, and sensitive towards accommodating its ethnic groups. The regime sought to eliminate controversy over the national question by accommodating the different ethnic identities, following Stalin's policy of institutionalising nationality rights to placate and counter potential opposition. So, although post-war Yugoslavia broke with Moscow in 1947, its approach drew on the Soviet Union's minority and language rights approaches (Isayev, 1977), but went further in its recognition of diverse nations and nationalities against a potential hegemonic nation. Yugoslav nationalities policy consciously sought to distance itself from the interwar Yugoslav Kingdom's Serbian assimilatory policies, and to counterbalance the largest national groups by fostering the status of other groups. So socialist Yugoslavia did not pursue equivalent Russification policies, elevating one national group, although some subsequent commentary erroneously makes this assumption.

The principle of equality of rights of all the national groups and cultures was central to official organisation of Yugoslav society (Majstorović, 1980, p. 49; Minić, 1961, p. 424). Legislation granted extensive ethnic cultural rights, as well as allocating posts to secure a plurality of ethnic representation, in efforts to defuse potential ethnic grievances. From 1945, it became a criminal offence to incite national, racial or religious hatred. According to area studies expert Paul Shoup, although there was not 'exact proportionality...at all levels or in regions of the country in relation to ethnicity', 'the law on incitement was vigorously enforced' (Shoup, 1968, p. 110, p. 120). Yugoslavia's Non-Aligned Movement role also encouraged internationalist, non-racist norms.

Consequently, while national political movements were suppressed, for example, secessionist demands by Croats in the 1970s and Kosovo Albanians in the 1980s, both Croatian and Albanian national identities, along with Macedonian, Montenegrin, Muslim, Serbian and others, were not only permissible but sponsored in the cultural sphere in an attempt to depoliticise identity. George Schöpflin, in his 1980s survey of Yugoslav politics, observes how the state actively fostered the creation of new nations (Schöpflin, 1980, p. 8). The Macedonians were recognised as a constituent nation by the 1943 Anti-Fascist Council for the People's Liberation of Yugoslavia (AVNOJ) declaration, while Muslims (in an ethnic sense) incrementally gained this status. As such, the Yugoslav constitution prefigures the ecolinguistic and linguistic human rights concerns for specific group identity recognition, and measures for their cultural survival (Grin, 2003a; Kontra *et al.*, 1999; May, 2003; Pennycook, 1998b; Phillipson, 1992; Réaume, 2003; Rickard, 1994; Skutnabb-Kangas, 1998; Skutnabb-Kangas and Phillipson, 1994; Taylor, 1992; 1994).

Ethnic cooperation was central to the legitimacy of the Yugoslav state, which was symbolically identified with its diversity. 'Yugoslavia has seven neighbours, six republics, five nations, four languages, three religions, two scripts and one goal: to live in brotherhood and unity', went the popular official refrain often cited to visitors. This idea is repeated in official documents (Majstorović, 1980). The state constantly endeavoured to balance the need to create a cohesive society and a collective identity, loyal to the state, without provoking a separatist ethnic backlash. Such was the concern over not offending ethnic identification that citizens were discouraged from identifying themselves as Yugoslav as a national identity. Instead, Yugoslav was treated as a shared socialist political identity, through which ethnic identity was realised. In other words, to be Yugoslav after 1945 was officially about the fulfilment of one's own distinct national identity, and the celebration of others.

Under the constitution, Yugoslavia consisted of various nations, nationalities and ethnic groupings. The term nation related to a national group primarily associated with the Yugoslav state as opposed to another, while the term nationalities referred to groups who were primarily associated with another (neighbouring) state (Majstorović, 1980, p. 45). The term 'ethnic groups', which included Romanies and Vlachs, referred to peoples with primarily an oral tradition, or in the process of codifying their written languages. These distinct categories can be viewed by rights advocates as failing to institutionalise group equality. Indeed, it was officially admitted that the Roma did not yet enjoy the national development or status of other ethnic groups (Majstorović, 1980, pp. 48–9). Nevertheless, as Pajić reminds us, the Yugoslav constitution went far further than any other constitution to date in attempting to recognise group identities (Pajić, 1994, p. 62).

This sensitivity can be seen in how no single Yugoslav nation was officially identified with the symbols of statehood (Majstorović, 1980, p. 45). So the idea of minority rights became viewed as a misnomer and the term 'national minority', implying inferior national rights, was thus replaced by the term 'nationality' in the 1963 constitution, to promote the idea of equal rights for all citizens, irrespective of their national origin.

> The former term 'national minority' has been rejected, as it offers a quantitative, and not a qualitative definition, and may mean that a minority has minor rights. To avoid this and to emphasize their terminological equality, the term 'nationality' has been adopted, although it is not without shortcomings. (Majstorović, 1980, p. 45)

The sensitivity towards multinationality was carried over into the country's official language policies:

> Many foreigners visiting Yugoslavia want to know how people in such a multinational and multilinguistic community can communicate with each other. The right to use one's mother tongue is guaranteed by the federal Constitution to every citizen, in his contacts with the

> administration, judicature and local authorities. In all communities where the members of several nations or nationalities live (the case of Vojvodina, for instance) the administration is bilingual, or even trilingual. The same applies to schools. If it is a monolingual community the courts and administrative agencies are bound to provide interpretation or translation whenever requested by an individual, or a group belonging to a different nation or nationality. In Vojvodina again (the 'most pluralistic' part of the country), the radio and television programmes are broadcast in five different languages. All languages are equal in Yugoslavia and all statutes and enactments of all Yugoslav importance are adopted in all national languages.... In terms of the size of its population, Yugoslavia is possibly the country with the most developed translation activity in Europe. (Majstorović, 1980, p. 50)

Tensions were played down in official reports on national cultural rights. Majstorović's report for UNESCO attributes problems to uneven development:

> in the early 1960s during the period of intensive industrial development, it became clear that national equality had not yet been fully established because nations at different levels of economic development could not but be economically unequal as well. The distribution of the national income, which is largely taking place through market mechanisms, still favours the more developed and economically stronger nations. In practical life, economic inequality is constantly disrupting and jeopardizing political equality, and increasingly threatens to reduce it to a mere political statement devoid of any real social and economic content. (Majstorović, 1980, p. 46)

Echoing UNESCO's policies today, Majstorović describes strategies at different levels to combat national chauvinism: 'all republics and provinces determine a cultural policy that will systematically encourage the confirmation of other cultures within their own communities' (Majstorović, 1980, p. 56). Ironically, official Yugoslav proclamations on cultural pluralism and 'unity in diversity' (Majstorović, 1980, p. 49) or bilingual education (Minić, 1961, p. 425) appear closer to UNESCO documents on multicultural diversity than in many countries even today – certainly Germany, along with the US, France and Britain, all of whom played decisive roles in the de-recognition of SFR Yugoslavia and the subsequent interventions in the region.

But the sensitivity of the socialist Yugoslav constitution towards ethnic groups, and the suspicion towards minority rights, were not understood, and were brushed aside by international mediators in the 1990s (Hayden, 1999; Woodward, 1995). Notably, the position was misunderstood by the

Badinter Commission, designated by the European Community to consider the minority rights guarantees as a prerequisite for the recognition of the republics as new states. In particular, the Badinter Commission failed to understand how minority rights status was viewed as demotion from full citizenship rights, and therefore regarded as threatening. International insistence on minority rights guarantees actually legitimised the hierarchical ethnicisation of citizenship, ignoring the lessons of fifty years previously in which minority status failed to provide protection (Arendt, 1968, pp. 268–75). For to be categorised a minority in the successor states signified being 'defined out of the body politic', as the regional constitutional expert Robert Hayden has analysed (Hayden, 1999, p. 15).

Post-war Yugoslav multi-ethnic policies were able to manage ethnic relations in a period of growing prosperity and international stability. However, Yugoslav emphasis on ethnic group rights reinforced ethnic identities, and held the potential for nurturing ethnic bureaucracies and undermining coexistence. So, although ethnic distinctions weakened culturally in the decades after the Second World War (Krejči and Velimsky, 1981, p. 144), distinct political loyalties were fostered through the institutionalisation of ethnicity. A major study by the Wilson Center in the 1980s documented how decision-making had become the outcome of political bargaining between rival ethnic political elites, leading to political stasis over both economic and political reform (Rusinow, 1988). In the erosion of shared loyalty consequent upon the Yugoslav socialism's loss of legitimacy, economic recession of the late 1970s, and IMF structural adjustment programmes of the 1980s, there was a growing perceived lack of group recognition, in spite of the country's 'unrivalled' recognition (Woodward, 1995). The granting of extensive ethnic rights, rather than satisfying demands, encouraged the politicisation of ethnicity and the articulation of discontent as ethnic differences. In short, the institutionalisation of ethnic rights fostered ethnic nationalists, contrary to the impression given by ethnic nationalists of their identity being suppressed.

In its final collapse into war, Yugoslavia all too vividly demonstrates how the politics of recognition may foster ungenerous attitudes towards others, and ultimately a politics of mutual recrimination. Nationalist politicians deployed culturalist arguments, essentialising ethnic difference and denying commonality (Hayden, 1999, pp. 142–4; Woodward, 1985). Nationalist claims to self-determination were on the basis that coexistence was a threat to their cultural identity, and each cultural nation required its state. The lived reality of multi-ethnic communities meant that violence was required to secure the separation of people. Yet the international politics of recognition endorsed these claims to separate identity against coexistence, whose consequences it has been trying to right. Equally, international rights approaches tended to legitimise language divisions in the former Yugoslavia.

When is a language?

In looking at the question of language rights politics in the former Yugoslavia, we need to consider the question of when is a language. Over a decade ago, there were calls for international clarification of the definition of a language (Phillipson *et al.*, 1994, p. 14), but confusion and contradictions still reign in international minority rights reports and international policy. Human rights documents, under the imperative to establish a linguistic human rights framework, have tended to assume the existence of distinct languages and treat minority language status as straightforward.

What criteria are to be deployed in determining the existence of a language? Broadly speaking, the question can be approached using either comparative linguistic criteria or subjective criteria, taking into account the views of the speakers themselves as to whether they share a distinct linguistic identity (Skutnabb-Kangas and Bucak, 1994, p. 364). Divergence over external or internal identifications of a language's existence typically revolves around the dialect/language distinction. For non-linguists, this issue has been usefully characterised as the apples and plums distinction, that is, 'classifying Opal, Clappes and Victoria (all varieties of plum) as a plum' versus 'calling a Victoria plum an apple' (Skutnabb-Kangas and Bucak, 1994, p. 370, note 12). Under external linguistic categorisation, British and American English are varieties of plum, as are Dutch and Flemish, although they may go under distinct internal names.

In recent years, socio-linguistic and minority rights thinking has become increasingly interested in subjective identification, influenced in part by post-modern approaches 'rejecting claims to objectivity in favour of more partial and particular versions of knowledge, truth and reason' (Pennycook, 1994, p. 298). Endorsement of subjective identification has been further encouraged by adopting 'a maximalist position for minorities' (Skutnabb-Kangas and Phillipson, 1994, p. 103). The Convention concerning Indigenous and Tribal Peoples in Independent Countries 1989 has stated: '*Self-identification* as indigenous or tribal shall be regarded as a fundamental criterion for determining the groups' (article 1.2; emphasis added). Subjective language identifications have been given recognition under human rights regimes, although language rights advocates would not necessarily endorse some of the specific language claims being made when external criteria would determine otherwise. The status of subjective identification is at the crux of the Serbo-Croatian language question.

Subjective criteria have been embraced by those championing the idea of distinct languages in the debates, whereas comparative linguistic criteria are regarded by the majority of foreign linguists as demonstrating that the language is one (Askew, 2011; Greenberg, 1996; Naylor, 1992; Pupavac, 2003). A useful summary for the general reader of the main regional differences in the language appears in Celia Hawkesworth's *Colloquial Serbo-Croat* (1986):

> There are three main dialects of Serbo-Croat, one of which was selected as the literary language in the mid-nineteenth century. This dialect is known as **štokavian** because in it the word for 'what' is **što**. (The other two are known as **kajkavski** and **čakavski** because in them the word for 'what' is respectively **kaj** and **ča**). Within **štokavian**, there are two major subdivisions, most conveniently described as the Western and the Eastern variant. The main distinguishing feature of these is the way in which a particular early Slavonic vowel sound has evolved: into **e** in the Eastern variant, and **je** or **ije** (depending on the length of the vowel) in the Western variant, e.g. **mleko** (milk) and **mlijeko**. The variants are thus known as **ekavski** and **jekavski** (or **ijekavski**). (There is a further sub-dialect, **ikavski**, spoken mainly on the Dalmatian coast, in which the word for 'milk' is **mliko**. This is not accepted as standard speech, however). There are certain other differences...These inevitably include some lexical variations, resulting from centuries of separate development. For example, the word for the basic foodstuff 'bread' is **kruh** in the Western and **hleb** in the Eastern variant. (Hawkesworth, 1986, p. xviii, bold in the original)

Here Hawkesworth notes how the standard languages spoken in Bosnia, Croatia, Montenegro and Serbia are all based on the štokavian dialect, which remains the case with the official standards in the successor states. How distinct are the standards? During SFR Yugoslavia, this was how the linguistic position was represented to UNESCO:

> Serbo-Croat and Croato-Serbian are very close, and only minor differences distinguish one from the other. These two versions are spoken by 70 per cent of the population (15 million out of the total of 22 million). Other Slavonic languages differ from Serbo-Croat (i.e. Croato-Serbian) to a greater or lesser degree, but these differences are never so great as to prevent general understanding in multinational milieu. (Majstorović, 1980, p. 17)

The Slavic linguist Thomas Magner has described the mutual comprehension and closeness of the standards:

> The correspondence of Croatian and Serbian sounds, vocabulary, nominal declensions, verb conjugations, and syntactic formulations ranges from 95 percent to 100 percent, and no Serb, Croat, or Bosnian Moslem today would have any difficulty in communicating, one with another. (Magner, 1991, p. ix)

The linguistic correspondence of the štokavian standards identified by Magner may be compared alongside the rich regional variation, notably within Croatian: kajkavian belonging to northern Croatia, and čakavian to the Adriatic islands and part of the coast, in addition to the ikavian dialect of the Dalmatian coast. However, these regional variations have not been politicised into declarations of linguistic independence, underscoring how objective linguistic criteria may be secondary to political or subjective criteria in determining the official status accorded to differences. There is greater divergence between British and American English, as Magner and other linguists and writers have observed, but these differences are not (or are no longer) politicised (Burchill, 1985; Bryson, 1994; Gustafson, 1992). International language rights and conflict management approaches have encouraged the idea of distinct Bosnian, Croatian, Montenegrin and Serbian language communities, although recognition of distinct linguistic identities has legitimised ethnic distance against ethnic integration.

Language rights politics and the demise of Serbo-Croatian

The earlier identification of a common Serbo-Croatian language is in opposition to the developments in official language policies since 1990. The break-up of the idea of a common Serbo-Croatian language community paralleled, or indeed prefigured, the break-up of the state of Yugoslavia. The Serbo-Croatian language question is integrally bound up with political developments over South Slav unity or division, as both foreign and local linguists highlight (Bugarski and Hawkesworth, 1992; Greenberg, 1996; 2004; Katičić, 2001; Magner, 1991). While contemporary nationalist identity politics tends to minimise the speech community, nineteenth-century nationalist movements tended to maximise the speech community. This stance was influenced both by the Enlightenment universalist ideals, stressing similarities over differences, and Romantic nation-building aspirations. Accordingly, members of the Illyrian Movement who aspired to South Slav unity declared the unity of the language under the Vienna Literary Agreement 1850 to realise Herder's ideal of one people, one language, although linguistically there was less correspondence in the language spoken across the region then than today.

Croatian nineteenth-century political figures, linguists and intellectuals, such as Ljudevit Gaj, were at the forefront of promoting codification of a common linguistic community (Okey, 2004). The very choice of štokavian as the basis of the standard in Croatia, as opposed to kajkavian with its then active literary corpus, was influenced by this desire. However, over the last few decades, Croatian linguists championed the idea of distinct languages towards legitimising claims to independent statehood. At the same time, their advocacy involved rewriting linguistic history, marginalising earlier Croatian initiatives helping forge a common language. In contrast, Serbs, politically attached to a unified state, were more reluctant to abandon the idea of a shared language. Serbian official policy has therefore been slower in endorsing a distinct standard.

Alongside declarations of new states, Bosnian, Croatian, Montenegrin and Serbian were declared separate languages, thereby allowing contemporary politics to comply with Herder's ideal of the unity of state, nation and language. New dictionaries and grammars were published across the region, codifying new distinct standard languages. Some of these publications represent revisions of older texts under new titles to reflect the break-up of the language (Pupavac, 2003). In the new Bosnian standard, Turkish words, for example, are now used to illustrate characteristics of a distinct Bosnian language (Isaković, 1995), whereas they were previously treated as a feature of a common Serbo-Croatian language (Škaljić, 1989).

The arguments of Croatian linguists are significant, because of the importance Croatian official policy has given to Croatian being a separate language from Serbian. To support a common language is regarded as giving succour to Yugoslavism and undermining the legitimacy of the Croatian state. The establishment of Croatian as a separate language preoccupied Croatian linguistics in the 1990s, as the *International Journal of the Sociology of Language* 2001 special issue on Croatia testifies (2001, no. 147). As one Croatian linguist outlines, a key activity of Croatian linguists has related to 'attempts at theoretical and empirical delimitation of the Croatian and Serbian standard languages, which had previously been considered by both Slavists and official policy a single (if polycentrically standardized) language' (Kalogjera, 2001, p. 1). 'Croatian linguistic loyalty', the title of an article in the edited volume (Katičić, 2001), is a matter of Croatian patriotism.

In declaring Croatian a distinct language, Croatian linguists have asserted the importance of subjective criteria over objective criteria to define a language. Stressing the subjective, the linguist Radoslav Katičič, a long-standing proponent of Croatian as a separate language, invokes 'the cultural and emotional individuality of the two languages' (Katičič, 2001, p. 26). The commonalities of the language in Serbia and Croatia are not denied. The linguist Ivo Pranjković concurs with Hawkesworth's account of the shared dialect of Croatian and Serbian standards:

> one is confronted with varieties that are for the most part the same, especially when taking into account only the grammatical system ... at that level, we are dealing with features that cannot possibly differ, for they belong to the same dialect – Novoštokavian – which served as the basis for both the Croatian and Serbian standards. Within the framework of one dialect there cannot, for example, be any difference in the number of cases, in the system of verb forms, or in the corpus of grammatical morphemes or personal pronouns. Therefore it could be said that between Croatian and Serbian there is no difference *where there is no possibility*

of choice, or in other words, where there cannot be any differences. (Pranjković, 2001, p. 35)

However, while acknowledging the shared grammatical system, Pranjković highlights how Croats distinguish themselves from Serbs in their *choice* of language. When they speak, Pranjković argues, they consciously choose to distinguish themselves from Serbian usage as far as is linguistically possible: 'as soon as *the possibility of choice appears*, then we are confronted with numerous differences between the two varieties on all levels of the linguistic system' (Pranjković, 2001, pp. 35–6, emphasis added). Nevertheless, Pranjković does not think linguistic distinctions could develop of the order of those between 'Croatian and Russian or Slovakian and Slovenian' (Pranjković, 2001, p. 49). Magner, however, has speculated that 'With sustained efforts at differentiation, Croatian and Serbian could become sometime in the twenty-first century as distinct as Slovenian and Bulgarian' (Magner, 1991, p. x). Pranjković is cautious about official policy attempting to create a mutually incomprehensible language, although some patriots have sometimes acted as if mutual incomprehension had already been achieved. The international mediator Carl Bildt, for example, has observed how some Croatian interpreters, interpreting for him were apparently unable to understand the ethnic Serb refugees he was interviewing. Pranjković warns against linguists attempting such a feat of differentiation: 'even could one succeed in this way, they would not only make communication impossible between Croats and Serbs, but among the Croats themselves' (Pranjković, 2001, p. 49). The limits of institutionalising a separate linguistic identity are determined by the necessity of internal communication within a country with rich regional variation.

The language divisions became highly significant in Bosnia, where language politics follows the ethnic divisions. In summary, Bosnian Croats have sought to follow Croatian language norms, and the Bosnian Serbs Serbian language norms, while the Bosnian Muslims or Bosniacs have sought to develop Bosnian language norms. We see a separate Bosnian language being elaborated, accompanying ethnic political developments, especially from the late 1990s (Bulić, 1999; Halilović, 1991; 1998; Isaković, 1995; Jahić, 1999a; 1999b). Linguistic advocates invoke historical references to a Bosnian language just as other ethnic groups have done (Halilović, 1998; Jahić, 1999a; 1999b). Yet they complain of Bosniacs' lack of identification with their language, and see the need to cultivate awareness and concern with their language identity (Halilović, 1998, p. 8; discussed in Askew, 2011). So the idea of the Bosnian language is simultaneously presented as historically given, but also to be constructed. Thus, Bosnian language books like *The Bosniac Nation and its Language* (Jahić, 1999b) or *The Bosnian Language: A hundred questions and a hundred answers* (Jahić, 1999a) have an important prescriptive function.

However, agreement on what constitutes Bosnian, and how it differs from Croatian and Serbian, is not settled, as is apparent from the 1998 Bihać symposium on the Bosnian language (Askew, 2011; Greenberg, 2004). In the early 1990s, there was readiness to adopt Croatian linguistic norms against Serbian linguistic norms, reflecting the broader political alliances. Following conflict between the Bosnian Croats and Bosnian Muslims, there was concern to distinguish Bosnian from Croatian. The use of the letter 'h', as in 'kahva' rather than 'kava' or 'kafa' (coffee), for example, was symbolically invoked to distinguish Bosnian religiously from the contemporary Croatian and Serbian standards respectively (Isaković, 1993, p. 4, discussed in Mačak, 2009, pp. 144–5). Interestingly, the association of the letter 'h' with the soul echoes Hamann's insistence on German retaining 'h' as the breath of God (Hamann, 2007, [1773], pp. 146–63; Haynes, 2007, p. xxiii). (My thanks to the anonymous reviewer for highlighting these parallels.) But, in seeking to distance themselves from contemporary Croatian and Serbian norms, there is also controversy over identifying Turkish Ottoman terms with Bosnian, as potentially undermining Bosnia's pro-western European orientation (Filipović, 1999 in Askew, 2011). For a common thread of East European nationalisms, since the end of the Cold War, has been competing claims to a western and European identity and status (Burgess, 1997; Todorova, 1997). Claims to a separate Bosnian language, as opposed to a Bosniac language, have provoked anxiety among Bosnian Croats and Bosnian Serbs as undermining Bosnian Croatian and Bosnian Serbian rights in Bosnia, although some have preferred the term Bosnian as more ethnically inclusive (Greenberg, 2004, p. 157).

The Bosnian Serb authorities have attempted to create stronger political links with Serbia through proclaiming the Serbian ekavian variant as the official language in Republika Srpska in 1993, and then again in 1996, although the population speak ijekavian, like Bosnian Croats and Bosniacs (Greenberg, 2004, p. 78). However, both attempts, with their attempted punitive sanctions, proved unpopular, and had to be abandoned amidst opposition and ridicule. Again, the Bosnian Serb ekavian decree would have implications for regional variation within Serbia. Meanwhile, there are concerns over the bureaucratisation of language (Klikovac, 2001). Overall, competing official efforts at forging distinct languages have not created distinct languages. Instead they have fostered symbolic identification, with separately defined names for the language, and symbolic use of specific words, which have become markers of ethnic linguistic identity (Askew, 2011; Greenberg, 2004).

How have these internal definitions influenced external definitions of the language, and vice versa? Some Slavic linguist specialists have been sympathetic to the internal definitions. Leonard Auburger refers to the 'illusion of closeness' in his discussion of the language (Auburger, 1999, pp. 351–5). Other foreign linguists have sought to avoid causing offence by adopting local terminology, even where they incline towards external definitions of the language affirming its commonality (Greenberg, 1996). Foreign linguists or foreign university departments not following the new internal definitions of distinct languages, and continuing to refer to a common language, have been criticised by the successor states. In Britain, the School of Slavonic and East European Studies (SSEES) at the University of London and the University of Nottingham now refer to Serbian/Croatian rather than Serbo-Croatian (previously SSEES also referred to the Bosnian language). The titles of textbooks reflect linguistic identities, for example, *Bosnian, Croatian, Serbian, A textbook: with exercises and basic grammar* (Alexander, 2006). Revised editions of language teaching books for foreign students were renamed to reflect contemporary political sensibilities: *Colloquial Serb-Croat* (Hawkesworth, 1986) to *Colloquial Croatian and Serbian* (Hawkesworth, 1998); *Introduction to the Serbo-Croatian Language* (Magner, 1986) to *Introduction to the Croatian and Serbian Language* (Magner, 1991); *Teach Yourself Serbo-Croat* (Norris, 1993) to *Teach Yourself Serbian* (Norris and Ribnikar, 2003) and *Teach Yourself Croatian* (Norris, 2003). Nevertheless, foreign Slavic linguists have been cautious about following declarations of linguistic independence, although making certain concessions. In practice, even academics committed to the conception of distinct Bosnian, Croatian, Montenegrin and Serbian languages would encounter difficulties strictly applying such a position – not least because of the financial constraints on foreign language teaching generally. The existence of many language departments is under threat, and some have closed or merged in Britain, since languages are declining in relative popularity as a subject to study at western universities.

International therapeutic governance in Bosnia

Understanding the Bosnian conflict primarily in culturalist terms, and attempting to satisfy recognition needs as understood in social psychology, the international community institutionalised a complex system of ethnic representation under the Dayton Agreement of 1995 and subsequent international decrees. Under the Dayton Agreement drawn up by US negotiators, Bosnia epitomises the idea of the 'culture state' proposed by Carr during the Second World War (Carr, 1941). In his conception of the culture state, Carr proposed that nations should be allowed to enjoy extensive cultural rights, but that economic, political and military power should be transferred to supranational institutions. Bosnia from 1995 was under the international supervision of Office of the High Representative (OHR), NATO, OSCE, UN and other international or regional organisations and donor states (Chandler, 1999; Knaus and Martin, 2003). Subsequently, the leading international supervisory role was transferred to the European Union, although the OHR has continued to play a significant role (ICG, 2011).

Under the constitutional arrangements drafted under Dayton, the Republic of Bosnia and Hercegovina consists of two entities: the Federation of Bosnia and Hercegovina, and Republika Srpska. The Presidency of the Republic of Bosnia and Hercegovina consists of three directly elected members: one Croat and one Bosniac from the Federation; one Serb from Republika Srpska (General Framework Agreement, 1995, Annexe 10, article V). Below the Presidency is the Council of Ministers, no more than two-thirds of whom are to be appointed from the Federation. The Council of Ministers is headed by two co-chairpersons, a Bosniac and Serb rotating weekly, and a Croat vice-chair, each minister having two deputies from the other two ethnic groups. Decisions are to be taken by consensus in the Council, echoing the previous Yugoslav approach. The Parliamentary Assembly consists of two chambers: the House of Peoples and the House of Representatives (article IV). The House of Peoples comprises fifteen delegates: five Bosniacs and five Croats from the House of Peoples of the Federation, and five Serbs from the National Assembly of the Republika Srpska. The House of Peoples has a rotating chair with two deputy chairs of different ethnicities. The House of Representatives comprises forty-two directly elected members: two-thirds from the Federation, one-third from Republika Srpska. There is a rotating chair and two deputy chairs of different ethnicities.

The provisions, amended provisions and subsequent decrees could continue to be reeled off to illustrate how the principle of ethnicity runs through public institutions at all levels (Chandler, 1999). There have, for example, been various further city agreements on joint administration, in which the international community has even decreed the allocation of seats in advance of election results, or rejigged them in order to achieve a particular balance of ethnic representation (OHR, 1996; 1997a; 1997b; 1997c). Similar measures to ensure multi-ethnicity are being carried over to private institutions and businesses, through internationally drafted employment discrimination legislation. Alongside the requirements for ethnic representation, there are complex procedures under which decisions may be declared destructive of the vital interests of an ethnic group.

Unsurprisingly, given SFR Yugoslavia's experience, ethnic representation and ethnic vetoes have not overcome ethnic divisions. Rather, the overall impact has been to institutionalise pork-barrel politics and recreate the impasses of the previous Yugoslav multi-ethnic system. Consequently, international institutions constantly step in to overcome impasses and force through decisions. The international community became progressively more involved in Bosnia, indefinitely extending the initial one-year supervisory role envisaged under the Dayton Agreement 1995 (General Framework Agreement, 1995). The Office of the High Representative, a key international supervisory institution created to supervise the civilian aspects of Dayton (General Framework Agreement, 1995, Annexe 10, article V), effectively enjoyed executive powers, drafting domestic laws, structuring public institutions and directing public policy. High Representatives have regularly imposed decisions and removed officials, measures endorsed by international NGOs (ICG, 2000; Petrisch, 1999a: OHR, 2000a). Yet the OHR enjoyed these extensive powers without any formal accountability to the population or any formal suspension of Bosnia's sovereignty. Conversely, the High Representative had to report to the UN, EU, US, Russian Federation or other governments or organisations (General Framework Agreement, 1995, Annexe 10, article II). An institutional dynamic was set in motion, unchecked by the weak and fragmented local institutions. International administration generally spiralled beyond inter-ethnic into public policy in the face of divided local institutions. Indicatively, the OHR had grown to nearly 700 staff – 236 international staff and 452 local support staff – five years after Dayton (OHR website, Spring 2000). Over fifteen years on, Bosnian institutions remain weak and fragmented (Bliesemann de Guevara, 2009; 2010).

To foster more cooperative relations, international administrators have sponsored civil society organisations, NGOs, and their role in public life. International officials have also sponsored so-called 'mandatory platforms' (OSCE, 1999b), in which political parties have to sign up to internationally drafted political economic and social policies to avoid political disputes. In this way, Bosnia well illustrates warnings on the authoritarian implications of culturalism, and its transformation of politics into administration (Chandler, 1999; Knaus and Martin, 2003). The internationally sponsored arrangements are characterised by periodic crises dependent on regular external intervention. Expert analysis has complained of there being 'no broadly respected authority in the country, only regional or partisan champions' and of the international community's 'over-involvement in local politics' and need to pull back from its micro-management (ICG, 2011). However, impasses are built into a system based on recognition of ethnic difference. Crucially, insofar as the sustained intense international intervention has established elite cooperation, it has been by marginalising dissenting elements at the expense of popular involvement, that is, by circumscribing democratic politics. At this point, Bosnians might feel with Goethe, 'We, seemingly free, are only more hemmed in than we were at the beginning' (Goethe, 1959, [1817], p. 231).

The multiculturalist understanding of rights does not see a contradiction between the formal upholding of Bosnian sovereignty and its effective suspension. This is possible because of the radically different view of the rights-holder held by multiculturalism from the classical view of the subject as an autonomous rational being. Multicultural critics of the classic model question the classical assumptions over the rights-holder as an exclusionary construct, highlighting how the model fails to recognise groups who are vulnerable and marginalised. Multiculturalism sees rights recognition as necessary for self-actualisation and empowerment (Taylor, 1994). This re-conception of rights necessary to realise the self fundamentally challenges the classic ideal, which assumes that rights-holders are moral agents capable of exercising their rights and freedoms. In distinction, multiculturalism subtly re-conceptualises civil and political rights as rights to third-party actualisation and empowerment, that is, positive rights supporting the self, as opposed to negative freedoms from inference. But third-party enablement cannot be relinquished, for self-actualisation is a process requiring continual affirmation, since the self is ever vulnerable to risk and dysfunction. Hence, external intervention in Bosnia is not conceived as violating the UN Charter on the right to national self-determination, but as supporting its realisation. Furthermore, in the multiculturalist understanding of rights, national self-determination is understood psychologically as a right to identity, rather than politically as a right to self-government (Pupavac, 1998).

International educational governance

To help secure cooperation, international negotiators, officials and human rights advocates have been ready to endorse nationalist declarations of linguistic independence. It is not uncommon for international documents to refer to distinct Bosnian, Croatian and Serbian languages or to provide three distinct translations of a particular document, thereby legitimising the idea of mutual incomprehensibility. The 1994 Washington Accords and the 1995 Dayton Agreement, for example, were translated from English into different versions. Again, objections were not raised over Croatia's declaration of Serbian as one of its minority languages, on its ratification in 1997 of the 1992 European Charter for Regional or Minority Languages. This is in line with the growing endorsement of self-definitions and the advocacy of maximalist positions for minorities. Indeed, international human rights experts have criticised Croatia for failing to provide specific Serbian language provision for its ethnic Serbs.

Yet international officials in Bosnia have been grappling with how linguistic identity rights may affirm divisions and marginalise minorities. Subsequently, they have realised how recognising subjectively defined linguistic identities may be divisive for inter-ethnic coexistence. In particular, international endorsement of three distinct Bosnian, Croatian and Serbian languages from what was formally considered a single language has been an obstacle to re-integrating Bosnian education. UNESCO's 1999 Bosnian education report highlighted the 'politically intended split up of the form Serbo-Croatian or Croatian-Serbian language in a "Serbian", "Bosnian" and a "Croat" language' (Lenhart *et al.*, 1999) as a problem for the re-integration of schools. Guidelines on education issued for field officers by the Human Rights Coordination Centre in Sarajevo stated: 'It is important for field monitors not to engage in this [language] debate' (Human Rights Coordination Centre, 1999, p. 12). Likewise, the World Bank singled out the politicisation of language as an obstacle to the re-integration of education (World Bank,

21 June 1999). Yet international policy-makers' stance has played an important role in legitimising the local language politics of difference. The divisive consequences can be seen in how people of different ethnicities from the same village, speaking the same dialect, have been demanding the right to be taught in their own Bosnian, Croatian and Serbian language and the funding of separate schools or classes. The Bosnian Minister of Education, echoing international linguistic human rights talk, defended a 1997 decree on segregated education as a response to minority demands. International officials were outraged at the decree, but it reflected the logic of the politics of recognition, which encouraged rights claims based on subjectively *perceived* cultural-linguistic needs.

The Peace Implementation Council's 1998 Madrid conference set out the necessity for Bosnian education to 'meet international standards and contribute to tolerance and stability' (Peace Implementation Council, section II, Item 7). The return of refugees was linked to curriculum reform. Under the follow-up 1998 Sarajevo Declaration, a review of school textbooks was conducted to identify and withdraw any textbooks contributing to ethnic hatred and intolerance (Spaulding, 1998). The internationally led reform initiative has been followed up by recurring international initiatives, attempting to achieve a coherent curriculum supporting a unified Bosnia. Numerous international reports on education reform and reform processes have been sponsored by a range of international bodies, including the Council of Europe, the European Commission, OECD, UNESCO, UNICEF, World Bank, and even SFOR (the NATO Stabilisation Force). In 2002, the OSCE gained the international mandate to pursue systematic education reform of primary, secondary and higher education (Perry, 2003, p. 93). A Framework Law on Primary and Secondary Education was passed in 2002 to standardise ethnically uncontroversial subjects like the sciences (article, 7), address segregated schools (article 5), and remove discriminatory material (Art 10) (Fisher, 2006). A few years later, the 2005 Memorandum of Understanding, whose guidelines stated that Bosnia 'should be the main reference point', drafted principles on politically ethnically controversial subjects like history, language and religion around a common core curriculum (Harroff-Tavel, 2005; OSCE, 2005b, p. 11).

Nevertheless, international reform efforts are still struggling a decade later. Reports over the years repeatedly observe failures to implement reforms and integrate education (Fischer, 2006; Harroff-Tavel, 2005; OSCE, 2005b; Perry, 2003; Popovic, 2006; Stabback, 2003). Reports over the years continue to observe the ethnicised character of the curriculum, and orientation of the Republika Srpska (RS) curriculum towards Serbia and that of Bosnian Croatian cantons towards Croatia (UN Human Rights Council, 2008, p. 19). The three ethnic groups have different political positions on Bosnia: the Bosniacs and Bosnian Muslims want a more centralised state, while the Bosnian Serbs and Bosnian Croats want a more decentralised state and to maintain stronger ethnic links with Serbia and Croatia respectively, and these differences are reflected in education politics. While the divided ethnic communities disagree of the form of the state they still look to the state as welfare and employment provider. However the erosion of the state's welfare and employment role under internationally driven reforms reinforces the importance of people's ethnic connections to their economic security. Linguistic and cultural barriers are invoked to legitimise some autonomy under international governance, whose security models recognise linguistic and cultural identity as part of conflict management, but do not allow independent political self-determination, which contradicts their vision for Bosnia. International interventions to punish the failure to implement reforms, like fines (Perry, 2003, p. 89) or removal of ministers (Harroff-Tavel, 2005), have not quickly resolved the problems of implementing education reform and a common curriculum.

Claude Kieffer, the OHR education minister, bemoaned how 'There is no feeling of community, and how can a state survive if the young show no will to build it, nor at least want it to exist? The state exists only thanks to a peace treaty – not because the people wish to live together' (Kieffer in Popović, 2006). International policy-makers see a common curriculum as vital to trying to build loyalty and common identity with the state. Conversely, resistance to education reforms persists, bound up with these broader political concerns. A report describes 'Virtual apartheid in the Bosnian school system' and how 'Although Bosniaks, Croats and Serbs speak almost identical languages, their political representatives insist that students must study separately' (Popović, 2006). The report is interesting in suggesting how international officials like Kieffer feel the potential legitimacy of separate curricula, if students speak separate languages and seek to reassure ethnic constituencies that fears that, 'they will not learn their language, or their history' are ungrounded (Kieffer in Popović, 2006). International reports constantly affirm how ethnic and linguistic identity may be secured in an integrated education system (Magill, 2010, pp. 32–6). The Constitutional Court ruled that teaching only Bosnian, Croatian or Serbian would constitute 'a violation of the constitutional principle of equality of all official languages' (in OSCE, 2005b, pp. 6–7). Yet issues of language, culture and history cannot be addressed in their own terms, because groups are seeking political self-determination, not simply cultural recognition. Thus, linguistic and cultural arguments should not be dismissed as merely irrational, but come back to opposing political interests in a unified state. The Bosnian language is asserted by Bosniacs towards supporting a more centralised state against Bosnian Croatian and Bosnian Serbian links with Croatia and Serbia respectively, while language differences continue to be asserted by Bosnian Serbs and Bosnian Croats, supporting a decentralised state against developments towards a more centralised state. Ironically, given the links conflict management models make between security and cultural and linguistic recognition, reports observe: 'The only schools that appear to surmount these intractable problems are elite academies that teach in English' (Popović, 2006). Significantly, we have here schools whose elite constituencies identify themselves and their interests more with the international community, rather than their local ethnic community.

Beyond the formal affirmation of linguistic and cultural identities, international conflict management efforts reveal tensions between respect for cultural recognition and cultural autonomy. For international cultural recognition has confronted the problem that the various post-war cultural identities and political allegiances are incompatible with each other.

Governance of political and cultural narratives

Repeatedly, international officials have stressed that education reforms will respect the culture of each ethnic group, seeking 'an agreement on revisions of curriculums, but in such a manner that would preserve the identity of all children in BiH [Bosnian and Herzegovina], regardless of where they live' (Lenart *et al.*, 1999). Repeatedly, international reports give education an important role in 'cultural identity preservation' and 'instilling pride in one's culture, history and heritage' (Perry, 2003, p. 15). Yet discussions over textbook reform show how international officials cannot reconcile conflicting cultural identities without circumscribing them and the region's culture, history and heritage. The review of Bosnian Serb literature textbooks is particularly interesting, because of involving the core South Slav cultural tradition. An international experts' report to UNESCO judged: 'in the people's (oral) literature there are some poems against the Turks and Austrians (not acceptable)' (Lenart *et al.*, 1999, p. 42). As another report explains, 'While the teaching of Serb poems might be viewed as study of legitimate cultural heritage by Bosnian Serbs, it can be seen as an expression of extreme nationalism by Bosniaks' (Perry, 2003, p. 36). International officials have also wanted to strike out passages from Ivo Andrić's (1892–1975) Nobel prize-winning novel *The Bridge Over the Drina* (1959) [1945], chronicling tales over three and a half centuries of Ottoman and Austro-Hungarian rule, which it deems culturally offensive to the Bosniacs and inimical to ethnic reconciliation. Extracts from the novel commonly appeared in school textbooks in the former Yugoslavia.

The proposed censorship of works from the oral tradition and other classical works has tremendous political and cultural significance. The rediscovery of the oral tradition in the nineteenth century and the flourishing of South Slav culture represented the stirrings of national self-determination, celebrated not just in the region, but across Europe. Previously, anti-Turkish or anti-Austrian elements were read in the context of centuries under foreign rule – whether the Ottoman or Austro-Hungarian empires – and are comparable to anti-British themes in Irish literature, or anti-European themes in anti-colonial or post-colonial literature such as Césaire's poetry. Indeed, were international officials to censor school books on the grounds of negative portrayals of Bosnian Muslims, Ottoman officials or Islamic clerics, this would affect the works of Meša Selimović (1910–1982), a key twentieth-century novelist of Bosnian Muslim ethnicity. His compelling novel *Death and the Dervish* (1996) [1966] explores totalitarian political oppression through a Kafkaesque treatment of Bosnia under Ottoman rule. Likewise, Croatia's most famous twentieth-century author Miroslav Krleža (1910–1982) could fall foul of censorship for negative portrayals of Austro-Hungarian officials, Catholic priests and fellow Croats and Yugoslavs. Similar observations can be made of key Serbian literature. Again, later works like those of Slobadan Selenić, attempting to explore national prejudices and political oppression through subversive literary devices such as unreliable narrators, have fallen foul of reductive literal readings by international experts who have condemned them as nationalist (Pupavac, 2006). Yet such works seek to develop more critical reading. Selenić was earlier known for challenging official censorship in one of the first fictional works to portray suffering in Yugoslav labour camps. Consequently, were works to be excised for their negative portrayals, this would excise some of region's most renowned historical works, ironically potentially affecting most the cultural expression of individuals within each group, since the most damning portrayals commonly come from within a cultural tradition.

At issue in the textbook reforms is not a question of replacing one verse or extract with another – quiet revisions were already contemplated by Bosnian Serbian officials, for example – but the symbolic and actual loss of self-determination. The international community's attempts to expunge negative portrayals of the Ottoman and Austro-Hungarian empires from Bosnian Serb textbooks represent a ridiculous sanitisation of history. Moreover, the unintended but predictable consequence of such international interventions is constantly to recreate nationalist grievances, fuelling ongoing ethnic insecurity and tensions, and discouraging responsibility for rebuilding cordial inter-ethnic relations. But it appears that some readers are more equal than others when it comes to determining what they may read; while the OHR was seeking to censor certain passages from Andrić's *The Bridge Over The Drina*, the then High Representative Wolfgang Petrisch, presiding over the textbook revisions, praised the novel in his diary (OHR, 1999b, 14 November).

The OHR, the OSCE and the European Commission have all repeatedly attempted to address the problem of separate education over the last decade (European Commission, 2009; OSCE, 2007a; 2007b). But efforts to de-ethnicise education go against the logic of internationally drafted constitutional arrangements institutionalising of ethnicity. Efforts to support refugee return and re-integrate schools in the Federation ossified into the phenomenon of 'two schools under one roof', that is, schools where Bosniac and Bosnian Croatian pupils each follow their own ethnic curriculum. There was ethnic re-integration of schools under the special international administration of Bihać, which was achieved through international non-democratic imposition. But, even in Bihać schools, there was not complete re-integration across the district. So, rather than Bihać setting the norm, it remained an exception. The Bosnian courts ruled against divided schools in 2012 after much external pressure, illustrating the continuing top-down governance of Bosnia to forge its unity.

Ironically, Bosnian school textbooks revised under the direction of international officials have referred to the language as 'naš jezik' ('our language') (Gazibara and Zekić, 2002). In other words, internationally directed education policies seek to avoid identifying language, that is, language rights as identity claims, and make the language anonymous in their drive to depoliticise the language question and work towards the re-integration of schooling. The easing of the security situation and the threat of a return to war has eased some of the language politics in Bosnia and the other successor states. There is a ritualistic dimension to assertions of language differences today. However, linguistic identity claims remain significant as normative claims to security and resource recognition in the Bosnian state. Meanwhile, young people may illicitly smoke together across the ethnic divisions (Hromadžić, 2009). However international anti-smoking campaigns, along with stranger danger and child abuse campaigns, unintentionally complicate building trust and forging informal relations across ethnic divisions.

Impatience with the slow, obstructed reform processes has led some international education reformers to criticise the international community for not intervening enough, and not fully utilising governance powers against obstacles to reforms (Magill, 2010, pp. 44–7). Conversely, some voices have raised questions over trying to impose a unified curriculum against the divided political understandings of the three ethnic constituencies. The internationally led education reforms and other projects like the International Criminal Court for Former Yugoslavia (ICTY) have effectively been attempting to 'impose a single perspective or a single truth' (Fischer, 2006, p. 321) against different, contested interpretations of the history, the present and the future. Licensing certain narratives and censoring others does not guarantee reception among hearers, because 'different experiences lead to different perspectives' (Fischer, 2006, p. 321). Moreover, passive resistance to internationally led official narratives has become reinforced through the recurring attempts to impose reforms against unwilling ethnic constituencies.

Hate speech legislation, which has replaced the earlier criminal libel and defamation laws, is becoming routinely invoked in public life to address continuing divisions and failures to establish political consensus around international arrangements. In July 2011 Bosnian Serb leader Milorad Dodik was accused of continuing to deny genocide in Srebrenica, and violating both Bosnian law on genocide denial and the European Parliament's 2009 declaration of 11 July as Srebrenica Genocide Remembrance Day. The ICTY's remit was to promote peace and reconciliation through legal truth making processes establishing definitive historical narratives. However, political perceptions of the trials follow ethnic divisions, and as such war crimes trials resemble the continuation of war by other means. Such political perceptions and divisions tend to be reinforced by international, regional or national laws mandating trial judgements as un-contestable historical truths and criminalising denial. Legalising specific interpretations of the war in divided societies tends to alienate, rather than reconcile, those with different interpretations, and thereby reinforce the societal security dilemmas. Official legal historical narratives do not address how people bring accessory ideas and experiences which influence how they interpret the trials and the historical events. Protecting beliefs or ideas as beyond contention, as Mill outlines, involves implicit claims to infallibility, but officially sanctioned opinions become a barrier to developing more thorough understanding of events where they close themselves to future contestation and thereby become held 'in a manner of a prejudice' (Mill, 1985, [1859], p. 116). So while human rights advocacy is opposed to forced language and cultural assimilation and increasingly opposes assimilation per se, it nevertheless ironically supports assimilation to official history narratives enforced through legal sanctions. Disturbingly, the internationally sanctioned narratives conveniently deter certain uncomfortable debates over the role, decisions and interests of external actors (Hayden, 2011). Not least, the disastrous western-backed international safe area policies, which forced refugees to remain in danger like Srebrenica, but contained refugee flows to western countries, have been marginalised in the internationally sanctioned narratives and war crimes prosecutions.

International refugee governance denying people free movement only contributed to deaths. Invocation of hate speech legislation goes beyond managing reception of war crimes judgements and issues of inter-ethnic relations. In May 2011, the head of the Bosnia's Islamic Community, Mufti Mustafa Cerić, was accused of hate speech for suggesting a 'Sarajevo Summer' against the education minister's decision to remove grades from religious studies, which were seen as inflating the levels achieved, from students' overall year grades. Mufti Cerić had earlier faced hate crime accusations over anti-homosexual statements – as have Catholic and Orthodox clerics in the region. But, rather than overcome prejudice or hostility, these laws are tending to perpetuate divisions through claims and counter-claims, rallying their respective audiences – hostile communication or non-communication, instead of real engagement with differences. Again, using hate laws to outlaw expression of prejudices such as anti-homosexual speech does not address how anti-homosexuality is both linked to conservative cultural identities, legitimised under international culturalism, and has also become a site to express resentment against the international community and the new younger English-speaking internationally orientated elite in Bosnia and neighbouring states. Indeed, international initiatives in this area tend to reinforce these associations and resentments, creating a dynamic of provocation and intervention as in other areas, complicating the position of local sexual minorities.

The rituals around linguistic and hate speech claims, counter-claims and interventions embody the sense of stasis under global governance, and the demise of national or international politics aspiring to transcend the past. International officials have repeatedly complained of a culture of dependency in Bosnia. But dependency is the logic of the extensive international cultural management. Along with stronger international intervention, some education reform advocacy has suggested giving children's voices and children's rights more of a role in the education reform process. In this vein, a UNESCO/ International Bureau of Education (IBE) report proposes:

> Given that the hopes, fears, and viewpoints of children and young people are likely to be different from those of adults, even parents/guardians, it is important to engage them directly and not rely exclusively on the views of older generations. (Magill, 2010, p. 49)

There is a view among international reformers that children's interests are different from those of their parents and community, and are not being properly represented by them. While international proposals to elevate the participation of children in decision-making processes may sound progressive, they have deeply undemocratic implications, in which the international community effectively legitimises itself through children's voices against the local community. A neo-colonial relationship is assumed in which the international community makes itself the saviour and representative of children against their own adult populations (Burman, 1994; Lewis, 1998). There is remarkably little self-consciousness among swathes of interveners of how their paternalistic assumptions towards Bosnian society echo Kipling, despite the growing critical studies of international governance of Bosnia (Bliesemann de Guevara, 2009, 2010; Chandler, 1999; Knaus and Martin, 2003).

Rule by international officials is reminiscent of a return to the days of the consuls, about which Andrić wrote so evocatively. Bosnians might recall Andrić's ironic observations on life under foreign determination, 'There'll be a flag flying!' people whispered and their eyes flashed defiantly as though it would be their very own flag' (Andrić, 1992, [1945], p. 11). Reading the well-meaning international reports and their frustration with the different ethnic groups feels rather like reading British colonial education reports and their frustrations with colonial subjects. Yet past foreign rulers in certain respects had more *laissez-faire* attitudes towards the beliefs of their subjects. Meanwhile, global governance of Bosnia has ironically expanded the role of English in Bosnian public life, and exacerbated the distance of the new internationally sponsored elites from non-English-speaking sections of the population.

Beyond language rights divisions?

The history of the former Yugoslavia shows how an ethnic rights approach may foster ethnic divisions. It is, therefore, ironic that the international human rights framework requires states to promote ethnicised rights as part of international security strategies and theories of justice. Tensions exist between international multicultural ideals and international de-legitimisation of socialist Yugoslavia's multicultural system. Minority rights advocacy follows the logic of ethnicised politics in representing minority ethnic interests against more powerful ethnic groups, but does not transcend its paradigm. Strategies of linguistic–cultural governance fix people into categories of difference, while undermining their political agency and potential to develop a politics beyond their divisions. These strategies tend to assume that identity-based groups can be reconciled through recognition. However, identity inevitably risks becoming divisive in circumstances of aborted modernisation, because identity is salient as a special claim for access to resources not universally available. The promotion of the third generation of rights represents a retreat from progressive politics to an ossifying bureaucratic administration of difference. Even as the international community demands inclusion within Bosnia, a process of international moral re-division between states goes apace, creating new international exclusions. Further tensions exist between international non-violent conflict resolution ideals and western humanitarian wars and the war on terror – tensions not lost on the Bosnian population or elsewhere.

International language rights advocacy has not re-assessed its politics of recognition in light of the former Yugoslavia or the governance of Bosnia. Language rights thinking romanticises difference and the social reproduction of difference. Ratification of a maximalist position for minorities endorses difference over commonality, and non-communication over communication. Ratification of linguistic identity rights risks colliding with fundamental rights, and colluding with exclusionary projects, while failing to address the common problems faced by marginalised groups globally.

While the ongoing governance of Bosnia is antithetical to real political and civil freedoms, further developments in linguistic human rights advocacy reinforce policy strategies institutionalising difference. Ecolinguistics advocacy, which equates linguistic diversity and biodiversity, implies maintaining ethnic difference and expanding external therapeutic governance of communities, with consequences for civil and political freedoms, as discussed in the next chapter.

9
Ecolinguistics and Post-Humanist Advocacy

Language death and ecolinguistics

Boa Senior died in January 2010 (Lawson, 2010). She was the last native speaker of Bo, a language of India's Andaman Islands, with ancient roots (ibid.). Viktors Bertholds died in February 2009 (Laakso, 2009). He was the last native speaker of the Livonian language. William Rozario died in August 2009 (Pradeep, 2009). He was the last speaker of Cochin Indo-Portuguese Creole. Marie Smith Jones died in 2008 (BBC, 2008a). She was the last native speaker of the Eyak language of Alaska. The obituaries narrate the loneliness of these speakers, and how their deaths announce the deaths of more world languages. Alarmed advocates report how one language is dying every two weeks, and that the disappearance of languages is accelerating (Pradeep, 2009).

The regularly updated edition of *Ethnologue* gives the figure of '6,909 known living languages' in its latest edition (Lewis, 2009). The estimated numbers of living or endangered languages diverge, largely because of classification differences over languages or dialects (Crystal, 2002, pp. 2–23). Irrespective of any disagreements over figures, advocates agree that the majority of the world's languages are endangered. *Ethnologue* classifies 473 languages as nearly extinct: forty-six in Africa, 182 in the Americas, eighty-four in The Americas, eight in Asia, nine in Europe and 152 in the Pacific (Lewis, 2009). Beginning with Cameroon, *Ethnologue* records the Baldemu language as having four remaining speakers, Bikya one, Bishuo one, Bung three, Busuu eight (ibid.). But so minuscule are the numbers of remaining speakers that they barely constitute living languages. For the last speakers are commonly reported as speaking other languages in daily communication. Narratives of language loss speak to human mortality, as captured in Yevtushenko's poem *People*:, 'In any man who dies there dies with him/ His first snow and kiss and fight/ It goes with him' (Yevtushenko, 1961). But key ecolinguistic strands appear driven by scepticism towards humanity as a species, rather than anguish towards human mortality and the tragic human condition.

Ecolinguistics joins environmental concerns with language identity rights and treats linguistic diversity as analogous to biodiversity. Ecolinguistic thinking has antecedents in European Romanticism and linguistic anthropology, but important distinctions exist between their ideas, particularly their view of humanity. The immediate origins of ecolinguistics may be traced to the linguist Einar Haugen's 1971 'Ecology of Language' paper (Haugen, 2001, [1971]). Ecolinguistics grew in the 1970s and 1980s, inspired by environmentalism and sustainable development. Just as environmentalism is concerned with loss of biodiversity, so ecolinguistics is concerned with loss of linguistic diversity.

Well-known socio-linguists, such as Joshua Fishman, author of the classic work *Language and Nationalism* (1973), and David Crystal, author of popular socio-linguistic texts, have taken up green linguistics. Literature on threatened languages is burgeoning, encompassing both academic and popular writing: Mark Abley's *Spoken Here: Travels Among Threatened Languages*, David Crystal's *Language Death*, Andrew Dalby's *Language in Danger: How Language Loss Threatens Our Future*, Joshua Fishman's *Can Threatened Languages Be Saved?*, David Harmon's *In Light of Our Differences: How Diversity in Nature and Culture Make Us Human*, Leanne Hinton and Ken Hale's *The Green Book of Language Revitalisation in Practice*, Luisa Maffi's *On Biocultural Diversity: Linking Language, Knowledge and Environment*, Peter Mühlhäusler's *Linguistic Ecology: Language Change and Linguistic Imperialism in the Pacific Region*, Daniel Nettle and Suzanne Romaine's *Vanishing Voices: The Extinction of the World's Languages*, to name just a few works. Publication of introductory texts such as *The Ecolinguistics Reader* (Fill and Mühlhäusler, 2001) reflects the greening of language debates. Not all these writers would explicitly identify themselves as 'ecolinguists', or subscribe to all ecolinguistic theories or policies, but ecolinguistic thinking captures certain currents in language rights advocacy.

Ecolinguistics underpins a number of language advocacy organisations, notably Terralingua: Partnerships for Linguistic and Biological Diversity, set up in 1996. Ecolinguistic concerns are also reflected in international organisations: UNESCO's Endangered Languages Project was set up in 1993, closely followed in 1995 by a series of university-linked organisations: the Endangered Language Fund, with Yale University links; Foundation for Endangered Languages (FEL), with Bristol University links; and the International Clearing House for Endangered Languages, linked to University of Tokyo. Linguistic associations have created sub-groups. In 1992 the Linguistic Society of America set up a Committee on Endangered Languages and their Preservation (CELP), and in 1997 members of the German Society of Linguistics set up the Society for Endangered Languages (GBS). Then there are organisations for specific language groups, such as the

Indigenous Language Institute formerly the Institute for the Preservation of the Original Languages of the Americas, established in 1992. A cluster of these organisations emerged in a five-year period between 1992 and 1997, coinciding with a raft of international minority rights documents, following the end of the Cold War.

These organisations are not simply concerned with documenting endangered languages and preserving them for posterity, but with revitalising and securing living language communities. Consider the mission of the Endangered Language Fund, supporting 'native efforts in maintaining endangered languages', or the Foundation for Endangered Languages, supporting 'the use of endangered languages in all contexts: at home, in education, in the media, and in social, cultural and economic life' (FEL website); while CELP is promoting strategies for maintaining and revitalising 'language varieties in language communities at risk of, or currently experiencing, significant language or dialect loss' (CELP website). Similarly, the Society for Endangered Languages aims 'to further the use, preservation, and documentation of endangered languages and dialects' (GBS website). Their concerns complement minority language organisations. The Indigenous Language Institute (ILI), for example, is 'dedicated to the preservation, revitalization and perpetuation of languages' and wants 'to assist in creating new language speakers at the grassroots level' (ILI website).

Environmental links are most explicitly made by Terralingua, but underpin the values of other organisations. Their advocacy is driven by profound doubts over the character of modern society, overlapping with the linguistic imperialism literature (Mühlhäusler, 1996; Phillipson, 1992). Significant strands of ecolinguistic thinking are hostile to modernity, as I explore below. Technological progress is charged with bringing neither freedom, nor social justice, but alienation (Chawla, 2001, pp. 120–1). Global English is indicted as globalising western materialist, anti-environmental values and homogenising cultures (Mühlhäusler, 1996; WWF and Terralingua, 2000). The Manifesto of the Foundation for Endangered Languages, for example, singles out how:

> the impacts of urbanization, Westernization and global communications grow daily, all serving to diminish the self-sufficiency and self-confidence of small and traditional communities. (Terralingua website)

The links between language rights advocacy, ecology and ecolinguistics are reinforced by the connections between NGOs, key ecolinguists and language rights academics. Consider Terralingua, whose advisors include Fishman, author of *Can Endangered Languages Be Saved?*, Grin, author of *Language Policy Evaluation and the European Charter for Regional or Minority Languages* (2003), Mühlhäusler, co-editor of *The Ecolinguistics Reader* (2001), and Phillipson, author of *Linguistic Imperialism* (1992) and co-editor of *Linguistic*

Human Rights (1994). At the same time, Terralingua has also reached out to nature conservation and environmental NGOs. Fascinatingly, Terralingua has collaborated with the World Wide Fund for Nature (WWF) on a project *Indigenous and Traditional Peoples and the Global 200 Ecoregions*, and a report *Indigenous and Traditional Peoples of the World and Ecoregion Conservation: An Integrated Approach to Conserving the World's Biological and Cultural Diversity* (WWF and Terralingua, 2000). In turn, UNESCO has teamed up with WWF and Terralingua in a later collaborative project and report *Sharing a World of Difference: the earth's linguistic, cultural and biological diversity* (Skutnabb-Kangas *et al.*, 2003).

Ecolinguistic thinking

Fill and Mühlhäusler's *Ecolinguistics Reader* (2001) usefully illustrates the evolving field. Two strands of ecolinguistics have been identified by Fill in his overview of ecolinguistics: ecology as a metaphor and environmentalism (Fill, 2001, pp. 43–53).

The first takes up Haugen's 'ecology of language' and conceptualises the world's languages as an ecosystem. Haugen's ecology of language is influenced by anthropology's adoption of the term 'human ecology' and associated concepts from biology (Haughen, 2001, [1972], p. 58). Haugen's understanding draws on Kroeber's anthropological model dividing humanity into cultures, seeing each culture as having its part in a holistic system (Kroeber, 1917; Malik, 2000b, p. 145).

An 'ecology of language' is not simply descriptive, but, in Haugen's words, 'the banner of a movement for environmental sanitation' (Haugen, 2001, p. 59). The metaphor 'ecology of language' took off in the 1980s (Fill, 2001, pp. 43–4), but the links made between ecology and the 'ecology of language' are becoming more literal, rather than just metaphorical. Biodiversity and linguistic diversity links suggest language as a finite, irreplaceable natural resource. These ideas influence language rights advocacy, most clearly Terralingua.

Language diversity is seen as vital for human physical and cultural survival, and is compared to 'a gene pool' (Pogson, 1998, p. 4 in Crystal, 2000, p. 34). Haugen explicitly acknowledges that his ecology of language revives a biological model (Haughen, 2001, [1972], p. 58). Biological analogies abound in ecolinguistics, including the idea of organic communities, historically associated with conservative and racial thought (Smuts, 1927). Famously, Burke counterposed traditional inherited organic communities established through generational ties to Painite rights of man, or social contract theories (Burke, 1986, [1790]). Models of organic communities have been treated sceptically by social scientists in the past (Williams, 1963, p. 253), but they recur as culturally compelling ideals against modernity. I highlight below tensions between ecolinguistic organic models and advocacy's cosmopolitan law-making and governance.

The second strand of ecolinguistics is concerned with how language relates to the physical environment, and may shape environmental attitudes. Unsurprisingly, German linguistics was at the forefront of developing ecological linguistics, paralleling the influence of German Green politics. But the convergence of linguistic and environmental thinking into ecolinguistics has occurred on both sides of the Atlantic, indicative of broad intellectual currents in western societies. A central theme in ecolinguistics is the idea that modern languages are dysfunctional, and hamper ecological thinking. Ecolinguists want language reform to promote 'ecoliteracy' (Fill, 2001, p. 51). The term ecoliteracy interestingly parallels the term 'emotional literacy'; both share similar views on expert empowerment and governance of communities.

Ecolinguistics is informed by Whorfian understandings of language related to linguistic determinism (language determines/shapes thought) and linguistic cultural relativism (different languages mean people understand the world differently) (Whorf, 1940a; 1940b; 1956; Sapir, 1924; 1929), as discussed in Chapter 4. In Whorf's much-cited words, 'We dissect nature along lines laid down by our native languages' (Whorf, 1940a, p. 231). A strong relationship is emphasised between language, culture and the physical environment in traditional societies, and language having correspondingly strong symbolic cultural power (Sapir, 2001, [1912], p. 22). Languages of primitive communities are regarded as being more heavily influenced by the physical environment, because their economies are based on hunting or agriculture, whereas language relating to plant and animal life in modern societies becomes specialised terminology through the division of labour, and only known to sections of the population.

Whorfian and ecolinguistic approaches stress how language constructs thought and behaviour. Mühlhäusler, as one prominent ecolinguist, emphasises limits to personal linguistic expression as against contrary approaches, stressing linguistic creativity beyond imitative or habitual use (Mühlhäusler, 2001b, p. 31). He believes that language shapes social behaviour, arguing, for example, that modern standard languages' loss of kinship terms has contributed to the breakdown of family ties (Mühlhäusler, 2001a, p. 162). Other linguists, sympathetic to the Sapir–Whorf thesis, see language as reflecting a group's experience of the world and speak of language influencing thinking. Since each language is regarded as expressing a unique world-view, language loss is equated with loss of thought (Nettle and Romaine, 2000).

The Sapir–Whorf thesis suggests that the relationship between environment, language and culture will become looser through history, because, although cultural or environmental changes influence language change, change is not at the same rate. Grammar forms, in particular, tend to be more conservative (Sapir, 2001, [1912], p. 23). Since the links between language and culture become more attenuated in modern societies, so too does language's symbolic power. We do not speak seriously, as translation studies have explored, and may freely swear to gods while being non-believing atheists (Gramsci, 1971, p. 450; Jakobson, 1992, [1959], pp. 146–7; Paz, 1992, [1971]; Salzmann, 1998, p. 47). Widely divergent world views may coexist within one language in modern societies, weakening linguistic determinism.

Yet, if the rapid cultural changes of the modern era, the division of labour, the growth of politics and individualism, have eroded earlier stronger correspondence between language and culture, revival of Whorfian ideas in the 1980s and 1990s needs to be explained. Tellingly, Whorfian ideas revived in an era characterised variously as 'the end of history', 'the end of utopianism', or a post-political age (Jacoby, 1999; Laïdi, 1998). The collapse of competing left and right political projects, the erosion of ideologically distinct world views, and the growth of identity-based politics have encouraged language identity models. If belief in modern linguistics that 'speakers of any language can express whatever they want' is related to wider societal beliefs concerning human progress (Mühlhäusler, 2001b, p. 31), equally revived interest in Whorfian ideas coincides with growing cultural perception of limits. Ecolinguistics views the looser relation between environment, language and culture as problematic, and seeks to rein in human action.

Ecology of language

Ecolinguist thinking regards humans as being 'as much a part of the landscape as plant and animal species', and is critical of modern cosmopolitan societies and languages severing ties to nature (WWF and Terralingua, 2000, p. 7). Ecolinguists draw on geography's distinctions between cosmopolitan societies and societies based around local ecosystems or 'cultures of habitat' (Dasmann, 1964 and Nabhan, 1997 in WWF and Terralingua, 2000, p. 10). 'Ecosystems peoples' are regarded as functional:

> Such societies, living in close contact with the environment, normally consider themselves as part of nature, not separate from it. They rely directly on the local environment for food, medicine, construction materials and other products essential for their subsistence and for their physical and spiritual well-being. (WWF and Terralingua, 2000, p. 10)

Conversely, complex modern cosmopolitan societies characterised by a global culture and high material consumption, 'living beyond the confines of local ecosystems', are regarded as dysfunctional (WWF and Terralingua, 2000, p. 13). Ecolinguistics criticises globalisation, global communications and the evolving global culture for eroding local cultures and ecosystems with their lower consumption levels. Haugen expressly describes his ecology of language as moving away from an industrial model in which language is treated as a tool or instrument of communication (Haughen, 2001, [1972], p. 58). Speed of communication, like technological progress, is not regarded as an inherent virtue, and is considered secondary to cultural preservation (Finke, 2001, p. 88). Ecolinguistics emphasises language as expressing identity, culture and place, rather than language's communicative role. Hence, strategies allowing languages to disappear are condemned as 'linguicide', and by implication should be prosecuted as genocide under international humanitarian law (Skutnabb-Kangas and Dunbar, 2010). Ecolinguistics parallels human rights advocacy for indigenous peoples, treating habitat loss as 'ecocide' (Haveman, 2009).

The ecolinguistic understanding of culture is informed by Boasian anthropological perspectives, seeing differences between humans as cultural, and values as culturally relative against ideas of cultural progression, as discussed in Chapter 4. But, while Boasian anthropology contests hierarchical racial and cultural classifications, it also makes culture itself absolute (Malik, 2008). Boasian anthropology, emphasising habituation over creativity, divides people into different cultures, and proposes the need to relate to different societies via culture. As such, culture becomes a universal category or metatheory, and key to social understanding and social stability. Kroeber's concept of the superorganic sees culture determining individual development and treats cultures as being analogous to biological sub-species with each culture forming part of a holistic system (Benedict, 1961, [1934]; Kroeber, 1917; Malik, 2000b, p. 145). Cultural diversity is to be cultivated as a bulwark against mass society (Boas, 1962, [1928], pp. 199–200), while cultural tolerance and intercultural understanding are to be promoted internationally towards, 'a world made safe for difference' (Benedict, 1946, p. 14). These ideas inform UNESCO's vision of international peace and cultural strategies (Malik, 2000b, pp. 115–47).

Maintaining a world of difference

The joint UNESCO, WWF and Terralingua publication, entitled *Sharing a World of Difference: the earth's linguistic, cultural and biological diversity* (2003), follows this anthropological cultural understanding, and alludes to Benedict's earlier phrase. The report treats culture as a universal category to understand the world:

> We think of ourselves as speakers of certain languages and we subscribe to certain religions, customs, values and worldviews which we take as self-evident. It is also on the basis of these same different distinctions that societies have handled their relationships with other societies. Those who

> speak the same language and have the same beliefs are felt to be parts of an 'us'; those who speak other languages and have different customs and beliefs, are seen as 'others'. (Skutnabb-Kangas *et al.*, 2003, p. 11)

The report suggests that language, culture, beliefs and world views are synonymous. Cultural linguistic identity is treated as fundamental: we relate to ourselves, the world and other people through specific cultural linguistic identities:

> Each language reflects a unique world-view and culture complex, mirroring the manner in which a speech community has resolved its problems in dealing with the world, and has formulated its thinking, its system of philosophy and understanding of the world around it. (Skutnabb-Kangas *et al.*, 2003, p. 28)

Ecolinguistic thinking echoes Lévi-Strauss' concern over progress ironing out cultural diversity (Lévi-Strauss, 1956, pp. 159–61). Lévi-Strauss wanted to maintain a pool of cultures for human survival, and each culture's 'individual way of solving problems' (Lévi-Strauss, 1956, p. 158; Malik, 1996, pp. 168–9; 2000b, pp. 141–5). The statement above, strikingly, uses the singular: one language, one world-view, one philosophy, one culture complex. Indeed, the report's formulation implicitly suggests that everybody or every culture should have a religious world-view. Furthermore, the vision of communities' having 'resolved' their 'problems in dealing with the world' suggests the end of politics, historical subjectivities, and political speech acts (Arendt, 1998, [1958])! Politicide as opposed to linguicide! Lévi-Strauss, nevertheless, recognised problems of cultural ossification in the maintenance of cultural traditions (Lévi-Strauss, 1956, pp. 159–60), but the problem is neglected in ecolinguistics.

While ecolinguists warn against homogenisation and celebrate diversity, their statements often suggest homogeneity of values and speech within a language community. Ecolinguistics envisages human settlements as small-scale, relatively isolated, traditional non-industrial communities, echoing anti-modernisation development philosophies like Schumacher's *Small is Beautiful* (1993) [1973]. Complex modern industrial societies, as well as the pre-modern expansive Chinese, Egyptian, Greek, Persian, Roman or medieval worlds, contradict its anthropological or ecological ideal. Accordingly, the WWF and Terralingua report *Indigenous and Traditional Peoples of the World and Ecoregion Conservation* states:

> It is generally agreed that small-scale societies with a history of continued and unchallenged occupation of given territories will, over time, tend to develop and maintain detailed and accurate knowledge about their ecological niches, as well as about sustainable ways of extracting

> and managing natural resources. Historically, where the balance between humans and the environment has not been sustained, the tendency has been for complex civilizations to arise, living beyond the confines of local ecosystems. (WWF and Terralingua, 2000, p. 6)

Terralingua and WWF's joint project *Indigenous and Traditional Peoples and the Global 200 Ecoregions* seeks to map language communities, and link areas of language diversity with areas of biodiversity. The project invites us to become engaged with language loss as part of environmental awareness. In the words of Terralingua, 'the global patterns of distribution of biodiversity coincide significantly with the patterns of distribution of linguistic diversity (as representative of cultural diversity as a whole)' (Terralingua website).

Ecolinguistic treatment of languages as given identities, and linguistic diversity as analogous to biodiversity, naturalises divisions between people and suggests different language groups as sub-species, just as Kroeber did earlier (Kroeber, 1917; Malik, 2000b, p. 145). Ecolinguistic mapping projects follow broader developments, shifting from mapping states to mapping peoples. The trends have been analysed as moves from geopolitics, or an international system based around national sovereignty, to what has been termed biopolitics, governance of peoples analogous to species (Duffield, 2007). Post-war international mapping emphasised sovereign borders and conscious (human) political borders, and human mastery of nature. Conversely, the new global ethical mapping involves ideas re-naturalising humanity and borders (Standish, 2009), as embodied in Terralingua and WWF's joint ecolinguistic mapping project.

Ecolinguistics proposes a quasi-biological model of adaptation to the environment, in which different cultures represent different adaptations. So preserving cultures becomes vital to ensuring that humanity has as many survival solutions as possible. The joint 2003 publication argues that 'The range of cross fertilisation becomes less as languages and cultures die and the testimony of human intellectual achievement is lessened' (Skutnabb-Kangas *et al.*, 2003, p. 10). Linguistic philosophers and anthropologists have long noted how so-called primitive languages may have more complex grammatical forms than modern languages, but not invariably (Boas, 1963, [1911]; 1965, [1911]; Humboldt, 1999, [1841]). Ecolinguistics associates losing indigenous languages with losing grammatical complexity, and therefore with losing complexity of thought. As such, ecolinguistics equates the range of human thought with the number of language forms in existence, implying that each language only permits a finite range of thoughts. Linguistic diversity, it is argued, 'offers the highest possible variety of solutions to the challenges of survival' (Skutnabb-Kangas *et al.*, 2003, p. 28). But, while ecolinguistics follows Lévi-Strauss (1956) in suggesting that humanity is only able to adapt existing or past solutions, as opposed to imagining new and better solutions or ways of organising human societies, it is more focused on the planet's survival than his earlier preoccupation with human survival. As such, it parallels the international policy thinking shifting from national and human security to the security of the biosphere, which is to be protected from human activity (Chandler, 2012; Reid, 2012).

Ecolinguistics and environmentalism

Ecolinguistic scepticism towards modernity echoes long-standing fears over mass society, expressed by both radical and conservative thinking, from the eighteenth-century counter-revolutionary writings, through Romanticism, through Le Bon's *The Crowd* (1995) [1895], Ortega y Gasset's *The Revolt of the Masses* (1961) [1930] and William Whyte's *Organisational Man* (1956), to Herbert Marcuse's *One Dimensional Man* (1964). They follow the recurring Romantic critiques which have accompanied modernity (Sayre and Löwy, 1984), discussed in earlier chapters. Indigenous languages are viewed as a defence against communities becoming like modern industrial countries, with mass uniform conglomerations (Schultz, 2001, p. 110). In the journalist Mark Abley's words, 'if a traditional language remained strong in a community, its people would be better equipped to resist the onslaughts of modernity' (Abley, 2003, p. 20). Assimilation of indigenous communities into modern societies is to be resisted, because of 'the health of the world's ecosystems and the goals of nature conservation' (Terralingua website). Ecolinguistics favours indigenous understanding against modern scientific knowledge, and seeks its integration into policy-making, science and education against the problems caused by humanity in industrial societies (Crystal, 2000, p. 47; WWF and Terralingua, 2000, pp. 6–8, p. 30, p. 58; Skutnabb-Kangas *et al.*, 2003, pp. 37–43). Terralingua argues that:

> Traditional ecological knowledge and practices often make indigenous peoples, minorities, and local communities highly skilled and respectful stewards of the ecosystems in greatest need of protection. (Terralingua website)

But, while ecolinguists want traditional ecological knowledge to be integrated into policy, they do not want indigenous language communities to be assimilated into mainstream culture (Skutnabb-Kangas *et al.*, 2003, p. 37). Consequently, tensions exist between minority language advocacy, seeking to increase the scientific and technical terminology of minority languages, and ecolinguistic advocacy, fearing that to modernise indigenous languages would undermine their potential to act as a refuge against modernity. Recent environmentalism has become more receptive to science, and now commonly invokes science in an expert-led form of politics. However, the new environmental enthusiasm for science and environmental technological innovation has been less evident in ecolinguistics.

A core ecolinguistic belief, informed by the Sapir–Whorf thesis, is that a 'close relationship' exists 'between language philosophy (or a world-view) and our handling of the natural environment' (Chawla, 2001, p. 115). Ecolinguists argue that a language's character fosters people's development approach, and whether or not they are environmentalist (Mühlhäusler, 2001b, p. 34). Indigenous languages as well as indigenous cultures are treated as intrinsically more ecologically aware. Conversely, modern languages are criticised as anti-environmental. Global English, in particular, is accused of spreading anti-environmental 'language habits' (Chawla, 2001, p. 121). Criticisms relate to lexical deficiencies and grammatical structures (Halliday, 2001). Ecolinguists criticise modern languages as languages of technology, and inadequate to express environmental ideas (Chawla, 2001, p. 121). Modern languages are accused of lacking vocabulary embodying environmental concerns, for example, a word for 'positive weeds' or 'a term for someone who does not recycle their bottles, papers, etc' (Mühlhäusler, 2001b, p. 34). European languages, such as English, are indicted for treating coal, water, oil, soil and air as unquantified in nature, and implicitly infinite (Halliday, 2001, p. 194), thereby encouraging their language communities to squander natural resources. The dearth of normative prefixes or suffixes in modern European languages, compared with various indigenous languages, is deplored by ecolinguists, since they could be used to embed greater environmental awareness (Mühlhäusler, 2001b, pp. 35–6). Ecolinguists have criticised how modern languages violate natural cyclical time, and encourage distorted development thinking out of harmony with the earth's natural rhythms. Namely, the complex tense schemes of standard modern languages are charged with 'fragmenting existence'. Conversely, indigenous languages with simple two-tense time schemes of earlier/later are commended for encouraging holistic thinking in tune with natural cycles (Chawla, 2001, p. 115–17).

Ecolinguists suggest grammar reforms to promote ecoliteracy. But ecolinguistic proposals to embed ecologism in our grammar repeat the fallacy of earlier philosophers, who wanted to fix meaning in language. Consider how the word 'revolution' was radically transformed during the turbulent political events in eighteenth-century France, from its original cyclical temporal meaning to the contrary meaning of radical historical rupture. Words change their meanings through people's experiences. As one ecolinguist acknowledges, 'We cannot transform language; it is people's acts of meaning that do that' (Halliday, 2001, p. 199). Words may gain different connotations; so too can parts of words, including prefixes. While ecolinguistics stresses differences between people, ecolinguistic grammar reforms presume uniform reception and culture within language groups, and no friction between communication and reception. Again, proposals to fix meaning in advance implicitly treat the public as automata, and share with strands of contemporary human rights advocacy a mistrust of political debate, which does not guarantee its norms being realised. Both strands of ecolinguistics tend to question people's capacity to think critically and engage in politics.

Indicatively, one ecolinguist refers to 'imprecision and misinterpretation' in language, where he is actually referring to language allowing the possibility of drawing different conclusions from environmental norms (Mühlhäusler, 2001b, p. 36). Another is prepared to subordinate truth to the sponsorship of ecological values, arguing, 'if our purpose is the long-term survival of the planet then truth will be whatever promotes that survival, and the metaphorical models will be selected accordingly' (Goatly, 2001, p. 222). The 'complex question of communication in highly industrialized societies' is highlighted as a problem (Mühlhäusler, 2001b, p. 40), against ecolinguistic portraits of modern societies as impoverished, undifferentiated, mass monocultures. Thus, while ecolinguists criticise modern society's uniformity, some apparently see the public sphere in modern society as too complex and not uniform enough! Implicitly, some ecolinguists would prefer to return to simpler forms of authority, and avoid the problems of negotiating in diverse, complex modern societies with contested political interests.

Ecolinguistics are attracted to holism, a philosophy which emphasises natural processes and organic relations and questions human uniqueness and its transcendence of nature (Chawla, 2001; Finke, 2001; Halliday, 2001). Ecolinguistics, it is argued, should deconstruct anthropocentric thinking in all its forms, 'including Marxist Humanism' (Fill, 2001, p. 49; also Goatly, 2001, p. 221). In the words of one ecolinguist, 'our image of the world has to become one in which processes predominate and human Actors disappear' (Goatly, 2001, p. 219). Ecolinguistics regards nature as creative, but humans as polluters, parasites, destroyers, or mere converters, not creators or producers (Finke, 2001, p. 87; Goatly, 2001, [1996], p. 218; Halliday, 2001, [1990]).

Ecolinguistic refutation of human creativity contrasts with past political movements of modern industrial society, which saw workers as producers, and capitalism as parasitical on workers' labour, as a basis for claims to ownership of the means of production and its profits. Instead, ecolinguistics questions humans as producers, and human claims in general. The ecolinguistic concept of alienation is closer to the old philosophical idea of alienation from God and nature, rather than a political economy understanding (Meszaros, 1970). So, although the ecolinguist Halliday has been praised for linking 'growthism, classism and speciesism' (Fill, 2001, p. 43), class is essentially an absent concern, or has been re-interpreted in ecological terms to have distinct anti-humanist social and political implications, reining in human agency and human needs against those of the planet. Human concerns are considered rather trivial in comparison to those of the planet (Chawla, 2001, p. 117). Indeed, the significance of human language, culture and art becomes questioned in their refutation of human uniqueness and creativity. (For discussion of the distinctiveness of human language, see Tallis, 2011, pp. 230–6).

Ecolinguistics' revulsion against contemporary society, and its turn to nature, fits with a recognisable classical philosophical tradition, seeking spiritual renewal for a tired civilisation. So what is distinct about the ecolinguistic critique, and its linguistic primordialism?

Ecolinguistics and linguistic primordialism

Ecolinguistic advocacy for indigenous peoples, and yearning for purer natural languages, echoes recurring leitmotifs of primitive man as an indictment against modern man, whether Rousseau's noble savages or Tolstoy's peasant–legislators (Rousseau, 1968, [1762], p. 127, p. 149; 1984, [1755], p. 144). Ecolinguistic primordialism firmly embodies an anti-modernity position. The cause of indigenous language rights rebukes modern civilisation and modern standard languages.

The idea of humanity's linguistic fall from grace is an abiding theme in linguistic primordialism. Le Guin's *Earthsea* quartet (1993) recreates the myth of an original world language, and links knowing the 'true names' of things with true meaning. Its underlying plot concerns how harmony may be restored to earth when a lost rune is understood. But language's power is also portrayed as a dangerous ambivalent force for humanity. Past western language origin myths tend to portray humanity's fall from divine grace and loss of divine language, whereas modern interpretations propose humanity's fall in humanity's very separation from nature, and language's role in separating humanity from nature. Older religious interpretations celebrated humanity's elevation from nature through sharing (divine) language, and allowed for humanity's redemption, as do the optimistic Romantic accounts of humanity's re-unification with nature at a higher moral level. Conversely, today's interpretations portray mute nature as ethical, and speaking humanity as morally degenerate. Thus, modern interpretations reverse the ethical relationship.

The novelist William Golding's story *The Inheritors* (1961) is a parable of humanity's corruption through its development of language and separation from nature. Golding's blunt message is that human language ushers in hatred, violence and destruction. Symbolically, the novel presents the more primitive, sensual Neanderthal tribe, with its simple, almost monosyllabic language, as ethically superior to the victorious Homo Sapiens tribe, who possess developed language. Golding's Neanderthals epitomise today's ethical ideal as gentle, affective, instinctual, non-violent, non-egotistical, non-materialist, feminised, childlike creatures. They are at one with each other and with nature. They do not distinguish themselves from animals, their word 'people' encompassing other living creatures. They achieve perfect communion beyond language through a deep (telepathic) awareness. Conversely, the new individuated linguistically developed people are brutal, corrupt, cruel, violent, selfish, capricious figures, alienated from nature and from each other. Hatred has displaced empathy with human's separation from nature. Human speech is used to command, human tools to kill. Thus, Golding associates the development of human language, culture and individuation with violence and injustice. The very awakening of human consciousness is a fall from grace, but without the redemption given in works like Milton's *Paradise Lost*.

Golding's themes anticipate ecolinguistic themes and the rise of what has been designated 'post-human' global ethics, that is, an ethics that fundamentally questions humans as moral actors. Ecolinguistics does not follow romantic belief in human language, and the 'wondrous power of words' (Wordsworth, *The Prelude*, 1995, [1850], Book VII, line 21, p. 256). The Romantic movement fiercely asserted the individual, whether the individual genius against the mediocrity of conventional society or the uniqueness of the individual soul, particularly the artistic soul, against mass industrial society. Romanticism expressed 'a belief in human potential taken beyond ordinary limits' (Wordsworth and Wordsworth, 2003, p. xxiii), as discussed in earlier chapters. Conversely, key ecolinguistic advocates want to counter egotism, minimise the human footprint, and re-merge humanity into nature. Romanticism turned away from Enlightenment universalism for the uniqueness of the individual, or the ethnic nation, but ecolinguistics questions human uniqueness and human moral agency, and invokes nature against humanity. Romantic writers consciously invoked nature as a pathetic fallacy to reinforce their ideal of human essence, but acknowledged nature's cruelties (Keats, 1970, [1818], pp. 381–3). However, the ecolinguistic ideal of nature appears to return to pre-Freudian understandings in its non-transcendent return to nature, and celebration of the earth and natural intuitive wisdom. As such, ecolinguistics represents a form of Romanticism without the Romantic human subject, heart or soul. Claims to human uniqueness are condemned as species-ism. Ultimately, ecolinguistic relativism ends up denying the significance of human language, against the idea of *linguistic human* rights and each language's uniqueness.

Tensions, therefore, exist between ecolinguistic holistic non-human-centred ethics and the political claims of ethnic groups, whose hopes are closer to the older Romantic aspirations of national political determination. Under ecolinguistic ethics, humanity appears ethical insofar as its existence is dictated by nature. This reverses earlier humanist ethics founded in humanity being both of nature and beyond nature (Tallis, 1999). In Fanon's words, 'I am a part of Being to the degree that I go beyond it' (Fanon, 2008, [1952], p. 179). Fanon is emphatic about there being 'no question of a return to Nature' (Fanon, 1967, [1961], p. 253). Logically, an ecolinguistic rights programme implies the rights of nature over humanity: human rights interpreted literally as *natural* rights, ensuring human ties to natural organic communities. Ecolinguistics, therefore, contrasts with the humanism which historically inspired human rights and emancipatory politics, including anti-colonialism, which sought to overcome the failures of European humanism. In this vein Césaire contests that humans 'parasite the world' and seeks a new humanist politics where 'man's work has only begun' to transcend a natural order (Césaire, 1995, p. 125).

Some problems in ecology of language

The two core strands in ecolinguistics, namely the ecology of language and ecological strands, have been highlighted above. Ecolinguistic texts often encompass ideas from both. However, they are at variance with each other in important respects, and there are also tensions within each strand. The ecological strand challenges claims to human uniqueness, and stresses continuities with nature, downplaying the significance of human culture versus nature, and emphasising interdependence between species. Symbolically, ecolinguistic writing often refers to humanity as a species. Classifications that distinguish humans from non-humans are questioned (for example, Chawla, 2001, p. 117). Yet ecological refutation of human uniqueness undermines the ecology of language's insistence on the uniqueness of each language and culture, and its demands for cultural classification through the promotion of identity rights, that is, rights of classified difference.

Simultaneously, classifying ethnolinguistic identities as if they were sub-species resurrects notions akin to biological difference. Ecolinguists acknowledge linguistic and ethnic categories as fluid concepts, but their repeated use of biological analogies of 'linguistic and cultural gene flow' naturalise linguistic and ethnic identities (WWF and Terralingua, 2000, p. 21). Treating people and language as an organism, and language loss as pathological, echoes European colonial or linguistic racial arguments against the 'deracinated native' (Malik, 2000b, 2008). Ecolinguists understand themselves as radical thinkers and are uncomfortable with these parallels (Fill, 2001, p. 45). Ecolinguistic metaphors of pollution repeat old chauvinist arguments over language purity and decay, and would raise political alarm bells if espoused in relation to standard European language speakers. So, while language rights advocates are ready to debunk purist pedantry over language change or dialects in modern European languages, they may accept it in relation to minority languages, as Crystal has criticised (Crystal, 2000, p. 23, pp. 139–41).

Ecolinguistic inclinations towards linguistic determinism, equating language loss with loss of social alternatives (WWF and Terralingua, 2000, pp. 14–15), end up denying human individuality and capacity for imagination and representing alternative ways of being (Arendt, 1998, [1958], pp. 176–9, pp. 246–7). Ecolinguistics risks mummifying language and identity, instead of treating them as active and fluid (Mackey, 2001, [1980], p. 67). Moreover, it is one thing to document languages, and quite another to preserve communities with specific language and cultural forms. Ecolinguistics assumes that people identify themselves as indigenous communities, overlooking their role in the construction of people as indigenous communities and how identity-based claim-making is legitimised in contemporary western policy-making. Communities' indifference may be expressed in their expectations that professionals will address language maintenance (Crystal, 2000, pp. 100–2).

Some social isolation from mainstream society appears to help preserve endangered languages. Consider the following situation where:

> the language has survived in geographical areas which are relatively isolated, the communities there being more likely to be economically self-sufficient and to have had little contact with outside groups (and thus few marriages to outsiders). In such places, the headman retained some measure of political control and social prestige, and there was no access to Thai-based education in schools. (Bradley, 1989, pp. 33–40 in Crystal, 2000, p. 128)

But would ecolinguists be prepared to keep communities isolated, and ensure that they have 'little contact with outside groups', that they do not go to mainstream schools, that they do not marry outside the community, that 'the headman' retains 'some measure of political control and social prestige' over other members of the community? Proposals supporting a headman, or a group of designated community elders, to retain authority over other individuals would endorse social hierarchies and undermine civil rights (Crystal, 2000, p. 156).

So how does ecolinguistic advocacy propose to support indigenous communities and preserve their endangered languages? Some would support social isolation, or as only a temporary approach (Mühlhäusler, 1996, p. 323). Others support community empowerment. Critics have argued that the more languages advocates attempt to preserve, the fewer they may ultimately preserve against global English (de Swaan, 2004). But, crucially, advocacy interventions expand external governance, and fail to preserve linguistic communities as the counter-cultural spaces they yearn for. I now want to consider ecolinguistic governance proposals to maintain endangered linguistic indigenous communities.

Ecolinguistic development approaches

Ecolinguistic development approaches stress the importance of natural harmonious development:

> To bring benefits to the local community through the provision of natural products and services

> To maintain the harmonious interaction of nature and culture and the continuation of traditional use
>
> To support lifestyles and economic activities that are in harmony with nature and the preservation of the social and cultural fabric of the communities concerned
>
> To provide a sustainable flow of natural products and services to meet community needs, without resulting in the decline of the area (WWF and Terralingua, 2000, p. 83)

Ecolinguistic development ideals resonate with the anti-materialist and spiritual development philosophies of Schumacher and Illich, who assume the essential harmony of interests in nature and traditional ways of being (Illich, 1976; Schumacher, 1977; 1993, [1973]). Their philosophies oppose both western and socialist modernisation and industrial economic growth approaches, which, they argue, cultivate greed and foster the seeds of conflict. Schumacher's *Small is Beautiful*, originally published in 1973, argues for anti-materialist Buddhist economics against material development (Schumacher, 1993, [1973]). Similarly, Illich's *Celebration of Awareness: A Call for Institutional Revolution*, which came out in the same year, argues for spiritual development against modernisation models:

> Underdevelopment is the result of a state of mind common to both socialist and capitalist countries. Present development goals are neither desirable nor reasonable. Unfortunately anti-imperialism is no antidote. Although exploitation of poor countries is an undeniable reality, current nationalism is merely the affirmation of the right of colonial elites to repeat history and follow the road travelled by the rich towards the universal consumption of internationally marketed packages, a road which can ultimately lead only to universal pollution and universal frustration. (Illich, 1973a, p. 148)

These anti-materialist ideas were taken up by NGOs, like Oxfam, and the international development sector more broadly. The joint WWF and Terralingua report wants human needs to be balanced against the environment, and advises the precautionary principle to inform development strategies (WWF and Terralingua, 2000, p. 15, p. 31, p. 52). Their vision, seeking a brake on modern development and increased consumption, may be described as an involuted form of 'non-evolutionary or non-revolutionary' development (Geertz, 1963; White, 1983). Their proposals follow other sustainable non-industrial NGO development approaches, which displaced the earlier western modernisation models promoting industrialisation, economic growth and cultural assimilation. Sustainable development thinking now informs mainstream global strategies in the UNDP's human development programme, the Millennium Development Goals, and also the World Bank's changed development approaches, which do not regard social justice as being dependent upon material prosperity. The World Bank *Voices of the Poor* report speaks of well-being as distinct from wealth or economic growth (Narayan *et al.*, 2000, p. 21):

> Wellbeing and illbeing are states of mind and being. Wellbeing has a psychological and spiritual dimension as a mental state of harmony, happiness and peace of mind. (Narayan *et al.*, 2000, p. 21)

So, when the WWF and Terralingua report writes of how 'Global notions of benefits, whether in terms of money, development or influence need to be replaced by or embrace local ideas of relevant benefits' (WWF and Terralingua, 2000, p. 78), it complements how poverty has become relativised in contemporary global development thinking. Ecolinguists, the UNDP, UNESCO, the World Bank and other major global development agencies suggest that the poor need only seek moderate material improvements to secure a sense of well-being. These ideas inform the Poverty Reduction Strategy Papers which have replaced the previous Structural Adjustment Programmes (Duffield, 2007; Harrison, 2004; Pender, 2002; 2007). They also inform reports like UNESCO's *Why Language Matters for the Millennium Development Goals* (UNESCO, 2012). They contrast earlier progressive politics linking material and social progress, from mainstream liberal approaches (Rostow, 1971, [1960]) to anticolonial approaches (Fanon, 1967; Fanon, 1980, [1959], p. 85).

Ecolinguistic livelihood proposals follow other human development or basic needs approaches, and revolve around supporting low-technological agricultural farming or alternatively small-scale income generation, fair trade, green products, crafts, and ecotourism or forestry (WWF and Terralingua, 2000, p. 51). The WWF and Terralingua report rejects large-scale mechanised farming, and condemns how traditional farming methods are threatened by 'agricultural policies, the promotion of mono-cropping, the introduction of high-yield crop varieties, lack of tenure security, use of pesticides and a range of other factors' (WWF and Terralingua, 2000, p. 77). They want to create incentives 'for traditional agricultural practices', including 'indigenous seed experimentation' (WWF and Terralingua, 2000, p. 77), stop incentives for high-tech agriculture, and 'eliminate subsidies and credit policies for high-yield varieties, fertilizers and pesticides' (WWF and Terralingua, 2000, p. 78). Although ecotourism is suggested, there are misgivings over tourism's impact on indigenous communities, undermining local ecosystems and their limited resource use (WWF and Terralingua, 2000, p. 6). Equally, there are misgivings over modern welfare benefits:

> Health-support activities may undermine traditional health practices, tourism activities risk destabilizing religious sites and practices, and

> formal education can threaten language and traditional knowledge. (WWF and Terralingua, 2000, p. 76)

Ecolinguists, echoing Illich's *Limits to Medicine, Medical Nemesis: The Expropriation of Health* (1976), suggest that traditional medical practices are superior to modern medicine. The later joint UNESCO, WWF and Terralingua report expresses concern that:

> Many younger people do not learn the names, characteristics, and uses of such plants which would constitute readily available and reliable medical resources. Instead they have to resort to generally poorer medical care they can obtain from the 'modern' medical system (Skutnabb-Kangas *et al.*, 2003, pp. 36–7).

Ecolinguistic proposals tend to romanticise the hard conditions and inherent insecurities of small-scale unmechanised labour-intensive family agriculture, overlooking the inequalities of its survival strategies (Duffield, 2001; de Waal, 1990; 1997), and its need for child labour (Pupavac, 2009; 2011). So, while they draw attention to the failures of modernisation, they do not analyse problems with the sustainable development approaches they follow (Bateman, 2010; Butcher, 2007; Duffield, 2007; Ilcan and Lacey, 2006; Rankin, 2001; Pupavac, 2010). Consider how they romanticise traditional healing and plants as offering 'reliable medical resources'. Local plants may be able to help alleviate some health problems, but they simply do not address the range of diseases and conditions that modern medicine treats or cures (Tallis, 1999, pp. 129–39). So, instead of indicting the appalling shortage of modern medical services available to people in the developing world, they indict modern medicine itself. We may contrast the ecolinguistic Romantic critique of modern medical technology with Fanon's anti-colonial critique of colonial medical relations, which outlines the decline of traditional medicine and embrace of modern medicine during the anti-colonial struggle (Fanon, 1980, [1952], pp. 99–128). Ecolinguists' scepticism towards modern medicine is linked to their fears over assimilation of indigenous communities. Similarly, they are cautious about ecotourism because commercial activities risk undermining the integrity of minority linguistic communities and traditions. Fanon would have identified their sustainable development approach with 'the stasis of Europe and its "motionless movement"', where 'dialectic is changing into the logic of equilibrium' (Fanon, 1967, [1961], p. 253).

In practice, the failure of national development has led populations in developing countries to increasingly rely on migration and remittances from abroad, which make more significant economic contributions to people's lives than global aid, as international development organisations have belatedly recognised (World Bank, 2008). The demise of national development has not prevented traditional communities from eroding; instead, they have disintegrated and evolved in distinct violent and non-violent forms (Duffield, 2001; 2007). Meanwhile, China and the other BRICs' ruthless economic growth strategies, which are antithetical to the UNDP's human development approach, have raised millions of people out of poverty, although unevenly, under illiberal, oligarchic regimes. China is most likely to realise the Millennium Development Goals by 2015, as the UN recognises (UN DESA, 2011, pp. 6–7). Yet UNESCO's 2012 *Why Language Matters for the Millennium Development Goals* blithely ignores the successes of the Chinese model in its uncritical endorsement of its sustainable development and participatory models (UNESCO, 2012, p. 4). It also ignores the debates over sustainable and participatory governance, and their exclusions and inclusions (Cooke and Kothari, 2001; Hickey and Mohan, 2005; Söderbaum and Sörensen, 2012).

Illich's and Schumacher's earlier development philosophies idealised traditional communities and tended to overlook their inequalities. Traditional communities, however, do not conform to global ethics on human rights, gender equality, children's rights, social inclusion, or, indeed, environmental awareness. Consequently, ecolinguistics, as other fields of global advocacy, supports expanding external governance of communities. Such imperatives become stronger as security concerns shift from human security to the security of the planet (Söderbaum and Sörensen, 2012).

Ecolinguistic governance

Ecolinguistic approaches believe in empowering communities in a way compatible with environmental concerns. The WWF and Terralingua report endorses 'Recognition of, and support to, indigenous peoples' right of self-determination in all aspects in which such right is relevant for conservation' (WWF and Terralingua, 2000, p. 27). WWF and Terralingua support 'Self-development (own decision-making on development options)' (ibid.), and assume, 'a coincidence of needs and aspirations with conservation organisations' (ibid., p. 27). Ecolinguistic ideals propose that indigenous populations are naturally ecological. WWF and Terralingua explicitly operate on this assumption:

> ***Principle 1:*** *Indigenous and other traditional peoples have long associations with nature and a deep understanding of it. Often they have made significant contributions to the maintenance of many of the Earth's most fragile ecosystems, through their traditional sustainable resource use practice and culture-based respect for nature. Therefore, there should be no inherent conflict between the objectives of protected areas and the existence, within and around their borders, of indigenous and other traditional peoples.* (WWF and Terralingua, 2000, p. 83, italics in original)

Operating on this principle, the authentic indigenous voices are those that are ecological.

Ecolinguistics assumes that a group's dependence on the local environment leads to ecological thinking, rather than a condition that people might want to escape. Disregard of environmental concerns is attributed to indigenous communities' oppression, exploitation or poverty. Nevertheless, ecolinguistic policy recommendations suggest that indigenous self-determination is not enough, and that ecological values need to be actively fostered. WWF and Terralingua observe:

> Some indigenous peoples, particularly well-organized ones in developed countries, have developed elaborate environmental agendas and perspectives concerning biodiversity. Others, although equally dependent on and connected to their environments, may be unacquainted with conservation terminology or lack the capacity to develop a biodiversity vision without recourse to professional assistance. (WWF and Terralingua, 2000, p. 39)

Recommendations for 'professional assistance' suggest that indigenous communities might not spontaneously follow ecological ideas, although ecolinguistic theories assume they are naturally ecological. Advocates acknowledge that some initiatives 'with indigenous communities are highly dependent on external advice and funding, and disappear once the supporting project comes to an end' (WWF and Terralingua, 2000, p. 85).

Tellingly, considerable space in WWF and Terralingua's *Indigenous and Traditional Peoples of the World and Ecoregion Conservation* report is dedicated to conflict management, and how to deal with conflicts between external advocates and indigenous communities in the course of implementing environmental projects. Tensions or conflicts between ecolinguists and communities are treated as arising from poor consultation, misunderstandings and miscommunications. Indicatively, WWF and Terralingua refer to 'major conflicts over perceptions' rather than conflicts of interest *per se* (WWF and Terralingua, 2000, p. 42). Improved professional communication and behavioural management is to address problems. WWF and Terralingua advise on some '"behavioural" basics' (WWF and Terralingua, 2000, p. 56). But, if ecolinguists do not feel their conflict management skills are sufficient, then the report suggests bringing in professional intervention. 'Collaborate with expert conflict resolution facilitators,' the report advises, and recommends that 'professional advice or hiring external facilitators or mediators in consultation with the communities can provide a means to reassess the situation together' (WWF and Terralingua, 2000, p. 53, p. 47). Strategies using expert mediators and conflict management approaches suggest how ecolinguistic advocacy follows therapeutic governance techniques. The perceived need of language advocacy for mediated communication is rather ironic, but illustrates its preference for regulation over freedom.

Consider protected areas schemes. It is admitted that past protected area schemes have caused suffering and have been experienced by indigenous communities as 'an odious and much despised imposition' (WWF and Terralingua, 2000, p. 29). Greater indigenous participation in the administration of protected areas seeks to give indigenous communities a stake in protected area schemes. But indigenous co-management is not the same as self-determination. Historically, indigenous participation has not necessarily implied respect for democratic rights, as illustrated by past colonial native administration, or the social psychological management pioneered in the US administration of Japanese internees during the Second World War (Herman, 1995). Nor is ecolinguistic governance immune to the temptations of bypassing local decision-making. In the words of WWF and Terralingua:

> in some cases it may be impossible to support collaborative management solutions owing to distrust or a restrictive policy environment. (WWF and Terralingua, 2000, p. 49)

Ecolinguistic human rights advocates assume compatibility between the different generations of rights, but their prescriptive proposals suggest tensions between the first generation of civil and political freedoms and any fourth generation of post-human earth rights. Ecolinguistic governance, like other global human rights advocacy, may be prepared to circumscribe communities' self-determination. But their governance also contradicts the social isolation and internal social control conducive to language maintenance highlighted above. Ecolinguistic thinking idealises indigenous cultures as cohesive groups in harmony with nature, and wants communities to maintain their traditional ways of life. Their proposals emphasise cultural respect, including consultation with village elders, religious leaders and community councils. But at the same time ecolinguists expect traditional societies to observe post-industrial cultural norms on ecology, gender, social inclusion, transparency and so on. Their tacit acknowledgement that traditional values may contradict the norms they are advocating is evident in proposals for extensive interventions, including verifying the authenticity of community leaders, and ensuring that 'indigenous leaders or representatives have transparent ways of communicating decisions and issues back to their communities' (WWF and Terralingua, 2000, p. 61). Further uneasy with the male village elders' authority, ecolinguists want to 'promote gender mainstreaming through hiring project staff who can voice women's issues explicitly in community meetings or through separate consultations, and by further engaging women in programme activities' (WWF and Terralingua, 2000, p. 57). The proposed extensive external interventions would hollow out linguistic communities, creating community elites orientated towards internationals.

Ecolinguistic post-humanist advocacy

Ecolinguistics and human rights advocacy share an ideal of international society as a global village. But the folksy image papers over tensions between global cosmopolitan law-making and its Balkanised identity-making, between global cosmopolitan intervention and its policies tying people to local organic communities, and between advocates' own cosmopolitan lives and the anti-cosmopolitan lives sustainable development entails for the majority of the world's population.

The tensions between people's self-determination and external intervention are underestimated, especially when we enter the area of 'preventive linguistics' (Crystal, 2000, p. 107, p. 159). Notably, tensions exist in ecolinguistics between its demands for cultural recognition and ecologism. Ecolinguistics effectively comes down on the side of far-reaching cultural management, rather than cultural autonomy (Finke, 2001, pp. 89–90). Problems also exist in advocates' understanding of culture as whole way of life, and their assumption that cultural norms can be changed without changing cultural expectations more generally. Change 'cannot be piecemeal – one element of a complex system can hardly be changed without seriously affecting the whole' (Williams, 1963, p. 229), earlier cultural studies and anthropological studies argued (Read, 1966). Ecological or sustainable interventions seeking to maintain linguistic communities unwittingly disturb communal interdependencies and responsibilities. External advisers or aid workers may seek to promote communal language, traditions and sustainable livelihoods fulfilling basic needs, but their presence unconsciously communicates to recipient communities messages of cosmopolitan affluence and mobility, and fuels frustrations over the gap between their lives and those of internationals (Duffield, 2010; Smirl, 2008).

Ecolinguists do criticise past environmental approaches for riding roughshod over indigenous people, but their ecolinguistic vision presupposes inherently unequal relations between the globalised advocates and locally bounded communities. Advocates are quick to presume conflicts of interests between states and populations, but slower to acknowledge conflicting interests between indigenous communities and their erstwhile saviours, as Crystal observes (Crystal, 2000, p. 156). But to concede that indigenous people are not necessarily ecological would undermine ecolinguistic claims to be grounded in community and represent the interests of indigenous people. Ecolinguistics moves language rights advocacy away from ethnic national minority causes, like the Bretons, the Kosovo Albanians, the Kurds or the Welsh, that dominated advocacy two or three decades ago. Their political aspirations appear antithetical to ecolinguistic governance seeking to restrain human ambition and activity.

The ecolinguistic pastoral trope of indigenous communities echoes the philosopher- king's preference for harmless docile subjects, creating further subconscious parallels between contemporary human rights culture and the philosopher-king's mistrust of politics and the masses. The growth of global advocacy on behalf of non-political subjects (refugees, children, animals, the environment and so on) has followed disillusion with the ideal of the common man and the decline of collective political movements or, even ethnic minority political movements (Pupavac, 2008). International advocacy as such becomes a flight from one's own society and its more complex accountable political relations. Yet ecolinguists express a loss of confidence in human imagination and humanity as political history-making subjects. So for all its insistence on preserving language diversity, its .vision simultaneously downgrades the meaning of speech and humans as beings with language and therefore subjects capable of speech acts (Arendt, 1992; 1998). Ecolinguistics represents a further anti-humanist retreat from the deconstructivist identification with God against humanity in the Tower of Babel myth (Derrida, 2007). And irony of ironies, its ecology of language requires limiting human speech acts. As such, ecolinguistics epitomises the growing anti-humanism in global ethics and human rights discourse.

The next chapter explores concerns over discriminatory speech, and the tensions between advocacy for hate speech prohibitions and freedom of speech and expression.

10
From Free Speech to Linguistic Governance

Introduction

In January 2011, US pastor Terry Jones was barred from entering Britain. He had called for an International Burn a Koran Day on the anniversary of the 9/11 terrorist attacks (BBC, 2011a, 20 January 2011). In June 2011, Palestinian activist Sheikh Raed Salah was detained under an exclusion order, barring him from visiting the UK amidst accusations of 'virulent anti-Semitism' (Hansard, 27 June 2011, p. 614). Salah had already spoken at a meeting in Leicester and had been due to attend a Palestine Solidarity Campaign meeting at the House of Commons (Travis, 2011). The Home Secretary Teresa May, supporting such bans, stated: 'Coming here is a privilege that we refuse to extend to those who seek to subvert our shared values' (Hansard, 27 June 2011, p. 614).

In February 2011, five Muslim men lost their High Court appeal against convictions for 'threatening, abusive or insulting words and behaviour likely to cause harassment and distress' against a march of a British army regiment of soldiers who had served in Iraq and Afghanistan (BBC, 2011b, 16 February 2011; Ford, 2010). In June 2011, Tommy Robinson, leader of the English Defence League (EDL), was banned from attending EDL activities, arising from charges related to anti-Islamist demonstrations. The June EDL ban follows earlier restrictions imposed on other EDL members (BBC, 2011c, 10 March 2011; Hayes, 2011a; National Extremism Tactical Coordination Unit (NETCU), 2012).

Increasing formal bans or prosecutions have been accompanied by informal codes or interventions against offending speech. Such measures are being applied beyond terrorism and racism concerns to encompass more and more areas deemed sensitive. Notably, academia and student politics, traditionally associated with free debate, have been important sites for developing and legitimising speech prohibitions. Many North American and UK universities have institutionalised speech codes circumscribing freedom of speech to ensure campus harmony (Harris, 2009; O'Neill, 2010b). Student organisations like the UK National Union of Students have also adopted 'No Platforms' policies to safeguard students against fascism and racism. Consider Leeds University's *Protocol on Freedom of Expression*, which authorises meetings to be banned where they might give offence:

> if the subject matter ... is or might reasonably be construed as 'controversial' (a 'controversial' meeting in this context being taken as one which might reasonably be construed as having the potential to occasion protest from, or give offence to, any sections of the University or wider community). (University of Leeds, 2008)

The Protocol is not idle, but has been invoked by the students' union to stop debates, including over secularism and Islamism, that is, matters central to contemporary national and global politics (Samarasinghe, 2010; Thomas, 2010). Such protocols are becoming routine elsewhere too. Many North American and UK universities have institutionalised speech codes circumscribing freedom of speech to ensure campus harmony (O'Neill, 2010c). Crucially, UK university guidelines today suggest that, where expression may be highly offensive, 'the balance is likely to lie in favour of restricting that activity' (Universities UK, 2005, p. 31). Student organisations like the UK National Union of Students have also adopted 'No Platforms' policies to safeguard students against fascism and racism. Furthermore, the regulatory climate is spilling over into alternative politics, which is increasingly preoccupied with the governance of speech and behaviour, ironically informally following official laws and codes (Hayes, 2011b).

These and similar cases illustrate readiness to accept growing speech regulation in Europe and North America. There is now extensive hate speech legislation internationally, especially in western European countries (Vanacker, 2009). Within the west, Europe has been more ready to restrict free speech than the United States, influenced by the distinct US and European progressive traditions (Knechte, 2008). Concerns over discriminatory discourse are leading to international initiatives seeking to harmonise national hate speech legislation, supported in particular by the Council of Europe and OSCE.

International linguistic human rights advocacy is becoming more involved in these efforts, although it has primarily focused on language identity claims. Advocates are concerned that existing language rights provisions do not address the power relations of discourse (Pennycook, 1994, pp. 295–321; 1998b). Pennycook argues: 'we cannot stop short by assuming that once someone has access to a language, they have access to doing what they need or want to do through language' (Pennycook, 1998b, p. 86).

This chapter considers hate speech governance and its implications for free speech. Mill's *On Liberty* warns that received opinion needs to be 'fearlessly discussed', or it becomes 'a dead dogma' (Mill, 1985, [1859], p. 97). Certain developments suggest that freedom of speech and expression is becoming 'a dead dogma', even among its traditional supporters on both sides on the Atlantic. Strategies to address discrimination and disempowerment assume the need for stronger speech restrictions to empower the vulnerable and protect them from disempowering speech. Anti-discrimination responses, grounded in more civil freedoms and more speech, appear to be anathema. In particular, global initiatives have focused on the new electronic media. Yet, as the UN Commission on Human Rights admitted in its deliberations, the global imperatives to regulate speech on the internet were driven by existing ambivalence towards global freedom of speech and presumptions of its dangers:

> There had been no discussion regarding the actual consequences of hate sites and the effect of regulation on racist propaganda. The whole debate therefore had been based on speculation. (UNHCHR, 1998, para. 72)

Effectively, advocacy strategies in this area are seeking freedom from offensive speech, rather than freedom of speech. This has profound implications for political life, and for us as autonomous moral subjects. Oppositional political movements have commonly been deemed offensive by the social interests they challenge. Strong speech governance risks stifling the character of the public sphere, as matters deemed sensitive to individuals or groups' identities are increasingly put off limits. But a public sphere exchanging safe, respectful, received opinions is a dead public sphere, antithetical to democratic politics. Historically, progressive, emancipatory political movements have pushed for greater freedoms of conscience, speech and expression. Moreover, if speech qualifies us as political beings, indeed defines our humanity, as Aristotle suggests, then growing speech governance is de-humanising, and degrades us as autonomous moral actors.

Expanding freedoms of speech and expression

Expanding global communications have opened up incredible new possibilities of international engagement. Authoritarian regimes are finding it harder to uphold their state monopoly on information and censor the dissemination of ideas, while the influence of big western media barons in shaping global opinion has diminished, since people can find alternative internet news sources. The last decade has witnessed global news outlets that rival CNN's global influence, such as Al Jazeera and Russia Today, breaking linguistic imperialism assumptions that English-language media necessarily reflect Anglo-American interests. Moreover, individuals are not simply following alternative sources; they are also writing and disseminating their own views through countless personal blogs or twitters. A global digital divide remains, but it has been modified. Isolated poorer communities are more connected today with cheaper access to mobile phones, bypassing the problem of expensive phone land-lines. These technical innovations have considerably facilitated the global transfer of vital remittances, which distribute more funds to developing populations than global development aid. The mobile phone is making the old long waiting lists for phone connection in East European or developing countries irrelevant.

Yet these new freedoms of global communication have been paralleled by other developments, encouraging more scepticism towards freedoms of speech and expression, and calls for more speech governance. Demands for circumscribing speech are coming not only from the authorities, whose former dominance over public opinion has been shaken, but from oppositional and advocacy groups on behalf of weaker social groups. Freedom of speech is still formally upheld, but its meaning is increasingly circumscribed. The next pages trace how thinking on freedom of speech has shifted in influential ways.

Freedom of speech is claimed as a fundamental right, inherent in recognition of our humanity and membership of a political community. The developing modern ideals of freedom of speech are expressed through the 1647 Putney Debates and works such as Milton's *Areopagitica* (1903) [1644], Paine's *The Rights of Man* (1996) [1791] and Mill's *On Liberty* (1985) [1859]. Mill treats freedom of speech as practically inseparable from liberty of conscience, thought, feeling and opinion (Mill, 1985, [1859], p. 71). He considers 'freedom of opinion and freedom of expression of opinion' as vital to humanity's mental well-being, and I quote his summary:

> First, if any opinion is compelled to silence, that opinion may for aught we can certainly know, be true. To deny this is to assume our own infallibility.
>
> Secondly, though the silenced opinion be an error, it may, and very commonly does, contain a portion of truth; and since the general or prevailing opinion on any subject is rarely or never the whole truth, it is only by the collision of adverse opinions that the remainder of the truth has any chance of being supplied.
>
> Thirdly, even if the received opinion be not only true, but the whole truth; unless it is suffered to be and actually is, vigorously and earnestly contested, it will, by most of those who receive it, be held in the manner of a prejudice, with little comprehension or feeling of its rational grounds. And not only this, but, fourthly, the meaning of the doctrine itself will be in danger of being lost or enfeebled, and deprived of its vital effect on the character and conduct. (Mill, 1985, [1859], p. 116)

Mill's famous harm principle sets out how the individual's liberty should only be restricted insofar as it harms others (Mill, 1985, [1859]). Here Mill refers to 'definite damage, or a definite risk of damage' (Mill, 1985, [1859],

p. 149). Mill argues that prohibitions are not necessarily justified, even where actions might offend or damage others:

> In many cases, an individual, in pursuing a legitimate object, necessarily and therefore legitimately causes pain or loss to others, or intercepts a good which they had a reasonable hope of obtaining. (Mill, 1985, [1859], p. 163)

Mill warns against a test of offence determining the limits of free speech and opinion, noting how people commonly feel offended by contrary arguments, especially when these are powerfully put and they struggle to answer them (Mill, 1985, [1859], p. 116). Mill allows for strong expression of opinion, but opposes speech inciting an excited crowd to violence towards specific individuals or groups (Mill, 1985, [1859], pp. 116–19). Classic liberal formulations support restrictions on free speech where there is 'clear and present danger', as stated in Oliver Wendell Holmes' famous judgement in the US case *Schenk v United States* (1917). For Holmes, the First Amendment did not protect a person 'falsely shouting fire in a theatre and causing a panic' (ibid.).

Free speech restrictions have historically been tighter towards ordinary people. The populace is more likely to find itself characterised negatively as a crowd susceptible to 'a positive instigation to some mischievous act' (Mill, 1985, [1859], p. 119). Restrictions on freedom of expression still tend to be heavier on the working class, as the recent Scottish football legislation indicates (Rooney, 2011; Scottish Government, 2012). Mill himself had reservations towards democracy, and believed that despotic rule over barbarians was legitimate if it realised their improvement (Mill, 1985, [1859], p. 69). Elite representations of people as the crowd or the masses questioned their rationality and their fitness for democracy (Le Bon, 1995, [1895]; Ortega y Gasset, 1961, [1930]), even as radical political struggles, from the seventeenth-century English Putney debates to anti-colonialism, challenged their exclusion from political rights (Césaire, 1995, [1939]; Fanon, 1967). This ambivalence informed the development of social psychological theories which attributed virulent nationalism and world war to the psychology of the masses (Herman, 1995).

Post-war international human rights documents, like the UN Declaration, the ECHR, and International Convention on the Elimination of All Forms of Racial Discrimination (1965) (CERD), reflect tensions between liberal ideals and political fears of the masses (Moravcsik, 2000; Sellars, 2002). Such fears inform the provisions circumscribing civil freedoms in the name of morality, public order or public safety, including CERD's restrictions on freedom of speech premised on people's susceptibility to racist propaganda. Nevertheless, negative representations of people as the masses were offset by wartime ideals of the heroic common man, forged by the mobilised populations and their capacity for sacrifice. Furthermore, the Cold War political ideals of the free world struggling against the Communist bloc, or oppression in post-independence states, invoked beliefs in civil and political freedoms (Laïdi, 1998). Consequently, the post-war period in the west witnessed developments consolidating civil rights and pushing for wider freedoms of speech and expression.

Within Britain, the famous *Lady Chatterley* censorship trial of fifty years ago pitted a liberal-left progressive belief in the public's capacity for moral judgement against paternalistic concerns, to protect the morally vulnerable from moral harm and indecency (Rolph, 1961). Those defending the book at the trial included writers, academics, publishers, politicians, clerics, and even a bishop. One of the defence witnesses was Richard Hoggart, a founder of British cultural studies and a director of UNESCO (Rolph, 1961, pp. 178–9). The infamous prosecution question, 'Is it a book which you would wish even your wife or your servants to read?', sounded ridiculously anachronistic (Griffith-Johns in Rolph, 1961, p. 17). Against the prosecution's social anachronism, the defence counsel's final speech suggested the capacity of ordinary people for greater freedom without undermining public morality:

> I do not want to upset the Prosecution by suggesting that there are a certain number of people nowadays who as a matter of fact don't *have* servants. But of course that whole attitude is one which Penguin Books was formed to fight against...the attitude that it is all right to publish a special edition at five or ten guineas so that people who are less well off cannot read what other people read. (in Rolph, 1961, p. 195)

The defence wryly noted how academics were already lecturing, nationally and internationally, on a book they were not supposed to have read (Rolph, 1961, p. 195). The trial's outcome affirmed freedom of speech against censorship. A culture expanding liberty ridiculed campaigners against liberalisation like Mary Whitehouse, who led the Clean-Up TV campaign and National Viewers and Listeners' Association (Barke, 2001; BBC, 2001; Kenny, 2001; Pearson, 1994).

Yet, while personal freedoms were liberalised, notably the decriminalisation of homosexuality, other developments fostered new demands for restrictions on free speech. Within Britain and the US these prominently related to the field of race and gender relations, while in continental Europe they related to fears over fascism. From the 1980s, the decline of collective politics witnessed left-liberal advocacy demanding new protections for minority identities and tighter speech regulation, including hate speech legislation, widening the meaning of incitement to racial hatred, and criminalising Holocaust denial.

The vulnerable citizen and expanding concepts of harm

Sixty years ago, George Orwell's 'Review of *Freedom of Expression*' (1945) complained of the left's self-censorship and failures to defend freedom of speech against commercial, institutional or political interests. Thirty years ago, Anthony Skillen also complained of the left's authoritarian socialism and neglect of free speech (Skillen, 1982). Today's left-liberal scepticism towards free speech commonly seeks to protect the vulnerable from abusive speech (Fish, 1994; Mackinnon, 1993).

Mill's harm principle sees harm as the exception, and subordinate to his strong belief in individual liberty (Beattie, 2004, p. 380; Mill, 1985, [1859], p. 149; Raz, 1988, p. 413). A narrow view of harm was underpinned by a culture affirming individual capacity, and risk as venture, articulated in popular literature like Kipling's 1909 poem *If*. However, a therapeutic culture emphasising vulnerability is expanding Mill's harm principle. Across the political spectrum, the citizen is represented as vulnerable and at risk. More and more citizens are deemed to fall within a vulnerable category, not just in health and social care, but throughout public policy. Politics merges into therapeutic governance where citizens are engaged in enabling processes to improve their self-esteem and capacity to make appropriate choices (Furedi, 2004; Herman, 1995; Nolan, 1998). Concerns over social exclusion, representation and access to discourse are not free speech arguments, but rather calls for mediation, empowering particular representations and understandings (Pennycook, 1998b, pp. 83–5). Imperatives to regulate interpersonal communication are spreading to more and more areas of life, driven by presumptions of vulnerability and abuse. Language rights advocacy also increasingly treats individuals as linguistically oppressed subjects to be empowered by (critical) enablers (Pennycook, 1994, p. 102; 1998b; Phillipson, 1998; Turner, 1993; discussed Holborow, 1999, pp. 84–86). Strikingly, key contemporary advocacy over harmful speech has related to protecting student identities where education implicitly takes on therapeutic governance functions (Fish, 1994, pp. 89–101, p. 108; Mackinnon, 1993, p. 7, pp. 107–8; Pennycook, 1994, p. 298, p. 311). At the same time, identity, culture and knowledge(s) become intertwined as the classroom becomes re-orientated around therapeutic empowerment (Pennycook, 1994, p. 311).

Moreover, the concept of vulnerability involves anticipatory victimhood and an imperative to take preventive action. Vulnerability and risk avoidance are mandated under the precautionary principle, originating in environmental thinking. The precautionary principle is codified in European Union law (European Commission, 2000; 2002, article 191) and its application is expanding into general policy approaches. US law has not mandated the precautionary principle in the same way as EU law, but precautionary approaches have become significant in practice (Sunstein, 2005).

Importantly, the precautionary principle shifts citizenship away from a social contract model, assuming citizens' capacity, towards a tort model, presuming their vulnerability. The harm principle's revision under the precautionary principle expands the restrictions on liberty deemed necessary to avoid risk of harm. Mill's concept of harm primarily concerns physical harm and excludes moral, psychological or cultural distress (Beattie, 2004, p. 381). But psychological harm has gained increased recognition, alongside the expanding concepts of risk and vulnerability, with implications for freedom of speech and expression.

Evolving western approaches effectively allow claims of moral distress, which Mill classically excluded. Libel laws have allowed the wealthy to make such claims. Now broader rights not to be offended are developing under national hate speech approaches, which effectively encompass insulting, not just abusive or threatening, speech, even if this is not strictly the law. Importantly, however, hate crimes are becoming defined in national legislation, not by defendants' intentions, but by others' perceptions of intention. The UK Home Office, for example, defines hate crimes subjectively:

> *A hate crime is any criminal offence which is perceived, by the victim or any other person, to be motivated by a hostility or prejudice based on a person's [race, religion etc] or perceived [race, religion etc].* (Home Office, 2009b, p. 8, italics in original)

As such, the burden of proof implicitly shifts onto the defendant, since speech by its nature involves intention, as Chomsky's critique of Skinner's behaviouralist model outlines (Chomsky, 1959). Simultaneously, we have the implied reversal of the legal principle of innocent until proven guilty, along with presumptions of speech regulation over free speech. But, ironically, blurring speech and action also undermines the individual moral responsibility of those who do commit violent acts, including terrorism (Malik, 2009, p. 190).

There's No Such Thing as Free Speech

Stanley Fish's *There's No Such Thing as Free Speech and Good Thing Too* explicitly questions free speech. Instead, Fish argues for regulating speech in the name of vulnerable groups (Fish, 1994, 102–19). First, he argues that speech is not free, as it has consequences, and potentially harmful consequences (Fish, 1994, pp. 105–6, p. 119). He therefore questions the distinction between speech and action, further arguing that existing legal prohibitions against incitement to violence, or 'fighting words', and provocative speech already blur the speech/action distinction (Fish, 1994, pp. 105–6). Second, he invokes how our speech is made in specific conditions. Our speech is not free from norms or accessory ideas, and is subject to contextual limits and discriminations

(Fish, 1994, p. 107). Speech necessarily involves discriminations for meaning-making; that is, when we speak we are silent about things we are not speaking about. Unbounded expression could not be articulation. Fish then compares the discriminations and exclusions of speech required for making-meaning with ethnic, gender or other social discriminations, and concludes that these features of speech justify speech regulation, codes and sanctions. Here his conclusions are diametrically opposed to earlier beliefs in rule-based creativity and freedom (Chomsky, 2002, p. 68; Humboldt, 1999, [1841], p. 144).

Essentially, Fish argues that, since public speech/discourse is not free but already conditioned, then arguments against speech codes regulating deliberation and outcomes are spurious (Fish, 1994, pp. 118–19). He contests the idea of a free market of ideas, and argues that the operation of free speech, just like the operation of the market, favours the more powerful. Here Fish echoes Rawlsian liberal doubts over the market realising social justice, and Rawlsian imperatives to regulate deliberation to ensure just outcomes (Rawls, 1973). He supports strategies addressing racism and other discrimination through speech codes and affirmative action (Fish, 1994, pp. 60–79). Fish sees the free speech position as politically serving neo-conservative interests rather than equality and progressive political opposition (Fish, 1994, p. 102). He fears that allowing prejudiced individuals or groups to appear in the media legitimises their discriminatory politics, because audiences are culturally susceptible to their discriminatory speech (Fish, 1994, p. 118). So he embraces state and non-state governance solutions, instead of strategies re-appropriating and re-invigorating free speech to a progressive politics.

Even more forcibly, Catherine Mackinnon's *Only Words* seeks tighter speech regulation to redress gender inequalities and violence. Mackinnon outlines women's reality as one of abuse, violence and silencing (Mackinnon, 1993, pp. 3–6). She sees women's lives as characterised by unspeakable trauma and terrors, which public discussion and law do not recognise (Mackinnon, 1993, p. 3). Mackinnon describes women as growing up to:

> learn that language does not belong to you, that you cannot use it to say what you know ... You learn that speech is not what you say but what your abusers do to you. (Mackinnon, 1993, p. 6)

Mackinnon contests the distinction between speech and action, particularly singling out pornography as the free speech of men silencing the free speech of women (Mackinnon, 1987; 1993). Male free speech constitutes violent acts against women, as well as causing further violent acts towards women. Mackinnon counterposes equality and freedom of speech, seeing free speech as protecting 'the speech of inequality' (Mackinnon, 1993, p. 72). Her scepticism towards negative freedoms also echoes Rawlsian post-liberal doubts about the market of ideas, which she sees operating in the interests of big business and male power (Mackinnon, 1993, p. 75, p. 102, p. 109;

Rawls, 1973). So Mackinnon wants pornography bans and other speech restrictions, to empower 'equal access to speech', to redress unequal gender power relations, empower victims and prevent speech harm (Mackinnon, 1993, p. 72). Again she follows governance solutions, regulating public and personal discourse to address social inequality, where politics takes the form of legal lobbying and regulation rather than collective political engagement. Underpinning Mackinnon's belief in 'legal intervention for social change' (Mackinnon, 1993, p. 73) is an intersubjective understanding of society as 'made of language' (Mackinnon, 1993, p. 106). Such strategies for speech regulation complement the influence of post-modern linguistics, viewing language itself as discriminatory, and seeking therapeutic governance solutions (Pennycook, 1994).

Globalising hate speech legislation

Expanding global communications have offered vast new opportunities to exchange ideas and material. Their potential use to spread extremism and hatred drives initiatives to harmonise hate speech legislation internationally (UNHCHR, 1998). Campaigners fear that the internet risks spreading pandemics of hate among susceptible users (ADL, 2000) – indicatively, users are represented as vulnerable. The Anti-Defamation League (ADL) campaigning in this area says:

> Whereas extremists once had to stand on street corners spewing their hate and venom – reaching only a few passersby – now they can rant from the safety of their own homes; anyone can easily create a Web site, propelling their message, good or bad, to the entire world. (ADL, 2000)

The United Nations Commission on Human Rights (UNHCHR) has been reviewing the challenges raised by the new media and use of the International Convention on the Elimination of All Forms of Racial Discrimination (CERD) (1965) (UNHCHR, 1998). The Convention's preamble declares:

> any doctrine of superiority based on racial differentiation is scientifically false, morally condemnable, socially unjust and dangerous, and that there is no justification for racial discrimination, in theory or in practice, anywhere.

Its provisions seek to outlaw racist propaganda internationally. Under article 4, state parties:

> Shall declare an offence punishable by law all dissemination of ideas based on racial superiority or hatred, incitement to racial discrimination, as well as all acts of violence or incitement to such acts against any

> race or group of persons of another colour or ethnic origin, and also the provision of any assistance to racist activities, including the financing thereof (article 4(a)).

The Commission treats CERD as mandatory international law, requiring state enforcement and preventative action (UNHCHR, 1998, paras 30, 33, 34 and 43). As such, it follows the shift from seeing international human rights documents as aspirational political declarations towards seeing them as firmly part of international law. The UNHCHR further contends that states' constitutional law is 'not superior to the principles of international law' (UNHCHR, 1998, para. 65). Here the Commission is implicitly challenging the strong US constitutional free speech provisions and its reservations to the Convention (UNHCHR, 1998, para. 40). The US Department of Justice delegate at the Commission summarises the US constitutional free speech philosophy:

> The animating principle of First Amendment jurisprudence was that such expression would meet with opposing expression – often described succinctly as 'more speech' – and that citizens could discern for themselves the truth or falsity of the contending viewpoints. That tolerant attitude to expression found its roots deep in the traditions of humanism itself, which proceeded from the fundamental belief that each person was (and must be) a moral actor. Under that philosophical approach, it was not the role of the State to dictate the views a citizen must hold; rather, each person must exercise his innate capacity for independent reason. (UNHCHR, 1998, para. 1)

The US constitutional approach to racist material believes 'racist dogma' would be 'soundly rebutted...through a clash of views in vigorous debate, and not through government censorship' (UNHCHR, 1998, para. 19). Other Commission delegates criticised the US for allowing internet sites to disseminate racist ideas under its strong free speech position, and were interested in how other states might prosecute US-based sites promoting racist material (UNHCHR, 1998, para. 41, para. 47).

The Commission believes that 'prohibition of the dissemination of all ideas based upon racial superiority or hatred' is 'compatible with the right to freedom of opinion and expression', since existing human rights are conditioned by provisions, including on incitement to violence, morality, public order and the general welfare in a democratic society and the rights of others (UNHCHR, 1998, para. 31, para. 41). The UN Universal Declaration of Human Rights 1948 allows free speech restrictions related to:

> securing due recognition and respect for the rights and freedoms of others and of meeting the just requirements of morality, public order and the general welfare in a democratic society. (article 29(2))

The European Convention for the Protection of Human Rights and Fundamental Freedoms (1950) similarly permits states to restrict freedoms of thought, expression or assembly 'in the interests of public safety, for the protection of public order, health or morals, or for the protection of the rights and freedoms of others' (ECHR, 1950, article 9, 10, 11). Here the Commission takes a positivist legal approach towards the post-war international human rights framework and the circumscribed rights provisions. It overlooks a 'quite distinct' libertarian tradition on civil freedoms (Starr, 2004, p. 125). This libertarian tradition treats freedom of speech as absolute, 'not negotiable or subject to being balanced' (Starr, 2004, p. 125). Against this tradition, the UNHCHR sees a trade-off between free speech and anti-racism. Consequently, it comes down on the side of regulation, believing: 'it would be unfortunate if the freedom of expression were to be given precedence over the right to life' (UNHCHR, 1998, para. 70). The report therefore considers that 'undue consideration should not be given to United States law' in interpreting international provisions (UNHCHR, 1998, para. 68).

Rather than US approaches, the Commission is interested in how west European legislation criminalises racist hate speech (UNHCHR, 1998, para. 69). More specifically, the Human Rights Committee has 'indicated that it would follow the jurisprudence of the European Court of Human Rights' rather than US jurisprudence (UNHCHR, 1998, para. 65 and para. 68).

The Council of Europe shares perceptions of the internet's dangers:

> the emergence of international communication networks like the Internet provides certain persons with modern and powerful means to support racism and xenophobia and enables them to disseminate easily and widely expressions containing such ideas. (Council of Europe, 2003b, para. 3)

The Council of Europe has led efforts to harmonise legislation in Europe through its Additional Protocol to the Convention on Cybercrime, 'concerning the criminalisation of acts of a racist and xenophobic nature committed through computer systems' (Council of Europe, 2003a). The Protocol represents the culmination of a four-year programme on combating illegal and harmful content on the internet and follows prevailing policy thinking, counterposing freedom of expression and eliminating racism. Accordingly, its preamble declares 'the need to ensure a proper balance between freedom of expression and an effective fight against acts of a racist and xenophobic nature' (Council of Europe, 2003a). The Protocol believes that freedoms of expression and communication should be qualified to prevent racism and xenophobia (ibid.). The document makes criminal offences of racist and xenophobically motivated threats or insults on the internet towards persons or groups 'distinguished by race, colour, descent or national or ethnic origin' (articles 4 and 5). The Protocol defines racist and xenophobic material as:

> any written material, any image or any other representation of ideas or theories, which advocates, promotes or incites hatred, discrimination or violence, against any individual or group of individuals, based on race, colour, descent or national or ethnic origin, as well as religion if used as a pretext for any of these factors. (Council of Europe, 2003a, article 2(1))

The Council of Europe has sought to clarify how the European Convention on Human Rights allows restrictions on freedom of speech and expression in an internet age (ECHR, article 10 (2)). Traditionally, as the Council of Europe's explanatory notes acknowledge, it has been considered that ECHR free speech protections under article 10 are applicable to materials that 'offend, shock or disturb the State or any sector of the population' (Council of Europe, 2003b). Such an interpretation follows Mill's *On Liberty*, which warns against a test of offence, observing how legitimate pursuits may offend others (Mill, 1985, p. 116, p. 163).Likewise, the Protocol's Explanatory Report affirms the usual legal defences 'like consent, self defence or necessity' and other exclusions, including 'for academic or research purposes', and maintains intention as an element of offences (Council of Europe, 2003b, para. 24 and para. 25).

The OSCE has followed up the Protocol with its 2004 Brussels Declaration which seeks participating States commit themselves to:

> Combat hate crimes, which can be fuelled by racist, xenophobic and anti-Semitic propaganda in the media and on the Internet, and appropriately denounce such crimes publicly when they occur. (OSCE, 2004a)

The OSCE sees hate crime policies as helping to build a sense of security and reduce a sense of fear and vulnerability (Lenarčič, 2009, p. 3). The OSCE has organised policy and practitioner conferences and published reports such as *Hate Crime Laws: A Practical Guide* (OSCE/ODIHR, 2009b) and *Combating Hate Crimes in the OSCE Region: An Overview of Statistics, Legislation, and National Initiatives* (OSCE, 2005a). Its Office for Democratic Institutions and Human Rights (ODIHR) has followed with annual reports on hate crimes in the OSCE region. The ODIHR has developed initiatives such as its Law Enforcement Officer Programme on Combating Hate Crimes (OSCE/ODIHR, undated). The OSCE directly links hate speech to social order and security concerns:

> the OSCE community has led the way by adopting international commitments in this field which reflect the knowledge that hate crimes, if not addressed properly, have the potential to escalate into wider scale

> violence, endangering social cohesion and affecting the security of individuals and communities. (Lenarčič, 2009, p. 1)

Social disorder fears add urgency to addressing hate crimes, which policymakers fear may escalate against minorities in periods of social crisis (Freeman, 2009; Lenarčič, 2009, p. 3). Human rights documents contain conditions qualifying freedoms, which lend themselves to subsequent interpretations, allowing states to invoke security concerns and circumscribe freedoms substantially, whether under the UN Universal Declaration of Human Rights 1948 (article 29) or the European Convention 1950 (article 10(2)), as the European Court of Human Rights has confirmed (Council of Europe, 2003b).

Similarly, the right of a state to ban material on the grounds of cultural offence was earlier confirmed by the European Court of Human Rights. Consider its decision in *Otto Preminger Institute v Austria* (1995):

> The Court cannot disregard the fact that the Roman Catholic religion is the religion of the overwhelming majority of Tyroleans. In seizing the film, the Austrian authorities acted to ensure religious peace in that region and to prevent that some people should feel the object of attacks on their religious beliefs in an unwarranted and offensive manner. (ECHR, 1995, cited in Dembour, 2001, p. 74)

Here cultural sensitivities and concerns over ensuring 'religious peace' are invoked, which circumscribe freedom of expression (ECHR, 1995, cited in Dembour, 2001, p. 74). Thus, the classic understanding of the European Convention as protecting offensive speech is not necessarily protected by either the European Court of Human Rights or national courts in practice.

A climate of heightened cultural and security fears has encouraged both governments and non-governmental organisations to be more ready to tilt the security–liberty balance against liberty in the name of security and societal peace. Broad support has existed among human rights and other NGOs for tighter hate crimes legislation and enforcement (OSCE, 2009). The last decade has witnessed the development of bodies like International Association of Internet Hotlines (INHOPE), supported by IGOs, governments, industry and NGOs to coordinate with national internet hotlines and remove material deemed illegal or harmful (Callanan, 2004). Tellingly the activities of organisations like INHOOPE have focused on promoting regulation and enforcement rather than defending freedom (Callanan, 2004). Thus, while freedom of speech is formally upheld internationally, its practice is becoming critically circumscribed under hate speech approaches. Here many would conclude with Fish that it is *'A Good Thing Too'* (1994). However, there are serious implications for weaker or dissenting individuals or groups in society.

Contesting speech regulation

Hate speech legislation shares aspects of earlier blasphemy and libel laws. It has long been criticised that libel law is only accessible to the wealthy, and blasphemy law to the established religion, and not to groups who face discrimination. The UK's Racial and Religious Hatred Act (2006) specifically superseded the older blasphemy laws to cover contemporary secular identity concerns. Fish contends that those opposing speech codes assume a 'weightless verbal exchange' (Fish, 1994, p. 109). But supporters of speech codes assume that speech codes are weighted and used against the powerful, rather than the marginal (Fish, 1994, pp. 75–6). Advocacy appealing to authority to regulate people's freedom of speech neglects the potential negative consequences of expanding governance of speech for those excluded or dissenting from the mainstream or polite society. Ironically, the problems of appealing to power to regulate speech were notoriously confirmed when the Canadian censorship laws, supported by Mackinnon, were invoked against feminist and anti-racist works (Dworkin, 1996, p. 243).

Indeed the UK public order legislation introduced during the 1930s against fascists was subsequently used against leftwing groups, while the first prosecution under the UK race relations was against a black man (Skillen, 1982). An earlier progressive politics believed in freeing speech, and saw limiting speech as protecting the privileged and established. Conversely, a cultural relativist climate, in which individuals and groups are not expected or prepared to defend their views, has been tempted into diverse measures to ban offending ideas from the public sphere rather than challenging them. Yet trust in expanding regulation, rather than expanding freedoms of speech and expression, represents an elitist form of politics, which implicitly mistrusts the public's capacity to make judgements and bypasses democratic debate and the problem of convincing people of one's views. Indicatively, advocates do not address the power relations involved in their third-party advocacy, or the problems of individuals or groups holding their advocates to account, whether state or non-state actors. Speech restrictions in the name of the vulnerable may limit public scrutiny of decision-making. The UK's strict reporting restrictions on family courts in the name of children, for example, have been criticised for shielding the courts' operation from proper public accountability (Greenslade, 2010).

One of the best-known critiques of speech regulation is by the legal theorist Richard Dworkin. Dworkin contests arguments counterposing free speech and equality and sees free speech as an egalitarian demand, based on equal rights to speech (Dworkin, 1996, pp. 234–8). The right of free speech asserts the right of all to speech, not determined by a higher authority. Speech codes seeking to protect minority identity and beliefs, Dworkin argues, are essentially asking for the 'right to respectful attention' or 'guaranteed conditions of being heard sympathetically' (Dworkin, 1996, p. 232,

p. 235). Speech reception claims recall the old philosophical schemes of perfecting our words, and they also flounder on the problem that reception of our words is not guaranteed. Attempts to regulate reception of speech may repress public expression of contrary opinions, but do not thereby eradicate them. This reality informs classic liberal arguments for state tolerance of religious belief and matters of conscience. Freedom of speech recognises freedom of reception against attempts to guarantee respect for what we say (Dworkin, 1996, p. 37). Free speech restrictions therefore deny not only opponents' rights to speak, but others' freedom to hear, interpret and contest. Simultaneously, speech governance has negative implications for individuals, dissenting from both mainstream and minority cultural identities or values and beliefs.

Restricting cultural offence and dissent

The *Satanic Verses* affair of twenty years ago signalled the rise of global demands for rights not to be offended. The affair was not only significant in showing the decline of left-wing politics among ethnic minority groups, but it also revealed how the western liberal-left was willing, along with the authorities, to allow new despotisms of custom to curtail freedom of speech and expression (Malik, 2009). Responses to Rushdie's *Satanic Verses* (2006) [1988] were very different from those towards Lawrence's *Lady Chatterley's Lover*, although the publisher Penguin defended its publication of both novels. A powerful left-liberal sensitivity against giving cultural offence condemned Rushdie's novel as orientalist, culturally and religiously offensive, and of little literary merit. Conversely, progressives had rallied to support Lawrence's novel, despite its publication offending those committed to traditional Christian morality (Malik, 2009, pp. 151–3; Rolph, 1961). Rushdie's novel was even condemned as 'a lethal weapon' comparable to *Mein Kampf* (Mazrui, 1990, p. 95 in Malik, 2009, pp. 188–9). Overall, western political responses proved uncommitted to defending Rushdie and freedom of speech as a fundamental principle (Malik, 2009).

In the wake of the Rushdie affair, precautionary approaches followed by the authorities and cultural advocates have continued to reinforce cultural conservatism against cultural experimentation, even in the absence of offence being expressed or violence threatened (Malik, 2009, pp. 192–7). Proponents believe hate speech legislation has a deterrent impact. However, speech laws and codes may rather legitimise claims and counter-claims to feeling offended.

Indicatively, groups exhibit double standards over claimed rights, illustrating how exclusion of ideas that offend us does not change contrary opinion, but, rather, changes the character of the public sphere into a more repressive, sectarian place dependent on ever tighter speech governance to keep public order (Malik, 2009, p. 195). A 'marketplace of outrage' is displacing a marketplace of ideas, where groups compete over recognition of their sense of moral or psychological hurt (Ali in Malik, 2009, p. 183). Thus, Islamists claim rights to protest against parades accompanying coffins of military casualties, while demanding rights to censor the Danish cartoons of Mohammed, Rushdie's novel or other material causing them offence. Or the US Christian preacher and his defenders claim the right to burn the Koran, but would deny the right to burn the US flag. Similarly, Wilders, a Dutch rightwing politician, condemns hate speech laws and expects his freedom to condemn Islam to be upheld, but calls for bans on burkas and the Koran. Left-wing groups support bans on the British National Party (BNP) or EDL. Notably, the Trade Union Congress (TUC) passed a motion in 2009 calling the government to ban all BNP members from employment in 'all public services' (Thomas, 2009; TUC, 2009). In turn, BNP or EDL members defend their freedom to protest, but want bans on Islamist organisations. Academics, defending freedom of speech against terrorism legislation, have supported prohibitions on genocide deniers, boycotts of Israeli speakers, or stricter advertising bans. Readiness to exclude ideas we do not like is characteristic across contemporary politics and culture, and is not confined to fringe groups.

Critics suggest, the deterrent impact of speech laws or codes is greatest on weaker or more isolated members of minority groups (Malik, 2009, p. 174). The powerful have historically cloaked themselves in the authority of sacred tradition, and a danger exists of hate speech prohibitions empowering the most conservative community elements, and silencing voices questioning traditional community norms (Malik, 2009, pp. 170–5). A climate opposing cultural offence has particular implications for women of minority communities dissenting from cultural tradition, illustrated in the closure of Gurpreet Bhatti's play *Behzti* (*Dishonour*) (Bhatti, 2004), and explored in her later play *Behud* (*Beyond Belief*) (Bhatti, 2010). Yet the voices of tradition seeking to suppress cultural dissent have been joined by liberal concern for cultural sensitivity. Writer Monica Ali, for example, was criticised by the feminist Germaine Greer for not properly respecting the Bengali community in her novel *Brick Lane* (Ali, 2004), not having an authentic voice for writing in English, and not knowing Bengali (Greer, 2006 in Malik, 2009, p. 171). Such liberal culturalist views, also displayed in language rights advocacy (May, 2003), tend to deny or downplay conflicts of interests within minority groups. But proponents of speech restrictions, like Fish (Fish, 2008), are reluctant to acknowledge 'censorship by fear'(Fish, 2008), and how new despotisms of cultural identity are pushing self-censorship. Conversely, a climate supporting free speech and expression gives women from minority communities greater space to dissent from cultural norms.

Defenders of free speech have noted the inevitability of giving offence when attempting to change society (Malik, 2009, p. 175; Mill, 1985, [1959], p. 116; Skillen, 1982). Earlier progressives and radicals were aware that minorities' cultural demands could be regressive. Wright, for one, wrote of the cultural pressures he felt under when planning his novel *Native Son*, particularly expectations to create positive representations of those racially discriminated against (Wright, 2000, [1940], p. 18). Against these pressures, Wright asserted, 'a human right, the right of a man to think and feel honestly' (Wright, 2000, [1940], p. 18). Wright's concerns over a cultural censor, or self-censor, restricting how he wrote about Black experience are even more relevant today (Malik, 2009). In the wake of the Rushdie affair, Said distanced himself from his interpreters, asserting the primacy of cultural identities, and voiced support for unqualified freedom of opinion and expression and the legitimacy of resisting cultural pressures (Said, 1994b, p. xvi, p. 27, pp. 88–9). Re-asserting the responsibility to speak truth to power, Said warned against 'all theocratic tendencies, not just against the conventionally designated ones' (Said, 1994b, p. 60).

The ambivalence of speech regulation for discriminated groups has become even clearer in subsequent counter-terrorism legislation and cultural pressures. Expanding concepts of harm parallel and help legitimise expanding security imperatives (Furedi, 2007). Yet the shift from liberty to the securitised concept of harm is mystified in the language of vulnerability and empowerment – a danger anticipated in Berlin's classic essay 'Two Concepts of Liberty' on negative and positive liberty (Berlin, 1969, pp. 118–72).

Cultural advocacy considering Rushdie's *Satanic Verses* (2006) [1988], 'a lethal weapon' inciting violence (Mazrui, 1990, p. 95, in Malik, 2009, p. 189), logically legitimises criminalising possession of other reading material under terrorism legislation. Securitising problems, the invocation of emergency conditions, leads to security becoming paramount over liberty, that is, harm trumping liberty, as critical security studies has explored. Victim advocacy supporting speech restrictions complements security measures restricting freedom of speech. Ali Mazrui argued against Rushdie's novel that it 'elevates the pleasure of art above the pain of society' (Mazrui, 1990, p. 98). But what about other works, touching other sensitive subjects? Some, but not all, relatives of the 7/7 London terrorist bombing victims opposed Chris Morris's comedy film *Four Lions* about a group of British terrorists (BBC 7 May 2010; Mckenzie, 2010; Morris, 2010). Mazrui's arguments against Rushdie's novel would justify banning *Four Lions* on the grounds of the 'real anguish' it could cause victims' families against film viewers' rights to 'titillation' (Mazrui, 1990, p. 98). A comedy about terrorism might seem offensive. Yet the film's satire of terrorists has arguably done more for undermining the status of terrorists and a culture of fear and resentment, and encouraging lived multicultural relations in the UK, than many an official counter-terrorism initiative.

Language advocates have not demanded counter-terrorism strategies restricting civil freedoms. Nevertheless, hate speech and language rights advocacy, treating individuals as vulnerable, and speech as violence, lend themselves to terrorism legislation, criminalising speech and expression. Ironic parallels exist between linguistic human rights advocacy, health and social care, and counter-terrorism constructing citizens as vulnerable. Tellingly, the UK Contest and Prevent documents speak of terrorist radicalisation in terms of those 'who are vulnerable to grooming' (HM Government, 2011, p. 83), using the language of children at risk from paedophilia. While the conflation of speech and action is illustrated in the case of the individual prosecuted for joking about bombing an airport on Twitter (Harris, 2010; Wainwright, 2010).

Security and the insecurity of speech rights

As highlighted above, the OSCE, as a security organisation concerned with regional minority rights governance, has been involved in harmonising hate speech legislation. Its human security model believes that terrorism cannot simply be combated militarily, but must involve more comprehensive approaches, overcoming social exclusions (OSCE, 2010, para. 13). Critics of existing counter-terrorism strategies seeking improved community relations (Lambert, 2011), or to protect minorities from victimisation under the war on terror, commonly look to stronger enforcement of hate crimes legislation. The OSCE's *Combating Hate Crimes* distinguishes between terrorist acts and hate crimes such as Islamophobia or anti-Semitism, but sees them as connected (OSCE, 2005a).

Yet, strikingly, since 9/11 we have not seen hordes of ordinary people, Muslims and non-Muslims, clashing with each other across western countries. Indeed, ordinary Europeans have been unenthusiastic about the prosecution of wars in Iraq and Afghanistan. Policy has assumed that racial, ethnic or religious hatred crimes must worsen, especially after terrorist attacks. Nevertheless, racist violence is considerably lower in Britain than in the 1970s and 1980s. Racial incident figures of recent years recorded by the police, which include non-violent crimes, decreased overall 'by two per cent from 56,387 in 2008/09 to 55,056 in 2009/10' (Home Office, 2010). Ambivalent attitudes towards Muslims and Islam are expressed, but the Citizenship 2009–2010 Survey for England reported perceptions of improved relations in the years after the 7th July bombings:

> In 2009–10, 85 per cent of people thought their community was cohesive, agreeing that their local area was a place where people from different backgrounds got on well together. This represents an increase from 2003 and 2005 (both 80 per cent) and 2007–08 (82 per cent), but is not significantly different from 2008–09 (84 per cent). (Citizenship Survey, 2009)

Negative attitudes also appear less common in more diverse large urban areas than in rural areas with far smaller numbers of ethnic minorities (Home Office, 2009b). This pattern suggests that more lived diversity fosters better inter-ethnic relations and perceptions. So, while the OSCE has documented the UK as having the highest levels of hate crimes reported in the world (OSCE/ODIHR, 2009a), the high figures are influenced by the promotion of tighter hate speech governance, and changed prosecution and reporting policies, rather than necessarily worsening UK inter-ethnic relations (CPS, 2009; Home Office, 2009a; 2009b; Natale, 2010). However, hate speech crimes risk worsening inter-ethnic relations, in that crimes between members of different ethnic groups become ethnicised. Similarly, conflating speech and action under the terrorism legislation risks amplifying the cultural and political impact of terrorist threats and their damage to society.

The OSCE emphasises that terrorists should not be identified with particular groups, and is concerned to overcome the social exclusion of minority communities. Accordingly, the OSCE Brussels Declaration rejects 'firmly the identification of terrorism and extremism with any religion, culture, ethnic group, nationality or race' (OSCE, 2004a, article 5). Nevertheless, hate crime approaches are encouraging the racialising or ethnicising of experience, and risk discriminatory official racial or ethnic profiling – that is, inferring certain (criminal) characteristics based on identity (FRA, 2010, p. 9). British legislation encourages crimes to become racialised and ethnicised by allowing subjectively defined offences, namely, any offences perceived by a victim of crime, or someone else, to be motivated by prejudice, to be defined as hate crimes (Home Office, 2009b, p. 8).

Furthermore, the hate speech legislation's treatment of speech as harmful and violent in itself reinforces counter-terrorism approaches circumscribing civil freedoms, especially of minorities, and undermining the values of rights and freedoms that counter-terrorism is supposed to be defending. Those caught up under the terrorism legislation may find themselves subject to curbs on their freedoms, even in the absence of arrest or charge. The OSCE Astana Declaration states:

> The respect and promotion of human rights are in themselves one of the most effective tools for preventing terrorism and the violent extremism and radicalization that lead to terrorism. Counter-terrorism measures which violate international human rights standards are counter-productive. They undermine the rule of law and the credibility and ability of public authorities to address the threat, thus diminishing participating States' long-term security. (OSCE, 2010, para. 7)

But the OSCE remains ambivalent over civil freedoms, as is evident in its views on the internet. On the one hand, the OSCE affirms the need 'to uphold privacy rights and freedom of expression' (OSCE, 2010, para. 11).

On the other, it seeks greater global surveillance of the internet because it may 'incite terrorist violence' or other concerns (OSCE, 2010, para. 11). The OSCE is particularly concerned about the impact of the internet on the young. Consequently, the OSCE gives a particular role to education in combating terrorism. Under the Astana Declaration, the OSCE declares:

> Academia has a vital role to play in preventing terrorism. Especially youth need to be made resilient to simplistic extremist propaganda that offers violence as a solution for tackling grievances. (OSCE, 2010, para. 9)

The OSCE approach parallels that of British official policies in the wake of the 7/7 London bombing. The Home Office's counter-terrorism strategy (CONTEST) is nervous about the ungoverned character of the internet and its circumvention of censorship laws (Home Office, 2011a, p. 63).

Simultaneously, official UK government responses have reiterated that core western values of freedom and instilling these values in young people are vital to combating terrorism (Home Office, 2011a). In this vein, the UK CONTEST strategy highlights how counter-terrorism strategies 'will reflect our fundamental values', and how 'we remain committed to protecting the freedom of speech which many of those same extremists set out to undermine' (Home Office, 2011a, p. 6, p. 9). Affirming core freedoms against radicalisation is reiterated in official policies directed towards colleges and universities. The UK Department of Business, Innovation and Skills (DBIS), previously the Department of Innovation, Universities and Skills (DIUS), which is responsible for higher education, has affirmed both freedom of speech and academic freedom in key policy reports aimed at universities (DIUS, 2008; Ebdon, 2005; Equality Challenge Unit, 2007). The DIUS states:

> We prize academic freedom and freedom of speech as ends in themselves and as the most effective way of challenging the views which we may find abhorrent but that remain within the law. (DIUS, 2008, p. 3)

Nevertheless, terrorism legislation is impacting on freedoms of speech and expression, both inside and outside universities.

Importantly, hate speech legislation expanding the meaning of incitement to hatred has helped criminalise speech under the terrorism legislation. Notably, the UK's Terrorism Act 2006 criminalises the possession of material glorifying terrorism. Its blurring of speech and action, as under hate speech legislation, has caused more of the population to be caught up under terrorist legislation or anti-terrorism codes, while its racialising or ethnicising of crime blurs identity and intention. Whorfian understandings of language and culture linking linguistic identity, knowledge and belief have implicitly been embraced in counter-terrorism surveillance associating linguistic knowledge with political sympathies. Competence in Middle Eastern or Asian languages may become grounds for suspicion, as academics have discussed in terrorism studies forums (for example, C-SAP, 2009). Even translating documents for an academic expert witness acting for the prosecution may lead to questioning by the police. Notwithstanding a defence of possession for lawful purposes, the idea that conduct is left 'unaffected' (Council of Europe, 2003b, para. 24) underestimates the impact of subjecting individuals to criminal investigation for possession when a climate of suspicion leads to individuals having to prove they are without criminal intent. So, while documents such as the Council of Europe's Additional Protocol seek to balance freedoms of expression and the security of minority groups, it is the freedoms of such groups which appear most threatened by the blurring of speech, intention and action.

Importantly, much counter-terrorism work has related to internet surveillance. Indeed, a number of cases listed as 'Major Islamist Terrorist Plots' in a report by the US Heritage Foundation used by the UK Home Office relate to internet speech and expression (Bromund and Roach, 2010). Internet-focused surveillance is better at collecting information than evaluating and identifying intention. Yet counter-terrorism approaches appear to conflate identity and knowledge in ways which impute intention in circumstances when individuals from ethnic minorities are proportionately more likely to be stopped and questioned under Schedule 7 of the Terrorism Act 2006 or other terrorism legislation (Equality and Human Rights Commission, 2010; Home Office, 2011b).

In the so-called lyrical terrorist case, Heathrow airport shop assistant Samina Malik, who wrote verses calling for martyrdom and beheadings, was convicted under section 58 of the Terrorism Act 2000 for possessing records or documents likely to be of use to a person committing or preparing an act of terrorism. Her conviction was subsequently quashed on appeal, thereby refining the scope of the terrorism legislation (BBC, 2008b; CPS, 2008). However, people have continued to find themselves caught under the terrorism legislation for showing interest in contemporary terrorism, and possession of literature has been treated as prima facie evidence of identification with its contents and commitment to action.

Criminalising studies

Strikingly, students have found themselves caught up under the terrorism legislation for papers they possess related to their studies. Consider the 2008 case concerning a student Rizwaan Sabir and administrator friend Hicham Yezza, who were arrested at the University of Nottingham and wrongly detained for seven days under section 41 of the Terrorism Act 2000 on suspicion of being involved in the 'commission, preparation or instigation of acts of terrorism'. Their arrests happened in the wake of the police being contacted and investigating the discovery of three documents found on the administrator's computer: two journal articles, one from *Foreign Affairs*, the other from *Middle East Policy Review*, and *The Al Qaeda Training Manual*. The latter internet edition was made available to the public from the US Department of Justice and highlighted for analysis in the popular textbook Gus Martin's *Understanding Terrorism*, now in its third edition (Martin, 2010, pp. 360–1). Various hard copy editions of *The Al Qaeda Training Manual*, including fuller editions, are also available for anybody to order from Amazon, Tesco and other retailers, or from libraries via inter-library loan, if not on the shelves. *The Al Qaeda Training Manual* is cited in leading terrorism studies by Rohan Gunaratna (2002) and others. Extracts commonly appear in student readers and edited collections of primary documents. On-line essay services, like AcaDemon, Essaytree, MightyStudents, Oppapers and Paperdue, even stock model essays on the *Al Qaeda Training Manual* for students who struggle writing their own. In other words, the two individuals were arrested for having legitimate sources in security studies. Indeed, *The Al Qaeda Training Manual* is not actually an Al Qaeda manual, but was only later given this name by the US authorities. Nevertheless, assumptions have been made over its Al Qaeda provenance and significance, including in the so-called ricin plot case and the case of Samina Malik, the so-called lyrical terrorist case (Campbell, 2005; CPS, 2008). The manual's original title translates as *Military Studies in the Jihad against the Tyrants*. The insurgency document, drawing on old standard military manuals, appears to have been created sometime towards the end of the Cold War, when Islamic groups were supported by the west. Indeed, its reference to tyrants probably refers to successive Middle Eastern rulers, as the terrorism expert Rod Thornton has analysed. It is of interest in understanding the history of contemporary terrorism, but of little practical value to terrorists today, since its tactics belong to a pre-internet and mobile phone age. Thornton was interviewed by the police in May 2008 over the arrests. However, the West Midlands police subsequently admitted they altered their interview notes to say that Thornton did not consider the document relevant to Sabir's academic research (*Nottingham Evening Post*, 2012; Townsend, 2012).

Moreover, the status of *The Al Qaeda Training Manual* was explicitly addressed in the Court of Appeal ruling in Zafar & Ors v R in February 2008. The appeal case turned on the question of intention under section 57 of the Terrorism Act 2000. It was argued that the legislation 'must be given a more restricted meaning' (Zafar & Ors v R [2008] 2 WLR 1013, 1018, para. 49). The legislation should be interpreted 'as if it reads':

> A person commits an offence if he possesses an article in circumstances which give rise to a reasonable suspicion that he intends it to be used for the purpose of the commission, preparation or instigation of an act of terrorism (para. 29).

The court emphasised that the law required 'certainty of meaning' and the terrorism legislation 'must be interpreted in a way that requires a direct connection between the object possessed and the act of terrorism' (para. 29). Possession of the relevant articles is an offence only if, the defendant having adduced evidence to show that there was 'an issue as to whether his possession of the relevant articles was for a purpose connected with the commission, preparation or instigation of an act of terrorism', the Crown proves beyond reasonable doubt that those were the defendant's purposes (paras 15 and 16).

Yet the well-established use of the document in terrorism studies was apparently not checked by the authorities prior to Yezza's and Sabir's arrests, according to documents incrementally released under the Data Protection Act and Freedom of Information legislation. Furthermore, the fact of its common reference was not acknowledged in subsequent official briefings according to official documents. An official PowerPoint presentation by an unnamed agency to the Home Office or DIUS declares:

> It is important to note that the Training Manual found WAS NOT the version you can purchase on "Amazon". (Anon, undated Slide 3, capitals in original)

The idea that the version downloaded was the 'most serious form' appears to have circulated among different bodies. It is not yet clear where or why this belief arose or persisted, although the altered interview evidence suggests official imperatives to show its possession as illegitimate. Nevertheless, the view was apparently crucial to the Home Office decision to subject the administrator to fast-track deportation after the two were released from terrorism custody, without charge. However, the internet edition in question is the same document you can buy on Amazon – and, insofar as there are differences, particular editions available on Amazon are actually more substantial. The downloaded US Department of Justice document, cited in leading terrorism studies, is essentially the same as the Pavillion Press edition, save for minor heading changes; they both omit chapters eight, nine, ten, eleven, and part of chapter seven (Anon, 2005). Jerry Post's edition contains these chapters, and just omits the section on ricin (Post, 2005b); similarly the US Airforce edition (Post, 2005a), while the latest Books Express edition includes the ricin section (Anon, 2010). Meanwhile, the campus Blackwells bookshop may also order you the book, and sells a paperback of Osama Bin Laden's speeches, as may other high street bookshops.

The DIUS media communications brief refers to 'extremist materials on campus' (DIUS, undated). Reference to 'extremist materials' sounds much more alarming than two respectable foreign policy journal articles and a popular primary text in terrorism studies made available to the public on the internet by respectable web sites like the US Department of Justice and the American Federation of Scientists, and available to buy through booksellers or borrow through libraries. Yet the 'Nottingham Two' case somehow ended up appearing among a list of UK serious 'Islamist Terrorist Plots', in a Heritage Foundation report, which was disseminated by the UK Home Office (Bromund and Roach, 2010, p. 3, p. 13) and held on a file that Europol held on Sabir. (Email from Rizwaan Sabir to the author dated 7 May 2012). Released documents show official preoccupation with communications problems and official dismissal of there being civil freedoms at stake. In this vein, the official PowerPoint presentation by the same unnamed agency complains about a 'comms problem', and refers to the threat to academic freedom in inverted commas:

> But the real comms problem was distortion of events by individual academics (plus University and College Union (UCU)) and how the 'threat to academic freedom' took off among wider academic community as chain emails; blogs. (Anon, undated, notes to Slide 7)

Is it distortion to raise questions and seek to hold the authorities to account over arrests related to a mainstream security studies text, legally available via public or academic libraries, booksellers or official websites for the public? The authorities' responses have implications for *public intellectual freedom*, not simply academic freedom, as set out, for example, by the International Federation of Library Associations and Institutions (IFLA, undated; 1999; 2003). Nor did the individuals' ordeals end with their release. The administrator was immediately re-arrested, threatened with deportation, and subsequently convicted on minor unrelated immigration offences. Strong support from students, staff and his local Member of Parliament, Alan Simpson, led to Yezza's deportation eventually being dropped, and his right to remain and his UK citizenship being established. Nevertheless, they found themselves under continuing suspicion from the authorities, whose responses appear more focused on justifying the arrests than on the rights and welfare of those affected. The student Sabir found himself repeatedly followed, stopped, searched and/or questioned. In a period of twelve months, for example, he was subjected to 13 stop-searches at the hands of the police, including for terrorism. (Email from Rizwaan Sabir to the author dated 7 May 2012). He subsequently brought a case against Nottinghamshire Police for 'false imprisonment, and breaches of the Race Relations Act 1976 and the Human Rights Act 1998', as well as 'under the Data Protection Act 1998 regarding false information on Nottinghamshire Police records' (Bhatt Murphy solicitors, 2011). Eventually, the police settled out of court in September 2011, and agreed to pay compensation and correct serious inaccuracies on their intelligence files (Bhatt Murphy solicitors, 2011). There may be yet further troubling revelations of official conduct following revelation of how the police altered interview evidence (Townsend, 2012).

The authorities' failure to robustly defend the freedoms of individuals to read published works legitimised interference with the freedoms of speech and expression of others, especially ethnic minority students. Consider the experience of an undergraduate student at another UK university, ironically writing a dissertation on the social impact of the war on terror on young British Muslims. His dissertation included reviewing Jihadi and Islamophobic-related papers. On one occasion in 2010, the student was searched and questioned for several hours by transport police. He was not arrested, nor was a warrant issued for any further investigation. Yet various possessions and his dissertation materials were confiscated. He was further informed he was not to travel on any form of public transport until further notice. After nearly two weeks, he was informed that no charges would be brought against him, and he was free to travel. Later his possessions were returned to him. His case illustrates how stop and search powers are informally extending bail-like curbs on individual freedom of movement, even in the absence of arrest or charge, or evaluation by an independent judge or magistrate. As such, the rights of students to follow their studies free from fear of arrest are compromised.

The Home Office's latest report is seeking 'to limit access to harmful content on-line in specific sectors or premises' (Home Office, 2011a, p. 76). Its implications are not yet clear, nor are the responses of educational institutions. The question is open whether the authorities will push academics to move towards more circumscribed curricula and reading materials, rather like Mrs Umbridge's defence of the dark arts 'risk free' class at Hogwarts (Rowling, 2003, pp. 216–21). Yet how effectively a sanitised terrorism studies would be able to 'challenge terrorist ideology', as the Home Office wishes, is in doubt (Home Office, 2011a, p. 63, para. 5.35).

Robert Lambert, author of *Countering Al Qaeda in London* (2011), and formerly of Special Branch, has cited the Nottingham case as 'ineffective counter-terrorism', fostering community loss of confidence in counter-terrorism policing and Prevent strategies (Powerpoint presentation to the Lancashire Police HQ, December 2011). He suggests that counter-terrorism has become 'too widely-focused', and ineffective due to targeting too many in the community. Yet the authorities still seem to be reluctant to take responsibility for the formal and informal restrictions they are fostering. Indicatively, government bodies and universities, instead of straightforwardly upholding the freedom of speech and expression in education, or alternatively outlining what material is proscribed, are displacing responsibility onto individual academics and students. The 2008 DIUS guidance refers to universities seeking legal guidance, but increasingly individuals are expected to clarify their legal position, although the authorities themselves consider it to be a complex area. Such is the climate that some university reading lists now even warn students to seek legal advice on the reading material they use. For example, a student has written how at his university, he is warned,

'ALL STUDENTS HOWEVER SHOULD BE FAMILIAR WITH THE CURRENT LEGAL SITUATION REGARDING POSSESSION OF MATERIALS "LIKELY TO BE OF USE TO A TERRORIST"' (quoted in Thorne, 2011, capitals in original). Here one might recall Milton's observation:

> for if we be so jealous over them, as that we dare not trust them with an English pamphlet, what do we but censure them for a giddy, vicious, and ungrounded people; in such a sick and weak state of faith and discretion, as to be able to take nothing down but through the pipe of a licenser? (Milton, 1903, [1644], p. 59).

Today the authorities do not want to be seen as censors, but are inviting self-censorship in a risk-averse culture, where robust comprehensive defence of civil liberties by institutions has been lacking. Milton's *Areopagitica* (1644) deplored how, 'Unoffensive books must not stir forth without a visible jailer in their title' (Milton, 1903, [1644], p. 59). Yet our institutional norms appear to be fostering such a timid regulated climate. The Enlightenment motto of 'Dare to know' appears rather forlorn under contemporary bureaucratic risk management and student politics. Instead, the expanding bureaucratic campus codes cultivate risk-averse subjectivities, seeking external governance and avoiding the moral responsibility of freedom.

Foolish defence of free speech

Two decades on from the *Satanic Verses* affair, we appear further away from Rushdie's injunction, 'Language is courage: the ability to conceive a thought, to speak it, and by doing so to make it true' (Rushdie, 2006, [1988], p. 281). Overall, speech codes are fostering personalities cautious how they speak or behave, anxious not to offend or judge anybody. Such personalities are less likely to have the courage of their convictions, and more likely to hesitate before daring to speak truth to power. But, untested convictions have the character of prejudices rather than true convictions (Mill, 1985, [1859], p. 97, p. 116). Renaissance philosopher Erasmus recognised the problem of cautious minds five centuries ago. His *Praise of Folly* suggests that the wise may know truth, but their very wisdom leads them to be too wise to the dangers of speaking truth to power (Erasmus, 1971, [1511]). Thus, their caution may lead them to keep quiet, reserve their judgement, and preserve their position. But, at the same time, their wisdom becomes limited as it conforms itself to the received cultural or political norms (Mill, 1985, [1859], pp. 94–5). Conversely, Erasmus praises fools as daring to speak truth to power (Erasmus, 1971, [1511], pp. 118–19). Foolish words, just like foolish tabloids, may be found irritating, stupid or offensive at times, but it is vital to defend freedom of speech against the growing codes of the 'unsayable'.

As Rushdie argues, foolish words or ideas are necessary to challenge vested interests and social stasis:

> What kind of idea are you? Are you the kind that compromises, does deals, accommodates itself to society, aims to find a niche, to survive; or are you the cussed, bloody-minded, ramrod-backed type of damnfool notion that would rather break than sway with the breeze? – The kind that will almost certainly, ninety-nine times out of hundred, be smashed to bits; but, the hundredth time, will change the world. (Rushdie, 2006, p. 335)

Shakespeare's tragedy *King Lear* ends with the injunction: 'Speak what we feel, not what we ought to say' (Shakespeare, Act V, Scene III). Yet terrorism laws, hate speech, libel laws and speech codes, supplemented with global speech, reinforce mainstream culture, emphasising what ought not to be said, from football matches to personal Twitters. Caliban in Shakespeare's *Tempest* cries out, 'I needs must curse' (Act II, Scene I, line 1085). But, in more and more areas of life, neither Calibans nor fools are free to curse.

Yet a striking, virtually uncontested exception exists to current speech prohibitions. Namely, left-liberal commentators feel able to freely curse the white working classes in language reminiscent of older racial or elite prejudices, suggesting they are primitive or apelike, even as they advocate tighter hate speech laws against them (O'Neill, 2012a; 2012b). Arguments, suggesting that those attracted to right-wing politics lack cognitive abilities (Monbiot, 2012), or implying their intelligence is akin to monkeys (Brooker, 2012), echo earlier colonial linguistic anthropology, which suggested that colonial subjects lacked the capacity for abstract thought (Malinowski, 1923).

Such arguments are anti-democratic and legitimise expert governance of populations against political and personal freedom. Authority, however, is not infallible, and only becomes true authority through being contestable (Mill, 1985, [1859], p. 97, p. 116). Unfortunately, a culture of governance over freedom is spilling over into oppositional politics and its practices and social demands, even among movements challenging state or private restrictions. Yet developments outside the west in recent years have suggested that there are people willing to speak truth to power and risk their lives to challenge repressive rule.

Afterword: Reclaiming Freedoms of Speech against Linguistic Governance?

Political re-awakening against undemocratic regimes

UNESCO's 1950 *Freedom and Culture* contrasts totalitarian and democratic systems: 'One is faith in an official truth and in the power of government to impose it. The other is faith in the continuing inventiveness of men' (Bryson, 1950, p. 144). The 2011 Arab Awakening saw people re-asserting faith in themselves, coming together collectively, and shaking regimes across the Middle East. However insecurely and temporarily, their 'acting and speaking together' recreated a *polis*, a space where people explicitly manifested themselves and distinguished themselves through their public words and deeds (Arendt, 1998, [1958], p. 198).

Simultaneously, they transformed themselves through speech and action from spectators into 'Privileged actors' of history (Fanon, 1967, p. 28) and re-*demonstrated* the potential of collective democratic politics and social revolutions globally. Thereby they also challenged culturalist prejudices, mistrusting their capacity for self-determination, and western assumptions over western democratic culture necessarily being stronger than elsewhere. People were willing to speak truth to power and risk their lives against repressive rule. In particular, protesters' tenacity in Egypt against the Mubarak regime, and their efforts to maintain non-sectarian ideals, inspired others globally.

The euphoria of the Arab Spring, at its zenith when Mubarak stepped down in February 2011, recaptures other liberatory historical moments, when suddenly the inconceivable seems conceivable, and 'word and deed' matter intensely (Arendt, 1977a, pp. 3–6). The writer Abu al-Qasim al-Shabi's poem *Life's Will* captured the times for many Arabs:

> When people choose
> To live by life's will,
> Fate can do nothing but give in;
> The night discards its veil,
> All shackles are undone.

When traditional divisions are challenged, new sympathies may spread, and more universal bonds between people seem possible. Negative concepts of the masses, the multitudes or the crowd are transformed from assuming their ignorance to admiring the virtues of 'a people risen up', seeing 'in rudest men/ self-sacrifice' (Wordsworth, 1995, [1850], lines 390–4). Participants and witnesses alike find themselves infused with the liberatory spirit of the times and become patriots. Here assimilation is not experienced as violence, as much language advocacy or theory emphasises today, but as humanising. So, even when the revolutionary moment recedes, is defeated or becomes degraded, the memory of 'the best of times' and 'the worst of times' points to how humanity might create a better world.

This book has argued that language rights advocacy has shifted from protecting civil and political freedoms to linguistic governance. There have been wide critiques of the erosion of civil and political freedoms under the war on terror. However, formal or informal limitations on speech and expression are not confined to a 'state of exception' and security imperatives (Agamben, 2005), but have ironically become an aspect of human rights advocacy. The rising status of international human rights following the end of the Cold War was greeted as embodying ideals of individual freedom and justice against traditional international relations. Yet international human rights governance is driven by ambivalence towards democratic politics. Contemporary language rights advocacy, like human rights advocacy more broadly, is wary of the *demos* and believes that it is necessary to circumscribe democracy in order to protect minority rights. In short, expert international or regional governance is preferred over popular national government. Language rights advocacy seeks to preserve diverse, plural societies, but its cultural and linguistic identity strategies are at the expense of political speech and experimentalism. Maximising such rights fixes divisions between people. Identity rights governance mummifies cultures in the name of cultural authenticity, and is antithetical to fostering diverse experiments in living and communication between people. Conversely, as Rushdie argues, ossified relations cannot be free:

> Free societies...are societies in motion, and with motion comes tension, dissent, friction. Free people strike sparks, and those sparks are the best evidence of freedom's existence (Rushdie, 2006, [1988], p. 215)

The counterpart to public recognition of our difference is the public surveillance of ourselves. Expectations that identities must be formally recognised have fostered expectations that individuals' identity should be formally protected, vetted and affirmed. Yet the expanding regulation is tending to legitimise offence and non-communication, even as identity claims are legitimising curbs on freedom of speech and expression which, where heeded, tend to silence marginal or dissenting voices within communities.

Myriad informal codes of therapeutic governance, supplementing laws, are expanding regulation of cultural identities and relations in ways which deny individuals' capacity for free speech, free expression and spontaneous interactions. Formal affirmations of principles of free speech and expression become hollow mantras when so many qualifications strip their meaning both conceptually and in practice. But, simultaneously, the substance of identities is also hollowed out as individuals' exercise of their political, moral and creative capacity is subject to external governance.

Human rights experts assume legitimacy and authority against the *demos*, paralleling the assumption of expert governance in other areas. A mummified Enlightenment is also being promoted alongside mummified cultures. Enlightenment ideals are subverted when legislation criminalises particular religious or traditional dress in the name of a particular model of individual autonomy. Equally, restrictions on free speech to protect the public from unenlightened views are antithetical to Enlightenment ideals. In this vein, some secularists are demanding restrictions on public expression of religious belief. As such, they follow other identity claims demanding freedom from other people's religious, political or cultural views that offend their own, and, in doing so, promote linguistic governance against freedom of speech and expression. Nevertheless, an enlightened response is more speech, not more regulation of speech. Political decision-making determined by the expert represents enlightened despotism, marginalising the citizen as political subject, and transforming politics into technical administrative matters (Berlin, 1969, p. 128). Concurrently, public engagement acquires a degraded understanding of the public as vessels to be filled with appropriate values. Undemocratic tendencies are marked in the European Union and its expanded technocratic governance of member states, which only seems to confirm Fanon's evaluation of Europe's political stasis (Fanon, 1967, p. 253).

Importantly, the EU has sought to legitimise itself and mitigate its democratic deficit through recognising cultural rights. Language rights advocates have commonly looked to the EU to promote their demands against national states, and have been slow to criticise its democratic deficit. Yet, while the Middle East has witnessed repressive regimes being challenged, Europe has witnessed serious encroachments on national democratic decision-making, notably on closer union under the Lisbon Treaty, and, more recently, on closer economic union under the EU's proposed Treaty on Stability, Coordination and Governance in the Economic and Monetary Union, and other economic crisis measures. The Treaty would embed fiscal austerity constitutionally, excluding alternative socialist, liberal or conservative economic visions from democratic electoral determination. As such, the EU is seeking to remove the economy from democratic politics. Yet, as *The Economist* has observed, 'Surely democratic politics is nothing if not about how wealth is created and distributed' (*The Economist*, 2012). Already in 2011, the EU effectively supplanted elected governments in Greece and Italy and replaced them with expert governments to implement its economic austerity policies. Thus political speech and action was usurped from the birthplace of the *polis* and democratic ideals. To add insult to democratic injury, the expert economic solutions, forged from narrow elite constituencies, have unsurprisingly shown narrow understanding of society and the economy, and reflected narrow interests. Serious questions exist, therefore, as to whether their economic strategies were promoting economic recovery, even as they have attacked ordinary people's living standards.

European human rights advocates have raised few, if any, objections to the undemocratic aspects of closer union, which they have largely supported. Language rights advocates have actively sought EU governance over national governments and majoritarian democracy to protect minority languages and communities. Overall, advocacy has shown 'faith in an official truth and in the power of [global or regional governance] to impose it', rather than 'faith in the continuing inventiveness' of the *demos* (Bryson, 1950, p. 144). So, while advocates may deplore the EU economic governance being imposed on populations, they have contributed to the EU's democratic deficit. As such, their objections to EU economic governance represent disputes between expert governance models, not principled objections to the EU's undemocratic, technocratic tendencies. To borrow from Arendt, 'they move in a world where speech has lost its power' (Arendt, 1998, [1958], p. 4).

The spirit of the Arab political awakening, and its popular demands for freedom and justice, not only challenged repressive state regimes, but were also antithetical to global and regional governance and their assumptions of a rather degraded humanity. The Arab uprisings were essentially spontaneous, but drew on long grievances (Dalacoura, 2012; Lawson, 2011). Indicatively, western media and policy-makers tended to overemphasise the role of electronic social media in societal mobilisation (Dalacoura, 2011, pp. 68–9; Lawson, 2011). Their rather ahistorical, technocratic understanding downplayed the role of people as 'privileged actors' originating the uprisings, and instead privileged the role of technological means. In doing so, western social media networkers also flattered their own activities and underestimated the collective political character of the Arab uprisings. Protesters obviously used contemporary technology, just as earlier movements, with their 'battle of the pamphlets', exploited the print technology of their day. Crucial is our humanity as speaking animals, and capacity to determine for ourselves 'what is just and unjust' (Aristotle, *Politics*, 1992, p. 60, [350BC], 1253a16), rather than the technical means actors choose to exploit.

The concluding pages highlight problems reclaiming the *polis* as a space for speaking and acting, in recent international human rights advocacy and the Occupy Movement. Both human rights interventions and Occupy's speech governance show ambivalence towards humanity as subjects capable of political and personal self-determination.

Human rights interventions in the Middle East

Influential strands in language rights advocacy are concerned that violations of language rights should be treated as linguicide or crimes against humanity. Contemporary international politics has seen crimes against humanity being invoked to support the concept of Responsibility to Protect (R2P), that is, military intervention in the name of humanitarian or human rights concerns. Human rights were invoked by western forces in the Kosovo, Afghan and Iraq wars, as well as less high-profile military operations in Sierra Leone and elsewhere. However, since the Iraq and Afghan wars, there has been more scepticism towards humanitarian interventions. R2P advocates are concerned over the concept being de-legitimised. Yet there are tensions between human rights governance and self-determination.

The Arab Spring witnessed protests breaking out across the region – Tunisia, Morocco, Egypt, Libya, Bahrain, Syria, Yemen – and showed people determined on self-determination in their demands for more freedom and justice. Those heady days of Spring 2011 insisted on autonomy from foreign intervention, even in the countries where international intervention, or the calls for international intervention, subsequently became intense. Posters or statements declaring 'No foreign intervention. We can do it alone' were reported in Benghazi, Libya in March 2011, shortly before NATO intervention. Likewise, earlier reports observed large opposition to foreign intervention in Syria (BBC, 2012; Daoudy, 2011, p. 23). Demands for democratic self-determination belie democratisation as an internationally governed process, for the experience of previous interventions shows that interveners do not stop at minority and human rights concerns, but expand into broader social and economic governance, as the cases of Bosnia or Kosovo illustrate. Thus we see the west's efforts to supervise post-Gaddafi Libyan politics through its sponsored interim national council. Nevertheless, populations are not just 'bare, forked' creatures to be written on by philosopher-kings, but people with their own beliefs and interests.

Unfortunately, however, the popular spontaneous political awakening was essentially without leadership, organisation or common collective goals, beyond deposing their regimes. Many of the young urban protesters, moreover, were sceptical towards hierarchies, power structures, and therefore formalising leadership and organisation around common collective goals. This position was dangerous where the uprisings also inspired counter-revolutions, and allowed counter-revolutionary, sectarian and external forces and interests to re-assert themselves (Shatz, 2012). Protesters across the Middle East found themselves losing the initiative against better-organised counter-revolutionary forces, and also foreign influences seeking to shape political developments. Among the insecure and threatened oppositional forces in the Middle East, some became tempted to shift from domestic political mobilisation and seek external sponsorship against their repressive regimes.

Influential human rights organisations called for international intervention to support opposition forces. Human Rights Watch (HRW) backed the Security Council resolution on Libya and NATO intervention. Kenneth Roth, director of HRW and long-time proponent of R2P, has called for similar protection to be taken elsewhere in the Middle East and in North Africa and beyond, including the Ivory Coast, Burma and Sri Lanka. Roth, writing in the US journal *Foreign Policy*, considers persistent anti-imperial objections to intervention anachronistic in the face of democratic and human rights demands (Roth, 2011). Unfortunately, ideals and good intentions to promote democracy and human rights do not guarantee good democratic and human rights outcomes. W.H. Auden warned half a century ago:

> When they speak of Principles, look out: perhaps
> Their generals are already poring over maps (Auden, 1966, p. 191).

Memories appear short among pro-interventionists, who forget how the western military interventions in Iraq and Afghanistan, under a declared strategy of 'non-negotiable demands of human dignity' (NSS, 2002, p. vi), failed to realise democratic freedoms or social justice, but precipitated worse sectarian violence, alongside their own violence at Abu Ghraib prison and elsewhere.

NATO military intervention in Libya was claimed 'an unqualified military success' (Joshi, 2011, p. 16). But similar claims were made at the time about the successes of the Afghan and Iraqi interventions. Even the earlier 'pristine' humanitarian intervention in Kosovo looks rather dubious from the perspective of progressive democratic politics. Both Bosnia and Kosovo show political ossification and retrenched sectarianism under global and regional governance, rather than democratic vibrancy.

So, while the west was able to mobilise military intervention in Libya, and probably speeded up the defeat of Gaddafi, the intervention fostered civil war, and complicated the development of authentic democratic politics. Policy analysts and human rights advocates have been concerned over western states being seen as honest brokers in the region. Advocates fear that NATO's tacit expansion of a responsibility to protect mandate to effectively authorise regime change in Libya has reinforced international opposition to the concept as legitimising western interference in weaker countries (Amnesty, 2012, pp. 47–9; Bolopion, 2011). Moreover, western states accepted the crushing of rebellion in Bahrain. They also reinforced the power of the Egyptian military through their continuing support. Yet the provisional Supreme Council of the Armed Forces (SCAF) actually reinforced emergency laws, although their abolition had been a core demand of demonstrators (Amnesty, 2012; Shatz, 2012). Hence, regional scepticism persists over external intervention due to ongoing experience, not only the decades of foreign support for repressive regimes in the region. Many in the Middle East may therefore beg to differ from Roth, and consider fears of neo-imperialism justified. Nevertheless, while the western powers may be ready to intervene in the internal affairs of other countries, interventions and occupations like that of Afghanistan have acquired a rather confused, purposeless character.

Meanwhile, international human rights advocacy continues to help re-legitimise western military and non-military intervention in the Middle East. Iran's mass opposition protests manifested themselves a couple of years earlier, in 2009, and the regime was able to crush them. Since 2010, opposition has struggled to revitalise itself as a mass collective movement. Moreover, western threats against Iran over its nuclear programme have tended to rally support for the regime and channel protests against the west. We see this in the mass demonstrations against the foreign assassinations of Iranian nuclear physicists, with demonstrators waving defiant placards declaring 'I am a nuclear physicist', as well as the patriotic surge of applications to study nuclear physics.

In spring 2012, western human rights attention turned from Libya to Syria, where the regime was using military force to hold onto power against a fractured opposition, and the country was descending into (sectarian) civil war. Amnesty International was among the international human rights organisations appealing to the UN Security Council to condemn Syria and refer Syria to ICC (Amnesty, 2012, p. 63). However, greater divisions existed internationally over formal intervention in Syria in the aftermath of the Libyan intervention. Nevertheless, external involvement in Syria, whether Chinese and Russian aid to Assad's regime or western-sponsored resolutions condemning Assad's regime, had already raised the internal and regional stakes and intensified internal conflict, entrenching the regime's brutal efforts to maintain power and tempting the threatened and divided opposition forces to seek external military backing. Thus, political determination moved away from locals and became subject to external forces.

While human rights advocacy was willing to support military intervention in Libya and Syria, it was also concerned with international monitoring of developments in other countries. Anxiety existed over the success of Islamist parties the post-Arab-spring elections. Suggestions were made that constitutional limits should be drafted prior to elections to protect weak secularist forces against the potential popularity of Islamist parties. However, the success of an Islamic party in Egypt was accepted, unlike the situation in Algeria in the 1990s, which witnessed the election results being annulled and the Islamist party being banned under military rule, precipitating a civil war that caused the deaths of over 100,000. Yet this violation of democracy received strikingly little attention or condemnation in the west, even among international human rights campaigners.

Western calls for international intervention to support democratic and human rights in the Middle East are ironic given the continuing western military occupations, the west's own attacks on civil liberties under the war on terror, and the EU's retreat from democratic politics. Demoralised western radical activism attempted to join the Arab Awakening 'To travel forward towards Liberty/With more success' (Wordsworth, 1995, [1850], Lines 215–19). Yet western radical activism is struggling to free itself from the contemporary norms of linguistic governance.

Radical politics and speech codes

The Occupy movement received significant media attention in 2011 as the cutting edge of a new oppositional politics in the west, inspired by the Arab Awakening, particularly the Egyptian protests, and also the Greek and Spanish anti-austerity protests. The call to Occupy Wall Street was initiated by *Adbusters*, the North American-based anti-consumerism organisation and magazine, which describes itself as 'a 90,000+ strong network of activists, cultural creative's [*sic*] and meme insurgents' (Adbusters in Greenberg, 2011a). The call was also echoed by the internet hacker campaigning group Anonymous. Thousands were attracted to Occupy Wall Street, inspired by the images of Tahrir Square in Egypt or Syntagma Square in Greece. Up to a couple of hundred regularly camped in Zuccotti Park, New York, through Autumn 2011. They, in turn, sparked other occupations internationally, from capitals like London and Amsterdam to provincial cities like Nottingham.

At their height, Occupy Wall Street, and elsewhere, enjoyed considerable media attention and striking public approval in opinion polls, against some negative responses. They also attracted numerous writers, journalists, and academics and non-academics organising informal 1968-like teach-ins, including speakers such as Samir Amin, Julian Assange and Slavoj Žižek. Their character is therefore interesting to examine to gain insights into contemporary political developments.

A core driving force behind Occupy was a feeling that a generation of activists had become overly preoccupied with a virtual world of electronic social media, and risked losing touch with physically grounded reality and interaction. Strikingly, participants emphasise Occupy as 'a *physical* space' for critical debate where people actually met together (Wehgman, 2012). Such concerns echo Arendt's emphasis on a *polis* as a 'space of appearance... the space where I appear to others as others appear to me' (Arendt, 1998, [1958], pp. 198–9). Nevertheless, their understandings of the political space and political speech diverged significantly from historical predecessors. Occupy preferred non-hierarchical forms of organisation and decision-making by consent, and was wary of claims to authority or representative politics, notwithstanding its popular slogan proclaiming 'We are the 99%.'

Occupy's eschewing of traditional political forms encouraged the phenomenon to be compared to dadaism and other cultural political movements. Nevertheless, unlike earlier movements, dadaist or otherwise, it did not draft its own manifesto (Danchev, 2011). The closest it came to was its slogan of 'We are the 99%', which invoked the division between the one per cent of the wealthy profiteers of capitalism and the vast majority of the world's population. The political theorist Wendy Brown enthused about the Occupy movement as representing a return of a 'Repressed Res-Publica' (Brown, 2011). She saw its slogan, 'We are the 99 %', as embodying a new populist political consciousness, inaugurating an inclusive politics of justice against interest or difference (Brown, 2011). Translation of this slogan into specific demands, however, proved more elusive. Diverse commentary suggested demands, or projected its own demands onto Occupy (for example, Connolly, 2011). No proposals, though, were formalised and adopted by the movement. Rather, the very absence of specific demands was celebrated by supporters as key to its success. As one supportive commentary wrote:

> To develop a list of specific demands will run the risk either of containing or limiting what the movement might accomplish, of breaking what is increasingly a global movement into local or national ones, or, if demands are not met, of weakening the movement in the eyes of the media, politicians, and the worldwide public. (Grusin, 2011)

These ideas originate in 1960s radicalism, which saw consciousness-raising as prior to developing political demands. There is a sense in which Occupy saw any set of demands as 'a kind of censorship' (Rushdie, 1983, p. 71), preventing other demands and excluding people they might want to attract. Again, Occupy echoed post-modern linguistic concerns over the discriminating character of speech. Writing a manifesto, like writing a story, means not writing another, at least at that moment (Rushdie, 1983, p. 71). But, while specific words and actions necessarily exclude speaking other words, or doing other acts, these exclusions are an aspect of creativity, whether creating arts or politics, and are neither inherently discriminatory not inherently ossifying, but a prelude to other words and acts. In other words, realising one manifesto may lead to another.

Instead of a written manifesto, Occupy has left a non-verbalised manifesto of its practices. Significantly, Occupy emphasised itself as an exemplar of a new form of living, counterposed to corporate greed, consumerism and mental pollution. John Protevi celebrated Occupy as empowering 'active joyous collective action, on and on in a horizontally radiating network', bringing together speech act theory and affect theory (Protevi, 2011). Its themes resonated with Romantic critiques of modernity, which influence ecolinguistic advocacy, and broader political ideas. Here we see Occupy's antecedents in anti-globalisation and environmental politics. Participants, however, expressed concern that the anti-globalisation movement succumbed to NGO-isation, and became elitist in its activities, focused on global summits and counter-summit activities, excluding those who did not speak global English or could not afford global travel expenses (Wehgman, 2012). Conversally, Occupy sought to re-focus activities, bringing people together locally and physically on the street as correctives to activism's more elite and virtual focus of the past decade.

But we come to a paradox in Occupy's politics: its apparent need to draft detailed codes of public and interpersonal communication, contrasting with its ambivalence towards drafting an explicit political manifesto. Newcomers to Occupy were instructed on the communication codes followed in Occupy's general assembly and its consensus decision-making (Greenberg, 2011a). These included the use of hand signals, which sought to facilitate inclusive exchanges of ideas with mutual respect, allowing everybody to speak, not speaking on behalf of others, and listening without cutting in on each other. They made its atmosphere distinct from traditional politics. Their practice of the 'people's mic', where people repeat the words of the speaker, for example, echoes the feel of a church congregation following the liturgy rather than classic protest meetings. The codes sought non-judgemental attitudes towards individuals, but the movement's insistence on being non-judgemental and consensus decision-making deterred drafting a collective political manifesto. Codes instructed, for example, 'Listen to the wisdom everyone brings to the group', 'Give each person the time and space to speak' and 'Recognize that we try not to judge, put each other down or compete' (Occupy London, 2011, discussed in Hayes, 2011b). Such codes echo the format of a seminar or formal mediation processes, rather than the urgency of political protest, but even in a seminar one knows not everyone brings wisdom to the group. Conversely, the very concept of political opposition is premised on the clash of opposing beliefs and ideas. As such, their practices have been criticised as conforming to mainstream US individualism, with participants cherry-picking their concerns, rather than forging a collective politics (Dean, 2011). Indicatively, discussion of class seemed to vanish in its consensual approach (Deseriis and Dean, 2012). Meanwhile, although Occupy sought to reclaim public spaces, it typically banned political parties from its sites, as conflicting with Occupy's participatory learning ways.

Furthermore, its codes embodied assumptions about human relations, and appropriate views and ways of communicating and behaving, antithetical to both liberal beliefs and collective politics. Implicit anxiety seemed to run through Occupy organisers over spontaneous, unregulated relations in their imperatives to draft communication codes, notwithstanding their defence of the right to protest. This anxiety was embodied in the London Occupy safety code instructing occupiers to, inter alia:

> Respect each other's physical and emotional boundaries, always get explicit verbal consent before touching someone or crossing boundaries. (Occupy London, 2011, discussed in Hayes, 2011b)

The accumulative instructions illustrate how the movement struggled, despite its counter-culture antecedents, to imagine or risk spontaneous informal relations – here non-verbal consent. Simultaneously, they echoed the therapeutic governance of late capitalism and its consumer-orientated culture, de-legitimising anger and grooming a pleasant personality (Hochschild, 1983; Stearns and Stearns, 1986). Yet earlier social movements have commonly fused both ideological and personal passions (Goodwin, 2001). Conversely, political and personal mistrust circumscribed aspects of Occupy. So, while Žižek warned Occupy protesters, 'Don't fall in love with yourselves...Carnivals come cheap' (Žižek, 2011), their elaborate codes were antithetical to carnival exuberance and spontaneity. As one reflective participant has commented, 'We were so busy building the infrastructure, we sometimes forgot to mobilise around actions.' Their activism did not simply become diverted into micro-management of daily living away from political demands (Greenberg, 2011b), but legitimised more governance of interpersonal relations and speech. Thus, whereas the 1960s counter-culture sought to liberate people from the 'policeman inside your head', today's radical politics appears to invite a permanent presence self-censoring speech and action.

At the same time, the weight of inhibiting codes deters clarification of political demands, leadership and collective organisation, leading to historical opportunities being missed. Occupation without clear political ideals loses its purpose and disengages support. (And radical occupation lacking purpose ironically echoes recent western military occupations lacking clear purpose.) Yet, again, a movement reluctant to engage in a struggle of ideas and formulate its own political manifesto risks allowing its political voice to pass from those in tents to established figures or interests, who read their politics onto activism. So, while Occupy has sought to be a movement without leadership, instead tacit leaders and managerial authorities developed, without collective democratic accountability. Indicatively, the safety codes themselves highlighted above were probably drafted by the tech group, one of the dozen or so process groups which supplemented the work of the general assembly. In other words, the codes were drafted by those exercising an implicit authority based on their superior command of technological expertise. Overall, these sorts of codes, if they were widely followed, would foster personalities cautious how they spoke or behaved, anxious not to offend or judge anybody. Occupy wanted to be an experiment in living, but it may have ended up offering a rather suffocating model of human communication and relations.

Again, the question of Occupy's reluctance as a movement to articulate a specific manifesto returns us to Sartre's warnings against the celebration of the non-communicable, and becoming complicit in political quietism or undemocratic solutions (Sartre, 1967, p. 210, discussed in Murdoch, 1989, pp. 64–80). Occupy claimed to represent the interests of the 99 per cent, without actually articulating its political ideas. Premature claims to represent the 99 per cent short-circuit the problem of building political support. Human rights advocates are often seen today at the forefront of demanding the exclusion of persons or views deemed harmful, instead of defending free speech. This undemocratic turn in advocacy is an evasion of the challenge of convincing people of our views, and a betrayal of earlier human rights activism. In this sense, they echo global human rights advocacy and global governance, which claim to speak on behalf of populations without having a popular democratic mandate. Such conditions are conducive to the people finding their will represented in ways which may contradict their actual will, as Berlin's essay 'Two Concepts of Liberty' warns (Berlin, 1969, pp. 118–72).

Reclaiming freedoms of speech and expression

Today we have expanding governance grounded in the political judgement of Platonic guardians, who move in a world increasingly excluding the *demos* and its power of speech (Arendt, 1998, [1958], p. 4). There is a need to revive a politics and culture grounded in the *demos*, and not afraid of political and civil freedoms of speech and expression. Such a revival is not given from above, but created by people themselves publicly reclaiming the political power of speech. People's power of speech may potentially be released wherever people appear together to speak and act publicly (Arendt, 1998, [1958], p. 199). Yet that very potentiality is widely seen as problematic in today's demoralised, anxious age, which assumes freedom of speech empowers dangerous, harmful voices. A culture of fear is pushing for more regulation of word and act to curb potential risks and harms.

Conversely, free speech demands assume that exercising freedoms involves uncertainty and does not guarantee outcomes. Hence, calls for freedom of speech imply more speech, not a relativist abdication of speech, unprepared to challenge obnoxious views (O'Neill, 2010a). It is precisely matters of grave human concern and serious political division where the freedom to speak should be most defended. For where discussion is heavily circumscribed and certain ideas are banned, then infallibility of understanding has been assumed. But such bans represent projections of power, not the pursuit of truth (Skillen, 1982). Understanding is not developed through banning offending ideas. Furthermore, those who have the moral courage to speak out are in a stronger position where a robust rights climate exists upholding the principle of free speech, than in an ambivalent climate where it is legitimate for the authorities to suppress dissent. But even oppositional politics, and its practices and social demands, are struggling to break out of linguistic governance and revive the power of speech. Thus, political radicalism today commonly pushes for greater freedom of (technological) communication and greater transparency, as shown in the wide protests against the Anti-Counterfeiting Trade Agreement (ACTA), but may accept more governance of speech. Disturbingly, a climate of cultural relativism uncomfortable with challenging different views is tempted towards censorship or self-censorship. The blurring of speech and action under hate speech legislation treats us as automata lacking the moral capacity to resist calls to violence, and thereby also denies our moral responsibility for our actions.

Key strands of contemporary language rights advocacy are ambivalent about free speech. Their concerns converge with influential post-Saussurean linguistic theories, emphasising language as discriminatory and violent. Treating language as communication may be an unsophisticated understanding of language. Nevertheless, it is historically associated with demands for more freedom of speech. Conversely, language advocacy, giving paramountcy to linguistic and cultural identity, favours more linguistic governance. In particular, ecolinguistics, combining linguistic identity and ecological concerns, seeks to affirm the worth of every language, but its linguistic determinism tends to degrade human language and creativity. Thus, linguistic and cultural identity advocacy ironically ends up repudiating our human identity.

In denying speech, we are, in Aristotle's understanding, renouncing our humanity. Speech is constitutive of humans as unique moral beings. Freedom of speech is a fundamental freedom without which we cannot be sure that we have any other freedoms (Harris, 2009; Skillen, 1982). Its restriction curbs human consciousness and our political, moral and creative potentiality. A humanist linguistic philosophy affirms individual and collective creativity. For it is through speech we realise both our individuality and our sociability (Humboldt, 1999, [1841]. However, contemporary linguistic governance embodies anti-humanist and anti-speech approaches. A living politics and culture requires freedoms of speech and expression. But regaining our freedoms of speech and expression from pervasive governance involves regaining a sense of ourselves, independent of formal recognition. Free speech needs to be lived, not treated as an ornament to be displayed on a mantle-piece and occasionally dusted. Too often freedom of speech is invoked as an abstract noun. We should treat free speech as a verb and an activity of speaking freely. We need to rediscover 'experiments of speaking' against the despotisms of contemporary linguistic governance, wherever they manifest themselves.

Bibliography

Abley, Mark (2003) *Spoken Here: Travels Among Threatened Languages.* London: Penguin.

Abrahamsen, Rita (2000) *Disciplining Democracy: Development Discourse and Good Governance in Africa.* London: Zed Books.

Abrams v. United States, 250 U.S. 616 (1919).

Abtahi, Hirad and Philippa Webb (2008) *The Genocide Convention: The Travaux Preparatoiries,* Vol. 1. Leiden: Martin Nijhoff.

AcaDemon (undated) Term Paper # 110519 Al Qaeda Training Manual http://www.academon.com/Term-Paper-Al-Qaeda-Training-Manual/110519. Accessed 15 April 2011.

Achebe, Chinua (1975) [1966] 'The African Writer and the English Language', in *Morning Yet on Creation Day.* New York: Anchor Press, pp. 91–103.

Achebe, Chinua (2001) *A Man of the People.* London: Penguin.

Adejunmobi, Moradewun (2004) *Vernacular Palaver. Imaginations of the Local and Non-Native Languages in West Africa.* Clevedon; Buffalo; Toronto: Multilingual Matters.

African Academy of Languages (ACALAN) http://www.acalan.org/. Accessed 15 April 2011.

African Academy of Languages (ACALAN) (2009a) Action Plan of the Bamako Commitment on Universal Multilingualism. http://www.acalan.org. Accessed 15 April 2011.

African Academy of Languages (ACALAN) (2009b) Bamako Commitment on Universal Multilingualism. http://www.acalan.org/eng/events/forum/commitment.pdf. Accessed 15 April 2011.

Agamben, Giorgio (2005) *State of Exception.* Chicago: Chicago University Press.

Akhmatova, Anna (1989) [1935–1943] *Selected Poems.* Translated by Stanley Kunitz with Max Hayward. London: Collins-Harvill.

Alexander, Ronelle (2006) *Bosnian, Croatian, Serbian, A Textbook: With Exercises and Basic Grammar.* Madison: University of Wisconsin Press.

Ali, Monica (2004) *Brick Lane.* London: Black Swan.

American Anthropological Association (AAA) (1947) 'Statement on Human Rights'. *American Anthropologist,* No. 49, pp. 539–43.

American Anthropological Association (AAA) (1999) Declaration on Anthropology and Human Rights Committee for Human Rights American Anthropological Association. http://www.aaanet.org/stmts/humanrts.htm.

Amin, Samir (1976) *Unequal Development.* Hassocks: Harvester.

Amnesty International (2012) *Year of Rebellion: The State of Human Rights in the Middle East and North Africa.* London: Amnesty International.

Anderson, Benedict (1991) *Imagined Communities: Reflections on the Origin and Spread of Nationalism.* London: Verso, revised edition.

Andrić, Ivo (1959) [1945] *The Bridge Over the Drina.* Translated by Lovett Edwards. London: Allan & Unwin.

Andrić, Ivo (1992) [1945] *The Days of the Consuls.* Translated by Celia Hawkesworth in collaboration with Bogdan Rakić. London: Allen & Unwin.

Anonymous (2005) *The Al Qaeda Training Manual*. New York: Pavilion Press.

Anonymous (2010) *Al Qaeda Training Manual: Military Studies in the Jihad Against the Tyrants*. Books Express. http://www.books-express.co.uk/book/9781907521249/Military-Studies-in-the-Jihad-against-the-Tyrants.html.

Anonymous (undated) Slide Presentation on Nottingham 2008 Arrests. http://nottinghamwhistleblower.files.wordpress.com/2011/06/footnote-309–312.pdf. Accessed 15 September 2011.

Anti-Defamation League (ADL) (undated) *Hate Crime Laws: Introduction*. http://www.adl.org/99hatecrime/intro.asp. Accessed 19 July 2011.

Anti-Defamation League (ADL) (2000) *Combating Extremism In Cyberspace: The Legal Issues Affecting Internet Hate Speech*. New York: ADL. http://Www.Adl.Org/Civil_Rights/Newcyber.Pdf. Accessed 19 July 2011.

Arendt, Hannah (1968) [1951] *The Origins of Totalitarianism*. San Diego: Harcourt.

Arendt, Hannah (1972) *Crisis of the Republic*. Harmondsworth: Penguin.

Arendt, Hannah (1973) *On Revolution*. London: Penguin.

Arendt, Hannah (1977a) *Between Past and Future*. London: Penguin.

Arendt, Hannah (1977b) *Life of the Mind*. San Diego: Harcourt.

Arendt, Hannah (1992) *Lectures on Kant's Political Philosophy*. Edited and with an interpretive essay by Ronald Beiner. Chicago: University of Chicago Press.

Arendt, Hannah (1998) [1958] *The Human Condition*. Chicago: University of Chicago Press.

Aristotle (1992) [350 BC] *The Politics*. Translated by T.A. Sinclair. Harmondsworth: Penguin.

Arnold, Matthew (1862) *On Translating Homer*. London: Longman, Green, Longman & Roberts. http://www.victorianprose.org/texts/Arnold/Works/on_trans_homer_last_w_1862.pdf. Accessed 23 October 2010.

Arnold, Matthew (1960) [1869] *Culture and Anarchy*. Cambridge: Cambridge University Press.

Arthur, Charles (2012) 'Acta Protests Break Out as EU States Sign Up to Treaty'. *Guardian*, 27 January. http://www.guardian.co.uk/technology/2012/jan/27/acta-protests-eu-states-sign-treaty. Accessed 5 February 2012.

Asamoa, E.A. (1955) 'The Problem of Language in Education in the Gold Coast'. *Africa: Journal of the International African Institute*, Vol. 25, No. 1, pp. 60–78.

Askew, Louise (2011) The Language Policy of the International Community in Bosnia-Herzegovina Since 1995. University of Nottingham doctoral thesis.

Auburger, Leopold (1999) *Die Kroactische Sprache und der Serbokroatismus*. Ulm/Donau: Gerhard Hess Verlag.

Auden, W.H. (1966) *Collected Shorter Poems 1927–1957*. London: Faber.

Baker, Catherine (2010) 'The Care and Feeding of Linguists: The Working Environment of Interpreters, Translators and Linguists during Peacekeeping in Bosnia-Herzegovina.' *War & Society*, Vol. 29, No. 2, pp. 154–75.

Baker, Mona (2006) *Translation and Conflict: A Narrative Approach*. London: Routledge.

Bakić-Hayden, Milica (1996) 'Nesting Orientalisms: The Case of Former Yugoslavia'. *Slavic Review*, Vol. 54, No. 4, pp. 917–32.

Balkan Insight (2011) 'Serbian Bishop's Hate Speech Trial on Hold'. *Balkan Insight*, 23 June. http://www.balkaninsight.com/en/article/serbian-bishop-on-trial-for-hate-speech. Accessed 19 July 2011.

Barkawi, Tarak (forthcoming) *Soldiers of Empire*.

Barke, Dennis (2001) 'Mary Whitehouse: Self-appointed Campaigner Against the Permissive Society on Television'.*Guardian*, 24 November 2001. http://www.guardian.co.uk/media/2001/nov/24/guardianobituaries.obituaries. Accessed 10 January 2011.

Barnett, H.G. (1948) 'On Science and Human Rights'. *American Anthropologist*, No. 50, pp. 352–5.

Barthes, Roland (1967) *Writing Degree Zero*. Translated by Annette Lavers and Colin Smith. London: Jonathan Cape.

Barthes, Roland (1977) 'Death of the Author', in *Image – Music*. Edited and translated by Stephen Heath. London: Fontana, pp. 42–8.

Bassnett, Susan (2002) *Translation Studies*. London: Routledge, third edition.

Bassnett, Susan and André Lefevere (1998) *Constructing Cultures: Essays on Literary Translation*. Clevedon: Multilingual Matters.

Bateman, Milford (2010) *Why Doesn't Microfinance Work?* London: Zed Books.

Bauman, Zygmunt (1989) *Modernity and the Holocaust*. Cambridge: Polity Press.

Bayley, John (1979) 'Introduction', in Alexander Puskin (ed.), *Eugene Onegin*. Translated by Charles Johnston. Harmondsworth: Penguin, pp. 9–28.

BBC (1986) *Blackadder*, second series, episode 3 entitled 'Head', http://www.bbc.co.uk/comedy/blackadder/, http://www.youtube.com/watch?v=lAHIcbTRDbI, http://humour.50megs.com/blackadder/ba22.html. Accessed 20 October 2010.

BBC (2001) 'Mary Whitehouse: Moral Crusader or Spoilsport?' *BBC News*, 23 November. http://news.bbc.co.uk/1/hi/uk/763998.stm. Accessed 19 July 2011.

BBC (2008a) 'Last Alaska Language Speaker Dies'. *BBC News*, 24 January. http://news.bbc.co.uk/1/hi/7206411.stm. Accessed 30 June 2010.

BBC (2008b) 'Lyrical Terrorist Wins Appeal'. *BBC News*, 17 June. http://news.bbc.co.uk/1/hi/uk/7459180.stm. Accessed 19 July 2011.

BBC (2010) 'Four Lions Film Boycott Urged by 7/7 Families'. *BBC News*, 7 May. http://news.bbc.co.uk/1/hi/uk/8663809.stm. Accessed 19 July 2011.

BBC (2011a) 'US Pastor Terry Jones Banned from Entering UK'. *BBC News*, 20 January. http://www.bbc.co.uk/news/uk-1223183.2. Accessed 19 July 2011.

BBC (2011b) 'Luton Army Parade Protesters Lose High Court Appeal'. *BBC News*, 16 February. http://www.bbc.co.uk/news/uk-12480509. Accessed 19 July 2011.

BBC (2011c) 'Lincoln Man Banned from English Defence League Meetings'. *BBC News*, 10 March. http://www.bbc.co.uk/news/uk-england-lincolnshire-12708120. Accessed 19 July 2011.

BBC (2012) 'Guide to the Syrian Opposition'. *BBC News*, 8 February. http://www.bbc.co.uk/news/world-middle-east-15798218. Accessed 15 March 2012.

Beano (2001) *Dennis and Gnasher: Seriously Silly Jokes*. New Lanark: Beano Books.

Beattie, James R. (2004) 'Taking Liberalism and Religious Freedom Seriously'. *The Catholic Lawyer*, Vol. 43, pp. 378–88.

De Beauvoir, Simone (1972) [1949] *The Second Sex*. Translated and edited by H.M. Parshley. Harmondsworth: Penguin.

Beck, Ann (1966) 'Colonial Policy and Education in British East Africa, 1900–1950'. *The Journal of British Studies*, Vol. 5, No. 2, pp. 115–38.

Bell, Daniel (1976) *The Cultural Contradictions of Capitalism*. London: Heinemann.

Benedict, Ruth (1946) *The Chrysanthemum and the Sword: Patterns of Japanese Culture*. Boston: Houghton Mifflin.

Benedict, Ruth (1961) [1934] *Patterns of Culture*. London: Routledge.

Benjamin, Walter (1992) [1923] 'The Task of the Translator', in Rainer Schulte and John Biguenet (eds), *Theories of Translation: An Anthology of Essays from Dryden to Derrida*. Chicago and London: University of Chicago Press, pp. 71–82.

Berlin, Isaiah (1969) *Four Essays on Liberty*. Oxford: Oxford University Press.

Berlin, Isaiah (2000) *Three Critics of the Enlightenment: Vico, Hamann, Herder*. Edited by Henry Hardy. Princeton: Princeton University Press.

Berlin, Brent and Paul Kay (1969) *Basic Color Terms: Their Universality and Evolution*. Berkeley: University of California Press.

Berman, Bruce (1996) 'Ethnography as Politics, Politics as Ethnology: Kenyatta, Malinowski and the Making of Facing Mount Kenya'. *Canadian Journal of African Studies / Revue Canadienne des Études Africaines*, Vol. 30, pp. 313–44.

Bernard, Russell (1992) 'Preserving Language Diversity'. *Human Organization*, Vol. 51, No. 1, pp. 82–9.

Bernasconi, Robert and Sybol Cook (eds) (2003) *Race and Racism in Continental Philosophy*. Bloomington: Indiana University Press.

Betjeman, John (1970) *John Betjeman's Collected Poems*. London: J. Murray.

Betts, Raymond (2005) *Assimilation and Association in French Colonial Theory, 1890–1914*. Lincoln: University of Nebraska Press.

Bhatt Murphy Solicitors (2011) 'Press Release: Nottinghamshire Police Pay £20,000 Damages to Rizwaan Sabir for Wrongful "Terror Arrest"'. London. 14 September.

Bhatti, Gurpreet Kaur (2004) *Behzti* (Dishonour). London: Oberon Books.

Bhatti, Gurpreet Kaur (2010) *Behud* (Beyond Belief). London: Oberon Books.

Bisong, Joseph (1995) 'Language Choice and Cultural Imperialism: A Nigerian Perspective'. *ELT Journal*, Vol. 49, No. 2, pp. 122–32.

Bliesemann de Guevara, Berit (2009) *States of Conflict: A Case Study on Peacebuilding in Bosnia and Herzegovina*. London: Institute of Public Policy Research.

Bliesemann de Guevara, Berit (2010) 'Introduction: The Limits of Statebuilding and the Analysis of State-Formation'. *Journal of Intervention and Statebuilding*, Vol. 4, No. 2, pp. 111–28.

Bloom, William (1990) *Personal Identity, National Identity and International Relations*. Cambridge: Cambridge University Press.

Boas, Franz (1904) 'Some Traits of Primitive Culture'. *Journal of American Folklore*, Vol. 17, pp. 243–54.

Boas, Franz (1940) *Race, Language and Culture*. New York: Macmillan.

Boas, Franz (1962) [1928] *Anthropology and Modern Life*. New York: WW Norton.

Boas, Franz (1963) [1911] *Introduction to Handbook of American Indian Languages*. Washington: Georgetown University Press.

Boas, Franz (1965) [1911] *The Mind of Primitive Man*. New York: Free Press.

De Boe-Buquicchio, Maud (2010) 'Balancing the Governance of Hate Speech and Freedom of Expression/the Free Flow of Information on the Internet'. Joint OSCE/CoE Internet Governance Forum. 15 September. Vilnius: OSCE. http://www.osce.org/documents/rfm/2010/09/46167_en.pdf. Accessed 10 July 2011.

Boettcher, Daniel (2010) 'Indian Language Is New to Science'. *BBC News*. 5 October. http://www.bbc.co.uk/news/science-environment-11479563. Accessed 20 December 2010.

Bolopion, Philippe (2011) 'After Libya: To Protect or to Depose'. *Los Angeles Times*. 25 August. http://www.hrw.org/news/2011/08/25/after-libya-question-protect-or-depose. Accessed 15 March 2012.

Bolton, Kingsley (2006) 'World Englishes', in Alan Davies and Catherine Elder (eds), *The Handbook of Applied Linguistics*. Oxford: Blackwell, pp. 367–96.

Bolton, Kingsley and Braj Kachru (2006) *World Englishes: Critical Concepts in Linguistics*. Abingdon; New York: Routledge.

Bookchin, Murray (1995) *Re-Enchanting Humanity: A Defense of the Human Spirit against Anti-Humanism, Misanthropy, Mysticism and Primitivism*. London: Cassell.

Boran, Idil (2003) 'Global Linguistic Diversity, Public Goods, and the Principle of Fairness', in Will Kymlicka and Alan Patten (eds), *Language Rights and Political Theory*. Oxford: Oxford University Press, pp. 189–209.

Bowring, Bill (2008) *The Degradation of the International Legal Order? The Rehabilitation of Law and the Possibility of Politics*. London: Routledge-Cavendish.

Bracken, Patrick (2002) *Trauma: Culture, Meaning and Philosophy*. London: Whurr Publishers.

Bradley, David (1989) 'The Disappearance of Ugong in Thailand', in Nancy Dorian (ed.), *Investigating Obsolescence: Studies in Language Contraction and Death*. Cambridge: Cambridge University Press, pp. 33–40.

Bradley, David and Maya Bradley (eds) (2002) *Language Endangerment and Language Maintenance: An Active Approach*. London: Routledge.

Bragg, Melvyn (2006) *In Our Time*. Newsletter, BBC Radio 4, 10 February.

Brierly, J.L. (1928) *The Law of Nations: An Introduction to the International Law of Peace*. Oxford: Clarendon Press.

Bromund, Ted, and Morgan Roach (2010) *Islamist Terrorist Plots in Great Britain: Uncovering the Global Network* No. 2329. Heritage Foundation, dated 26 October 2009; and revised and updated 4 January 2010. http://www.heritage.org/research/reports/2009/10/islamist-terrorist-plots-in-great-britain-uncovering-the-global-network. Accessed 19 July 2011.

Brooker, Charlie (2012) 'When the Daily Mail Calls Rightwingers Stupid, the Result Is Dumbogeddon'. *Guardian*, 5 February. http://www.guardian.co.uk/commentisfree/2012/feb/05/daily-mail-calls-rightwingers-stupid. Accessed 10 March 2012.

Brookes, Heather and Shirley Brice Heath (1997) 'Book Review: *Overcoming Linguistic Discrimination*, edited by Tove Stutnabb-Kangas and Robert Phillipson'. *International Journal of the Sociology of Language*, Vol. 27, pp. 197–208.

Brooks, Alan and Jeremy Brickhill (1980) *Whirlwind before the Storm*. London: International Defence and Aid Fund for Southern Africa.

Broome, Benjamin J. (1993) 'Managing Differences in Conflict Resolution: The Role of Relational Empathy', in Dennis Sandole and Huge van der Merwe (eds), *Conflict Resolution Theory and Practice: Integration and Application*. Manchester and New York: Manchester University Press, pp. 97–111.

Broomfield, G.W. (1930) 'The Development of the Swahili Language'. *Africa*, Vol. 3, No. 4, pp. 516–22.

Brown, Wendy and Janet Halley (eds) *Legalism/Left Critique*. Durham and London: Duke University Press.

Brown, Wendy (2011) 'Occupy Wall Street: Return of a Repressed Res-Publica'. *Theory and Event*, Vol. 14, No. 4, Occupy Wall Street supplement.

Brownlie, Ian (ed.) (1971) *Basic Documents on Human Rights*. Clarendon Press: Oxford University Press.

Brutt-Griffler, Janina (2002) *World English: A Study of Its Development*. Cleveland: Multilingual Matters.

Bryson, Bill (1994) *Made in America: An Informal History of the English Language in the United States*. New York: W. Morrow.

Bryson, Lyman (1950) 'Freedom of Information', in Julian Huxley (ed.), *Freedom and Culture*. London: Unesco/Wingate, pp. 116–56.

Buell, John (2011) 'Occupy Wall Street's Democratic Challenge'. *Theory and Event*, Vol. 14, No. 4, Occupy Wall Street supplement.

Bugarski, Ranko and Celia Hawkesworth (eds) (1992) *Language Planning in Yugoslavia*. Columbus: Slavica.

Bugarski, Ranko (2001) 'Language, Nationalism and War in Yugoslavia'. *International Journal of the Sociology of Language*, No. 151, pp. 69–88.

Bulić, Refik (1999) *Bosanski jezik u praksi i normi*. Tuzla: Printcom.

Burchill, Richard (1985) *The English Language*. Oxford: Oxford University Press.

Burgess, Adam (1997) *Divided Europe: The New Domination of the East*. London: Pluto.

Burke, Edmund (1986) [1790] *Reflections on the Revolution in France*. Harmondsworth: Penguin.

Burke, Roland (2006) 'The Compelling Dialogue of Freedom: Human Rights at the Bandung Conference'. *Human Rights Quarterly*, Vol. 28, No. 4, pp. 947–65.

Burman, Erica (1994) 'Innocents Abroad: Western Fantasies of Childhood and the Iconography of Emergencies'. *Disasters*, Vol. 18, No. 3, pp. 238–53.

Burton, John (1997) *Violence Explained: The Sources of Conflict, Violence and Crime and Their Provention*. Manchester and New York: Manchester University Press.

Butcher, Jim (2003) *The Moralisation of Tourism: Sun, Sand and Saving the World?* London: Routledge.

Butcher, Jim (2007) *Ecotourism, NGOs and Development: A Critical Analysis*. London: Routledge.

Butler, Alan (2005) *Times Higher Educational Supplement*, Letters, 9 September, p. 15.

Callanan, Cormac (2004) 'Best Practices for Internet Hotlines', in OSCE, *The Media Freedom Internet Cookbook*. Vienna: OSCE, pp. 150–60. http://www.osce.org/fom/13836?download=true. Accessed 17 July 2011.

Campbell, Aiden (1997) *Western Primitivism, African Ethnicity: A Study in Cultural Relations*. London: Cassell.

Campbell, Colin (2005) *The Romantic Ethic and the Spirit of Modern Consumerism*. Oxford: Alcuin Academic.

Campbell, Duncan (2005) 'The Ricin Ring That Never Was'. *Guardian*, 1 April. Corrected Version. http://www.guardian.co.uk/world/2005/apr/14/alqaida.terrorism. Accessed 19 July 2011.

Cannadine, David (2002) *Ornamentalism: How the British Saw Their Empire*. London: Penguin.

Carey, John (1992) *The Intellectuals and the Masses: Pride and Prejudice among the Literary Intelligentsia. 1880–1939*. London: Faber & Faber.

Carr, E.H. (1939) *The Twenty Years Crisis 1919–39: An Introduction to the Study of International Relations*. London: Macmillan.

Carr, E.H. (1941) *The Future of Nations: Independence or Interdependence*. London: Kegan Paul, Trench, Trubner & Co.

Carr, E.H. (1942) *Conditions of Peace*. London: Macmillan.

Carroll, John (1963) 'Linguistic Relativity, Contrastive Linguistics, and Language Learning'. *International Review of Applied Linguistics in Language Teaching*, Vol. 1, No. 1, pp. 1–20.

Casaba, Sogor (2009) 'There Is Linguistic Genocide In the European Union', European Parliament speech, 24 November. http://www.sogorcsaba.eu/mywork/?l=en&m=4&sm=22&id=214. Accessed 19 February 2012.

Cassese, Antonio (1994) *Human Rights in a Changing World*. Cambridge: Polity Press.

Césaire, Aimé (1972) *Discourse on Colonialism*. Translated by Joan Pinkham. New York: Monthly Review Press.

Césaire, Aimé (1995) [1939] *Notebook of a Return to My Native Land*. Translated by Mireille Rosello and Annie Pritchard.Tarset. Highgreen: Bloodaxe Books.

Chandler, David (1999) *Bosnia: Faking Democracy after Dayton*. London: Pluto.

Chandler, David (2002) *From Kosovo to Kabul: Human Rights and International Intervention*. London: Pluto.

Chandler, David (2004) *Constructing Global Civil Society: Morality and Power in International Relations*. Basingstoke: Palgrave Macmillan.

Chandler, David (2010) *International Statebuilding: The Rise of Post-Liberal Governance*. London: Routledge.

Chandler, David (2012) 'Development as Freedom? From Colonialism to Countering Climate Change' *Development Dialogue*, No. 58, pp. 115–29.

Chase, Malcolm (1988) *The 'People's Farm': English Radical Agrarianism 1775–1840*. Oxford: Clarendon Press.

Chatterjee, Partha (1992) 'Their Own Words? An Essay for Edward Said', in Michael Sprinker (ed.) *Edward Said: A Critical Reader*. Oxford: Blackwell, pp. 194–220.

Chawla, Saroj (2001) 'Linguistic and Philosophical Roots of Our Environmental Crisis', in Alvin Fill and Peter Mühlhäusler (eds), *The Ecolinguistics Reader: Language Ecology and the Environment*. London: Continuum, pp. 115–23.

Chomsky, Noam (1959) 'A Review of B. F. Skinner's Verbal Behavior'. *Language*, Vol. 1, pp. 26–58.

Chomsky, Noam (1965) *Aspects of the Theory of Syntax*. Cambridge, Mass.: MIT Press.

Chomsky, Noam (1988) *Language and Problems of Knowledge*. Cambridge, Mass.: MIT.

Chomsky, Noam (1999) *The New Military Humanism: Lessons from Kosovo*. London: Pluto Press.

Chomsky, Noam (2000) *A New Generation Draws the Line: Kosovo, East Timor and the Standards of the West*. London: Verso.

Chomsky, Noam (2002) *Cartesian Linguistics: A Chapter in the History of Rationalist Thought*. Second edition edited by James McGilvray. Christchurch: Cybereditions.

Chomsky, Noam (2006) 'Why Are There So Many Languages? Diversification from an Underlying Unity', Lecture at the Endangered Languages Fund, New Haven. 15 November. http://www.endangeredlanguagefund.org/chomsky.php. Accessed 23 November 2010.

Citizenship Survey (2009) *Citizenship Survey: 2009–10 (April 2009 – March 2010), England*. http://www.communities.gov.uk/publications/corporate/statistics/citizenshipsurveyq4200910. Accessed 17 July 2011.

Clark, Jon and Lord Wedderburn (1987) 'Juridification – A Universal Trend? The British Experience in Labour Law', in Gunther Teubner (ed.), *Juridification of Social Spheres. A Comparative Analysis in the Area of Labor, Coroporate, Antitrust and Social Welfare Law*. Berlin and New York: Walter de Gruyter, pp. 163–90.

Coetzee, J.M. (1983) *Life and Times of Michael K*. South Yarmouth: John Curley.

Cohn, Bernard (1996) *Colonialism and Its Forms of Knowledge: The British in India*. Princeton: Princeton University Press.

Collins, Harold (1953) '"Cry, the Beloved Country" and the Broken Tribe'. *College English*, Vol. 14, No. 7, pp. 379–85.

Coleridge, Samuel Taylor (2001) [1817] *Biographia Literaria*. Vol. 1, Elecbook.

Comas, Juan (1956) 'Racial Myths', in UNESCO (1956) *The Race Question in Modern Science*. Paris: Unesco, pp. 11–53.

Committee on Endangered Languages and their Preservation (CELP) http://www.lsadc.org/info/lsa-comm-endanger.cfm. Accessed 20 July 2010.

Condillac, Etienne Bonnot de (2001) [1746] *Essay on the Origin of Human Knowledge*. Translated and edited by Hans Aarsleff. Cambridge: Cambridge University Press.

Connolly, William (2011) 'What Is to Be Done?' *Theory and Event*, Vol. 14, No. 4, Occupy Wall Street supplement.

Constituent Assembly of India (1948) *Report of the Linguistic Provinces Commission*. New Delhli: Government Press.

Constituent Peoples' Decision of the Bosnia-Herzegovina Constitutional Court dated 14 September 2000. http://www.ohr.int/ohr-dept/legal/const/default.asp?content_id=5853. Accessed 3 November 2010.

Constitution of the Federation of Bosnia-Herzegovina. http://www.ohr.int/const/bih-fed/default.asp?content_id=5907. Accessed 29 October 2010.

Cooke, Bill and Uma Kothari (eds) (2001) *Participation: The New Tyranny?* London: Zed Books.

Cosgrove, Richard A. (1980) *The Rule of Law: Albert Venn Dicey, Victorian Jurist*. London and Basingstoke: Macmillan.

Council of Europe (1950) *Convention for the Protection of Human Rights and Fundamental Freedoms* (ECHR). http://conventions.coe.int/treaty/Commun/QueVoulezVous.asp?NT=005&CL=ENG. Accessed 5 January 2011.

Council of Europe (1992a) *European Charter for Regional or Minority Languages. CETS No. 148*. http://www.coe.int/t/e/legal_affairs/local_and_regional_democracy/regional_or_minority_languages/ or http://conventions.coe.int/Treaty/Commun/QueVoulezVous.asp?NT=148&CM=8&DF=07/10/2010&CL=ENG. Accessed 10 November 2010.

Council of Europe, *Committee of Experts on European Charter for Regional or Minority Languages*. http://www.coe.int/t/dg4/education/minlang/aboutcommittee/default_en.asp. Accessed 10 November 2010.

Council of Europe (1992b) *Explanatory Report: European Charter for Regional or Minority Languages*. CETS No. 148. http://conventions.coe.int/Treaty/en/Reports/Html/148.htm. Accessed 10 November 2010.

Council of Europe (1995) *Framework Convention for the Protection of National Minorities and Explanatory Report*. Doc. No. H(1995)010 http://www.coe.int/t/dghl/monitoring/minorities/1_AtGlance/PDF_H(1995)010_FCNM_ExplanReport_en.pdf. Accessed 10 November 2010.

Council of Europe (2001) European Charter for Regional or Minority Languages. Report of the Committee of Experts on the Application of the Charter in Croatia. Strasbourg: Council of Europe, dated 20 September. Accessed 19 June 2012. http://www.coe.int/t/dg4/education/minlang/report/EvaluationReports/CroatiaECRML1_en.pdf.

Council of Europe (2003a) Additional Protocol to the Convention on Cybercrime, Concerning the Criminalisation of Acts of a Racist and Xenophobic Nature Committed through Computer Systems, Strasbourg, 28 January, Document No. STE 189. Accessed 5 January 2011.

Council of Europe (2003b) Explanatory Report, Additional Protocol to the Convention on cybercrime, Concerning the Criminalisation of Acts of a Racist and Xenophobic Nature Committed through Computer systems, Strasbourg: CoE, Document STE No. 189. http://conventions.coe.int/Treaty/en/Reports/Html/189.htm. Accessed 5 January 2011.

Cowan, Jane K. Marie-Bénédicte Dembour, and Richard Wilson (eds) (2001) *Culture and Rights: Anthropological Perspectives*. Cambridge: Cambridge University Press.

Cox, Roger (1996) *Shaping Childhood. Themes of Uncertainty in the History of Adult-Child Relationships*. London: Routledge.

Criminal Justice Act 2003 http://www.legislation.gov.uk/ukpga/2003/44/contents. Accessed 6 January 2011.

Crowder, Michael (1964) 'Indirect Rule: French and British Style'. *Africa: Journal of the International African Institute*, Vol. 34, No. 3, pp. 197–205.

Crowley, Tony (1991) *Proper English? Readings in Language, History and Cultural Identity*. London: Routledge.

Crowley, Tony (2003) *Standard English and the Politics of Language*. Basingstoke: Palgrave, second edition.

Crown Prosecution Service (CPS) (2008) 'CPS response to Samina Malik appeal'. 17 June. http://www.cps.gov.uk/news/press_releases/143_08/. Accessed 14 January 2011.

Crown Prosecution Service (CPS) (2009) *Hate Crime Report 2009*. London: CPS. http://www.cps.gov.uk/publications/docs/CPS_hate_crime_report_2009.pdf. Accessed 19 January 2011.

C-SAP (2009) *C-SAP Special Interest Group Teaching About Terrorism Residential*. London, 9–10 June.

Crystal, David (1997) *English as a Global Language*. Cambridge: Cambridge University Press.

Crystal, David (2002) *Language Death*. Cambridge: Cambridge University Press.

Currie, James (1934) 'The Educational Experiment in the Anglo-Egyptian Sudan, 1900–33. Part I'. *Journal of the Royal African Society*, Vol. 33, No. 133, pp. 361–71.

Currie, James (1935) 'The Educational Experiment in the Anglo-Egyptian Sudan, 1900–33. Part II'. *Journal of the Royal African Society*, Vol. 34, No. 134, pp. 41–59.

Dalby, Andrew (2003) *Language in Danger: How Language Loss Threatens Our Future*. London: Penguin.

Dalacoura, Katerina (2012) 'The 2011 Uprisings in the Arab Middle East: Political Change and Geopolitical Implications'. *International Affairs*, Vol. 88, pp. 63–79.

Danchev, Alex (ed.) (2011) *100 Artists' Manifestos: From the Futurists to the Stuckists*. London: Penguin.

Daoudy, Marwa (2011) 'Syria: Revolution and Repression', in Conservative Middle East Council (ed.), *The Arab Spring*. London: Conservative Middle East Council, pp. 20–23.

Dasmann, Raymond (1964) *Environmental Conservation*. New York; London: Wiley.

Davies, Alan (1996) 'Review Article: Ironising the Myth of Linguicism'. *Journal of Multilingual and Multicultural Development*. Vol. 17, No. 6, pp. 485–596.

Davies, Alan (1997) 'Response to a Reply'. *Journal of Multilingual and Multicultural Development* Vol. 18, No. 3, p. 248.

Davies, Alan and Catherine Elder (eds) (2006) *The Handbook of Applied Linguistics*. Oxford: Blackwell.

Davis, Merle (1967) *Modern Industry and the African*. London: Frank Cass, second edition.

Dayton Peace Agreement or the General Framework Agreement for Peace in Bosnia and Herzegovina (1995) Dayton, Ohio, US, 21 November, in Snežana Trifunovska (ed.) (1999), *Former Yugoslavia through Documents: From Dissolution to the Peace Settlement*. The Hague: Martinus Nijhoff Publishers, pp. 472–83 or http://www.ohr.int/gfa/gfa-home.htm.

Dean, Jodi (2011) 'Claiming Division, Naming a Wrong'. *Theory and Event*, Vol. 14, No. 4, Occupy Wall Street supplement.

Decision on Constitutional Amendments in the Federation dated 19 April 2002. http://www.ohr.int/decisions/statemattersdec/default.asp?content_id=7475. Accessed 23 November 2010.

Decision on Constitutional Amendments in the Republika Srpska dated 19 April 2002. http://www.ohr.int/decisions/statemattersdec/default.asp?content_id=7474. Accessed 23 November 2010.

Defoe, Daniel (1702) *The Reformation of Manners: A Satyr.* London. Eighteenth Century Collections Online. Gale. Gale Document Number: CW116484008

Defoe, Daniel (2001) [1719] *Robinson Crusoe.* London: Penguin.

Dembour, Marie-Bénédicte (2001) 'Following the Movement of a Pendulum: Between Universalism and Relativism', in Jane Cowan, Marie-Bénédicte Dembour and Richard Wilson (eds), *Culture and Rights: Anthropological Perspectives.* Cambridge: Cambridge University Press, pp. 56–79.

Department for Innovation, Universities and Skills (DIUS) (2008) Promoting Good Campus Relations, Fostering Shared Values and Preventing Violent Extremism in Universities and Higher Education Colleges. March. http://www.bis.gov.uk/assets/biscore/corporate/migratedD/ec_group/22-07-HE_on. Accessed 20 January 2011.

Department for Innovation, Universities and Skills (DIUS) (undated) Media Communications Brief.

Derrick, Jonathan (2008) *Africa's Agitators: Militant Anti-Colonialism in Africa and the West, 1918–1939.* New York: Columbia University Press.

Derrida, Jacques (1973) *Speech and Phenomena and Other Essays on Husserl's Theory of Signs.* Translated by David Allison. Evanston: Northwestern University Press.

Derrida, Jacques (1976) *Of Grammatology.* Translated by Gayatri Spivak. Baltimore: John Hopkins University.

Derrida, Jacques (1981) 'Semiology and Grammatology', in *Positions.* Translated by Alan Bass. Chicago: Chicago University Press, pp. 17–61.

Derrida, Jacques (1982) 'Différance'. *Margins of Philosophy.* Translated by Alan Bass. Chicago: Chicago University Press, pp. 3–27.

Derrida, Jacques (1990) *Writing and Difference.* Translated by Alan Bass. London: Routledge.

Derrida, Jacques (1992) 'Force of Law: The "Mystical Foundations of Authority" ', translated by Mary Quaintance in Drucilla Cornell, Michel Rosenfeld and Benjamin Cardozo (eds), *Deconstruction and the Possibility of Justice.* New York: Routledge, pp. 3–67.

Derrida, Jacques (2007) [1985] 'Des Tours de Babel', in *Psyche: Inventions of the Other, Vol. 1.* Stanford: Stanford University Press, pp. 191–225.

Deseriis, Marcos and Jodi Dean (2012) 'A Movement Without Demands'. *Possible Futures,* 3 January. http://www.possible-futures.org/2012/01/03/a-movement-without-demands/. Accessed 8 April 2012.

Deutscher, Guy (2005) *The Unfolding of Language.* London: Arrow Books.

Deutscher, Guy (2010) *Through the Language Glass: How Words Colour Your World.* London: William Heinemann.

Dewey, John (1916) *Democracy and Education: An Introduction to the Philosophy of Education.* New York: Macmillan.

Dewey, John (1940) *Freedom and Culture.* New York: Henry Holt & Co.

Dicey, Albert Venn (1959) [1889] *Introduction to the Study of the Law of the Constitution.* London: Macmillan.

Dickens, Charles (1985) [1854] *Hard Times: For These Times.* Harmondsworth: Penguin.

Dingwaney, Anuradha (1995) 'Introduction: Translating "Third World" Cultures', in Anuradha Dingwaney and Carol Maier (eds), *Between Languages and Cultures: Translation and Cross-Cultural Texts*. Pittsburgh and London: University of Pittsburgh Press, pp. 3–15.

Dingwaney, Anuradha and Carol Maier (eds) (1995) *Between Languages and Cultures: Translation and Cross-Cultural Texts*. Pittsburgh; London: University of Pittsburgh Press.

Dirks, Nicholas (2001) *Castes of Mind: Colonialism and the Making of Modern India*. Princeton: Princeton University Press.

Divan Orchestra http://www.west-eastern-divan.org/. Accessed 15 October 2011.

Donnelly, Jack (2003) *Universal Human Rights in Theory and Practice*. Ithaca; London: Cornell University Press, second edition.

Douzinas, Costas (2000) *The End of Human Rights: Critical Legal Thought at the Turn of the Century*. Oxford: Hart Publishing.

Dryden, John (1992) [1680] 'On Translation', in Rainer Schulte and John Biguenet (eds), *Theories of Translation: An Anthology of Essays from Dryden to Derrida*. Chicago; London: University of Chicago Press, pp. 17–31.

Duffield, Mark (1996) 'Symphony of the Damned: Racial Discourse, Complex Emergencies and Humanitarian Aid'. *Disasters*, Vol. 20, No. 3, pp. 173–93.

Duffield, Mark (2001) *Global Governance and the New Wars: The Merging of Development and Security*. London: Zed Books.

Duffield, Mark (2007) *Development, Security, and Unending War: Governing the World of Peoples*. Cambridge: Polity.

Duffield, Mark (2010) 'Risk-Management and the Fortified Aid Compound'. *Journal of Intervention and Statebuilding*, Vol. 4, No. 4, pp. 453–74.

Dworkin, Ronald (1996) *Freedom's Law; the Moral Reading of the American Constitution*. Oxford: Oxford University Press.

Ebdon, Les (2005) *Promoting Good Campus Relations – Dealing with Hate Crimes and Intolerance*. London: Equality Challenge Unit. http://www.ecu.ac.uk/publications/files/promoting-good-campus-relations-dealing-with-hate-crimes.pdf/view. Accessed 20 January 2011.

Eagleton, Terry (1996) *The Function of Criticism*. London: Verso.

East, R.M. (1936) 'A First Essay in Imaginative African Literature'. *Africa*, Vol. 9, No. 3, pp. 350–8.

East Africa Commission (1925) *Report of the East Africa Commission*. London: HMSO.

Economist (2012) 'Angela the Lawgiver: a Pact to Cut Budget Deficits Is Achieved at the Cost of a Growing Democratic Deficit'. 4 February. http://www.economist.com/node/21546024. Accessed 20 March 2012.

Eckermann, Johann (1883) *Conversations of Goethe, with Eckermann and Soret*. Translated by John Oxenford. London: George Bell.

Eekman, Thomas (1978) *Yugoslav Literature 1945–1975*. Ann Arbor: Michigan University Press.

Einzinger, Kurt (2004) Media Regulation on the Internet', in OSCE, *The Media Freedom Internet Cookbook*. Vienna: OSCE, pp. 142–9. http://www.osce.org/publications/rfm/2004/12/12239_94_en.pdf. Accessed 8 January 2011

El-chebbi, Abou-Al-kacem [Abu al-Qasim al-Shabi] (1991) 'Life's Will', translated by Sargon Boulat and Christopher Middleton, in Salma Khadra Jayyusi (ed.), *Modern Arabic Poetry*. New York: Columbia University Press.

Eliot, T.S. (1965) *Dante*. London: Faber.

Elliott, A.V.P. (1938) 'The Teaching of African Languages in African Schools: A Need for Improvement'. *Africa*, Vol. 11, No. 1, pp. 73–9.

Endangered Language Fund (ELF) http://www.endangeredlanguagefund.org/. Accessed 20 July 2010.

Engels, Friedrich (1849a) 'The Magyar Struggle'. *Neue Rheinische Zeitung* No. 194, 13 January. http://www.marxists.org/archive/marx/works/1849/01/13.htm. Accessed 20 September 2010.

Engels, Friedrich (1849b) 'Democratic Pan-Slavism'. *Neue Rheinische Zeitung*. Nos. 222 and 223, 15 and 16 February. http://www.marxists.org/archive/marx/works/1849/02/15.htm. Accessed 20 September 2010.

Engle, Karen (2001) 'From Skepticism to Embrace: Human Rights and the American Anthropological Association from 1947–1999'. *Human Rights Quarterly* Vol. 23, No. 3, pp. 536–59.

Equality and Human Rights Commission (2010) *Warning from Commission Over Disproportionate Use of Stop and Search by Police*. 15 March. http://www.equalityhumanrights.com/media-centre/2010/march/warning-from-commission-over-disproportionate-use-of-stop-and-search-by-police/. Accessed 18 January 2011.

Equality Challenge Unit (2007) *Promoting Good Campus Relations*. Briefing. London: Equality Challenge Unit.

Erasmus (1971) [1511] *Praise of Folly*. Harmondsworth: Penguin.

Eriksen, Thomas Hylland (1993) *Ethnicity and Nationalism: Anthropological Perspectives*. London and East Haven: Pluto Press.

Eriksen, Thomas Hylland (2001) 'Between Universalism and Relativism: A Critique of the unesco Concept of Culture', in Jane K. Cowan, Marie-Bénédicte Dembour and Richard Wilson (eds), *Culture and Rights: Anthropological Perspectives*. Cambridge: Cambridge University Press, pp. 127–48.

Erikson, Erik (1959) *Identity and the Life Cycle*. New York; London: W.W. Norton.

Essay Tree (undated) *al Qaeda Training Manual*. http://essaytree.com/criminology/al-qaeda-training-manual-and-pres-bushs/ or http://essaytree.com/communication-strategies/al-qaeda-training-manual/.

EU-ICBE (2008) *Strategic Directions for the Development of Education in Bosnia and Herzegovina, with the Implementation Plan 2008–2015*. EU-ICBE. http://www.erisee.org/downloads/library_bih/EducStrategy2008_2015_engl.pdf. Accessed 23 November 2010.

European Commission (2000) *Communication from the Commission on the Precautionary Principle*. http://eur-lex.europa.eu/LexUriServ/LexUriServ.do?uri=CELEX:52000DC0001:EN:NOT. Accessed 18 January 2011.

European Commission (2002) *Consolidated Version of the Treaty on the Functioning of the European Union* in *Official Journal of the European Union*, C 83/49. http://eur-lex.europa.eu/LexUriServ/LexUriServ.do?uri=OJ:C:2010:083:0047:0200:EN:PDF. Accessed 23 November 2010.

European Commission (2009) *Bosnia and Herzegovina 2009 Progress Report*. SEC (2009) 1338. http://www.delbih.ec.europa.eu/docs/ProgressReport20092.pdf. Accessed 23 November 2010.

European Union Agency for Fundamental Rights (FRA) (2010) *Towards More Effective Policing: Understanding and Preventing Discriminatory Ethnic Profiling: A Guide*. Luxembourg: Publications Office of the European Union. http://fra.europa.eu/fraWebsite/attachments/Guide_ethnic_profiling.pdf. Accessed 18 January 2011.

Evans, Tony (1996) *US Hegemony and the Project of Universal Human Rights*. Basingstoke: Palgrave Macmillan.

Everett, Daniel L. (2005) 'Cultural Constraints on Grammar and Cognition in Piraha: Another Look at the Design Features of Human Language'. *Current Anthropology*, Vol. 46, No. 4, August–October, pp. 621–46. http://llc.illinoisstate.edu/dlevere/docs/currentanthroarticle.web.pdf. Accessed 18 July 2010.

Fanon, Frantz (1967) [1961] *The Wretched of the Earth*. Translated by Constance Farrington and preface by Jean-Paul Sartre. London: Penguin.

Fanon, Frantz (1970) *Toward the African Revolution*. Translated by Haakon Chevalier. Harmondsworth: Penguin.

Fanon, Frantz (1980) [1959] *A Dying Colonialism: Freedom for Algeria*. Translated by Haakon Chevalier. London: Writers and Readers.

Fanon, Frantz (2008) [1952] *Black Skin, White Masks*. Translated by Charles Lam Markmann. London: Pluto.

Ferré, Rosario (1995) 'On Destiny, Language, and Translation; or, Ophelia Adrift in the C.&O. Canal', in Anuradha Dingwaney and Carol Maier (eds), *Between Languages and Cultures: Translation and Cross-Cultural Texts*. Pittsburgh; London: University of Pittsburgh Press, pp. 39–50.

Filipović, Muhamed (1999) 'Amaterski rječnik'. *BH Dani*, 19 November. http://www.bhdani.com/arhiva7129/t292a.htm. Accessed 1 July 2011.

Filipović, Rudolf and Damir Kalogjera (eds) (2001) *International Journal of the Sociology of Language*, No. 147.

Fill, Alvin and Peter Mühlhäusler (eds) (2001) *The Ecolinguistics Reader: Language Ecology and the Environment*. London: Continuum.

Fill, Alvin (2001) 'Ecolinguistics: State of the Art 1998', in Alvin Fill and Peter Mühlhäusler (eds), *The Ecolinguistics Reader: Language Ecology and the Environment*. London: Continuum, pp. 43–53.

Finke, Peter (2001) 'Identity and Manifoldness: New Perspectives in Science, Language and Politics', in Alvin Fill and Peter Mühlhäusler (eds), *The Ecolinguistics Reader: Language Ecology and the Environment*. London: Continuum, pp. 84–90.

Fischer, Astrid (2006) *Integration or Segregation: Reforming the Bosnian Education Sector*. Berlin: Berghof Research Center for Constructive Conflict Management. http://www.zapravicnoobrazovanje.ba/Istrazivanja/10.%20Integration%20or%20segregation.pdf. Accessed 3 February 2012.

Fish, Stanley (1994) *There's No Such Thing as Free Speech and It's a Good Thing Too*. Oxford and New York: Oxford University Press.

Fish, Stanley (2008) 'Crying Censorship'. *New York Times*, 24 August. http://opinionator.blogs.nytimes.com/2008/08/24/crying-censorship/. Accessed 18 January 2011.

Fishman, Joshua (1973) *Language and Nationalism: Two Integrative Essays*. Rowley, Mass.: Newbury House.

Fishman, Joshua (ed.) (2000) *Can Threatened Languages Be Saved? Reversing Language Shift, Revisited – A 21st Century Perspective*. Clevedon: Multilingual Matters.

Fitzpatrick, Peter (ed.) (1995) *Nationalism, Racism and the Rule of Law*. Aldershot: Ashgate.

Fitzpatrick, Peter (2001) *Modernism and the Grounds of Law*. Cambridge: Cambridge University Press.

Fitzpatrick, Peter and Patricia Tuitt (eds) (2004) *Critical Beings: Law, Nation, and the Global Subject*. Aldershot: Ashgate.

Ford, Richard (2010) 'Five Guilty for Islamist Protests In Luton'. *The Times*. 12 January. http://www.timesonline.co.uk/tol/news/uk/crime/article6984005.ece. Accessed 19 January 2011.

Brandenburg v. Ohio, 395 U.S. 444 (1969).
Forster, Michael (2002) 'Introduction', in Johan Gottfried Herder (ed.), *Philosophical Writings*. Port Chester; New York: Cambridge University Press, pp. vii–xxxv.
Foucault, Michel (1972) *The Archaeology of Knowledge*. Translated by A.M. Sheridan Smith. London: Tavistock Publications.
Foundation for Endangered Languages (FEL) . Accessed 20 October 2010.
Framework Law on Primary and Secondary Education in Bosnia and Herzegovina (2003) http://www.oscebih.org/documents/14-eng.pdf. Accessed 23 November 2010.
Freeman, Steven M. (2009) 'United States Mission to the OSCE SHDM on Hate Crimes – Effective Implementation of Legislation as prepared for delivery by Anti-Defamation League'. PC.SHDM.DEL/2/09, 5 May. Vienna: OSCE. http://www.osce.org/documents/odihr/2009/07/38747_en.pdf. Accessed 17 January 2011.
Frank, Andre Gunder (1971) *Capitalism and Underdevelopment in Latin America*. Harmondsworth: Penguin.
Frobenius, Leo (2007) *Leo Frobenius on African History, Art, and Culture: An Anthology*. Edited by Eike Haberland with preface by Leopold Senghor. Princeton: Markus Wiener Publishers.
Furedi, Frank (1998) *The Silent War: Imperialism and the Changing Perception of Race*. New Brunswick: Rutgers University Press.
Furedi, Frank (2004) *Therapy Culture: Cultivating Vulnerability in an Age of Uncertainty*. London and New York: Routledge.
Furedi, Frank (2007) *Invitation to Terror*. London: Continuum.
Furnivall, J.S. (1948) *Colonial Policy and Practice: A Comparative Study of Burma and Netherlands India*. New York: New York University Press.
Fukuyama, Francis (1992) *The End of History and the Last Man*. London: Penguin.
Galtung, Johan (1971) 'A Structural Theory of Imperialism'. *Journal of Peace Research*, Vol. 8, No. 2, pp. 81–117.
Galtung, Johan (1973) *The European Community: A Superpower in the Making*. Oslo: Prio; London: George Allen & Unwin.
Galtung, Johan (1985) 'Social Communication and Global Problems', in Philip Lee (ed.), *Communication for All: New World Information and Communication Order*. Maryknoll, New York: Orbis, pp. 1–16.
Galtung, Johan (1989) *Europe in the Making*. New York: Crane Russak.
Gaskell, Elizabeth (1970a) [1850] *Mary Barton: A Tale of Manchester Life*. Harmondsworth: Penguin.
Gaskell, Elizabeth (1970b) [1855] *North and South*. Harmondsworth: Penguin
Gazibara, S. and Z. Zekić (2002) *Naš jezik za 5. razred osnovne škole*. [Our Language for the Fifth Year of Primary School]. Sarajevo: Svjetlost.
Geertz, Clifford (1963) *Agricultural Involution: The Process of Ecological Change in Indonesia*. Berkeley: University of California Press.
Geertz, Clifford (1983) *Local Knowledge: Further Essays in Interpretive Anthropology*. New York: Basic Books.
Gellner, Ernst (1992) *Reason and Culture*. Oxford: Blackwell.
Gellner, Ernest (1998) *Language and Solitude: Wittgenstein, Malinowski and the Habsburg Dilemma*. Cambridge: Cambridge University Press.
Greer, Germaine (2006) 'Reality Bites'. *Guardian*. 24 July. http://www.guardian.co.uk/film/2006/jul/24/culture.books. Accessed 23 June 2012.
Gilchrist, John (1787) *a Dictionary, English and Hindoostanee, in Which the Words Are Marked with Their Distinguishing Intials; as Hinduwee, Arabic, and Persian. Whence the*

Hindostanee .Is Evidently Formed. Calcutta: Stuart and Cooper. Electronic reproduction. Farmington Hills, Michigan: Thomas Gale, 2003.

Gledhill, John (1997) 'Liberalism, Socio-economic Rights and the Politics of Identity: From Moral Economy to Indigenous Rights', in Richard Wilson (ed.), *Human Rights, Culture and Context: Anthropological Perspectives.* London: Pluto, pp. 70–111.

Goatly, Andrew (2001) [1996] 'Green Grammar and Grammatical Metaphor, or Language and Myth of Power, or Metaphors We Die By', in Alvin Fill and Peter Mühlhäusler (eds), *The Ecolinguistics Reader: Language Ecology and the Environment.* London: Continuum, pp. 203–25.

Goethe, Johann Wolfgang (1932) 'Goethe's Reflections on Nature'. *Nature,* Vol. 129, No. 3255, 19 March, pp. 425–6. Translated by T.H. Huxley.

Goethe, Johann Wolfgang (1957) [1817] 'Necessity', in Leonard Forster (ed.), *The Penguin Book of German Verse.* Harmondsworth: Penguin, p. 231.

Goethe, Johann Wolfgang (1992) [1819] 'Translations', in Rainer Schulte and John Biguenet (eds), *Theories of Translation: An Anthology of Essays from Dryden to Derrida.* Chicago and London: University of Chicago Press, pp. 60–3.

Goethe, Johann Wolfgang (1998) [1819/1827] *Poems of the West and East: West-Eastern Divan – West-Oestlicher Divan: Bi-Lingual Edition of the Complete Poems.* Translated by John Whaley and introduced by Katharina Mommsen. Berlin: Peter Lang Publishing.

Golding, William (1961) *The Inheritors.* London. Faber & Faber.

Goldsmith, Oliver (1910) [1770] 'The Deserted Village' in *The Poems and Plays of Oliver Goldsmith.* London: Dent, pp. 23–4.

Goodwin, Jeff (ed.) (2001) *Passionate Politics: Emotions and Social Movements.* Chicago: University of Chicago Press.

Gordon, Cyrus (1971) *Forgotten Scripts: The Story of Their Decipherment.* Harmondsworth: Penguin.

Gramsci, Antonio (1971) [1929–1935] *Selections from the Prison Notebooks.* Translated and edited by Quniton Hoare and Geoffrey Nowell Smith. New York: International Publishers.

Gramsci, Antonio (1985) [1913–1935] *Selections from Cultural Writings.* Edited by David Forgacs and Geoffrey Nowell-Smith; translated by William Boelhower. London: Lawrence & Wishart.

Green, Leslie (1987) 'Are Language Rights Fundamental?' *Osgoode Hall Law Journal,* Vol. 25, pp. 639–69.

Greenberg, Robert (1996) 'The Politics of Dialects Among Serbs, Croats, and Muslims in the Former Yugoslavia', *East European Politics and Society,* Vol. 10, No. 3, pp. 393–415.

Greenberg, Robert (2004) *Language and Identity in the Balkans.* Oxford: Oxford University Press.

Greenberg, Michael (2011a) 'In Zuccoti Park'. *New York Review of Books,* 10 November.

Greenberg, Michael (2011b) 'Zuccoti Park: What Future?'. *New York Review of Books,* 8 December.

Greenslade, Roy (2010) 'Publishers Protest at Reporting Restrictions in Family Court Cases'. *Guardian,* 16 September. http://www.guardian.co.uk/media/greenslade/2010/sep/16/newspapers-medialaw. Accessed 20 January 2011.

Grigg-Spall, Ian and Paddy Ireland (eds) (1992) *The Critical Lawyers' Handbook.* London and Concord, Mass: Pluto Press

Griffith, John (1977) *The Politics of the Judiciary.* London: Fontana.

Griffiths, Anne (2001) 'Gendering Culture: towards a Plural Perspective of Kwena Women's Rights', in Jane K. Cowan, Marie-Bénédicte Dembour, and Richard Wilson (eds), *Culture and Rights: Anthropological Perspectives*. Cambridge: Cambridge University Press, pp. 102–26.

Grimm, Jacob and Wilhelm Grimm (2002) [1857] *Complete Fairy Tales*. London: Routledge.

Grin, Francois (1999) 'Market Forces, Language Spread and Linguistic Diversity', in Miklós Kontra, Robert Phillipson, Tove Skutnabb-Kangas and Tibor Varady (eds), *Language, a Right and a Resource: Approaches to Linguistics Human Rights*. Budapest: Central European University Press, pp. 169–86.

Grin, Francois (2003a) *Language Policy Evaluation and the European Charter for Regional or Minority Languages*. London: Palgrave Macmillan.

Grin, Francois (2003b) 'Diversity as Pardigm, Analytical Device, and Policy Goal', in Will Kymlicka and Alan Patten (eds), *Language Rights and Political Theory*. Oxford: Oxford University Press, pp. 169–88.

Grin, Francois (2005) 'Linguistic Human Rights as a Source of Policy Guidelines: a Critical Assessment'. *Journal of Sociolinguistics*, Vol. 9, No. 3, pp. 448–60.

Grossfeld, Bernhard (1990) *The Strengths and Weaknesses of Comparative Law*. Translated by Tony Weir. Oxford: Clarendon Press.

Grovogui, Siba (1996) *Sovereigns, Quasi Sovereigns, and Africans: Race and Self-Determination in International Law*. Minneapolis: University of Minnesota Press.

Grusin, Richard (2011) 'Premediation and the Virtual Occupation of Wall Street'. *Theory and Event*, Vol. 14, No. 4, Occupy Wall Street supplement.

Gunaratna, Rohan (2002) *Inside Al Qaeda: Global Network of Terror*. London: Hurst.

Gupta, Anthea (1997) 'When Mother-Tongue Education Is *Not* Preferred'. *Journal of Multilingual and Multicultural Development*, Vol. 18, No. 6, pp. 496–506.

Gustafson, Thomas (1992) *Representative Words: Politics, Literature, and the American Language, 1776–1865*. Cambridge: Cambridge University Press.

Le Guin, Ursula (1993) *The Earthsea Quartet*. London: Penguin.

Le Guin, Ursula (2005) *Changing Planes: Armchair Travel for the Mind*. London: Gollancz.

Habermas, Jürgen (1971) *Knowledge and Human Interests*. Translated by Jeremy Shapiro. Boston, Massachusetts: Beacon Press.

Habermas, Jürgen (1976) *Legitimation Crisis*. Translated by Thomas McCarthy. London: Heinemann Educational.

Habermas, Jürgen (1987) *The Theory of Communicative Action: Volume 2: Lifeworld and System*. Translated by Thomas McCarthy. Boston: Beacon Press.

Habermas, Jürgen (1995) 'Reconciliation through the Public Use of Reason: Remarks on John Rawls' Political Liberalism'. *The Journal of Philosophy*, Vol. 92, No. 3, pp. 109–31.

Habermas, Jürgen (1997) *Between Facts and Norms: Contributions to a Discourse Theory of Law and Democracy*. Translated by William Regh. Cambridge: Polity Press.

Habermas, Jürgen (2001) 'Remarks on Legitimation through Human Rights', in *The Postnational Constellation: Political Essays*. Translated by Max Pensky. Cambridge: Polity Press, pp. 113–29.

Hacking, Ian (1995) *Rewriting the Soul: Multiple Personality and the Sciences of Memory*. Princeton, New Jersey: Princeton University Press.

Haggard, H. Rider (2002) [1885] *King Solomon's Mines*. Peterborough, Ontario: Broadview Press.

The Hague Recommendations Regarding The Education Rights Of National Minorities 1996. http://www.unesco.org/most/ln2pol6.htm.

Halilović, Senahid (1991) *Bosanski jezik*. Sarajevo: Biblioteka Ključanin.

Halilović, Senahid (1998) *Bosanski jezik*. Sarajevo: Baština, second edition.

Halliday, M.A.K (2001) [1990] 'New Ways of Meaning: The Challenge to Applied Linguistics', in Alvin Fill and Peter Mühlhäusler (eds), *The Ecolinguistics Reader: Language Ecology and the Environment*. London: Continuum, pp. 175–202.

Hamel, Rainer Enrique (1997a) 'Introduction: Linguistic Human Rights in a Sociolinguistic Perspective'. *International Journal of the Sociology of Language*, No. 127, pp. 1–24.

Hamel, Rainer Enrique (1997b) 'Language Conflict and Language Shift: A Sociolinguistic Framework for Linguistic Human Rights'. *International Journal of the Sociology of Language*, No. 127, pp. 105–34.

Hamann, Johann Georg (2007) [1759–1786] *Writings on Philosophy and Language*. Translated and edited by Kenneth Haynes. Cambridge: Cambridge University Press.

Handwerker, W. Penn (1997) 'Universal Human Rights and the Problem of Unbounded Cultural Meanings'. *American Anthropologist*, Vol. 99, No. 4, pp. 799–809.

Hansard (2011) *House of Commons, Official Report, Parliamentary Debates*. London: House of Commons, Vol. 530, No. 177, 27 June. http://www.publications.parliament.uk/pa/cm201011/cmhansrd/chan177.pdf

Hardt, Michael and Antonio Negri (2000) *Empire*. Cambridge, Mass.: Harvard University Press.

Hardy, Thomas (1978) [1891] *Tess of the D'Urbervilles: A Pure Woman*. London: Pan.

Harmon, David (2002) *In Light of Our Differences: How Diversity in Nature and Culture Make Us Human*. Washington, DC: The Smithsonian Institute Press.

Harris, Evans (2010) 'Twitter Jokes: Free Speech on Trial'. *Guardian*, 12 November. http://www.guardian.co.uk/commentisfree/libertycentral/2010/nov/12/twitter-jokes-free-speech-on-trial

Harris, Roy (2009) 'Freedom of Speech and Philosophy of Education'. *British Journal of Educational Studies*, Vol. 57, No. 2, pp. 111–26.

Harrison, Graham (2004) *The World Bank and Africa: The Construction of Governance States* London: Routledge.

Harroff-Tavel, Helene (2005) 'Tackling School Textbook Reform in Bosnia and Herzegovina'. Sarajevo: OSCE. 14 November. http://www.osce.org/bih/57453.

Hart, H.L.A. (1961) *The Concept of Law*. Oxford: Clarendon Press.

Harvey, David (2003) *The New Imperialism*. Oxford: Oxford University Press.

Haugen, Einar (2001) [1972] 'The Ecology of Language', in Alvin Fill and Peter Mühlhäusler (eds), *The Ecolinguistics Reader: Language Ecology and the Environment*. London: Continuum, pp. 57–66.

Hawkesworth, Celia (1986) *Colloquial Serbo-Croat*. London; New York: Routledge & Kegan Paul.

Hawkesworth, Celia (1998) *Colloquial Croatian and Serbian*. London; New York: Routledge.

Haveman, Paul (2009) 'Indigenous Peoples Human Rights', in Michael Goodhart (ed.), *Human Rights: Politics and Practice*. Oxford: Oxford University Press, pp. 260–78.

Hayden, Robert (1999) *Blueprints for a House Divided: The Constitutional Logic of the Yugoslav Conflicts*. Ann Arbor: The University of Michigan Press.

Hayden, Robert (2011) 'What's Reconciliation Got to Do with It? The International Criminal Tribunal for the Former Yugoslavia) as Antiwar Profiteer'. *Journal of Intervention and Statebuilding*, Vol. 5, No. 3, pp. 313–30.

Hayes, Patrick (2011a) 'You Can't Say That: Whatever Happened to Our Free and Open Society?' *The Free Society*. 16 March. http://www.thefreesociety.org/Patrick-Hayes/whatever-happened-to-our-free-and-open-society. Accessed 23 June 2012.

Hayes, Patrick (2011b) 'Occupy London Reveal Their True Colours'. *The Free Society*, 19 November. http://www.thefreesociety.org/Articles/Features/occupy-london-reveal-their-true-colours. Accessed 23 June 2012.

Hayes, Carlton Joseph (1968) *The Historical Evolution of Modern Nationalism*. New York: Russell & Russell.

Haynes, Kenneth (2007) 'Introduction', in Johann Georg Hamann, *Writings on Philosophy and Language*. Translated and edited by Kenneth Haynes. Cambridge: Cambridge University Press, pp. vii–xxv.

Heartfield, James (undated) 'Rights and the Legal Subject'. Unpublished paper.

Heartfield, James (2002) *The 'Death of the Subject' Explained*. Sheffield: Sheffield Hallam Press.

Heartfield, James (2009) 'Review: Pessimism of the Intellect'. *Forth Magazine*. 4 December. http://forth.ie/index.php/content/article/review_pessimism_of_the_intellect/#axzz0Z1JEYe05. Accessed 28 November 2011.

Heartfield, James (2011) *The Aborigines' Protection Society: Humanitarian Imperialism in Australia, New Zealand, Fiji, Canada, South Africa, and the Congo, 1837–1909*. London: Hurst.

Hegel, Georg (2004) [1842] *Introductory Lectures on Aesthetics*. Translated by Bernard Bosquet and edited by Michael Inwood. London: Penguin.

Herman, Ellen (1995) *The Romance of American Psychology: Political Culture in the Age of Experts*. Berkeley: University of California Press.

Herder, Johann Gottfried (1800) *Outlines of a philosophy of the history of man*... London. *Eighteenth Century Collections Online*. Gale Group. http://galenet.galegroup.com/servlet/ECCO. Accessed 24 September 2011.

Herder, Johan Gottfried (1966) [1772] 'On the Origin of Language', translated by Alexander Gode in Jean-Jacques Rousseau, Johann Gottfried Herder, *On the Origin of Language*. Chicago: University of Chicago Press, pp. 85–166.

Herder, Johan Gottfried (1969) [1769–1791] *J.G. Herder on Social and Political Culture*. Translated and edited by F.M. Barnard. Cambridge: Cambridge University Press.

Herder Johan Gottfried (2002) [1765–1797] *Philosophical Writings*. Edited and translated by Michael Forster Port Chester, New York: Cambridge University Press.

Herder, Johann Gottfried (2008) [1773] *Shakespeare*. Translated and edited by Gregory Moore. Princeton: Princeton University Press.

Hermans, Theo (ed.) (1985) *The Manipulation of Literature School: Studies in Literary Translation*. Beckenham: Croom Helm.

Hermans, Theo (ed.) (2006) *Translating Others*. Manchester: St. Jerome.

Hermans, Theo (2007) *The Conference of the Tongues*. Manchester: St. Jerome.

Hickey, Samuel and Giles Mohan (eds) (2005) *Participation: From Tyranny to Transformation? Exploring New Approaches to Participation in Development*. London. Zed Books.

Hill, Christopher (1975) *The World Turned Upside Down*. Harmondsworth: Penguin.

Hinton, Leanne and Ken Hale (eds) (2000) *The Green Book of Language Revitalisation in Practice*. San Diego: Academic Press.

Hirson, Baruch (1981) 'Language in Control and Resistance in South Africa'. *African Affairs*, Vol. 80, No. 319, pp. 219–37.

HM Government (2011) *Prevent Strategy*. London: HM Stationers. http://www.met.police.uk/prevent/prevent-strategy-review.pdf. Accessed 23 June 2012

Hobsbawm, E.J. (1965) *Primitive Rebels: Studies in Archaic Forms of Social Movement in the 19th and 20th Centuries*. New York: Norton.

Hobsbawm, E.J. (1990) *Nations and Nationalism Since 1780: Programme, Myth, Reality*. Cambridge: Cambridge University Press, revised edition.

Hobsbawm, Eric (1994) *The Age of Empire, 1875–1914*. London: Abacus.

Hobsbawm, Eric (1996) 'Identity Politics and the Left'. *New Left Review*, No. I/217.

Hobsbawm, Eric and Terence Ranger (eds) (1992) *The Invention of Tradition*. Cambridge: Cambridge University Press, Canto edition.

Hochschild, Arlie Russell (1983) *The Managed Heart: Commercialization of Human Feeling*. Berkeley: University of California Press.

Hogan-Brun and Stefan Wolff (eds) (2004) *Minority Languages in Europe: Status, Frameworks, Prospects*. Basingstoke: Palgrave Macmillan.

Hoggart, Richard (1958) *The Uses of Literacy*. Harmondsworth: Penguin.

Hoggart, Richard (1978) *An Idea and Its Servants: UNESCO from within*. London: Chatto & Windus.

Holborow, Marnie (1999) *Politics of English*. London: Sage.

Holborow, Marnie (2006) 'Putting The Social Back into Language: Marx, Vološinov and Vygotsky Re-examined'. *Studies in Language and Capitalism*, Vol. 1, pp. 1–28. http://www-staff.lboro.ac.uk/~ssjer/SLC1/SLC1-1_Holborow.pdf. Accessed 15 October 2010.

Holbrook, John (2002) 'Humanitarian Intervention and the Recasting of International law', in David Chandler (ed.), *Rethinking Human Rights: Critical Approaches to International Politics*. Basingstoke: Palgrave Macmillan, pp. 136–54.

Holmes, James S (1994) *Translated! Papers on Literary Translation and Translation Studies*. Amsterdam: Rodopi.

Holt, Sally and John Packer (2001) 'OSCE Developments and Linguistic Minorities'. *International Journal on Multicultural Societies*, Vol. 3, No. 2, pp. 99–126. http://unesdoc.unesco.org/images/0014/001457/145796e.pdf. Accessed 27 November 2010.

Holt, Sally and John Packer (2007) 'Protecting Linguistic Minorities – the Role of the osce', in Matthias Koenig and Paul de Guchteneire (eds), *Democracy and Human Rights in Multicultural Societies*, Paris: Unesco, pp. 127–66.

Homburger, Lilias (1949) *The Negro African Languages*. London: Routledge & Kegan Paul.

Home Office (2009a) *Cross-Government Action Plan on Hate Crime Equality Impact Assessment – report. London: Home Office.* http://webarchive.nationalarchives.gov.uk/20100418065544/http:/www.homeoffice.gov.uk/documents/hate-crime-action-plan/hate-crime-action-plan-eia2835.pdf?view=Binary. Accessed 24 June 2012.

Home Office (2009b) *Hate Crime The Cross-Government Action Plan 2008–11* London: HM Government. http://www.homeoffice.gov.uk/documents/hate-crime-action-plan/hate-crime-action-plan2835.pdf?view=Binary. Accessed 24 June 2012

Home Office (2010) *Home Office Statistical Findings: Racist Incidents, England and Wales, 2009/10*, 30 November, second edition. http://data.gov.uk/dataset/racist-incidents-england-wales. Accessed 24 June 2012.

Home Office (2011a) *CONTEST: The United Kingdom's Strategy for Countering Terrorism*. London: HM Government. http://www.homeoffice.gov.uk/publications/counter-terrorism/counter-terrorism-strategy/contest-summary?view=Binary. Accessed 24 June 2012.

Home Office (2011b) Operation of police powers under the Terrorism Act 2000 and subsequent legislation: Arrests, outcomes and stop and searches, Statistical Bulletin Quarterly update to December 2010. London: Home Office. http://www.

homeoffice.gov.uk/publications/science-research-statistics/research-statistics/counter-terrorism-statistics/hosb1411/. Accessed 24 June 2012.

Hooks, Bell (1995) '"This Is the Oppressor's Language/ Yet i Need It to Talk to You": Language, a Place of Struggle', in Anuradha Dingwaney and Carol Maier (eds), *Between Languages and Cultures: Translation and Cross-Cultural Texts*. Pittsburgh and London: University of Pittsburgh Press, pp. 295–302.

Hopgood, C.R. (1948) 'Language, Literature, and Culture'. *Africa*, Vol. 18, No. 2, pp. 112–19.

Hopkins, Gerald Manley (1996) *Selected Poetry*. Oxford. Oxford University Press.

Horkheimer, Max and Theodor Adorno (1997) [1944] *Dialectics of Enlightenment*. Translated by John Cumming. London: Verso.

Horobin, Simon (2007) *Chaucer's Language*. Basingstoke: Palgrave Macmillan.

Hromadžić, Azra (2009) '"Smoking doesn't kill, it unites!" Cultural Meanings and Practices of "Mixing" in Post-conflict Bosnia and Herzegovina,' in Claire McGlynn, Michalinos Zembylas, Zvi Bekerman, and Tony Gallagher (eds), *Peace Education in Conflict and Post-conflict Societies: Comparative Perspectives*. Basingstoke: Palgrave Macmillan, pp. 109–25.

Hughes, Caroline and Vanessa Pupavac (2005) 'Framing Post-Conflict Societies: International pathologisation of Cambodia and the post-Yugoslav states'. *Third World Quarterly*, Vol. 26, No. 6, pp. 873–89.

Human Rights Coordination Centre (1999) *Overview of Educational Problems in BiH and Guidelines for Intervention*. Sarajevo: OHR.

Humboldt, Wilhelm von (1992) [1816] 'Introduction to his Translation of Agamemnon', in Rainer Schulte and John Biguenet (eds), *Theories of Translation: An Anthology of Essays from Dryden to Derrida*. Chicago and London: University of Chicago Press, pp. 55–61.

Humboldt, Wilhelm von (1999) [1841] *On Language*. Edited by Michael Losonsky and translated by Peter Heath. Cambridge: Cambridge University Press.

Hunia, Fran (1979) *The Magic Stone*. Read It Yourself Series 777. Loughborough: Ladybird Books.

Hussey, E.R.J. (1932) 'The Languages of Literature in Africa'. *Africa*, Vol. 5, No. 2, pp. 169–75.

Hymes, Dell (1974) *Foundations in Sociolinguistics: The Ethnography of Communication*. Philadelphia: University of Pennsylvania Press.

Ignatieff, Michael (1998) *The Warrior's Honor: Ethnic War and the Modern Conscience*. London: Chatto & Windus.

Illich, Ivan (1973a) *Celebration of Awareness: A Call for Institutional Revolution*. Harmondsworth: Penguin.

Illich, Ivan (1973b) *Deschooling Society*. Harmondsworth: Penguin.

Illich, Ivan (1976) *Limits to Medicine: Medical Nemesis: The Expropriation of Health*. London: Boyars.

Illich, Ivan (1981a) *Shadow Work*. Boston: M Boyars.

Illich, Ivan (1981b) 'Taught Mother Tongue and Vernacular Tongue', in D.P. Pattanayak (ed.), *Multilingualism and Mother Tongue Education*. Delhi: Oxford University Press, pp. 1–39.

Illich, Ivan and Etienne Verne (1976) *Imprisoned in the Global Classroom*. London: Writers and Readers.

Indigenous Language Institute http://www.ilinative.org/. Accessed 20 July 2010.

Inghilleri, Moira and Sue-Ann Harding (2010) 'Translating Violent Conflict'. *The Translator Special Issue: Translation and Violent Conflict*, Vol. 16, No. 2, pp. 165–73.

International Clearing House for Endangered Languages University of Tokyo.

International Commission on Intervention and State Sovereignty (ICISS) (2001) *The Responsibility to Protect: Report of the International Commission on Intervention and State Sovereignty.* Ottawa: IDRC. http://www.iciss.ca/report-en.asp. Accessed 15 September 2010.

International Crisis Group (ICG) (2000) *Denied Justice: Individuals Lost in a Legal Maze.* 23 February. http://www.crisisweb.org/

International Crisis Group (ICG) (2011) *Bosnian Briefing,* No. 62, 6 May. http://www.crisisgroup.org. Accessed 15 March 2012.

International Federation of Library Associations and Institutions (IFLA) (1999) *Statement on Libraries and Intellectual Freedom.* The Hague, Netherlands, 25 March. http://archive.ifla.org/faife/policy/iflastat/iflastat.htm. Accessed 17 January 2011.

International Federation of Library Associations and Institutions (IFLA) Free Access to Information and Freedom of Expression (FAIFE) Committee. http://www.ifla.org/en/about-faife. Accessed 17 January 2011.

International Federation of Library Associations and Institutions (IFLA) (2003) 'Council Resolution on National Security Legislation'. World Library and Information Congress: 69th IFLA General Conference and Council. Berlin, Germany 1–9 August. http://archive.ifla.org/IV/ifla69/resolutions.htm#5. Accessed 17 January 2011.

International Journal on Minority and Group Rights (1996/1997) Special Issues, Vol. 4, No. 2.

International Journal on Multicultural Societies (IJMS) (2001) Vol. 3, No. 2, Special Issue on The Human Rights of Linguistic Minorities and Language Policies. http://unesdoc.unesco.org/images/0014/001457/145796e.pdf. Accessed 27 November 2011.

International Labour Organisation (ILO) (1957) Indigenous and Tribal Populations Convention, C107. http://www.ilo.org/public/english/region/ampro/mdtsanjose/indigenous/derecho.htm.

International Labour Organisation (ILO) (1969) The World Employment Programme. Report of the Director General of the ILO (part 1) to the International Labour Conference. ILO: Geneva. Accessed 24 June 2012.

International Labour Organisation (ILO) (1989) Indigenous and Tribal Peoples Convention, C169. http://www.ilo.org/public/english/region/ampro/mdtsanjose/indigenous/derecho.htm. Accessed 24 June 2012.

International Social Science Journal (1961) Part One: 'The Yugoslav Commune'. UNESCO, Vol. 13, No. 3.

InZone http://inzone.eti.unige.ch. Accessed 24 June 2012.

Isaković, Alija (1993) *Rječnik karakteristične leksike u bosanskome jeziku* [Dictionary of characteristic words of the Bosnian language]. Wurppertal: Bambi.

Isaković, Alija (1995) *Rječnik bosanskoga jezika: karakteristična leksika* [Dictionary of the Bosnian language: characteristic lexicon]. Sarajevo: Bosanska knjiga.

Isayev, M.I. (1977) *National Languages in the USSR: Problems and Solutions.* Moscow: Progress Publishers.

Israel, Jonathan (2002) *Radical Enlightenment: Philosophy and the Making of Modernity 1650–1750.* Oxford: Oxford University Press.

Ives, Peter (2004a) *Gramsci's Politics of Language: Engaging the Bakhtin Circle and the Frankfurt School.* Toronto: University of Toronto Press.

Ives, Peter (2004b) *Language and Hegemony in Gramsci.* London: Pluto Press.

Ives, Peter (2004c) 'Language, Representation and Suprastate Democracy: Questions Facing the European Union', in David Laycock (ed.), *Representation and Democratic Theory.* Vancouver: UBC Press, pp. 23–47.

Ives, Peter (2004d) 'Managing or Celebrating Linguistic Diversity in the E.U.?' paper presented as 'Multiple Diversities: European Experiences/Diversités Multiples: Les expériences européennes' at the Consortium for European Studies, Université de Montréal and McGill University, Montreal, 1 October.

Ives, Peter (2005) 'Language, Agency and Hegemony: A Gramschian Response to Post-Marxism'. *Critical Review of International Social and Political Philosophy*, Vol. 8, No. 4, pp. 455–68.

Ives, Peter (2006) '"Global English": Linguistic Imperialism or Practical Lingua Franca?' *Studies in Language and Capitalism*, Issue 1, pp. 121–42. http://www.languageandcapitalism.info/.

Ives, Peter (2010) 'Cosmopolitanism and Global English: Language Politics in Globalisation Debates'. *Political Studies*, Vol. 58, No. 3, pp. 516–35.

Ives, Peter and Rocco Lacorte (eds) (2010) *Gramsci, Language and Translation*. Lanham: Lexington.

Ivić, Pavle (2001) 'Language Planning in Serbia Today'. *International Journal of the Sociology of Language*, No. 151, pp. 7–18.

Jacoby, Russell (1999) *The End of Utopia: Politics and Culture in the Age of Apathy*. New York: Basic Books.

Jahić, Dževad (1999a) *Bosanski jezik u 100 pitanja i 100 odgovora*. Sarajevo: Ljiljan. [The Bosnian Language: a Hundred Questions and a Hundred Answers.]

Jahić, Dževad (1999b) *Bošnjački narod i njegov jezik*. Sarajevo: Ljiljan. [The Bosniac Nation and Its Language.]

Jakobson, Roman (1992) [1959] 'On Linguistic Aspects of Translation', in Rainer Schulte and John Biguenet (eds), *Theories of Translation: An Anthology of Essays from Dryden to Derrida*. Chicago; London: University of Chicago Press, pp. 144–51.

James, C.L.R. (1977) *Nkrumah and the Ghana Revolution*. London: Allison and Busby.

James, C.L.R (2001) [1938] *The Black Jacobins*. London: Penguin.

Janhunen, Juha (2006) 'In a Manner of Speaking, Change Is Constant', *THES*, 10 February, pp. 26–7.

Jenkins, Tiffany (2010) *Contesting Human Remains in Museum Collections: the Crisis of Cultural Authority*. London: Routledge.

Jensen, Steffen (2008) *Gangs, Politics and Dignity in Cape Town*. Chicago: University of Chicago Press.

Joan, Bernat i Marí (2005) *Ecolinguistics Project*. Eivissa: Mediterrania.

Johnson, Samuel (1792) A Letter to James Boswell, Esq. With some remarks on Johnson's Dictionary, and on language, &c. London. Available at *English Short Title Catalogue. Eighteenth Century Collections Online*. Gale Group. http://galenet.galegroup.com/servlet/ECCO

Johnston, Charles (1979) 'Translator's Note' in Alexander Puskin, *Eugene Onegin*. Harmondsworth: Penguin, pp. 29–30.

Joshi, Shashank (2011) 'Six Lessons from Libya', in Conservative Middle East Council (ed.), *The Arab Spring*. London: Conservative Middle East Council, pp. 16–19.

Journal of the Royal African Society (1927) 'Editorial Notes'. Vol. 27, No. 105, pp. 77–88.

Journal of the Royal African Society (1928) 'Editorial Notes'. Vol. 28, No. 110, pp. 200–7.

Journal of the Royal African Society (1939) 'Editorial Notes'. Vol. 38, No. 153, pp. 407–18.

Joyce, James (1964) *Daniel Defoe*. Translated by Joseph Prescott. *Buffalo Studies*, Vol. 1, No. 1: Buffalo: State University of New York, pp. 1–27.

Kahn, Andrew (1972) 'The Translator's Preface', in Yevgeny Yevtushenko, *Stolen Apples*. St Albans: Panther Books, pp. xxiii–xxiv.

Kalogjera, Damir (2001) 'Foreword'. *International Journal of the Sociology of Language*, No. 147, pp. 1–3.

Kant, Immanuel (1952) [1790] *Critique of Judgement*. Translated by James Meredith. Oxford: Clarendon Press.

Kant, Immanuel (1967) *Kant: Philosophical Correspondence 1759–99*. Edited and translated by Arnulf Zweig. Chicago: University of Chicago Press.

Kant, Immanuel (1968) *Selected Pre-Critical Writings and Correspondence with Beck/ Immanuel Kant*. Translated and introduced by G.B. Kerferd and D.E. Walford, with a contribution by P.G. Lucas. Manchester: Manchester University Press.

Kant, Immanuel (1974) [1798] *Anthropology from a Pragmatic Point of View*. Hague: Martinus Njihoff.

Kant, Immanuel (1991) *Political Writings*. Edited with an introduction and notes by Hans Reiss; translated by H.B. Nisbet. Cambridge: Cambridge University Press.

Kant, Imannuel (1997) [1775] 'On the Different Races of Man', in Emmanuel Chukwudi Eze (ed.), *Race and the Enlightenment: A Reader*. Oxford: Blackwell, pp. 38–64.

Kant, Immanuel (1998) [1781] *Critique of Pure Reason*. Edited and translated by Paul Guyer; Allen W. Wood. Cambridge: Cambridge University Press.

Kant, Immanuel (2001) [1784] 'An Answer to the Question: "What Is Enlightenment?" ' Konigsberg, Prussia in Allan Wood (ed.), *Basic Writings of Kant*. New York: Modern Library, pp. 133–42.

Karadžić, Vuk (1992) [1824] *Red Knight: Serbian Women's Songs*. Edited and translated by Daniel Weissbort and Tomislav Longinović. London: Menard Press/King's College London.

Karadžić, Vuk (1997) [1814–1833] *Songs of the Serbian People: From the Collections of Vuk Karadžić*. Edited and translated by Milne Holton and Vasa D. Mihailovich. Pittsburgh: University of Pittsburgh Press.

Karamcheti, Indira (1995) 'Aimé Césaire's Subjective Geographies: Translating Place and the Difference It Makes' in Anuradha Dingwaney and Carol Maier (eds), *Between Languages and Cultures: Translation and Cross-Cultural Texts*. Pittsburgh and London: University of Pittsburgh Press, pp. 181–98.

Katičić, Radoslav (2001) 'Croatian Linguistic Loyalty'. *International Journal of the Sociology of Language*, No. 147, pp. 17–29.

Kavanagh, Trevor (2012) 'This Witch-Hunt Has Put Us behind Ex-Soviet States on Press Freedom'. *The Sun*, 11 February. http://www.thesun.co.uk/sol/homepage/news/4124870/The-Suns-Trevor-Kavanagh-Witch-hunt-puts-us-behind-ex-Soviet-states-on-Press-freedom.html. Accessed 20 March 2012.

Keats John (1970) [1814–1821] *Poetic Works*. Edited by H. W. Garrod. Oxford: Oxford University Press.

Keats, John (1970) [1816] 'On First Looking into Chapman's Homer', in *Keats: Poetic Works*. Edited by H.W. Garrod. Oxford: Oxford University Press, p. 38.

Keats, John (1970) [1818] 'To J. H. Reynolds Esq', in *Keats: Poetic Works*. Edited by H.W. Garrod. Oxford: Oxford University Press, pp. 381–3.

Kedourie, Elie (1960) *Nationalism*. London: Hutchinson.

Kelman, Herbert (1993) 'Foreword', in Dennis Sandole and Hugo van der Merwe (eds), *Conflict Resolution Theory and Practice: Integration and Application*. Manchester; New York: Manchester University Press, pp. ix–xii.

Kenny, Mary (2001) 'In Defence of Mary Whitehouse'. *The Spectator*, 7 June. http://www.spectator.co.uk/coffeehouse/6064488/in-defence-of-mary-whitehouse.thtml. Accessed 16 January 2011.

Kenyatta, Jomo (1962) *Facing Mount Kenya*. New York: Vintage.

Kenyatta, Jomo (1965) *African Socialism and Its Application to Planning in Kenya*. Republic of Kenya.

King, Michael (1997) *A Better World for Children? Explorations in Morality and Authority*. London: Routledge.

King, Richard (1996) *Civil Rights and the Idea of Freedom*. Athens; London: University of Georgia.

King, Richard (2004) *Race, Culture and Intellectuals, 1940–1970*. Washington, DC: Woodrow Wilson Center.

Kirkpatrick, Andrew (2007) *World Englishes: Implications for International Communication and English Language Teaching*. Cambridge: Cambridge University Press.

Klikovac, Duška (2001) 'On the Bureaucratisation of Serbian'. *International Journal of the Sociology of Language*, No. 151, pp. 111–16.

Klug, Francesca (2000) *Values for a Godless Age: The Story of the United Kingdom's New Bill of Rights*. London: Penguin.

Knaus, Gerald and Felix Martin (2003) 'Travails of the European Raj: Lessons from Bosnia and Herzegovina'. *Journal of Democracy*, Vol. 14, No. 3, pp. 60–74.

Knechte, John (2008) 'Holocaust Denial and the Concept of Dignity in the European Union'. *Florida State University Review*, Vol. 36, pp. 41–65.

Koestler, Arthur (1964) *The Sleepwalkers: A History of Man's Changing Vision of the Universe*. Harmondsworth: Penguin.

Kontra, Miklós, Robert Phillipson, Tove Skutnabb-Kangas and Tibor Varady (eds) (1999) *Language, a Right and a Resource: Approaches to Linguistics Human Rights*. Budapest: Central European University Press.

Kosonen, Kimmo and Catherine Young (2009) *Mother Tongue as Bridge Language of Instruction: Policies and Experiences in South East Asia*. Bangkok: SEAMEO with World Bank.

Krejči, Jaroslav and Vitezslav Velimsky (1981) *Ethnic and Political Nations in Europe*. London: Croom Helm.

Kroeber, A.L. (1915) 'Eighteen Professions'. *American Anthropologist*, Vol. 17, No. 2, pp. 283–8.

Kroeber, A.L. (1917) 'The Superorganic'. *American Anthropologist*, Vol. 19, No. 2, pp. 163–213.

Kuper, Adam (1988) *The Invention of Primitive Society: Transformations of an Illusion*. London: Routledge.

Kuper, Adam (2000) *Culture: The Anthropologists' Account*. Cambridge, Mass.; London: Harvard University Press.

Kuper, Adam (2003) 'The Return of the Native'. *Current Anthropology*, Vol. 44, No. 3, pp. 389–402.

Kymlicka, Will (1995) *Multicultural Citizenship*. Oxford: Oxford University Press.

Kymlicka, Will (2004) 'Justice and Security in the Accommodation of Minority Nationalism', in Stephen May, Tariq Modood, Judith Squires (eds), *Ethnicity, Nationalism and Minority Rights*. Cambridge: Cambridge University Press, pp. 144–76.

Kymlicka, Will and Alan Patten (eds) (2003) *Language Rights and Political Theory*. Oxford: Oxford University Press.

Laakso, Johanna (2009) 'The Last Livonian Is Dead'. http://tangyra.voila.net/eng.html

Lacan, Jacques (1977) *Écrits: A Selection*. Translated by Alan Sheridan. New York: Norton.

Lacey, Anita and Suzan Ilcan (2006) 'Volunteer Labour, Responsible Citizenship and International NGOs'. *International Journal of Comparative Sociology*. Vol. 47, No. 1, pp. 35–53.

Laïdi, Zaki (1998) *A World without Meaning: The Crisis of Meaning in International Politics*. Translated by June Burnham and Jenny Coulon. London: Routledge.

Laitin, David and Rob Reich (2003) 'A Liberal Democracy Approach to Language Justice', in Will Kymlicka and Alan Patten (eds), *Language Rights and Political Theory*. Oxford: Oxford University Press, pp. 80–104.

Lambert, Robert (2011) *Countering Al Qaeda in London: Police and Muslims in Partnership*. London: Hurst.

Langendoen, D. Terence (1968) *The London School of Linguistics: a Study of the Linguistic Theories of B. Malinowski and J.R. Firth*. Cambridge, Mass.: MIT Press.

Languages at War http://www.reading.ac.uk/lanaguages-at-wars. Accessed 24 April 2012.

Lansing, Robert (1921) *Notes on Sovereignty: From the Standpoint of the State and of the World*. Washington: Carnegie Endowment for International Peace.

Lasch, Christopher (1984) *The Minimal Self: Psychic Survival in Troubled Times*. New York: W.W. Norton.

Laughland, John (2002) 'Human Rights and the Rule of Law: Achieving Universal Justice' in David Chandler (ed.), *Rethinking Human Rights: Critical Approaches to International Politics*. Basingstoke: Palgrave Macmillan, pp. 38–56.

Laughland, John (2008) *A History of Political Trials from Charles I to Saddam Hussein*. Oxford: Peter Lang.

Laughton, William H. (1938) 'The Teaching of African Languages in Schools: A Note on the Position in Kenya'. *Africa*, Vol. 11, No. 2, pp. 221–5.

Lauterpacht, Hersch (1950) *International Law and Human Rights*. London: Stevens.

Law on Ministries and Other Bodies of Administration of Bosnia-Herzegovina 2003 http://www.ohr.int/ohr-dept/legal/oth-legist/doc/BH-LAW-ON-MINISTRIES.doc. Accessed 24 November 2010.

Lawson, Alastair (2010) 'Last Speaker of Ancient Language of Bo Dies in India'. *BBC News*, 4 February. http://news.bbc.co.uk/1/hi/world/south_asia/8498534.stm. Accessed 28 October 2010.

Lawson, George (2011) 'Halliday's Revenge: Revolutions and International Relations'. *International Affairs*, Vol. 87, pp. 1067–85.

Leavis, F.R. (1962) *Two Cultures? The Significance of C. P. Snow: Being the Richmond Lecture*. London: Chatto & Windus.

Le Bon, Gustave (1995) [1895] *The Crowd: A Study of the Popular Mind*. New Brunswick, New Jersey: Transaction Publishers.

Lee, J.M. (1967) *Colonial Development and Good Government: A Study of the Ideas Expressed by the British Official Classes in Planning Decolonization 1939–1964*. Oxford: Clarendon Press.

Lefevere, André (ed.) (1992a) *Translation, History, Culture: A Sourcebook*. London: Routledge.

Lefevere, André (1992b) *Translation, Rewriting, and the Manipulation of Literary Fame*. London: Routledge.

Lieber, Francis (1881) *Miscellaneous Writings: Contributions to Political Science*. Philadelphia: Lippincott.

Leibniz, Gottfried Wilhelm (1978) *Leibniz and Ludolf on Things Linguistic: Excerpts from Their Correspondence, 1688–1703*. Edited and translated by John T. Waterman. Berkeley: University of California Press.

Leibniz, Gottfried Wilhelm (1981) [1704] *New Essays on Human Understanding*. Edited and translated by Peter Remnant and Jonathan Bennett. Cambridge: Cambridge University Press.

Leiris, Michel (1956) 'Race and Culture', in UNESCO (1956) *The Race Question in Modern Science*. Paris: Unesco, pp. 85–122.

Lenarčič, Janez (2009) Supplementary Human Dimension Meeting Hate Crimes – Effective Implementation Of Legislation, Opening Remarks by Ambassador Janez Lenarčič, Director of the Office for Democratic Institutions and Human Rights, Vienna, 4 May. Vienna: OSCE. http://www.osce.org/odihr/37035. Accessed 18 January 2011.

Lenhart, Volker; Anastasia Kediou and Stephan Stockmann (1999) The Curricula of the 'National Subjects' in Bosnia and Herzegovina: A Report to UNESCO. Heidelberg, August.

Lenin, Vladimir (1965) [1924] *A Caricature of Marxism and Imperialist Economism*. Moscow: Progress Publishers.

Lenin, Vladimir (1972a) [1913] *Critical Remarks on the National Question*. Moscow: Progress Publishers. Moscow. Marxist Internet Archive. http://www.marxists.org/archive/lenin/works/1913/crnq/. Accessed 3 July 2010.

Lenin, Vladimir (1972b) [1914] 'Is a Compulsory Official Language Needed?' *Lenin Collected Works*. Moscow: Progress Publishers, Vol. 20, pp. 71–3. Marxist Internet Archive. http://www.marxists.org/archive/lenin/works/. Accessed 3 July 2010.

Lenin, Vladimir (1977) [1913] 'Liberals and Democrats on the Language Question'. *Lenin Collected Works* Vol. 19, pp. 354–7. Moscow: Progress Publishers. Marxists Internet Archive. http://www.marxists.org/archive/lenin/works/. Accessed 3 July 2010.

Lenin, Vladimir (1996) [1916] *Imperialism: The Highest Form of Capitalism*. London: Pluto.

Leon, Abram (1970) [1950] *The Jewish Question: A Marxist Interpretation*. New York: Pathfinder.

Lermontov, Mikhail (1966) [1840] *A Hero of Our Time*. Translated with an introduction by Paul Foote. Harmondsworth: Penguin.

Levi, Primo (1986) *The Periodic Table*. London: Abacus.

Levi, Primo (1988) *If This Is a Man; The Truce*. London: Abacus.

Lévi-Strauss, Claude (1956) 'Race and History', in UNESCO (1956) *The Race Question in Modern Science*. Paris: Unesco, pp. 123–63.

Lévi-Strauss, Claude (1958) *Race and History*. Paris: Unesco.

Lévi-Strauss, Claude (1966) *The Savage Mind*. London: Weidenfeld & Nicolson.

Lévi-Strauss, Claude (1977) [1958] *Structural Anthropology*. Translated by Monique Layton. London: Allen Lane.

Lévi-Strauss, Claude (1992) [1955] *Tristes Tropiques*. Translated by John and Doreen Weightman. New York; London: Penguin Books.

Lévi-Strauss, Claude (2001) [1978] *Myth and Meaning*. London: Routledge.

Levitas, Ruth, 1998. *The Inclusive Society?* Basingstoke: Palgrave Macmillan.

Levy, Jacob (2003) 'Language Rights, Literacy,and the Modern State', in Will Kymlicka and Alan Patten (eds), *Language Rights and Political Theory*. Oxford: Oxford University Press, pp. 230–49.

Lewis, M. Paul (ed.) (2009) *Ethnologue: Languages of the World*, Sixteenth edition. Dallas, Texas: SIL International. Online version: http://www.ethnologue.com/. Accessed 8 July 2010

Lewis, Norman (1998) 'Human Rights, Law and Democracy in an Unfree World', in Tony Evans (ed.), *Human Rights Fifty Years On: A Reappraisal*. Manchester: Manchester University Press, pp. 77–104.

Lijphart, Arend (1977) *Democracy in Plural Societies: A Comparative Exploration*. New Haven: Yale University Press.

Little, Kenneth (1956) 'Race and Society', in UNESCO (1956) *The Race Question in Modern Science*. Paris: Unesco, pp. 165–214.

Locke, John (2001) [1690] *An Essay Concerning Human Understanding*. Kitchner, Ontario: Batoche Books.

Locke, John; David Hume and Jean Jacques Rousseau (1947) *Social Contract: Essays by Locke, Hume and Rousseau*. Edited Ernest Barker. London: Oxford University Press.

Losonsky, Michael (1999) 'Introduction', in Wilhelm von Humboldt (1999) [1841] *On Language*. Edited by Michael Losonsky and translated by Peter Heath. Cambridge: Cambridge University Press, pp. vii–xxxxiv.

Lugard, F.D. (1926) *The Dual Mandate in British Tropical Africa*. Edinburgh & London: William Blackwood.

Lugard, Frederick, Morris Ginsberg and H.A. Wyndham (1926) 'The Problem of Colour in Relation to the Idea of Equality'. *Journal of Philosophical Studies*, Vol. 1, No. 1, pp. 211–33.

Lugard, Lord (1933) 'Education and Race Relations'. *Journal of the Royal African Society*, Vol. 32, No. 126, pp. 1–11.

Lukács, Georg (1968) *Goethe and His Age*. Translated by Robert Anchor. London: Merlin.

Macartney, C.A. (1934) *National States and National Minorities*. London: Oxford University Press.

Macaulay, Thomas Babington (1935) [1835] *Speeches by Lord Macaulay, with his Minute on Indian education*. Edited by G.M. Young. London: Oxford University Press.

MacIntyre, Alasdair (1985) *After Virtue: A Study in Moral Theory*. London: Duckworth, second edition.

MacIntyre, Alasdair (2006) *Ethics and Politics: Selected Essays*, Vol. 2. Cambridge: Cambridge University Press.

Mackey, William (2001) [1980] 'The Ecology of Language Shift', in Alvin Fill and Peter Mühlhäusler (eds), *The Ecolinguistics Reader: Language Ecology and the Environment*. London: Continuum, pp. 67–74.

MacKinnon, Catherine (1987) *Feminism Unmodified: Discourses on Life and Law*. Cambridge Massachusetts: Harvard University Press.

MacKinnon, Catherine (1993) *Only Words*. Cambridge, Mass.: Havard University Press.

Macmillan, W.M. (1934a) '*The African Today*, Diedrich Westermann'. *Journal of the Royal African Society*, Vol. 33, No. 133, pp. 426–7.

Macmillan, W.M. (1934b) 'The Importance of the Educated African'. *Journal of the Royal African Society*, Vol. 33, No. 131, pp. 137–42.

Mačak, Ivana (2009) *Sarajevo under Siege: Anthropology in Wartime*. Philadelphia: University of Pennsylvania Press.

Maffi, Luisa (ed.) (2001) *On Biocultural Diversity: Linking Language, Knowledge and Environment*. Washington, DC: The Smithsonian Institute Press.

Magill, Claire (2010) *Education and Fragility in Bosnian Herzegovina*. Paris: International Institute for Education Planning/UNESCO. http://www.iiep.unesco.org/fileadmin/user_upload/Info_Services_Publications/pdf/2010/Bosnia-Herzegovina.pdf. Accessed 23 June 2012.

Magner, Thomas (1956) *Introduction to the Serbo-Croatian Language*. Philadelphia: Pennsylvania State University Press.

Magner, Thomas F. (1991) *Introduction to the Croatian and Serbian Language*. Philadelphia: Pennsylvania State University Press, revised edition.

Mahalanobis, P.C. (1959) 'Industrialization of Underdeveloped Countries – A Means to Peace'. *Bulletin of the Atomic Scientists*, Vol. XV, No. 1, pp. 12–17.

Maier, Carol (1995) 'Towards a Theoretical Practice for Cross-Cultural Translation', in Anuradha Dingwaney and Carol Maier (eds), *Between Languages and Cultures: Translation and Cross-Cultural Texts*. Pittsburgh and London: University of Pittsburgh Press, pp. 21–38.

Majstorović, Stevan (1980) *Cultural Policy in Yugoslavia Self-management and Culture*. Paris: UNESCO.

Malik, Kenan (1996) *The Meaning of Race: Race, History and Culture in Western Society*. London: Macmillan.

Malik, Kenan (2000a) 'Let Them Die'. *Prospect*, No. 57, 20 November. http://www.prospectmagazine.co.uk/magazine/letthemdie/ Accessed 26 July 2012.

Malik, Kenan (2000b) *Man, Beast and Zombie: What Science Can Tell Us and Not Tell Us about Human Nature*. London: Weidenfeld and Nicolson.

Malik, Kenan (2008) *Strange Fruit: Why Both Sides are Wrong in the Race Debate*. Oxford: Oneworld.

Malik, Kenan (2009) *From Fatwa to Jihad: The Rushie Affair and Its Legacy*. London: Atlantic Books.

Malik, Kenan (2010) 'CLR James: *The Black Jacobins*'. Normblog, 17 August. http://www.kenanmalik.com/reviews/james_jacobins.html. Accessed 23 June 2012.

Malinowski, Bronislaw (1922) *Argonauts of the Western Pacific*. London: Routledge.

Malinowski, Bronislaw (1923) 'The Problem of Meaning in Primitive Languages', in Charles Kay Ogden and I.A. Richards (1949) *The Meaning of Meaning: A Study of the Influence of Language upon Thought and the Science of Symbolism*. London: Routledge and Kegan Paul, 10th edition, pp. 296–336.

Malinowski, Bronislaw (1935) *Coral Gardens and Their Magic*, Vol. I. New York: American Book Company.

Malinowski, Bronislaw (1938) *Methods of Study of Culture Contact in Africa*. Oxford: Oxford University Press.

Malinowski, Bronislaw (1945) *The Dynamics of Culture Change: An Inquiry into Race Relations in Africa*. Edited by Phyllis M. Kaberry. New Haven: Yale University Press..

Mandelbaum, David (1949) 'Culture: The General View: Editor's Preface', in Edward Sapir (1949) *Selected Writings of Edward Sapir: Language, Culture and Personality*. Edited by David Mandelbaum. Berkeley and Los Angeles: University of Califonria Press, pp. 305–7.

Manguel, Alberto (2007) *Homer's The Illiad and the Odyssey: A Biography*. London: Atlantic.

Marchand, Suzanne (1997) 'Leo Frobenius and the Revolt against the West'. *Journal of Contemporary History*, Vol. 32, No. 2, pp. 153–70.

Marcuse, Herbert (1964) *One Dimensional Man: Studies in the Ideology of Advanced Industrial Society*. London: Routledge and Kegan Paul.

Marks, Susan (2000) *The Riddle of All Constitutions*. Oxford: Oxford University Press.

Martel, Angeline (1999) 'Heroes, Rebels, Communities and States in Language Rights Activism and Litigation', in Miklós Kontra, Robert Phillipson, Tove Skutnabb-Kangas and Tibor Varady (eds), *Language, a Right and a Resource: Approaches to Linguistics Human Rights*. Budapest: Central European University Press, pp. 47–80.

Martin, Gus (2010) *Understanding Terrorism: Challenges, Perspectives, and Issues*. London: Sage, third edition.

Marx, Karl (1844) *On the Jewish Question*. http://www.marxists.org/archive/marx/works/1844/jewish-question/index.htm. Accessed 3 July 2010.

Marx, Karl (1972) [1891] *Critique of the Gotha Programme.* Peking: Foreign Languages Press.
Marx, Karl (1973) [1857] *Grundrisse.* Translated by M. Nicolaus. Harmondsworth: Penguin.
Marx, Karl (1976) [1867] *Capital.* Vol. 1. Translated by Ben Fowkes. London: Penguin.
Marx, Karl (2007) [1852–1854] *Dispatches for the New York Tribune: Selected Journalism of Karl Marx.* London: Penguin.
Marx, Karl and Frederick Engels (1960) [1845] *The German Ideology.* New York: International Publishers.
Marx, Karl and Frederick Engels (1975) [1843–1844], *Collected Works,* Vol. 3. London: Lawrence & Wishart.
Marx, Karl and Friedrich Engels (2002) [1848] *The Communist Manifesto.* Translated by Samuel Moore with an introduction and notes by Gareth Stedman Jones. London: Penguin.
Matthews, Z.K. (1937) 'An African View of Indirect Rule in Africa'. *Journal of the Royal African Society,* Vol. 36, No. 145, pp. 433–7.
May, Stephen (2001) *Language and Minority Rights: Ethnicity, Nationalism and the Politics of Language.* Harlow/London: Longman/Pearson Education.
May, Stephen (2003) 'Misconceiving Minority Language Rights: Implications for Liberal Political Theory', in Will Kymlicka and Alan Patten (eds), *Language Rights and Political Theory.* Oxford: Oxford University Press, pp. 123–52.
Mayhew, Arthur (1933) 'A Comparative Survey of Educational Aims and Methods in British India and British Tropical Africa'. *Africa,* Vol. 6, No. 2, pp. 172–86.
Mazrui, Ali A. (1966) 'The English Language and Political Consciousness in British Colonial Africa'. *Journal of Modern African Studies,* Vol. 4, No. 3, pp. 661–76.
Mazrui, Ali (1989) 'The Satanic Verses or a Satanic Novel? Moral Dilemmas of the Rushdie Affair', in Commission for Racial Equality (ed.), *Free Speech: Report of a Seminar.* London: Commission for Racial Equality, pp. 79–103.
Mazrui, Ali (1990) *Cultural Forces in World Politics.* London: Currey.
Mazrui, Ali (2004) *English in Africa: After the Cold War.* Clevedon: Multilingual Matters.
Mbeki, Govan (1964) *The Peasants' Revolt.* Harmondsworth: Penguin.
McGilvray, James (2002) 'Introduction for Cybereditions', in Noam Chomsky, *Cartesian Linguistics: A Chapter in the History of Rationalist Thought.* Christchurch, New Zealand: Cybereditions, second edition edited by James McGilvray, pp. 7–44.
McKenzie, Greg (2010) '7/7 relative reviews terror comedy Four Lions'. *BBC Newsbeat.* 6 May. http://www.bbc.co.uk/newsbeat/10100390. Accessed 31 July 2012.
Mead, Margaret (ed.) (1953) *Cultural Patterns and Technical Change.* Paris: Unesco.
Mieville, China (2005) *Between Equal Rights: A Marxist Theory of International Law.* Leiden and Boston: Brill.
Mieville, China (2011) *Embassytown.* Basingstoke: Palgrave Macmillan.
Menendez, Agustin (2004) 'No Legitimacy Without Politics: Comments on Jens Steffek', in Christian Joerges, Inger-Johanne Sand and Gunther Teubner (eds), *Transnational Governance and Constitutionalism.* Oxford: Hart Publishing, pp. 103–14.
Mendus, Susan (1995) 'Human Rights in Political Theory'. *Political Studies,* Vol. 43, pp. 10–24.
Merry, Sally Engle (1992) 'Anthropology, Law and Transnational Processes'. *Annual Review of Anthropology,* Vol. 21, pp. 357–79.

Merry, Sally Engle (1997) 'Legal Pluralism and Transnational Culture', in Richard Wilson (ed.), *Human Rights, Culture and Context: Anthropological Perspectives*. London: Pluto, pp. 28–48.

Merry, Sally Engle (2001) 'Changing Rights, Changing Culture', in Jane K. Cowan, Marie-Bénédicte Dembour and Richard Wilson (eds), *Culture and Rights: Anthropological Perspectives*. Cambridge: Cambridge University, pp. 34–41.

Messer, Ellen (1993) 'Anthropology and Human Rights'. *Annual Review of Anthropology*, Vol. 22, pp. 221–49.

Meszaros, Istvan (1970) *Marx's Theory of Alienation*. London: Merlin.

Michaels, Walter Benn (1995) *Our America: Nativism, Modernism and Pluralism*. Durham, North Carolina: Duke University Press.

Mighty Students (undated) *Paper Topic: Al Qaeda Training Manual*. http://www.mightystudents.com/essay/Al.Qaeda.Training.134499. Accessed 28 June 2011.

Milanović, Dragan (1992) *Postmodern Law and Disorder*. Liverpool: Deborah Charles Publications.

Mill, John Stuart (1962) [1861, 1859, 1838] *Utilitarianism, On Liberty, Essay on Bentham*. London: Collins/Fontana, edited by Mary Warnock.

Mill, John Stuart (1984) [1859] 'A Few Words on Non-Intervention', in John M. Robson (ed.), *Essays on Equality, Law and Education: Vol. XXI*. Toronto and Buffalo. University of Toronto Press, pp. 109–24.

Mill, John Stuart (1985) [1859] *On Liberty*. Harmondsworth: Penguin.

Mill, John Stuart (1991) [1861] *Considerations on Representative Government*. Buffalo: Prometheus Books.

Miller, Arthur (1991) *Salesman in Beijing*. London: Methuen.

Milton, John (1903) [1644] *Areopagitica*. London: Constable.

Milton, John (2003) [1667] *Paradise Lost*. London: Penguin.

Minić, Milka (1961) 'The Role of the Commune in Education and Culture'. *International Social Science Journal*, Vol. 13, No. 3, pp. 422–6.

Minority Rights Group (1990) *World Directory of Minorities*. Harlow: Longman.

Misra, Maria (2008) 'Colonial Officers and Gentlemen: The British Empire and the Globalization of "Tradition"'. *Journal of Global History*, Vol. 3, pp 135–61.

Molière, Jean-Baptiste (2000) [1670] *The Misanthrope and Other Plays*. London: Penguin.

Monbiot, George (2012) 'The Right's Stupidity Spreads, Enabled by a Too-Polite Left'. *Guardian*, 6 February. http://www.guardian.co.uk/commentisfree/2012/feb/06/right-stupidity-spreads-enabled-polite-left. Accessed 24 April 2012.

Monboddo, James Burnet, Lord (1773–1792) *Of the Origin and Progress of Language. Volumes 1–6*. Edinburgh. Available at *English Short Title Catalogue. Eighteenth Century Collections Online*. Gale Group. http:/galenet.galegroup.com/servlet/ECCO. Accessed 8 September 2010.

Monboddo, James Burnet, Lord. (1774) *Of the Origin and Progress of Language. Vol. 2*. Edinburgh. Available at *English Short Title Catalogue. Eighteenth Century Collections Online*. Gale Group. http://galenet.galegroup.com/servlet/ECCO. Accessed 8 September 2010.

Monier-Williams, Monier (1858) *An Easy Introduction to the Study of Hindústání Words*. London: Longman, Brown, Green, Longmans, and Roberts.

Montagu, Ashley (1963) *Race, Science and Humanity*. London: Van Nostrand.

Montesquieu, Baron de (1949) [1748] *The Spirit of the Laws*. New York: Hafner Publishing.

Moore, Gregory (2008) 'Introduction', in, Johann Gottfried Herder, *Shakespeare*. Translated and edited by Gregory Moore. Princeton: Princeton University Press, pp. vii–xlii.

Moravcsik, Andrew (2000) 'The Origins of Human Rights Regimes: Democratic Delegation in Post-War Europe'. *International Organization*, Vol. 54, No. 92, 2000, pp. 217–52.

Morgan, Jonathan (2002) 'Law's British Empire'. *Oxford Journal of Legal Studies*, Vol. 22, No. 4, pp. 729–46.

Morris, Chris (2010) *Four Lions*. http://www.four-lions.co.uk/. Accessed 24 April 2012.

Mühlhäusler, Peter (1996) *Linguistic Ecology: Language Change and Linguistic Imperialism in the Pacific Region*. London; New York: Routledge.

Mühlhäusler, Peter (2001a) 'Ecolinguistics, Linguistic Diversity, Ecological Diversity', in Luisa Maffi (ed.), *On Biocultural Diversity: Linking Language, Knowledge and the Environment*. Smithsonian Institution Press, pp. 133–44.

Mühlhäusler, Peter (2001b) 'Talking about Environmental Issues', in Alvin Fill and Peter Mühlhäusler (eds), *The Ecolinguistics Reader: Language Ecology and the Environment*. London: Continuum, pp. 31–42.

Murdoch, Iris (1989) *Sartre: Romantic Rationalist*. London: Penguin.

Myrdal, Gunnar (1944) *An American Dilemma: The Negro Problem and American Democracy*. New York: Harper & Brothers.

Myrdal, Gunnar (1957) *Economic Theory and the Under-Developed Regions*. London: Duckworth.

Nabhan, Gary (1997) *Cultures of Habitat: On Culture, Nature, and Story*. Washington, DC: Counterpoint.

Nabokov, Vladimir (1992) [1955] 'Problems of Translation: *Onegin* in English', in Rainer Schulte and John Biguenet (eds), *Theories of Translation: An Anthology of Essays from Dryden to Derrida*. Chicago; London: University of Chicago Press, pp. 127–44.

Nandy, Ashis (1983) *The Intimate Enemy: Loss and Recovery of Self Under Colonialism*. Delhi; Oxford: Oxford University Press.

Narayan, Deepak; R. Chambers, M. Kaul Shah and P. Petesch (eds) (2000) *Voices of the Poor: Crying Out for Change*. Oxford: Oxford University Press.

Nasson, Bill (2004) *Britannia's Empire: Making a British World*. Stroud: Tempus.

Natale, Lara (2010) *FACTSHEET- Hate Crime*. London: Civitas. http://www.civitas.org.uk/crime/factsheet-HateCrime.pdf. Accessed 18 January 2011.

National Security Strategy of the United States of America (NSS) (2002) Washington: Office of the President of the United States of America. http://www.whitehouse.gov/nsc/nss. Accessed 10 March 2012.

Naylor, Kenneth (1992) 'The Sociolinguistic Situation in Yugoslavia with Special Emphasis on Serbo-Croatian', in Ranko Bugarski and Celia Hawkesworth (eds), *Language Planning in Yugoslavia*. Columbus: Slavica, pp. 80–92.

NETCU (National Extremism Tactical Coordination Unit) (2010) 'First EDL Crasbo Given to Duo'. 17 December 2010. Accessed 30 January 2011. http://www.netcu.org.uk/media/article.jsp?id=667&chkx=2e564901d3272a1100d18704762448ae. Accessed 18 January 2011.

Neisser, Charlotte (1955) 'Community Development and Mass Education in British Nigeria'. *Economic Development and Cultural Change*, Vol. 3, No. 4, pp. 352–65.

Nettle, Daniel and Suzanne Romaine (2002) *Vanishing Voices: The Extinction of the World's Languages*. Oxford: Oxford University Press.

Neumann, Franz (1986) *The Rule of Law: Political Theory and the Legal System in Modern Society*. Leamington Spa: Berg.

Neumann, Franz (1996) 'The Concept of Political Freedom', in William Scheuerman (ed.), *The Rule of Law under Siege. Selected Essays of Franz L. Neumann and Otto Kirchheimer*. Berkeley: University of California Press, pp. 195–230.

Nevins, Andrew; David Pesetsky, Cilene Rodrigues (2009a) 'Pirahã Exceptionality: A Reassessment'. *Language*, Vol. 85, No. 2, pp. 355–404.

Nevins, Andrew; David Pesetsky, Cilene Rodrigues (2009b) 'Discussion Note: Evidence and Argumentation: A reply to Everett'. *Language*, Vol. 85, No. 3, pp. 671–81. http://www.ucl.ac.uk/psychlangsci/staff/linguistics-staff/nevins-publications/npr09b.

Ngũgĩ wa Thiong'o (1986) *Decolonising the Mind: The Politics of Language in African Literature*. London: James Currey.

Nicolson, Adam (2004) *Power and Glory: Jacobean England and the Making of the James Bible*. London: Harper Perennial.

Nietzsche, Friedrich (1996) [1887] *On the Genealogy of Morals: A Polemic*. Translated by Douglas Smith. Oxford: Oxford University Press.

Nkrumah, Kwame (1970) *Consciencism*. New York: Monthly Review Press.

Nolan, James (1998) *The Therapeutic State: Justifying Government at Century's End*. New York: New York University.

Norgaard, Richard (2001) 'Possibilities after Progress', in Luisa Maffi (ed.), *On Biocultural Diversity: Linking Language, Knowledge and the Environment*. Washington, DC: Smithsonian Institution Press, pp. 533–9.

Norris, David (1999) *In the Wake of the Balkan Myth: Questions of Identity and Modernity*. Basingstoke: Palgrave Macmillan Press.

Norris, David (1993) *Teach Yourself Serbo-Croat*. London: Hodder & Stoughton.

Norris, David (2003) *Teach Yourself Croatian*. London: Hodder & Stoughton.

Norris, David and Vladislava Ribnikar (2003) *Teach Yourself Serbian*. London: Hodder & Stoughton.

Nottingham Evening Post (2012) 'Terrorism evidence against Nottingham student was 'made up' by police.' 17 July. http://www.thisisnottingham.co.uk/Terrorism-evidence-Nottingham-student-police/story-16548005-detail/story.html

NU (2011) 'Meeste Nederlanders niet eens met Srebrenica-uitspraak'. 10 July. Posted on JUSTWATCH-L@LISTSERV.BUFFALO.EDU. http://www.nu.nl/binnenland/2561431/meeste-nederlanders-niet-eens-met-srebrenica-uitspraak.html. Accessed 20 July 2011.

Nyerere, Julius (1968) *Ujamaa: Essays on Socialism*. Dar es Salaam: Oxford University Press.

Office of the High Representative (OHR) http://www.ohr.int.

OHR (1995) Annex to the Dayton Agreement on Implementing the Federation of Bosnia and Herzegovina, Agreed Principles for the Interim Statute for the City of Mostar, 10 November 1995. http://www.ohr.int/docu/d951110b.htm. Accessed 8 November 2010.

OHR (1996) 'Agreement on Joint Town Administration'. *Office of the High Representative Bulletin*, No. 13, 6 August. http://www.ohr.int/bulletins/b960806.htm#1. Accessed 17 December 1999.

OHR (1997a) Brcko Arbitral Tribunal for Dispute Over the Inter-Entity Boundary in Brcko Area Order on Multi-Ethnic Administration in the RS Municipality of Brcko, 10 October. http://www.ohr.int/docu/d971010b.htm Accessed 17 December 1999.

OHR (1997b) *Federation Forum, Chairman's Conclusions*, Sarajevo, 12 November 1997 http://www.ohr.int/docu/d971112a.htm. Accessed 17 December 1999.

OHR (1997c) *Statute of the City of Sarajevo*, Sarajevo, 27 March 1997 http://www.ohr.int/docu/d970327e.htm. Accessed 17 December 1999.

OHR (1999a) *High Representative's Diary for Dnevni Avaz.* 12 November. http://www.ohr.int/articles/a991120a.html. Accessed 17 December 1999.

OHR (1999b) *High Representative's Diary for Dnevni Avaz.* 14 November. http://www.ohr.int/articles/a991120a.html. Accessed 17 December 1999.

OHR (1999c) High Representative's Decisions on the Restructuring of the Public Broadcasting System in BiH and on Freedom of Information and Decriminalization of Libel and Defamation, 30 July. http://www.ohr.int/mediares/d990730a.htm Accessed 17 December 1999.

OHR (2000a) *OBN News Review*, 13 January. OHR@LISTSERV.CC.KULEUVEN.AC.BE. Accessed 28 September 2010.

Okey, Robin (2004) 'Serbian, Croatian, Bosnian? Language and Nationality in the Lands of Former Yugoslavia'. *East European Quarterly*, Vol. 38, No. 4, pp. 419–41.

Oldham, J.H. and B.D. Gibson (1931) *The Remaking of Man in Africa*. London: Humphrey Milford.

O'Neill, Brendan (2010a) 'Can We Have Our Voltaire Back?' *Spiked*, 13 January. http://www.spiked-online.com/index.php/site/article/7931/. Accessed 23 June 2012.

O'Neill, Brendan (2010b) 'Students Are Supposed to Read Books, Not Burn Them'. *Spiked*. 18 November. http://www.spiked-online.com/index.php/site/article/9905/. Accessed 23 June 2012.

O'Neill, Brendan (2012a) 'An Accepted Hatred'. *Spectator*, 4 February. http://www.spectator.co.uk/essays/all/7620968/an-acceptable-hatred.thtml. Accessed 23 June 2012.

O'Neill, Brendan (2012b) 'Racist Right-Wingers Once Used 'Science' to Prove Their Superiority'. *Telegraph*, 8 February. http://blogs.telegraph.co.uk/news/brendanoneill2/100135633/racist-right-wingers-used-to-use-science-to-prove-their-superiority-now-leftists-like-george-monbiot-do-it/. Accessed 23 June 2012.

O'Neill, Sean (2008) 'Terror Law in Tatters as Extremists Go Free'. *Times*, 14 February. http://business.timesonline.co.uk/tol/business/law/article3365890.ece. Accessed 18 January 2011.

Oppapers (undated) *Al Qaeda Training Manual*. http://www.oppapers.com/essays/Al-Qaeda-Training-ManuAl/519160. Accessed 23 June 2012.

Organisation of African Unity (1986) 'Language Plan of Action for Africa'. http://www.bisharat.net/Documents/OAU-LPA-86.htm. Accessed 15 March 2011.

Ortega y Gasset, José (1961) [1930] *The Revolt of the Masses*. London: Allen & Unwin, second edition.

Ortega y Gasset, Jose (1992) [1937] 'The Misery and the Splendor of Translation', in Rainer Schulte and John Biguenet (eds), *Theories of Translation: An Anthology of Essays from Dryden to Derrida*. Chicago and London: University of Chicago Press, pp. 93–112.

Orwell, George (1945) 'Review of *Freedom of Expression*'. *Tribune*, 12 October. http://georgeorwellnovels.com/journalism/review-of-freedom-of-expression-12-oct-1945/

Organisation for Security and Cooperation in Europe (OSCE) http://www.osce.org/. Accessed 24 June 2012.

OSCE (1999a) Employment Discrimination in BiH. June.

OSCE (1999b) Women Can Change Bosnia. June, http://www.oscebih.org/events/events15–7-interview.htm Accessed 17 December 1999.

OSCE (2003) From Quill to Cursor Freedom of the Media in the Digital Era. Vienna: OSCE http://www.osce.org/fom/13834. Accessed 19 January 2011.

OSCE (2004a) Brussels Declaration, CIO.GAL/86/04, 14 September. http://www.osce.org/documents/cio/2004/09/3567_en.pdf. Accessed 19 January 2011.

OSCE (2004b) The Media Freedom Internet Cookbook. Vienna: OSCE. http://www.osce.org/fom/13836. Accessed 19 January 2011.

OSCE (2005a) Combating Hate Crimes in the OSCE Region: An Overview of Statistics, Legislation, and National Initiatives. Vienna: OSCE. http://www.osce.org/publications/odihr/2005/09/16251_452_en.pdf. Accessed 19 January 2011.

OSCE (2005b) Raising Debate: Is BiH Respecting Its International Commitments in the Field of Education? Questions for the Citizens of BiH. http://www.zapravicnoobrazovanje.ba/Dokumenti//Zakoni%20i%20konvencije/OSCE.pdf. Accessed 29 November 2010.

OSCE (2007a) *Tailoring Catchment Areas: Schools Catchment Areas in Bosnia and Herzegovina,* A Status Report. http://www.oscebih.org/documents/9769-eng.pdf. Accessed 29 November 2010.

OSCE (2007b) *Lessons from Education Reform in Brčko.* http://www.oscebih.org/documents/9994-eng.pdf. Accessed 29 November 2010.

OSCE (2009) Supplementary Human Dimension Meeting on Hate Crimes – Effective Implementation of Legislation Side Event: Roundtable for Civil Society, 4–5 May 2009, Hofburg, Vienna Recommendations by Civil Society Representatives. Pc.Shdm.Gal/5/09. Vienna: OSCE. http://www.osce.org/odihr/62875. Accessed 19 January 2011.

OSCE (2010) Astana Declaration. October. Vienna: OSCE. http://www.osce.org/documents/osce/2010/10/47138_en.pdf. Accessed 19 January 2011.

OSCE/ODIHR (2009a) *Hate Crimes in the OSCE Region – Incidents and Responses: Annual Report for 2008.* Warsaw: ODIHR. http://www.osce.org/odihr/40203. Accessed 19 January 2011.

OSCE/ODIHR (2009b) *Hate Crime Laws: A Practical Guide.* Warsaw: ODIHR. http://www.osce.org/odihr/36426. Accessed 19 January 2011.

OSCE/ODIHR (undated) *Law Enforcement Officer Programme on Combating Hate Crimes.* Warsaw: ODIHR. http://www.osce.org/odihr/20699. Accessed 19 January 2011.

The Oslo Corpus of Bosnian Texts http://www.tekstlab.uio.no/Bosnian/Corpus.html. Accessed 26 November 2010.

The Oslo Recommendations Regarding the Linguistic Rights of National Minorities & Explanatory Note. 1998. http://www.unesco.org/most/ln2pol7.htm. Accessed 15 September 2010.

Otto Preminger Institute v Austria, Judgement of 20 September 1994, Series A, No. 295-A; (1995) 19 European Human Rights Reports 34.

Ouane, Adama and Christine Glanz (2010) *Why and How Africa Should Invest in African Languages and Multilingual Education.* Hamburg UNESCO Institute for Lifelong Learning http://unesdoc.unesco.org/images/0018/001886/188642e.pdf. Accessed 8 July 2011.

L'Ouverture, Toussaint (2008) [1793–1802] *The Haitian Revolution.* London: Verso.

Owiredu, P.A. (1964) 'Proposals for a National Language for Ghana'. *African Affairs,* Vol. 63, No. 251, pp. 142–5.

Owiredu, P.A. (1957) 'Towards a Common Language for Ghana'. *African Affairs,* Vol. 56, No. 225, pp. 295–9.

Packer, John (2003) 'The Practitioner's Perspective: Minority Languages and Linguistic Minorities in the Work of the OSCE High Commissioner on National Minorities', in G. Hogan-Brun and S. Wolff (eds), *Minority Languages in Europe: Status – Frameworks – Prospects*. London: Palgrave Macmillan, pp. 75–96.

Paine, Thomas (1996) [1791] *Rights of Man*. Ware: Wordsworth Editions.

Pajić, Zoran (1994) 'The Former Yugoslavia', in Hugh Miall (ed.), *Minority Rights in Europe: The Scope for a Transnational Regime*. London: Pinter Publishers, pp. 56–65.

Paperdue (undated) *Al Qaeda Training Manual*. http://www.paperdue.com/Details/Al+Qaeda+training+manual/12630. Accessed 5 July 2011.

Parton, Nigel (1985) *The Politics of Child Abuse*. Basingstoke: Palgrave Macmillan.

Pashukanis, Evgeny (1978) [1924] *Law and Marxism: A General Theory*. Translated by Barbara Einhorn. London: Pluto.

Pateman, Carole (1988) *The Sexual Contract*. Cambridge: Polity Press.

Paton, Alan (1958) *Cry the Beloved Country*. Harmondsworth: Penguin.

Patten, Alan (2003) 'What Kind of Bilingualism?', in Will Kymlicka and Alan Patten (eds), *Language Rights and Political Theory*. Oxford: Oxford University Press, pp. 296–321.

Patten, Alan and Will Kymlicka (2003) 'Introduction: Language Rights and Political Theory: Context, Issues and Approaches', in Will Kymlicka and Alan Patten (eds), *Language Rights and Political Theory*. Oxford: Oxford University Press, pp. 1–51.

Paulston, Christina Bratt (1997) 'Epilogue: Some Concluding Thoughts on Linguistic Human Rights'. *International Journal of the Sociology of Language*, Vol. 27, pp. 187–95.

Paz, Octavio (1992) [1971] 'Literature and Letters', in Rainer Schulte and John Biguenet (eds), *Theories of Translation: An Anthology of Essays from Dryden to Derrida*. Chicago and London: University of Chicago Press, pp. 152–62.

Peace Implementation Council (1998) Madrid Conference.

Pearson Allison (1994) 'Mary, Mary, Quite Contrary'. *Independent on Sunday*, 29 May. http://www.independent.co.uk/arts-entertainment/television – mary-mary-quite-contrary-1439331.html.

Peil.nl (2011) 'Schadevergoeding slachtoffers Srebenica'. https://n10.noties.nl/peil.nl/. Accessed 16 July 2011.

Penn, Julia (1972) *Linguistic Relativity Versus Innate Ideas: The Origins of the Sapir-Whorf Hypothesis in German Thought*. The Hague: Mouton.

Pender John (2002) 'Empowering the Poorest? The World Bank and "The Voices of the Poor"' in David Chandler (ed.), *Rethinking Human Rights: Critical Approaches to International Politics*. Basingstoke: Palgrave Macmillan, pp. 97–114.

Pender John (2007) 'Country Ownership: The Evasion of Donor. Accountability,' in Chris Bickerton, Philip Cunliffe and Alex Gourevitch (eds), *Politics without Sovereignty*. London: Routledge, pp. 112–30.

Pennycook, Alastair (1990) 'Towards a Critical Applied Linguistics for the 1990s'. *Issues in Applied Linguistics*, Vol. 1, No. 1, pp. 9–28.

Pennycook, Alastair (1994) *The Cultural Politics of English as an International Language*. Harlow: Longman.

Pennycook, Alastair (1998a) *English and the Discourses of Colonialism*. London: Routledge.

Pennycook, Alastair (1998b) 'The Right to Language: Towards a Situated Ethics of Language Possibilities'. *Language Sciences*, Vol. 20, No. 1, pp. 73–87.

Perrin, Colin (2004) 'Breath from Nowhere: The Silent Foundation of Human Rights'. *Social and Legal Studies*, Vol. 13, No. 1, pp. 133–51.

Perry, Valery (2003) *Reading, Writing and Reconciliation: Educational Reform in Bosnia and Herzegovina*, ECMI Working Paper 18. Flensburg: European Centre for Minority Rights. http://www.ecmi.de/download/working_paper_18.pdf. Accessed 23 November 2010.

Petrisch, Wolfgang (1999a) 'The Future lies with Its People'. *The Wall Street Journal Europe*, 17 September. http://www.ohr.int/articles/a990917a.htm. Accessed 4 November 2010.

Petrisch, Wolfgang (1999b) 'Odgovornost Is the Key to Returns, and Sarajevo, the Capital, Must Lead'. *Dani*, 1 October. http://www.ohr.int/articles/a991001a.htm. Accessed 4 November 2010.

Phillipson, Robert (1992) *Linguistic Imperialism*. Oxford: Oxford University Press.

Phillipson, Robert (1996) 'Linguistic Imperialism: African Perspectives'. *ELT Journal*, Vol. 50, No. 2, pp. 160–7.

Phillipson, Robert (1998) 'Globalizing English: Are Linguistic Human Rights an Alternative to Linguistic Imperialism?' *Language Sciences*, Vol. 20, No. 1, pp. 101–12.

Phillipson, Robert (2003) *English-Only Europe?* London: Routledge.

Phillipson, Robert (2009a) *Linguistic Imperialism Continued*. London: Routledge.

Phillipson, Robert (2009b) 'The Tension between Linguistic Diversity and Dominant English', in Tove Skutnabb-Kangas, Robert Phillipson, Ajit Mohanty and Minati Panda (eds), *Social Justice through Multilingual Education*. Bristol; Buffalo; Toronto: Multilingual Matters, pp. 85–102.

Phillipson, Robert; Tove Skutnabb-Kangas and Mart Rannut (1994) 'Introduction', in Tove Skutbnabb-Kangas and Robert Phillipson (eds), *Linguistic Human Rights: Overcoming Linguistic Discrimination*. Berlin: M. de Gruyter, pp. 1–22.

Pickard-Cambridge, A.W. (1940) 'The Place of Achimota in West African Education'. *Journal of the Royal African Society*, Vol. 39, No. 155, pp. 143–53.

Pigott, Charles (1792) *The Jockey Club, or a Sketch of the Manners of the Age. Part the First*. The seventh edition. London. Eighteenth Century Collections Online. Gale. http://galenet.galegroup.com/servlet/ECCO. Accessed 24 June 2012.

Pigott, Charles (1794) *The Female Jockey Club, Or a Sketch of the Manners of the Age*. The fourth edition. London. Eighteenth Century Collections Online. Gale Group. http://galenet.galegroup.com/servlet/ECCO. Accessed 24 June 2012.

Pigott, Charles (1795) *A Political Dictionary Explaining the True Meaning of Words*. London: D. I. Eaton. Eighteenth Century Collections Online. Gale Group. http://galenet.galegroup.com/servlet/ECCO . Accessed 24 June 2012.

Pigott, Charles (2004) [1795] *A Political Dictionary Explaining the True Meaning of Words*. Edited by Robert Rix. Aldershot, Hants: Ashgate.

Pigs' Meat; Or, Lessons for the Swinish Multitude (1795) Vol. 1. The third edition. London. 2 vols. Eighteenth Century Collections Online. Gale Group. http://galenet.galegroup.com/servlet/ECCO. Accessed 24 June 2012.

Pogge, Thomas (2003) 'Accommodation Rights for Hispanics in the United States', in Will Kymlicka and Alan Patten (eds), *Language Rights and Political Theory*. Oxford: Oxford University Press, pp. 105–22.

Pogson, Geoff (1998) 'Digital Technology Will Save Your Language'. Conférence des Services de Traduction des Etats Européens, The Hague, pp. 1–5

Popović, Predrag (2006) 'Virtual Apartheid in the Bosnian School System'. *Balkan Insight*, 13 October. http://www.bosnia.org.uk/bosrep/report_format.cfm?articleid=3134&reportid=172. Accessed 23 June 2012.

Porter, Roy (2000) *Enlightenment: Britain and the Creation of the Modern World*. London: Penguin.

Post, Jerrold (ed.) (2005a) *Declaration of Jihad Against the Country's Tyrants, Military Series: The Al-Qaeda Terrorism Manual.* Maxwell Air Force Base: USAF Counterproliferation Center.

Post, Jerry (ed.) (2005b) *Military Studies in the Jihad against the Tyrants: The Al-Qaeda Training Manual.* London: Frank Cass. http://www.amazon.co.uk/Military-Studies-Jihad-against-Tyrants/dp/0714682748/ref=sr_1_1?s=books&ie=UTF8&qid=1311621287&sr=1-1. Accessed 18 January 2011.

Povelja o bosanskom jeziku (2002) [Charter of the Bosnian Language] http://www.bosnjaci.rs/

Pradeep, K. (2010) 'Tribute to Cochin Creole Portuguese'. *The Hindu Times*, 26 September. http://www.thehindu.com/life-and-style/society/article795353.ece. Accessed 16 October 2011.

Pranjković, Ivo (2001) 'The Croatian Standard Language and the Serbian Standard Language'. *International Journal of the Sociology of Language*, No. 147, pp. 31–50.

Prashad, Vijay (2008) *The Darker Nations: A People's History of the Third World.* New York: New Press.

Pratt, Cranford (1999) 'Julius Nyerere: Reflections on the Legacy of his Socialism'. *Canadian Journal of African Studies* Vol. 33, No. 1, pp. 137–52.

Priestly, Joseph (1784) *The Rudiments of English Grammar, Adapted to the Use of Schools; with Notes and Observations, for the Use of Those Who Have Made Some Proficiency in the Language.* Dublin: Byrne, fourth edition.

Protevi, John (2011) 'Semantic, Pragmatic and Affective Enactment at OWS'. *Theory and Event*, Vol. 14, No. 4, Occupy Wall Street supplement.

Pupavac, Vanessa (1998) 'The Post-Yugoslav States'. *Peace Review*, Vol. 10, No. 2, pp. 143–50.

Pupavac, Vanessa (2001) 'Therapeutic Governance: Psychosocial Intervention and Trauma Risk Management'. *Disasters*, Vol. 25, No. 4, pp. 358–72.

Pupavac, Vanessa (2002) 'Pathologizing Populations and Colonizing Minds: International psychosocial programmes in Kosovo'. *Alternatives*, Vol. 27, No. 4, pp. 489–511.

Pupavac, Vanessa (2003) 'Politics and Language Rights: A Case Study of Language Politics in Croatia', in G. Hogan-Brun and S. Wolff (eds), *Minority Languages in Europe: Status, Frameworks, Prospects.* Basingstoke: Palgrave Macmillan, pp. 138–54.

Pupavac, Vanessa (2004) 'The Emotionology of the New International Security Paradigm'. *European Journal of Social Theory*, Vol. 7, No. 2, pp. 149–170.

Pupavac, Vanessa (2005) 'Human Security and the Rise of Global Therapeutic Governance'. *Conflict, Security and Development*, Vol. 5, No. 2, pp. 161–81.

Pupavac, Vanessa (2006) 'The Politics of Emergency and the Demise of the Developing State: Problems for Humanitarian Advocacy'. *Development in Practice*, Vol. 16, Vols 3–4, pp. 255–69.

Pupavac, Vanessa (2008) 'Refugee Advocacy, Traumatic Representations and Political Disenchantment'. *Government and Opposition.* Vol. 43, No. 2, pp. 270–92.

Pupavac, Vanessa (2009) 'International Children's Rights Advocacy', in Michael Goodhart (ed.), *Human Rights Politics and Practice.* Oxford: Oxford University Press, pp. 219–38.

Pupavac, Vanessa (2010) 'The Consumerism Security-Development Nexus'. *Security Dialogue*, Vol. 41, No. 6, pp. 1–23.

Pupavac, Vanessa (2011) 'Punishing Childhoods: Contradictions in Children's Rights and Global Governance'. *Journal of Intervention and Statebuilding*, Vol. 5, No. 3, pp. 285–312.

Pupavac, Vanessa (2012) 'Global Disaster Management and Therapeutic Governance of Communities'. *Development Dialogue*, No. 58, pp. 81–98.

Pushkin, Alexander (1964) [1833] *Eugene Onegin: A Novel in Verse*. Translated by Vladimir Nabokov. London: Routledge and Kegan Paul.

Pushkin, Alexander (1979) [1833] *Eugene Onegin*. Translated by Charles Johnston. Harmondsworth: Penguin.

Pushkin, Aleksander (2006) [1827] *The Gypsies and Other Narrative Poems*. Translated with an introduction and notes by Antony Wood. London: Angel Books.

Radovanović, Milorad and Randall Major (eds) (2001) *International Journal of the Sociology of Language*, No. 151.

Rai, Amrit (1984) *A House Divided: The Origin and Development of Hindi/Hindavi*. Delhi and Oxford: Oxford University Press.

Ramanathan, Vaidehi (2005) *The English-Vernacular Divide: Postcolonial Language Politics and Practices*. Clevedon, UK: Multilingual Matters.

Rankin, Katharine (2001) 'Governing Development: Neoliberalism, Microcredit, and Rational Economic Woman'. *Economy and Society*, Vol. 30, No. 1, pp. 18–37.

Rannut, Mart (1999) 'The Common Language Problem', in Miklós Kontra, Robert Phillipson, Tove Skutnabb-Kangas and Tibor Varady (eds), *Language, a Right and a Resource: Approaches to Linguistics Human Rights*. Budapest: Central European University Press, pp. 99–114.

Rawls, John (1958) 'Justice as Fairness'. *The Philosophical Review*, Vol. 67, No. 2, pp. 164–94.

Rawls, John (1973) *A Theory of Justice*. Oxford: Oxford University Press.

Rawls, John (1999) *The Law of Peoples: With, 'The Idea of Public Reason Revisited'*. Cambridge, Mass.: Harvard University Press.

Raz, Joseph (1988) 'Autonomy, Toleration, and the Harm Principle', in Susan Mendus (ed.), *Justifying Toleration; Conceptual and Historical Perspectives*. Cambridge University Press: Cambridge, pp. 155–76.

Réaume, Denise (1988) 'Individuals, Groups, and Rights to Public Goods'. *University of Toronto Law Journal*, Vol. 38, pp. 1–27.

Réaume, Denise (1991) 'The Constitutional Protection of Language: Survival Or Security?', in David Schneiderman (ed.), *Language and the State: The Law and Politics of Identity*. Quebec: Less Editions Yvon Blais, pp. 37–57.

Réaume, Denise (2003) 'Beyond Personality: The Territorial and Personal Principles of Language Policy Reconsidered', in Will Kymlicka and Alan Patten (eds), *Language Rights and Political Theory*. Oxford: Oxford University Press, pp. 271–96.

Reece, Helen (2003) *Divorcing responsibly*. Oxford: Hart.

Reece, Helen (2009) 'Feminist Anti-Violence Discourse as Regulation', in Shelley Day Sclater, Fatemeh Ebtehaj, Emily Jackson and Martin Richards (eds), *Regulating Autonomy: Sex, Reproduction and Family*. Oxford: Hart, pp 37–51.

Read, Margaret (1966) *Culture, Health and Disease: Social and Culture Influence on Health Programmes in Developing Countries*. London: Tavistock.

Reed, John (2007) [1919] *Ten Days That Shook the World*. London: Penguin.

Reid, Walter and Kenton Miller (1993) *Keeping Options Alive: The Scientific Basis for Conserving Biodiversity*. Washington, DC: World Resources Institute. http://pdf.wri.org/keepingoptionsalive_bw.pdf

Reid, Julian (2012) 'The Disastrous and Politically Debased Subject of Resilience'. *Development Dialogue*, No. 58, pp. 67–80.

Reus-Smith, Christian (2001) 'Human Rights and the Social Construction of Sovereignty'. *Review of International Studies*, Vol. 27, No. 3, pp. 519–38.

Rickard, Maurice (1994) 'Liberalism, Multiculturalism and Minority Protection'. *Social Theory and Practice*, Vol. 20, No. 2, pp. 143–70.

Rix, Robert (2004) 'Introduction', and 'Annotated Notes', in Charles Piggot (ed.), *A Political Dictionary Explaining the True Meaning of Words*. Aldershot, Hants: Ashgate, pp. xiii–xxxi; pp. 1–114.

Robertson, Geoffrey (1999) *Crimes against Humanity: The Struggle For Global Justice*. London: Penguin.

Robeson, Paul (1955) 'Here's my Story: Freedom', in Paul Robeson, *Paul Robeson Speaks: Writings, Speeches, Interviews, 1918–1974*. Edited by Philip Foner. London: Quartet Books, pp. 270–2.

Robin, Corey (2004) *Fear: The History of a Political Idea*. New York and Oxford: Oxford University Press.

Rodriquez, Felipe (2003) 'Burning the Village to Roast the Pig: Censorship of Online Media', in OSCE, *From Quill to Cursor Freedom of the Media in the Digital Era*. Vienna: OSCE, pp. pp. 85–109. http://www.osce.org/fom/13834. Accessed 16 January 2011

Rolph, C.H. (ed.) (1961) *The Trial of Lady Chatterley: Regina v. Penguin Books Limited: The Transcript of the Trial*. Harmondsworth: Penguin.

Ronsbo, Henrik (2004) 'Decentering Struggle: Traumatizing Central Americans'. *Psyke & Logos* Vol. 25, No. 1, pp. 143–55.

Rooney, Kevin (2011) Offensive Behaviour at Football and Threatening Communications (Scotland) Bill. Written Submission to the Justice Committee.

Rosenstein, Lucy (2002) 'Theory versus Practice: Some Thoughts on Postcolonial Translation with Special Reference to Hindi', Translations and Translation Theories East and West Workshop, SOAS, London.

Rosello, Mireille (1995) 'Introduction', in Aimé Césaire (1995) *Notebooks of a Return to My Native Land*. Translated by Mireille Rosello with Annie Pritchard. Tarset: Bloodaxe, pp. 9–64.

Rostow, W.W. (1971) [1960] *Stages of Economic Growth: A Non-Communist Manifesto*. Cambridge: Cambridge University Press.

Roth, Kenneth (2011) 'The Security Council Has at Last Lived Up to Its Duty'. *Foreign Policy*, 19 March. http://www.hrw.org/news/2011/03/18/security-council-has-last-lived-its-duty. Accessed 15 March 2012.

Rothwell, W. (2004) 'Henry of Lancaster and Geoffrey Chaucer: Anglo-French and Middle English in Fourteenth-Century England'. *The Modern Language Review*, Vol. 99, No. 2, pp. 313–27.

Rousseau, Jean-Jacques (1966) [1781] 'On the Origin of Language', translated by J.M. Cohen in Jean-Jacques Rousseau, Johann Gottfried Herder, *On the Origin of Language*. Chicago: University of Chicago Press, pp. 1–83.

Rousseau, Jean-Jacques (1968) [1762] *The Social Contract*. Translated and introduced by Maurice Cranston. Harmondsworth: Penguin Books.

Rousseau, Jean-Jacques (1984) [1755] *A Discourse on Inequality*. Translated with an introduction and notes by Maurice Cranston. Harmondsworth: Penguin.

Rowling J.K. (2003) *Harry Potter and the Order of the Phoenix*. London: Bloomsbury.

Rushdie, Salman (1983) *Shame*. London: Picador.

Rushdie, Salman (2002) *Step Across This Line*. London: Random House.

Rushdie, Salman (2006) [1988] *The Satanic Verses*. London: Vintage.

Rusinow, Dennison (ed.) (1988) *Yugoslavia: A Fractured Federalism*. Washington: Wilson Center Press.

Ruxton, F.H. (1930) 'An Anthropological No-Man's-Land'. *Africa*, Vol. 3, pp. 1–12.

Ruzzo, Carlo (2000) 'Language and Nationalism in Italy: Language as a Weaker marker of Identity', in Stephen Barbour and Cathie Carmichael (eds), *Language and Nationalism in Europe*. Oxford: Oxford University Press, pp. 168–82.

Said, Edward (1991) [1978] *Orientalism: Western Conceptions of the Orient*. London: Penguin.

Said, Edward (1994a) *Culture and Imperialism*. London: Vintage.

Said, Edward (1994b) *Representations of the Intellectual*. New York: Vintage Books.

Said, Edward (2003) 'a Window on the World: 25 Anniversary of His Book *Orientalism*'. *Guardian*, 2 August. http://www.guardian.co.uk/books/2003/aug/02/alqaida.highereducation. Accessed 16 September 2010.

Salzmann, Zdenek (1998) *Language, Culture and Society: An Introduction to Linguistic Anthropology*, second edition. Boulder, CO: Westview Press.

Samarasinghe, Gayan (2010) 'Defend the Freedom Campaign'. *Freedom in a Puritan Age* http://www.freedominapuritanage.co.uk/?p=388. Accessed 15 January 2011.

Sandel, Michael (1982) *Liberalism and the Limits of Justice*. Cambridge; London; New York; New Rochelle; Melbourne; Sydney: Cambridge University Press.

Sands, Philippe (2005) *Lawless World: America and the Making and Breaking of Global Rules*. London. Penguin/Allen Lane.

Santos, B. de Sousa (1987) 'Law: A Map of Misreading: Toward a Postmodern Conception of Law'. *Journal of Law and Society*, Vol. 14, No. 3, pp. 279–302.

Santos, Boaventura de Sousa (1995) *Toward a New Common Sense: Law, Science and Politics in the Paradigmatic Transition*. New York: Routledge.

Sapir, Edward (1921) *Language: An Introduction to the Study of Speech*. New York: Harcourt, Brace.

Sapir, Edward (1924) 'Culture, Genuine and Spurious'. *American Journal of Psychology*, Vol. 29, pp. 401–29 in Edward Sapir (1949) *Selected Writings of Edward Sapir: Language, Culture and Personality*. Berkeley and Los Angeles: University of Califonia Press, pp. 308–31.

Sapir, Edward (1929) 'The Status of Linguistics as a Science'. *Language*, Vol. 5, pp. 207–14 in Edward Sapir (1949) *Selected Writings of Edward Sapir: Language, Culture and Personality*. Berkeley; Los Angeles: University of Califonia Press, pp. 160–6.

Sapir, Edward (1949) *Selected Writings of Edward Sapir: Language, Culture and Personality*. Edited by David Mandelbaum. Berkeley and Los Angeles: University of California Press.

Sapir, Edward (2001) [1912] 'Language and Environment', in Alvin Fill and Peter Mühlhäusler (eds), *The Ecolinguistics Reader: Language Ecology and the Environment*. London: Continuum, pp. 13–23.

Santos, Boaventura de Sousa (1995) *Toward a New Common Sense: Law, Science and Politics in the Paradigmatic Transition*. New York: Routledge.

Sardar, Ziauddin (2008) 'Forewood to the 2008 Edition', in Frantz Fanon (2008) [1952] *Black Skin, White Masks*. Translated by Charles Lam Markmann. London: Pluto, pp. vi–xx.

Sartre, Jean-Paul (1948) *Existentialism and Humanism*. Translated by Philip Mairet. London: Methuen.

Sartre, Jean-Paul (1964–1965) 'Black Orpheus'. Translated by John MacCombie. *The Massachusetts Review*, Vol. 6, No. 1, pp. 13–52.

Sartre, Jean-Paul (1967) *What Is Literature?* Translated by Bernard Frechtman London: Methuen.

Sartre, Jean-Paul (1995) [1946] *Anti-Semitism and the Jew*. Translated by George Becker. New York: Schocken Books.

Satterlee, Thom (1996) 'Robert Frost's Views on Translation'. *Delos*, pp. 46–52.

Sauer, Charles A. (1943) 'The Place of the Vernacular Language in Colonial Education'. *The Modern Language Journal*, Vol. 27, No. 3, pp. 180–3.

Saussure, Ferdinand de (1974) [1916] *Course in General Linguistics*. London: Fontana.

Sayre, Robert and Michael Löwy (1984) 'Figures of Romantic Anti-Captialism'. *New German Critique*, Vol. 32, pp. 42–92.

Scheper-Hughes, Nancy (1995) 'The Primacy of the Ethical: Propositions for a Militant Anthropology'. *Current Anthropology* Vol. 36, No. 3, pp. 409–40.

Schleiermacher, Friedrich (1992) [1813] '*From* on the Different Methods of Translating' in Rainer Schulte and John Biguenet (eds), *Theories of Translation: An Anthology of Essays from Dryden to Derrida*. Chicago; London: University of Chicago Press, pp. 36–54.

Schmidt, P.W. (1930) 'The Use of the Vernacular in Education in Africa'. *Africa*, Vol. 3, No. 2, pp. 137–49.

Schopenhauer, Arthur (1992) [1851] 'On Language and Words', in Rainer Schulte and John Biguenet (eds), *Theories of Translation: An Anthology of Essays from Dryden to Derrida*. Chicago and London: University of Chicago Press, pp. 32–35.

Schöpflin, George (1980) 'Nationality in the Fabric of Yugoslav Politics'. *Survey*, Vol. 25, No. 3, pp. 1–19.

Schulte, Rainer and John Biguenet (eds) (1992) *Theories of Translation: An Anthology of Essays from Dryden to Derrida*. Chicago; London: University of Chicago Press.

Schultz, Beth (2001) 'Language and Natural Environment', in Alvin Fill and Peter Mühlhäusler (eds), *The Ecolinguistics Reader: Language Ecology and the Environment*. London: Continuum, pp. 109–14.

Schumacher, E.F. (1993) [1973] *Small Is Beautiful: A Study of Economics as if People Mattered*. London: Vintage.

Schumacher, E.F. (1977) *A Guide for the Perplexed*. London: Jonathan Cape.

Scottish Government, Offensive Behaviour at Football and Threatening Communications (Scotland) Act 2012. http://www.scotland.gov.uk/Topics/Justice/law/sectarianism-action-1/football-violence/bill. Accessed 24 June 2012.

Selimović, Mesa (1996) [1966] *Death and the Dervish*. Translated by Bogdan Rakić and Stephen Dickey. Illinois: North Western University Press.

Sellars, Kirsten (2002) *The Rise and Rise of Human Rights*. London Sutton Publishing.

Sen, Amartya (1981) *Poverty and Famines: An Essay on Entitlement and Deprivation*. Oxford: Oxford University Press.

Sen, Amartya (2001) *Development as Freedom*. Oxford: Oxford University Press.

Senghor, Léopold Sedar (1971) *The Foundations of "Africanité" or "Negritude" and "Arabité"*. Translated by Mercer Cook. Paris: Présence Africaine.

Senghor, Léopold Sédar (2000) [1961] 'What Is "Negritude"'?', in Robert Bernasconi and Tommy Lott (eds), *The Idea of Race*. Indianapolis: Hackett, pp. 136–8.

Senghor, Léopold Sédar (2003) [1939] 'What the Black Man Contributes', translated by Mary Beth Mader in Robert Bernasconi and Sybol Cook (ed.), *Race and Racism in Continental Philosophy*. Bloomington: Indiana University Press, pp. 287–301.

Senghor, Léopold Sédar (2007) [1971] 'The Lessons of Leo Frobenius' in Leo Frobenius, *Leo Frobenius on African History, Art, and Culture: An Anthology*. Edited by Eike Haberland. Princeton: Markus Wiener Publishers, pp. vii–xiii.

Sennett, Richard (1998) *The Corrosion of Character: The Personal Consequences of Work in the New Capitalism*. New York: W.W. Norton.

Seth, Vikram (1993) *A Suitable Boy*. London: Phoenix House.

Seton-Watson, Hugh (1977) *Nations and States: An Inquiry into the Origins of Nations and the Politics of Nationalism*. Boulder, CO: Westview Press.

Shakespear, John (1817) *A Dictionary, Hindūstānī and English*. Shakespear. London: Cox and Baylis.

Shakespeare, William (1992) [1608] *The Tragedy of King Lear*. Cambridge: Cambridge University Press.

Shakespeare, William (1994) [1623] *The Tempest*. New York: Washington Square Press.

Shapiro, Ian (1986) *The Evolution of Rights in Liberal Theory*. Cambridge: Cambridge University Press.

Sharpe, Jenny (2000) 'Postcolonial Studies in the House of US Multiculturalism', in Henry Schwarz and Sangeeta Ray (eds), *A Companion to Postcolonialism Studies*. Oxford: Blackwell, pp. 112–25.

Shatz, Adam (2012) 'Whose Egypt?' *London Review of Books*, 5 January.

Shelley, Percy (1822) *Queen Mab*. London: Carlile.

Shelley, Percy (1998) [1821] 'A Defence of Poetry', in W.R. Owen and Hamish Johnson (eds), *Romantic Writings: An Anthology*. Milton Keynes: Open University, pp. 341–66.

Shelley, Percy (1998) [1819] 'Sonnet: England in 1819', in W.R. Owen and Hamish Johnson (eds), *Romantic Writings: An Anthology*. Milton Keynes: Open University, p. 333.

Shoup, Paul (1968) *Communism and the Yugoslav National Question*. New York: Colombia University Press.

Shuibhne, Niamh Nic (2002) *EC Law and Minority Language Policy: Culture, Citizenship and Fundamental Rights*. The Hague; London: Kluwer Law International.

Shute, Stephen and Susan Hurley (eds) (1993) *On Human Rights: The Oxford Amnesty Lectures*. New York: Basic Books.

Singh, Rajendra (1998) *Linguistic Theory, Language Contact, and Modern Hindustani*. New York: Peter Lang.

Škaljić, Alija (1989) *Turcizmi u srpskohrvatskom jeziku*. [Turkish words in the Serbo-Croatian language] Sarajevo: Svjetlost, sixth edition.

Skillen, Anthony (1982) `Freedom of Speech', in Keith Graham (ed.) *Contemporary Political Philosophy*. Cambridge: Cambridge University Press, pp. 139–59.

Skutnabb-Kangas, Tove (1998) 'Human Rights and Language Wrongs – A Future for Diversity'. *Language Sciences*, Vol. 20, No. 1, pp. 5–27.

Skutnabb-Kangas, Tove (1999) 'Linguistic Diversity, Human Rights and the "Free" Market', in Miklós Kontra, Robert Phillipson, Tove Skutnabb-Kangas and Tibor Varady (eds), *Language, a Right and a Resource: Approaches to Linguistics Human Rights*. Budapest: Central European University Press, pp. 187–222.

Skutnabb-Kangas, Tove (2000) *Linguistic Genocide in Education – or Worldwide Diversity and Human Rights?* Mahwah, New Jersey: Lawrence Erlbaum.

Skutnabb-Kangas, Tove (2001) 'Linguistic Human Rights in Education for Language Maintenance', in Luisa Maffi (ed.), *On Biocultural Diversity: Linking Language, Knowledge and the Environment*. Smithsonian Institution Press, pp. 397–411.

Skuttnabb-Kange, Tove (2006) 'Linguistic Human Rights'. *Sociolinguistics*, Vol. 3, No. 3, pp. 2575–84.

Skutnabb-Kangas, Tove (2009) 'Multilingual Education for Global Justice: Issues, Approaches, Opportunities', in Tove Skutnabb-Kangas, Robert Phillipson, Ajit Mohanty and Minati Panda (eds), *Social Justice through Multilingual Education*. Bristol; Buffalo; Toronto: Multilingual Matters, pp. 36–62.

Skutnabb-Kangas and Sertaç Bucak (1994) 'Killing a Mother Tongue – How Kurds are Deprived of their Linguistic Human Rights', in Tove Skutbnabb-Kangas and Robert Phillipson (eds), (1994) *Linguistic Human Rights: Overcoming Linguistic Discrimination*. Berlin: M. de Gruyter, pp. 347–70.

Skutnabb-Kangas, Tove and Robert Dunbar (2010) 'Indigenous Children's Education as Linguistic Genocide and a Crime Against Humanity?' *Guovdageaidnu/Kautokeino: Galdu Cala – Journal of Indigenous Peoples Rights*, No. 1. http://www.e-pages.dk/grusweb/55/.

Skutnabb-Kangas, Tove, Luisa Maffi and David Harmon (2003) *Sharing a World of Difference: The Earth's Linguistic, Cultural and Biological Diversity*. UNESCO, WWF and Terralingua.

Skutbnabb-Kangas, Tove and Robert Phillipson (eds) (1994) *Linguistic Human Rights: Overcoming Linguistic Discrimination*. Berlin: M. de Gruyter.

Skutnabb-Kangas, Tove and Robert Phillipson (1994) 'Linguistic Human Rights, Past and Present', in Tove Skutbnabb-Kangas and Robert Phillipson (eds), *Linguistic Human Rights: Overcoming Linguistic Discrimination*. Berlin: M. de Gruyter, pp. 71–110.

Skutnabb-Kangas, Tove, Robert Phillipson, Minati Panda and Ajit Mohanty (2009a) 'Multilinguial Education Concepts, Goals, Needs and Expense: English for all or Achieving Justice', in Tove Skutnabb-Kangas, Robert Phillipson, Ajit Mohanty and Minati Panda (eds), *Social Justice through Multilingual Education*. Bristol; Buffalo; Toronto: Multilingual Matters, pp. 320–44.

Skutnabb-Kangas, Tove, Robert Phillipson, Ajit Mohanty and Minati Panda (eds) (2009b) *Social Justice through Multilingual Education*. Bristol; Buffalo; Toronto: Multilingual Matters.

Smirl, Lisa (2008) 'Building the Other, Constructing Ourselves: Spatial Dimensions of International Humanitarian Response'. *International Political Sociology*, Vol. 2, No. 3, pp. 236–53.

Smith, Anthony (1986) *The Ethnic Origins of Nations*. Oxford: Basil Blackwell.

Smith, Anthony (1991) *National Identity*. London: Penguin.

Smith, Anthony (2004) *The Antiquity of Nations*. Cambridge: Polity Press.

Smith, Rennie (1932) 'Education in British Africa'. *Journal of the Royal African Society*, Vol. 31, No. 122, pp. 54–76.

Smuts, Jan (1927) *Holism and Evolution*. London: Macmillan.

Snow, C.P. (1964) *The Two Cultures*. Cambridge: Cambridge University Press.

Society for Endangered Languages (GBS) http://www.uni-koeln.de/gbs/e_index.html. Accessed 24 June 2012.

Spaink, Karin (2003) 'Introduction', in OSCE, *From Quill to Cursor Freedom of the Media in the Digital Era*. Vienna: OSCE pp. 6–30. http://www.osce.org/fom/13834. Accessed 18 January 2011.

Spaulding, Seth (1998) *An Assessment of Educational Renewal and Reform in Bosnia-Herzegovina*. Sarajevo: USIS. 14 March. http://www.pitt.edu/~ginie/bosnia/pdf/AsseBiH98.pdf. Accessed 22 November 2010.

Spence, Thomas (1796) The Meridian Sun of Liberty; or, the whole rights of man displaed and most accurately defined in a lecture read at the Philosophical Society in Newcastle, on he 8th of November 1775. London. Electronic reproduction. Farmington Hills, Mich.: Thomson Gale, 2003.

Spivak, Gayatri Chakravorty (1976) 'Translator's Preface', in Jacques Derrida, *Of Grammatology*. Baltimore; London: John Hopkins University, pp. ix–lxxxvii..

Spivak, Gayatri Chakravorty (1988) 'Can the Subaltern Speak?', in Cary Nelson and Larry Grossberg (eds), *Marxism and the interpretation of Culture*. Chicago: University of Illinois Press, pp. 271–313.

Spivak, Gayatri Chakravorty (1992) 'The Politics of Translation', in Michele Barrett and Anne Phillips (eds), *Destabilizing Theory*. Stanford: Stanford University Press, pp. 177–200.

Spivak, Gayatri Chakravorty (2000) 'Translation as Culture'. *Parallax*, Vol. 6, No. 1, pp. 13–24 Spivak, Gayatri Chakravorty (2001) 'Questioned on Translation: Adrift'. *Public Culture*, Vol. 13, No. 1, pp. 13–22

Söderbaum, Fredrik and Jens Stilhoff Sörensen (ed.) (2012) *Development Dialogue*, Special Issue: The End of the Development-Security Nexus? The Rise of Global Disaster Management, No. 58.

Sogge, David (ed.) (1996) *Compassion and Calculation: The Business of Private Foreign Aid*. London: Pluto Press.

Stabback, Philip (2003) *Bosnia and Herzegovina. Synopsis of the Case Study*. Geneva: UNESCO International Bureau of Education. http://www.see-educoop.net/education_in/pdf/educ-bosnia-case-study-bih-enl-t06.pdf. Accessed 24 June 2012.

Stabback, Philip (2003) *Bosnia and Herzegovina: Synopsis of the Case Study*. Project on Curriculum Change and Social Cohesion in Conflict-affected Societies. Geneva: UNESCO International Bureau of Education. http://www.ibe.unesco.org/Regional/social_cohesion/schome.htm. Accessed 24 June 2012.

Stabback, Philip (2007) 'Common Curriculum, Core Curriculum Or Common Curriculum Standards – Finding a Solution for Bosnia and Herzegovina'. *Prospects*, Vol. 37, No. 4, pp. 449–67. Accessed 24 June 2012.

Standish, Alex (2009) *Global Perspectives in the Geography Curriculum: Reviewing the Moral Case for Geography*. Abingdon: Routledge.

Starr, Sandy (2003) 'The Diminishing Importance of Constitutional Rights in the Internet Age', in OSCE, *From Quill to Cursor: Freedom of the Media in the Digital Era*. Vienna: OSCE, pp. 57–72. http://www.osce.org/fom/13834. Accessed 18 January 2011.

Starr, Sandy (2004) 'Understanding Hate Speech', in OSCE, *The Media Freedom Internet Cookbook*. Vienna: OSCE, pp. 125–41. http://www.osce.org/publications/rfm/2004/12/12239_94_en.pdf. Accessed 18 January 2011.

Stearns, Carol and Peter Stearns (1986) *Anger: the Struggle for Emotional Control in America's History*. Chicago: University of Chicago Press.

Steiner, George (1969) *Language and Silence*. Harmondsworth: Penguin.

Steiner, George (1996) *No Passion Spent: Essays 1978–1996*. London and Boston: Faber & Faber.

Steiner, George (1998) [1975] *After Babel: Aspects of Language and Translation*. Oxford: Oxford University Press, third edition.

Steward, Julian (1948) 'Comments on the Statement on Human Rights'. *American Anthropologist*, No. 50, pp. 351–2.

Stonequist, Everett (1961) *The Marginal Man: A Study in Personality and Culture Conflict*. New York: Russell & Russell.

Summerfield, Derek (2001) 'The Invention of Post-Traumatic Stress Disorder and the Social Usefulness of a Psychiatric Category'. *British Medical Journal*, Vol. 322, No. 7278, pp. 95–8.

Sunnemark, Fredrick (2003) *Ring Out Freedom! The Voice of Martin Luther King and the Making of the Civil Rights Movement*. Bloomington: Indiana University Press.

Sunstein, Cass R. (2005) *Laws of Fear: Beyond the Precautionary Principle*. New York: Cambridge University Press.

de Swaan Abram (2004) 'Endangered Languages, Sociolinguistics, and Linguistic Sentimentalism'. *European Review*, Vol. 12, No. 4, pp. 567–80.

Swift, Jonathan (2001) [1726] *Gulliver's Travels*. London: Penguin.

Tallis, Raymond (1988) *Not Saussure: A Critique of Post-Saussurean Literary Theory*. Basingstoke: Palgrave Macmillan.

Tallis, Raymond (1999) *Enemies of Hope: A Critique of Contemporary Pessimism: Irrationalism, Anti-Humanism and Counter-Enlightenment*. Basingstoke: Palgrave Macmillan.

Tallis, Raymond (2003) *The Hand: A Philosophical Inquiry in Human Being*. Edinburgh: Edinburgh University Press.

Tallis, Raymond (2011) *Aping Mankind: Neuromania, Darwinitis and the Misrepresentation of Humanity*. Durham: Acumen.

Tawney, R.H. (1921) *The Acquisitive Society*. London: Bell.

Taylor, Charles (1985) *Human Agency and Language: Philosophical Papers 1*. Cambridge: Cambridge University Press.

Taylor, Charles (1989) *Sources of the Self: the Making of the Modern Identity*. Cambridge, Mass.: Harvard University Press.

Taylor, Charles (1992) 'Heidegger, Language, and Ecology', in Hubert Dreyfus and Harrison Hall (eds), *Heidegger: A Critical Reader*. Oxford: Oxford University Press, pp. 247–69.

Taylor, Charles (1994) 'The Politics of Recognition', in Amy Gutman (ed.), *Multiculturalism: Examining the Politics of Recognition*. Princeton: Princeton University Press, pp. 25–73.

Temples, Placide (1959) *Bantu Philosophy*. Paris: Presence Africaine.

Terralingua: Partnerships for Linguistic and Biological Diversity. Accessed 20 July 2010.

Terralingua (undated) Statement of Purpose. http://www.terralingua.org/basics/intro.html. Accessed 20 July 2010.

Thomas, Paul (2009) 'TUC and the Dangers of Far-Right Obsession'. *Freedom in a Puritan Age*. http://www.freedominapuritanage.co.uk/?p=186. Accessed 15 January 2011.

Thomas, Paul (2010) 'Fettering Freedom of Expression'. *Freedom in a Puritan Age* http://www.freedominapuritanage.co.uk/?p=594. Accessed 17 January 2011.

Thompson, Duncan (2007) *Pessimism of the Intellect: A History of the New Left Review*. London: Merlin.

Thompson, E.P. (1964) *The Making of the English Working Class*. Harmondsworth: Penguin.

Thompson, E.P. (1997) *The Romantics: England in a Revolutionary Age*. Woodbridge: Merlin.

Thoreau, Henry (1986) [1854] *Walden; and, Civil Disobedience*. London: Penguin.

Thorne, Nick (2011) 'Textbooks Don't Make Terrorists'. *Spiked*, 17 March. http://www.spiked-online.com/index.php/site/printable/10302/. Accessed 6 July 2011.

Thorson, Per (1936) *Anglo-Norse Studies: An Inquiry into the Scandinavian Elements in the Modern English Dialects. Part 1*. Amsterdam: Swets en Zeitlinger.

Tisdall, William St. Clair (1911) *A Conversation-Grammar of the Hindūstānī Language*. London: J. Groos.

Todorov, Tzvetan (1993) *On Human Diversity: Nationalism, Racism, and Exoticism in French Thought*. Translated by Catherine Porter. Cambridge, Mass.: Harvard University Press.

Todorov, Tzvetan (2009) *In Defence of the Enlightenment*. Translated by Gila Walker. London: Atlantic.

Todorova, Maria (1997) *Imagining the Balkans*. New York, Oxford: Oxford University Press.

Tomlinson, John (1991) *Cultural Imperialism: A Critical Introduction*. London: Continuum.

Tooke, John Horne (1786) *Epea pteroenta. Or, The Diversions of Purley. Part I*. London, Eighteenth Century Collections Online. Gale Group. http://galenet.galegroup.com/servlet/ECCO. Accessed 17 September 2010.

Toulmin, Stephen (1992) *Cosmopolis: The Hidden Agenda of Modernity.* Chicago: University of Chicago Press.

Townsend, Mark (2012) 'Police "made up" evidence against Muslim student'. *Guardian,* 14 July. http://www.guardian.co.uk/uk/2012/jul/14/police-evidence-muslim-student-rizwaan-sabir

Trade Union Congress (TUC) (2009) 'Motion: C6 Opposing the Far Right'. Congress 2009. http://www.congressvoices.org/2009/09-fighting-the-bnp-and-far-right/. Accessed 7 July 2011.

Travis, Alan (2011) 'Leading Palestinian Activist Arrested In London'. *Guardian,* 29 June. http://www.guardian.co.uk/world/2011/jun/29/sheikh-raed-salah-arrest-london. Accessed 7 July 2011.

Trotsky, Leon (1927) *Radio, Science, Technique and Society,* Vol. 21 of the Collected Works of L.D. Trotsky. Moscow State Publishing House. Internet Leon Trotsky Internet Archive www.marxists.org. Accessed 6 October 2010.

Trotsky, Leon (1934) 'Nationalism and Economic Life'. *Class Struggle,* Vol. 4, Nos.9–10, October.

Tunstall, J. (1977) *The Media are American.* London: Constable.

Turner, Bryan (1993) 'Outline of a Theory of Human Rights'. *Sociology,* Vol. 27, No. 3, pp. 489–512.

Turner, Terence (1997) 'Human Rights, Human Difference: Anthropology's Contribution to an Emancipatory Cultural Politics'. *Journal of Anthropological Research,* Vol. 53, No. 3, pp. 272–92.

Tyutchev, Fyodor (1830) *Silentium.* Translated by Vladimir Nabokov. Available in Vladimir Nabokov (1947) *Pushkin, Lemontov, Tyutchev: Poems.* London. Lindsay Drummond Limited. http://lib.ru/NABOKOW/silent.txt. Accessed 17 September 2010.

Ugresić, Dubravka (1998) 'Balkan Blues', in *Culture of Lies: AntiPolitical Essays.* Translated by Celia Hawkesworth. London: Phoenic House, pp. 128–50.

UN (1945) Charter of the United Nations. http://www.un.org/en/documents/udhr/index.shtml

UN (1948) Universal Declaration of Human Rights. http://www.un.org/en/documents/udhr/index.shtml. Accessed 23 June 2012.

UN (1965) International Convention on the Elimination of All Forms of Racial Discrimination (CERD) http://www2.ohchr.org/english/law/cerd.htm. Accessed 23 June 2012.

UN (1966) International Covenant on Civil and Political Rights, General Assembly resolution 2200A (XXI) of 16 December 1966. http://www2.ohchr.org/english/law/ccpr.htm. Accessed 23 June 2012.

UN (1992) Declaration on the Rights of Persons Belonging to National or Ethnic, Religious and Linguistic Minorities UNGA Doc. No. A/RES/47/135. http://www.un-documents.net/a47r135.htm. Accessed 23 June 2012.

UN (1989) UN Convention on the Rights of the Child, General Assembly Resolution 44/25 20 November 1989, Entry into force 2 September 1990. http://www.ohchr.org/english/law/pdf/crc.pdf. Accessed 23 June 2012

UN (2007) United Nations Declaration on the Rights of Indigenous Peoples, Adopted by General Assembly Resolution 61/295 on 13 September 2007 http://www.un.org/esa/socdev/unpfii/en/drip.html. Accessed 23 June 2012.

UNESCO (1945) Conference for the Establishment of the United Nations Educational, Scientific and Cultural Organisation. Paris: UNESCO. Accessed 23 June 2012.

UNESCO (1948) Constitution. http://www.unesco.org/education/information/nfsunesco/pdf/UNESCO_E.PDF. Accessed 23 June 2012.

UNESCO (1950) 'The UNESCO Statement by Experts on Race Problems', in Ashley Montagu (1963) *Race, Science and Humanity*. Princeton: Nostrand, pp. 172–8.

UNESCO (1952) 'Statement on the Nature of Race and Race Differences', in Ashley Montagu (1963) *Race, Science and Humanity*. Princeton: Nostrand, pp. 178–83.

UNESCO (1953) Monograph on Fundamental Education: The Use of Vernacular Languages in Education. Monographs on Fundamental Education, No. 8. Paris: UNESCO.

UNESCO (1982) *Final Report of the World Conference on Cultural Policies*. Mexico City. Paris: UNESCO.

UNESCO (1995) *Our Creative Diversity: Report of the World Commission on Culture and Development*. Paris: UNESCO. Further information available at: http://www.unesco.org/culture_and_development/ocd/ocd.html. Accessed 23 June 2012.

UNESCO (1997) Recommendation Concerning the Status of Higher-Education Teaching Personnel, 11 November 1997. http://portal.unesco.org/en/ev.php-URL_ID=13144&URL_DO=DO_TOPIC&URL_SECTION=201.html. Accessed 22 November 2010.

UNESCO (1998a) Preliminary Consolidated Report to the United Nations on a Culture of Peace. Executive Board. Paris: UNESCO, 155 EX/49, 11 August.

UNESCO (1998b) Evaluation Report on the Transdisciplinary Project 'Towards a Culture of Peace'. Executive Board. Paris: UNESCO, 155 EX/48, 14 September.

UNESCO (2002) UNESCO Universal Declaration on Cultural Diversity, 21 February. http://www.unesco.org/education/imld_2002/unversal_decla.shtml. Accessed 23 June 2012.

UNESCO (2006) *Intergovernmental Conference on Language Policies in Africa Harare*, Zimbabwe 17–21 March 1997. Final Report. Paris: Unesco, Intangible Heritage Section. http://unesdoc.unesco.org/images/0014/001457/145746e.pdf. Accessed 23 June 2012.

UNESCO (2010) Unesco's Work to Foster Linguistic Diversity and Promote Multilingualism: 1946–2010. CLT/CEI/CID/2010/PI/147. fhttp://www.worldfamily-organization.org/wfs6/bg/UNESCO's%20work%20to%20foster%20linguistic%20diversity%20and%20promote%20multilingualism%201946%202010.pd. Accessed 23 June 2012.

UNESCO (2012) *Why Language Matters for the Millennium Development Goals*. Bangkok: UNESCO. http://unesdoc.unesco.org/images/0021/002152/215296e.pdf. Accessed 23 June 2012

UNESCO MOST Clearing House on Linguistic Rights http://www.unesco.org/most/ln1.htm; http://www.unesco.org/most/ln2int.htm. Accessed 23 June 2012.

UN General Assembly (1974) *Declaration on the Establishment of a New Economic Order*, GA Resolution 3201 (S-VI), 1 May 1974.

UNHCHR (1998) *Racism, Racial Discrimination, Xenophobia and Related Intolerance*. Report of the Expert Seminar on the Role of the Internet in the Light of the Provisions of the International Convention on the Elimination of All Forms of Racial Discrimination in Geneva dated 10–14 November 1997. E/CN.4/1998/77/Add.2 http://www.unhchr.ch/Huridocda/Huridoca.nsf/TestFrame/5069557b561c0fd4c1256619003267d2?Opendocument. Accessed 23 June 2012.

UN Human Rights Council (2008) Report of the Special Rapporteur [on the Right to Education], Vernor Muñoz: addendum: mission to Bosnia and Herzegovina (24 September–2 October 2007), 27 May. A/HRC/8/10/Add.4, http://www.unhcr.org/refworld/docid/484d1c142.html. Accessed 23 June 2012.

UN Millennium Development Goals. http://www.un.org/millenniumgoals/. Accessed 24 June 2012.

UN Department of Economic and Social Affairs (UN DESA) (2011) *The Millennium Development Goals Report 2011*. New York: UN DESA. http://www.un.org/millenniumgoals/pdf/(2011_E)%20MDG%20Report%202011_Book%20LR.pdf. Accessed 24 June 2012.

Universal Declaration of Linguistic Rights (1996) http://www.unesco.org/cpp/uk/declarations/linguistic.pdf. Accessed 24 June 2012.

Universities UK (2005) Promoting good campus relations: dealing with hate crimes and intolerance. London: Universities UK. http://www.ecu.ac.uk/publications/files/promoting-good-campus-relations-dealing-with-hate-crimes.pdf/view. Accessed 19 January 2011.

University of Leeds (2008) Protocol on Freedom of Expression. http://www.leeds.ac.uk/timetable/codeofpr.htm. Accessed 16 January 2011

Del Valle, Sandra (2003) *Language Rights and the Law in the United States: Finding Our Voices*. Clevedon: Multilingual Matters.

Vanacker, Bastiaan (2009) *Global Medium, Local Laws: Regulating Cross-Border Cyberhate*. El Paso, TX: LFB Scholarly Publishing LLC.

Van den Berghe, Pierre (1970) *Race and Ethnicity: Essays in Comparative Sociology*. New York: Basic Books.

De Varennes, Fernand (1996) *Language, Minorities and Human Rights*. The Hague: Martinus Nijhoff.

De Varennes, Fernand (1999) 'Equality and Non-Discrimination: Fundamental Principles of Minority Language Rights'. *International Journal* on *Minority* and *Group Rights*, Vol. 6, No. 3, pp. 307–18.

De Varennes, Fernand (2001a) *A Guide to the Rights of Minorities and Language*. Budapest COLPI. http://www.osi.hu/colpi/files/COLPI4.pdf. Accessed 23 June 2012.

De Varennes, Fernand (2001b) 'Language Rights as an Integral Part of Human Rights'. MOST *International Journal on Multicultural Societies*, Vol. 3, No. 1, pp. 15–25.

De Varennes, Fernand (2008) 'International Law and Education in a Minority Language'. *Encyclopedia of Language and Education*, Part 1 and 2, pp. 121–36.

Väyrynen, Tarja (2001) *Culture and International Conflict Resolution: A Critical Analysis of the Work of John Burton*. Manchester: Manchester University Press.

Vaux, Tony (2001) *The Selfish Altruist: Relief Work in Famine and War*. London: Earthscan.

Vennebusch, Joachim (1966) *Gottfried Wilhelm Leibniz: Philosopher and Politician in the Service of a Universal Culture*. Bad Godesberg, Inter-Nationes.

Venuti, Lawrence (1986) 'The Translator's Invisibility'. *Criticism*, Vol. 28, No. 2, pp. 179–212.

Venuti, Lawrence (1992) (ed.) *Rethinking Translation: Discourse, Subjectivity, Ideology*. New York: Routledge.

Venuti, Lawrence (1993) 'Translation as Cultural Politics: Regimes of Domestication in English'. *Textual Practice*, Vol. 7, No. 2, pp. 208–23.

Venuti, Lawrence (1995) *The Translator's Invisibility: A History of Translation*. London: Routledge.

Venuti, Lawrence (1998a) *The Scandals of Translation: Towards an Ethics of Difference*. London: Routledge.

Venuti Lawrence (ed.) (1998b) *Translation and Minority*. Manchester: St. Jerome.

Venuti, Lawrence (ed.) (2004) *The Translation Studies Reader*. New York; London: Routledge, second edition.

Vico (2002) [1725] *The First New Science*. Edited and translated by Leon Pompu. Cambridge: Cambridge University Press.

Vincent, Andrew (2010) *The Politics of Human Rights*. Oxford: Oxford University Press.
Visoka, Gezim (2012) 'Interpreters in Kosovo'. Presentation to AHRC Languages and NGOs (LINGOs) Workshop, Royal Soceity of Arts, London, 22 June.
Voegelin, Charles and Florence Voegelin (1957) *Hopi Domains: A Lexical Approach to the Problem of Selection*. Indiana University Publications in Anthropology and Linguistics, memoir 14 of the International Journal of American Linguistics. Baltimore: Waverly Press.
Vollebaek, Knut (2008) 'Linguistic Rights in the Work of the HCNM: New and Old Challenges in Promoting Comprehensive Security'. Opening speech to to the Conference on Linguistic Rights of National Minorities: Ten Years after the Oslo Recommendations and Beyond. Oslo – 18 June. http://www.osce.org/documents/hcnm/2008/06/32045_en.pdf. Accessed 16 October 2010.
Voltaire (2006) [1759] *Candide, Or Optimism*. London: Penguin.
Vygotsky, Lev (1986) [1934] *Thought and Language*. Edited and translated by Alex Kozulin. Cambridge, Mass.: MIT.
De Waal, Alex (1990) 'A Re-Assessment of Entitlement Theory in the Light of the Recent Famines In Africa'. *Development and Change*, Vol. 21, pp. 469–90.
De Waal, Alex (1997) *Famine Crimes*. Bloomington: Indiana University Press.
Wachtel, Andrew Baruch (1998) *Making a Nation, Breaking a Nation: Literature and Cultural Politics in Yugoslavia*. Stanford: Stanford University Press.
Wainwright, Martin (2010) 'Twitter Joke Trial: Paul Chambers Loses Appeal against Conviction'. *Guardian*, 11 November. http://www.guardian.co.uk/uk/2010/nov/11/twitter-joke-trial-appeal-verdict. Accessed 15 January 2011.
Wallbank, T. Walter (1935) 'Achimota College and Educational Objectives in Africa'. *The Journal of Negro Education*, Vol. 4, No. 2, pp. 230–45.
Washburn, Wilcomb E. (1987) 'Cultural Relatvism, Human Rights and the AAA'. *American Anthropologist*, Vol. 89, No. 4, pp. 939–43.
Washington Agreement 1994. http://www.usip.org/library/pa/bosnia/washagree_03011994.html. Accessed 22 November 2010.
Watt, Ian (1987) [1957] *The Rise of the Novel*. London: Hogarth.
Watt, Ian (1997) *Myths of Modern Individualism: Faust, Don Quixote, Don Juan, Robinson Crusoe*. Cambridge: Cambridge University Press.
Weber, Max (1954) *Max Weber on Law in Economy and Society*. New York: Simon & Schuster.
Wehgman, Vera (2012) 'Occupy Movement: Reclaiming Public Spaces to Think about and Practice Alternatives', talk at CSSGJ, University of Nottingham dated 6 February.
Weinstock, Daniel (2003) 'The Antinomy of Language Policy', in Will Kymlicka and Alan Patten (eds), *Language Rights and Political Theory*. Oxford: Oxford University Press, pp. 250–70.
West, Michael (2002) *Rise of an African Middle Class: Colonial Zimbabwe 1898–1965*. Bloomington: Indiana University Press.
Westendorp, Carlos (1999) 'Lessons Bosnia Taught Us'. *The Wall Street Journal*, 19 May.
Westermann D. (1929) 'The Linguistic Situation and Vernacular Literature in British West Africa'. *Africa*, Vol. 2, No. 4, pp. 337–51.
Westermann, Diedrich (1934) *The African Today and Tomorrow*. Oxford: Oxford University Press.
Westermann, D. (1939) 'The Study of African Languages: Present Results and Future Needs'. *Africa*, Vol. 12, No. 1, pp. 12–26.
White, B. (1983) ' "Agricultural involution" and Its Critics: Twenty Years after Clifford Geertz'. Working paper series no. 6, Institute of Social Studies.

Whitehead, Clive (2003) *Colonial Educators: The British Indian and Colonial Education Service 1858–1983*. London; New York: I.B.Tauris.
Whiteley, W.H. (1956) 'The Changing Position of Swahili in East Africa'. *Africa: Journal of the International African Institute*, Vol. 26, No. 4, pp. 343–53.
Whorf, Benjamin Lee (1936) 'The Punctual and Segmentative Aspects of Verbs In Hopi'. *Language*, 12, pp. 127–31.
Whorf, Benjamin Lee (1940a) 'Science and Linguistics'. *Technology Review*, Vol. 42, No. 6, pp. 229–31, 247–8.
Whorf, Benjamin Lee (1940b) 'Linguistics as an exact science'. *Technology Review*, Vol. 43, No. 1, pp. 61–3, 80–3.
Whorf, Benjamin Lee (1956) *Language, Thought, and Reality*. Cambridge, Mass.: MIT Press.
Whyte, William (1956) *Organizational Man*. New York: Simon and Schuster.
Wilder, Lisa (1997) 'Local Futures? From Denunciation to Revalorization of the Indigenous Other', in Gunther Teubner (ed.), *Global Law Without a State*. Aldershot: Dartmouth, pp. 215–56.
Williams, Raymond (1963) *Culture and Society 1789–1950*. Harmondsworth: Penguin.
Williams, Raymond (1973) *The Country and the City*. New York: Oxford University Press.
Williams, Raymond (1988) *Keywords: A Vocabulary of Culture and Society*. London: Fontana.
Wilson, Edmund (1965) 'The Strange Case of Pushkin and Nabokov'. *New York Review of Books*, Vol. 4, No. 12, 15 July. http://www.nybooks.com/articles/12829. Accessed 6 October 2010.
Wilson, Richard (1997) 'Human Rights, Culture and Context: An Introduction', in Richard Wilson (ed.), *Human Rights, Culture and Context: Anthropological Perspectives*. London: Pluto, pp. 1–27.
Windmiller, Marshall (1954) 'Linguistic Regionalism in India'. *Pacific Affairs*, Vol. 27, No. 4, pp. 291–318.
Wolfe, Alan (1977) *Limits of Legitimacy: Political Contradictions of Contemporary Capitalism*. New York: Free Press.
Wolpe, Harold (1990) *Race, Class and the Apartheid State*. Trenton: Africa World Press.
Wollenstonecroft, Mary (1992) [1792] *A Vindication of the Rights of Women*. London: Penguin.
Wolton, Suke (2000) *Lord Hailey, the Colonial Office and the Politics of Race and Empire in the Second World War*. Basingstoke: Palgrave Macmillan.
Wood, Barbara (1983) *E. F. Schumacher: His Life and Thought*. New York: Harper & Row. Available via E.F Schumacher Society. http://www.schumachersociety.org/Wood%20bio/index.html. Accessed 10 July 2011.
Woodward, Susan (1995) *Balkan Tragedy: Chaos and Dissolution after the Cold War*. Washington DC: Brookings Institute.
Woodward, Susan (2001) 'Humanitarian war: a consensus?' *Disasters*, Vol. 25, No. 4, pp. 331–44.
Wordsworth, Jonathan and Jessica Wordsworth (eds) (2003) *The New Penguin Book of Romantic Poetry*. London: Penguin.
Wordsworth, William (1995) [1805–1850] *The Prelude*. Edited by Jonathan Wordsworth. London: Penguin.
Wordsworth, William (1998a) [1802] 'Preface to Lyrical Ballards (1802)', in W.R. Owen and Hamish Johnson (eds), *Romantic Writings: An Anthology*. Milton Keynes: Open University, pp. 82–101. . Accessed 23 June 2012.

Wordsworth, William (1998b) [1798] 'Tintern Abbey', in W.R. Owen and Hamish Johnson (eds), *Romantic Writings: An Anthology*. Milton Keynes: Open University, pp. 70–3.

World Bank (1999) *Bosnia-Herzegovina, Education Development Project*: Project ID: BAPE58512, 21 June.

World Bank (2005) *In Their Own Language…Education for All*. New York: World Bank. http://siteresources.worldbank.org/EDUCATION/Resources/Education-Notes/EdNotes_Lang_of_Instruct.pdf. Accessed 24 June 2012.

World Bank (2008) *The Migration and Remittances Factbook 2008*. Washington, DC: World Bank.

World University Service (1988) The Lima Declaration on Academic Freedom and Autonomy of Institutions of Higher Education.

Wright, Richard (1964) *White Man, Listen!* New York: Anchor.

Wright, Richard (1994) [1956] *The Color Curtain: A Report on the Bandung Conference*; with a foreword by Gunnar Myrdal and an afterword by Amritjit Singh. Jackson, Mississippi: University Press of Mississippi.

Wright, Richard (2000) [1940] *Native Son*. London: Vintage.

Writh, Jason (2003) 'Beyond Black Orpheus: Preliminary Thoughts on the Good of African Philosophy', in Robert Bernasconi and Tommy Lott (eds), *The Idea of Race*. Indianapolis: Hackett, pp. 268–85.

WWF International and Terralingua (2000) *Indigenous and Traditional Peoples of the World and Ecoregion Conservation: An Integrated Approach to Conserving the World's Biological and Cultural Diversity*. Gland, Switzerland: WWF International and Terralingua.

Yevtushenko, Yevgeny (1972) *Stolen Apples*. St Albans: Panther Books.

Yevtushenko, Yevgeny (1979) *The Face behind the Face*. London; Boston: Marion Boyars.

Yuill, Kevin (2006) *Richard Nixon and the Rise of Affirmative Action*. Lanham, Maryland: Rowman & Littlefield.

Zafar and Ors v R [2008] EWCA Crim 184 (13 February 2008). http://www.bailii.org/ew/cases/EWCA/Crim/2008/184.html or http://news.bbc.co.uk/1/shared/bsp/hi/pdfs/13_02_08beaumont.pdf. Accessed 18 January 2011.

Zechenter, Elizabeth (1997) 'In the Name of Culture: Cultural Relativism and the Abuse of the Individual'. *Journal of Anthropological Research*, Vol. 53, No. 3, pp. 319–48.

Zimmern, Alfred (1927) *Third British Empire: Being a Course of Lectures Delivered at Colombia University, New York*. London: Humphrey Milford.

Žižek, Slavoj (1991) *For They Know Not What They Do: Enjoyment as a Political Fac*tor. London: Verso.

Žižek, Slavoj (1997) 'Multiculturalism, or, the Cultural Logic of Multinational Capitalism'. *New Left Review*, No. I/225, Sept–Oct, pp 28–51.

Žižek, Slavoj (1999a) 'Human Rights and Its Discontents', Olin Auditorium Bard College, 15 November. . Accessed 9 September 2010.

Žižek, Slavoj (1999b) *The Ticklish Subject: The Absent Centre of Political Ontology*. New York: Verso.

Žižek, Slavoj (2001) 'Have Michael Hardt and Antonio Negri Rewritten the Communist Manifesto for the Twenty-First Century?' *Rewriting Marxism*, Vol. 13, No. 3–4, pp. 190–8. http://actpolitik.org/forum/Attachments/ZizekReviewofEmpire.pdf. Accessed 9 September 2010.

Žižek, Slavoj (2005) 'Against Human Rights'. *New Left Review*. No. 34, July-August, pp. 115–31.

Žižek, Slavoj (2011) 'Actual Politics'. *Theory and Event*, Vol. 14, No. 4, Occupy Wall Street supplement. http://muse.jhu.edu/login?auth=0&type=summary&url=/journals/theory_and_event/v014/14.4S.zizek.html. Accessed 31 July 2012.

Zolo, Danilo (2009) *Victor's Justice: From Nuremberg to Bagdad*. London: Verso.

Index